RAGE AND GLORY

RAGE AND GLORY

THE VOLATILE LIFE AND CAREER OF

George C. Scott

DAVID SHEWARD

APPLAUSE
THEATRE & CINEMA BOOKS

AN IMPRINT OF HAL LEONARD CORPORATION

NEW YORK

Published in 2008 by Applause Theatre & Cinema Books
An Imprint of Hal Leonard Corporation
7777 West Bluemound Road
Milwaukee, WI 53213

Trade Book Division Editorial Offices
19 West 21st Street, New York, NY 10010

Printed in the United States of America

Book design by Mark Lerner

Library of Congress Cataloging-in-Publication Data is available upon request.

ISBN: 978-1-55783-670-0

www.applausepub.com

For Jerry, who gives me everything

TABLE OF CONTENTS

INTRODUCTION

THE LIGHTS DIM TO CONCLUDE the evening's performance of Noel Coward's frothy comedy *Present Laughter* at the Circle in the Square theatre on Broadway. The audience is applauding as the lights come back up. The cast enters to take their curtain calls. The applause swells as the star and director of the show George C. Scott enters. Usually, an actor looks happy when he's receiving the audience's love. But Scott's granite features are fixed in a scowl. The rest of the company can tell he hasn't liked this audience. Maybe they weren't smart enough. Maybe they didn't laugh in the right places. Maybe they unwrapped too many of those little hard candies.

Whenever Scott didn't like an audience, he would refuse to give them a solo curtain call. Instead he would have the entire cast bow with him. He would signal his fellow players to get up from where they were sitting after taking their own calls and joining him center stage, usually muttering under his breath, "I'm not going to bow for these horses' asses."

Tonight Scott enters quickly, begins gesturing for the cast to get up, and moves to his center stage position. The audience—this stupid audience—thinks Scott is directing them to rise and give him a standing ovation, which makes him even madder. By the time the company is all in place, the entire audience is on its feet and the star is furious. The cast takes a fast bow and Scott bounds off in a huff.

At the moment of supreme adulation, the actor rejects his public. This defiant gesture, imperceptible to the cheering crowd at the Circle in the Square, was emblematic of Scott's love-hate relationship with his audience and his craft, indeed with the entire world. He craved affection, but wanted it only at his own price. He turned down an Oscar nomination for *The Hustler* and the award itself for *Patton* only after he had experienced the crushing disappointment of losing on his first nomination for 1959's *Anatomy of a Murder*.

He often threatened to quit acting, but never did. He thought it was a crazy way to earn a living, but, as he expressed to a fellow performer after many drinks, he didn't know how to do anything else. There were directing and producing projects (some more successful than others) and a few attempts to return to his college major of journalism (an article for *Esquire* on Vietnam, an unfinished historical novel). But he always found himself back in front of the camera or onstage.

He took risks on and offstage, twice investing his own money in vehicles for himself and losing his shirt. "Safe actors hold back, experiment not, dare not, change nothing and have no artistic courage," Scott told an interviewer. "I call them walkers. I may stagger a little now and then, but I have never been accused of walking."

He was never accused of being safe, either. He never wanted to repeat himself. The gallery of George C. Scott portrayals is studded with villains, heroes, criminals, con men, gamblers, and, most of all, rebels—the most famous of all being General George S. Patton. The actor and subject shared more than a first name. Patton bucked the military establishment as Scott chafed at the restraints of the Hollywood hierarchy. The general was a brilliant strategist but lacked tact and diplomatic skills. He said what he thought, consequences be damned. The actor was an equally brilliant practitioner of his craft who spoke his opinions regardless of their effect on his career.

William Goldman in his book *The Season* described Scott as being one of only two actors whom he believed was actually capable of coming down off the stage or screen and killing him. The other was Burt Lancaster, but Goldman theorized that Lancaster would murder him with charm, whereas Scott would just bludgeon him. With the possible exceptions of Robert Duvall, Robert De Niro, and Al Pacino, there are no star-level actors today who could pass such a killer-instinct test—and certainly none in the up-and-coming generation.

Scott carried an air of authority and power with him. The critic Harold Clurman wrote of him, "He is always vivid, never less than arresting. He is one of the few American actors who create the impression of a mature manliness: most others strike me as grown-up boys."

His physique helped lend him this authority. At a towering height of six feet two inches, he possessed a nose like a bald eagle's beak, craggy features, and a muscular frame. His voice was equally distinctive, a guttural rasp that sounded like rocks rattled inside a dented tin can.

He was a man's man in an age of men's men. As Scott was coming of age, the ideal American male in fiction and film was the archetypical figure made famous in the works of Ernest Hemingway: a macho drinker who was free with his fists and stingy with his emotions. Appropriately, one of his subtlest performances is in an adaptation of Hemingway's *Islands in the Stream*.

Like the protagonists of Hemingway, Scott could be a drunken brawler and a binge drinker. By the time he was forty, his nose had been broken five times—four times in fights and once in a mugging. But, as actress Dana Ivey observed, "He was a deeply felt person and sensitive which he covered up with that rough masculinity."

Married five times to four women, and distant with his six children, Scott was as restless in his personal relationships as he was quixotic in his professional life. The current wife didn't support him enough, the current job wasn't fulfilling enough (even *Patton* missed somehow, according to him).

He would not even deal with death on any terms but his own. In 1994, he was diagnosed with an aortic aneurysm, a swelling of the blood vessel which could prove fatal. An operation would have prolonged his life, but as the problem worsened he refused proper medical attention and eventually died of the condition. He was George C. Scott, goddamn it, and no one was going to tell him what to do.

1

Coal Miner's Son

CHANCES FOR THE BABY'S SURVIVAL weren't strong. The boy was born on October 18, 1927, on a kitchen table in the modest home of George Dewey Scott and Helena Agnes Slemp Scott. The young couple lived on the second floor of the drugstore owned by Helena's father, Judge Campbell Slemp, on Coburn Road in the mining town of Wise (population: 1,200), a tiny hamlet situated in the southwest corner of Virginia. George Campbell Scott, named for his father and his maternal grandfather, would later tell an interviewer, "I was a very sickly child. But I was big, long—I weighed twelve and a half pounds when I was born. It was all bone. There was no meat on me then."

George Dewey recalled to his cousin Nancy Clark Brown that the baby was not breathing: "I ran to the creek and got cold water and dipped the baby [in] first cold and then hot water. He began to breathe. George C. was a sickly baby; nothing he ate would stay down. The baby lost weight and was very frail. We didn't think we would raise him."

But, just as he would be in later life, this baby proved to be contrary. He would not do what was expected of him. He lived. The family, which included an older sister named Helen for her mother, experimented with a formula. George Dewey continued the story: "One day, I went to the post office for my father-in-law, Campbell Slemp . . . In the mail was a sample of a new food for babies. . . . His mother prepared the food, and the baby ate the whole box. It stayed down. The food was Pabulum, a cereal for babies." Little George grew stronger and actually won second prize in the Wise County Fair's baby contest at the age of two.

It's not clear if the prize was a cash one, but the Scotts could have used it. In 1929, the general economy of the United States collapsed, and with it the coal mining industry. Many mines shuttered and the hardest of times fell on Wise.

The Scotts were typical of the region. Baby George, like the majority of Wise, was the son and grandson of coal miners. A typical miner's day ran from nine to eleven hours. He was responsible for extracting several tons of the black gold from the dark interior of the mine with nothing more than his pick and explosives. In addition, he was required to lay the track for the cars that held the coal and transported it to the tipple (the giant container for the precious mineral), erect timber to prevent cave-ins, and clean up any "jack rock" or useless, unburnable coal. The exhausting demands had their rewards. When the country's hunger for fuel was high, as it was during World War I, a miner could command the dizzying fee of $1.50 a day. But those princely wages were by no means steady. By the early 1920s, supply was beginning to outstrip demand and competition from oil was driving down prices.

George Dewey Scott realized a coal miner's life was not a reliable one and that, if he was going to make any sort of a future beyond sustenance for his young family, it would be wise to leave Wise.

Born in a mountain log cabin in 1902, George D. Scott was put to work early on his parents' farm. Many families of that era would supplement their mining income with agriculture: the father would report to the mines while the family raised crops, and as soon as the sons were old enough they followed the older generations into the earth. George D., or Dewey as everyone called him, wanted more than coal dust and dirt for his offspring, and educated himself by studying at night. In between work and his books, he did allow himself some fun: as a respite from the darkness of the mines and the rigor of his self-improvement, he played the banjo in an amateur quartet. But his drive to succeed, which elevated him from miner to surveyor at the age of only eighteen, was never in doubt.

While George C.'s father placed a premium on hard work and only occasionally gave vent to his lighter side by plucking a banjo, his mother Helena was more artistic, an aspiring poet with the gentle nickname of Honey. She contributed verse to local newspapers and gave readings to small groups and occasionally over the radio. While the Scotts were coal miners, Helena Agnes Slemp came from a distinguished family; her first cousin, once removed, was Campbell Bascom Slemp, a Virginia congressman and later chief of staff to President Calvin Coolidge. Helena's father, Judge Campbell Slemp, who was not a judicial official but carried the name of one, worked his way up from clerk to owner of the drugstore and respected community leader. He served on the town council and was a supporter of all the local churches and civic organizations.

Given his poor prospects when the mines closed, Dewey saw that he could not follow his father-in-law's example of rising to financial security without leaving his hometown. The Scotts' destination was Pontiac, Michigan, a suburb of Detroit with a population of 50,000. Compared to the ruined Wise, it offered ample opportunity. Founded in 1818 and named for the eccentric Native American chief, the town had been a center of carriage-making. When the horseless kind took over the country's roadways, it heeded the call of changing times and switched to automobiles. In addition to cars, this bustling burg was a manufacturer of bricks, clayworks, sockets, and machine parts. But it was no smoggy slum. Its natural attractions of woods and waterways just outside the town center earned it the nickname "Land o' Lakes."

Once ensconced with his family in their new home, Dewey found work at General Motors' Buick assembly plant in Flint, outside of Pontiac. He was set to work in the tool crib for thirty-three cents an hour. George Junior recalled a steady diet of macaroni and cheese with tuna fish for special occasions. "I worked my ass off," George D. would later recall, "and the family never missed a meal. It was drive, drive, drive."

He didn't intend to stay in the tool crib for long. The 1930 census of Pontiac reported that the head of the Scott household's occupation was clerical and that the family rented their home for $60 a month and owned a radio. But this relative prosperity meant more hours at work for Dewey than at home. George Campbell drew closer to this mother as a result. His father was distant emotionally as well as physically, and left the child-rearing to his dreamy wife. His only physical contact with his son was probably administered in the name of discipline.

Dewey would surpass his coal-miner dad and expected his son to do the same. There was tremendous pressure on the sensitive boy. His father's goal-oriented, career-driven personality and his mother's artistic leanings would set up a conflict within George Campbell that would last well into adulthood. He wanted to please his dad by emulating his masculine, tough exterior, but was frightened of his gruff, distancing demeanor. He also sought to return his mother's love by pursuing his natural talents, first on the page by writing stories and later on the stage. The macho he-man would constantly be at war with the sensitive artist. He was always uncomfortable in scenes that required the open display of affection, as many of his leading ladies would report. Offstage, he would cover up his more feminine, artistic side with drinking and brawling.

Before he was old enough to adopt such tactics, however, he suffered from embarrassment at getting up in front of a crowd and reciting. As the adult George C. would relate, his mother encouraged him to entertain visitors with recitations she would teach him. "But it put me off performing," he said, "because one was obliged to do it to please mommy and daddy. I lost interest when I was about seven, and it never came back until I was in college."

There was one exception: George C.'s theatrical debut at elementary school. He claimed it was a role that would prove prophetic both professionally and personally. "I played Disaster," he later recalled. "That was my name. It was in one of those safety-pageant plays. And

I've sort of been a disaster ever since. I came on stage . . . in a black cloak. I was about six or seven and I had one long speech about all the rotten things I'd done—car wrecks, boats sinking, earthquakes. . . . That was the extent of my stage career for a number of years."

He remembered being taken to only two stage productions—touring companies of the popular attractions *Tobacco Road* and *Porgy and Bess*. The movies were more affordable. His first recalled cinema experience was *The Three Little Pigs* in 1934. Walt Disney's animated porkers and their ilk soon gave way to the exploits of cowboys, private eyes, and gangsters as George's favorite movie fare.

Many a Saturday afternoon was spent in the local movie house. Scott idolized Warner Brothers tough guys like Humphrey Bogart, Edward G. Robinson, and James Cagney, and would learn many useful lessons from the screen, as he related to Michael Billington of the *Times of London*: "I was brought up on movies—they kept me off the streets and out of the pool room. I found myself walking down the street like Cagney and doing his famous spring-heeled glide; or even adopting the explosive technique of Robinson. He would blow up certain words in a sentence, adjectives particularly. Myself I'm a verb man—I stress words like 'do,' 'be' and 'go' that suggest purpose or activity."

Another Warner Brothers star he admired was one of the few females with a reputation for toughness equal to that of her male counterparts: Bette Davis. "The most fascinating film actress I've ever seen," Scott told the *Los Angeles Times*. "I've never known her to play the same thing the same way twice, to repeat a character. She gives you incredible nuance."

It was a childhood of film fantasy and lakeside romps. By a quirk of economic fate, George Campbell Scott had been rescued from a life in the mines and was growing up in the Land o' Lakes rather than poverty-stricken Appalachia. His father was a distant source of fear, but a strong provider: young George, his sister, and their mother were eating regularly and had a roof over their heads and clean clothes. Helena encouraged her son's love of stories. He had even attempted writing a few of his own. Then in 1935, the family moved again and his creative parent was taken away from him.

On January 1, the Scotts took up residence in Detroit. Several months later, young George received an even greater shock. It was two weeks before his eighth birthday when the gentle Honey came down with peritonitis, a form of blood poisoning that causes pain and fever. Dewey took his wife to the hospital and told young Helen to watch her brother. When he returned without Helena the next morning, he only informed his children their mother would not be coming back.

His own emotional reticence, and the custom of the time of keeping children in the dark about life's deeper aspects, prevented Dewey from opening up to his son about the grief they both felt. Young George would later say, "With a couple of exceptions, I was completely unloved." Those exceptions were provided by his older sister Helen, all of twelve years old, and his Aunt Sally, wife of his mother's younger brother Byron Baker "Bud" Slemp. Scott would later relate: "Aunt Sally and my sister raised me. They were two very important females in my life. Bud is a mountain man, a very large, powerful man." Scott borrowed his Uncle Bud's drawling accent for the cantankerous judge in the Broadway comedy *Sly Fox*. Bud's daughter Dianne recalled,

> As a small child, I can remember him playing some kind of board game where you flipped checker-type pieces into the corner pockets. He played this with George C. many hours. Whoever won the game would flip the other person with thumb and finger into the forehead unmercifully. Many times they ended up with a very red forehead. He was very fun-loving and liked to play practical jokes on his friends. He loved to played Santa Claus and give out eggnog at Christmas.

While Uncle Bud would play games with young George, Dewey continued to push himself at work, and had little time to spend with his children. In November 1936, he was hired as a salesman for the

Ex-Cell-O Corporation, a manufacturer of parts, tools, and assemblies, some of which had found their way into Charles Lindbergh's Atlantic-crossing aircraft *Spirit of St. Louis*. The company's very name lived up to Dewey's credo: "Excel."

There would be more changes for George Campbell. Five years after his mother's death, his father remarried. Three years later, his stepmother, the former Betty Hurd, gave birth to a boy, Robert. In another two years—when Scott was seventeen—another half-brother, James, was born. It was a world of constant adjustment. Nothing was permanent.

His loving, creative mother was gone, and for many years young George shut off the side of himself that she had influenced. He stopped writing stories, starting getting into fights at school, and tenaciously went out for sports. He had grown into a tall, strong teenager, always ready for roughhousing. As a result, he suffered a series of accidents both on and off the field. Sister Helen would later tell Mary Cronin of *Time*, "He never cried or complained. He broke his nose playing football; he cut his head open diving into somebody in a swimming pool; he was hit by a golf club and run over by a car."

The adult Scott recalled the latter incident: "I was in junior high school and was on my way to class on a cold, rainy day. I was crossing the street and I was hit by a car. Luckily the boy was driving very slowly, or I would have been killed. As it was, I was unconscious for twenty minutes and woke up in the hospital. . . . It messed up all the calf muscles in my left leg and I still have a bad right knee. At times, I still have a pretty bad pain in my left leg."

This injury prevented Scott from triumphing at baseball, his favorite sport. But by now, he had renewed his interest in writing. "In my teens I wrote two novelettes, fifty short stories and got rejection slips for all of them," Scott recalled, "Faulkner, Hemingway and Steinbeck were my heroes."

While the son was facing constant rejection, the father was excelling at Ex-Cell-O, gaining a promotion to sales executive in charge of the Pur-Pak milk machines that the company had acquired the right to manufacture. George Campbell would later detail his dad's achievements to *Penthouse* magazine: "My dad was in milk. . . . He even put Pur-Pak machines in the hospital ship *Hope*. He also put in a desalinization machine—it drew in seawater, desalted it, purified it, zapped it with powdered milk, ran it through the machine, and out it came—cartoned milk just like that." Helen's son Kip Hamilton recalled of his grandfather, "Because of his efforts [in placing Pur-Pak on the *Hope*], untold thousands and thousands of children all over the world were given milk that was pasteurized and packaged on the ship and distributed to them."

When he grew up, Scott came to enjoy and appreciate his father. He would describe Dewey as "a character. He's a gas. And what a voice. The most marvelous speaking voice—if I had that voice I'd rule the fucking world" (this from a man whose own distinctive voice had become an unmistakable force in the theatre and on film). He admired his father's achievements—pushing his way from near poverty to an executive position at a national company. But the constant coming up short in comparison with his old man must have been wearing.

His relationship with his stepmother was trying as well. George Campbell did not get along with his father's second wife, and at sixteen he ran away from home. It was only a brief rebellion, and he soon returned. But a year later, young George would leave his father's house again, this time leaving his childhood behind him as well.

2

Growing Up in a Hurry

FEELING AS IF HE HAD been pushed aside by his father in favor of a new wife and new sons, George Campbell Scott sought a replacement family in the military with the toughest outfit he could find, the Marines. Enlistment in the few and the proud would fulfill his father's idea of what a man should be—devoted to duty, silent about emotions, tough as hell—while toning down his mother's feminine, artistic influence. To make the deal even sweeter, George Dewey had never fought in a war nor even served in the military. As a Marine—the branch of the armed forces he thought was most likely to see action before World War II ended—George Campbell could potentially cover himself in glory and best the old man. Young Scott had graduated from Redford High School in Detroit. He was seventeen, strong as a bull at six feet and 185 pounds, and had nowhere else to go. Like a boy, he had tried running away the year before. Now he would leave home as a man and maybe return as a hero.

Not only was he isolated from his family, he had collected a mountain of rejection slips as a writer. Perhaps in joining this brutal surrogate clan he could garner material for future stories and finally achieve literary success. In 1945, thousands of young men had the same idea of seeing the world and gaining maturity, and World War II was offering overseas romance and adventure. In *The Glass Menagerie*, then on Broadway,

Tennessee Williams's dreamy protagonist Tom Wingfield described the burning desires of ordinary kids to grab glory off the movie screen:

> Hollywood characters are supposed to have all the adventures for everyone in America, while everyone in America sits in a dark room and watches them have them. Yes, until there's a war. That's when adventure becomes available to the masses! Everyone's dish, not only Gable's! . . . It's our turn now, to go to the South Sea Islands—to make a safari—to be exotic, far-off!

Like Tom Wingfield, Scott had spent hundreds of hours at the movies, and now here was the opportunity to really live the screenland scenarios. In July, he bid goodbye to his unwelcoming home and shipped out for Parris Island, South Carolina, for basic training.

Scott was willing to endure the deprivations of military service—a shaved head, push-ups in the mud, endless hikes loaded down with a lead-heavy pack—if it meant he could battle for his country like his movie heroes. But, like his ambitions of being published and winning his father's approval, his John Wayne–inspired dreams were never realized. The plan was to ship out at the end of training and join the Seventh Marine division for the invasion of Japan. "I was very gung-ho . . ." he would later relate. "Then, right in the middle of my training, they dropped the bomb and the war was over. I felt a little like General Patton—they stole my war."

The "gung-ho" private had forty-five months left to serve. The remaining days of his term of peacetime service must have loomed before him like a prison sentence. Perhaps taking into account his literary aspirations, his superiors sent Scott to language school, then to a desk job in Washington, D.C., where he taught correspondence courses for the Marine Corps Institute in English literature and in speaking and writing for radio. Fellow leathernecks from around the world seeking to further their education would submit essays and answer tests for degrees while serving.

Scott was also assigned the funeral detail at Arlington National Cemetery. His duties included carrying the coffin from the chapel to the graveside. There were treacherous hills that made carrying the burden in strict formation a challenge.

Rather than fighting on the front lines, Scott would now be helping to bury soldiers who had had the misfortune to be born just a few years, or even months, earlier than him. Instead of writing his own stories, he would be teaching others to appreciate classic works and to pen their own scripts for radio. Guilt over getting out of the war with his skin intact, along with boredom and frustration, drove the youthful recruit to the barrooms of the capital city. He later said,

> I was there four years, and it was the dullest four years I ever spent. . . . I played a little baseball, did a little boxing, got on all right with the ladies, and made sergeant's stripes. But nothing much helped. I guess you might say I was suffering from a sort of life disappointment. Anyway, beginning with my arrival in Washington, a great liberty town, no matter what else you may say against it, I picked up a solid drinking habit that stayed with me from then on.

Scott claimed that half of his detail was drunk at Arlington every day. Fellow Marine Bob Morrissey, however, stated in an article published on a Marine website that neither Scott nor any of their company imbibed while on duty.

Morrissey served with Scott both as an instructor at the Marine Corps Institute and on the funeral detail. In addition to the grim duty of carrying fallen soldiers, the two friends also marched in ceremonial events such as presidential inaugural parades. There were a few perks to the job, such as a cross-country train ride, but even that journey had its onerous side. Scott and another noncom were required to keep the eternal flame from the Tomb of the Unknown Solider constantly lit during the trip.

A typical day would start at first light. After a quick meal, there was marching and drilling to perfect the form required of the unit entrusted with the task of escorting heroes to their final rest. Morrissey said Scott marched "with the grace of a gazelle" and was assigned the lead bearer duty. The young Marines were then bused to a broken-down former schoolhouse with ancient desks and worn floors, where they would assign and grade work for the correspondence courses.

The schoolhouse's heating system was decrepit and during the winter rarely provided enough warmth to fill the cavernous structure. Like a platoon of Bob Cratchits in a giant Scrooge-and-Marley counting house, Scott, Morrissey and company would huddle at their rotting desks, shivering in their fur-lined field jackets, grading papers with gloved hands. Morrissey reported that many threatened to set fire to the school just to provide a little heat. At noon, mess personnel would bring field rations for lunch. If you wanted something warm to drink, you had to tote your own thermos of hot coffee.

Following his pattern from school, when Scott got disappointed, he threw punches. According to writer Tedd Thomey, Scott got into one of his first fights as a Marine with a sergeant major over the talents of Ava Gardner. His opponent "broke the bridge of Scott's nose, twisted an ear into a soft pulp and sent him crashing twice to the floor." But Scott won the fight. That the alluring Gardner was the subject of the conflict seems unlikely—not to mention highly coincidental, since Scott would become embroiled romantically with the screen goddess about twenty years later. When asked by *Playboy* interviewer Lawrence Grobel about Thomey's account of the fight, Scott called the anecdote "ludicrous."

Regardless of the pretexts for his brawls, Scott got into a number of them. Like the drinking, fighting would become a steady habit. Scott's aversion to conformity and his short temper would often send him into battle mode. In a culture founded on lack of individuality, such as the Marines, he would have numerous provocations. One was the rivalry between the barracks Marines and Scott's division of instructors, who

were perceived by the former as pencil-pushers. The barracks detachment had control over their shared living quarters and lorded it over
the Marine Corps Institute crew. One barracks Marine corporal named
Holmes habitually volunteered for gate duty and would routinely give
liberty-bound M.C.I. guys rigorous inspections. If he found a dirty
fingernail or a dull brass button, he would deny the pass.

One evening, as Morrissey recalled, Scott responded to Holmes's
overly enthusiastic once-over. The future General Patton portrayer
drew himself up to his full height of over six feet and declaimed down
to the obnoxious, five-foot-six-inch corporal that Marines should
stick together, and that sometime they would "meet outside the gate
and have a very serious discussion about your biased, chicken-shit antics." Scott and Morrissey were waved through and Holmes rarely left
the barracks after that.

Some of his fellow soldiers, such as Bob Morrissey, continued in
the Marines as a career. But that wasn't for Scott. Doing his patriotic
duty and winning his father's attention were his prime motivations in
enlisting. He was too much of an individual to be content as a cog in
the military machinery. All social units lacking room for individuality
repelled him.

After four years of service, Scott was discharged in July of 1949.
Many of his contemporaries would stay in the service and ship out for
Korea when war broke out there in 1950, chasing the glory they had
missed when the bomb dropped on Hiroshima. About half of his friends
were killed in that conflict. Scott would count himself both lucky and
ashamed that he had avoided combat in two wars.

Where to go next? He still burned to be a writer, but concluded his
prospects for financial independence as an author of fiction were shaky
at best. A news reporter could at least depend on a weekly salary. As
a veteran, he was entitled to a college education through the G.I. Bill
of Rights, and enrolled at the University of Missouri at Columbia as a
journalism major.

The School of Journalism at Mizzou, the first of its kind in America, was founded in 1908 by Walter Williams, a Missouri newspaperman who believed reporters' careers should be professionalized. The university is located in the sleepy college town of Columbia, midway between Kansas City and St. Louis. Scott roomed with seven other students in a World War II barracks in Rollins Field on campus.

Scott had an advantage going into the program. Over the past four years he had witnessed real life up close in the form of grieving young widows and the dead bodies of numerous soldiers. In addition to those extra years, Scott's established drinking habit would have set him apart from his fellow Mizzous. Thanks to an ironclad constitution inherited from his robust father, he could consume prodigious amounts of alcohol, while most of his fellow freshmen, just out of high school, were probably still eager for their first taste of beer.

After a few months, Scott realized that journalism school, like the Marines, was merely a temporary stop on the way to his ultimate, unknown career. Even though he was taking only preliminary courses, he sensed a job requiring him to ask probing questions of complete strangers would be too taxing of his sensitive nature. The macho ex-Marine could not overcome his basic shyness.

He later explained to W. H. Manville in *Cosmopolitan*, "So I was bored, frustrated, unhappy, and I saw a notice on a bulletin board about a theatrical production. And I wondered what it would be like to be an actor. So I went to the library, got the script, and memorized the entire part I wanted by heart. I came in to the tryouts and began playing the scene without the book . . . not using the script is just about the most hick, unprofessional way to go at it—but I got the part."

The play was Terence Rattigan's *The Winslow Boy,* a teddibly British drawing-room drama centering on a thirteen-year-old cadet expelled from the naval academy based on an accusation of stealing a five-shilling postal note and forging the name of a friend to cash it. Despite his protestations of innocence, he is booted out without a trial and this seemingly minor crime leads to major disgrace for the boy's family. Pat McClarney, a professional actress with Broadway credits, had been cast as the boy's suffragette sister. The role Scott was interested in was the lead, Sir Robert Morton, a haughty barrister who takes up the boy's case. One of Scott's roommates, Jack Drake, would later claim that the journalism major was attracted to one of the actresses and auditioned to get to know her better. Whether it was attraction for a pretty girl, whim, curiosity, or sheer boredom that drove him to the audition, Scott was determined to win the role.

The production was presented by the Missouri Workshop Theatre under the aegis of the Department of Speech and Dramatic Art. Donovan Rhynsburger, head of the department since the 1920s, first met Scott during pre-audition interviews in his office. Rhynsburger explained in a radio interview in 1970,

> During this audition, I discovered that he had never been onstage before and he was here to play the barrister, the leading male role. . . . He was determined that he could do it. The risk was pretty great but I was interested in his dedication, his sincerity and his purposefulness. He was willing to argue with me that that he could do the role in spite of all my [negative] experience with first-timers. And so I invited him to tryouts. . . . It was evident he was the best person for this role.

"I'll never forget that day," Scott recalled to Cleveland Amory in *Parade*. "I was terrified when I went on, and I was certain I'd been terrible. I was even more sure of it when Donovan Rhynsburger . . . held up his hand. Then he didn't say anything for what seemed to me an hour, and I didn't know what to do. I was just kind of backing off the stage when he beckoned for me to come down to the front of the stage. 'You're good,' he said. 'Where have you been?'"

He had been wandering in search of a home and now he had finally found it. He felt comfortable onstage, pulling on the skin of another person and living a different life for a while. He told interviewer Lewis

Funke of his realization that acting was a job he could do, "I can only say that it was as though I had turned a dial on a safe and felt a click and a locking and a door opened. That's the only image I can bring to you. It was something that just felt right; it fit."

While he dreaded imposing himself on people as journalism required—he'd seen enough of real-life tragedy on the burial detail—he had found release in inhabiting fictional lives. He could unleash his frustrations and anger while remaining safely behind the protective covering of the character. In this case, Scott was able to convincingly portray Sir Robert's steely determination and haughty manner despite his total lack of formal training. His only classroom had been the movies, observing Cagney, Robinson, Bogart, and Davis. In fact, he would never attend an acting class. His training would be entirely practical.

Joe Koenan, a fellow journalism student who later became a theatre columnist for *Newsday*, recalled Scott had a natural bent for the stage, "He was something of a figure on campus. He had a certain flair for drama even then. He was a fairly imposing figure. When he walked across the campus, people noticed him."

On the opening night of *The Winslow Boy*, March 14, 1950, the fifty theatergoers who paid their eighty cents at the Jesse Auditorium certainly noticed him. The anonymous critic of a local paper described Scott's first big scene in which he interrogates his prospective young client: "The lawyer finished his staccato examination. As the young defendant burst into tears his family rushed to comfort him, hurling denunciations at the barrister. In the momentary lull, England's foremost attorney spoke calmly, 'The boy is clearly innocent—I accept the case.' As the curtain lowered, a breathless audience broke into enthusiastic applause. It was an ovation in honor of a young man in his first stage role."

When asked years later why he had added the C. to his name, he replied, "It took up space. I tell people that nobody knows who Edward Robinson is, but everybody knows who Edward G. Robinson is."

The Winslow Boy played for four more nights and Scott performed in a total of six plays at the University of Missouri in 1950. He went right from *The Winslow Boy* to Herman Wouk's *The Traitor*, a recent Broadway drama. This time he played Allan Carr, an idealistic young scientist bent on sharing atomic technology with the Soviets in the belief that the more countries who possess the knowledge, the less dangerous the world will be. Local critic Robert Skeetz praised Scott's "adroit characterization of a befuddled idealist."

Scott stayed at Mizzou for the summer session to participate in the department's Starlight Theatre program, consisting of two productions performed in the round on the roof of the Education Building. As one of only two players ever to be cast in both Starlight productions in one season, he had ample opportunity to stretch as an actor. In George Kelly's *The Show-Off*, he played the sixteen-year-old juvenile. Then, in *Laburnum Grove,* by J. B. Priestley, he was the elderly counterfeiter originated by Edmund Gwenn, the actor best known as Kris Kringle in the holiday classic *Miracle on 34th Street*.

Allene Preston Jones, who played opposite Scott in *Laburnum Grove*, would tell the *Columbia Daily Tribune* decades later: "I remember that he was rather reserved, more so than some of the other cast members, but very good. As I think back, I think he learned his lines faster than anyone else in the play. He was good from the start, don't you know. He picked up his character and developed it beautifully."

Scott threw himself into the theatre and, while still taking his journalism classes, began reading plays for possible future Workshop or Starlight productions. He wrote evaluations for Rhynsburger's perusal, grading Broadway fare such as *Our Town*, *The Little Foxes*, *Boy Meets Girl*, and *The Man Who Came to Dinner* on their difficulties in casting, potential datedness, and appropriateness for college-level performers. Rhynsburger continued to nurture his young star, relishing the versatility evident in one so unschooled and young. The department chairman planned the upcoming 1950–51 season around Scott's talents, another unprecedented move. Rhynsburger later related he didn't detect "any seeds of genius," but his student was "energetic and willing to work hard to develop his talent."

The fall season began with November performances of Samuel Spewack's *Two Blind Mice*, a slight comedy satirizing government bureaucracy. The plot centered on an abolished government office of medicinal herbs reactivated as a practical joke. Scott played a sarcastic reporter modeled on H. L. Mencken.

This featherweight doodle was followed by the metaphysics of *Shadow and Substance*, Paul Vincent Carroll's religious drama, in December. Scott was cast as Canon Skerritt, an Irish clergyman battling with a cynical schoolmaster for the soul of his parlor maid, who claims to have seen an earthly manifestation of a saint. "George C. Scott's portrayal of Canon Skerritt is an actor's masterpiece," an unsigned local review read. "The whole man is present in the severity of his acting. Scott plays with classic calm and modern compassion a very trying role."

Though Rhynsburger had planned the rest of the season for Scott and supplied him with odd jobs such as babysitting, *Shadow and Substance* was the last Workshop production for the young actor. During the summer, he had appeared at nearby Stephens College, an all-female institute, in *Family Portrait*, a sprawling religious epic about Christ's family, as "A Disciple." Stephens was known, according to Koenan, as a "fancy girls' school which had strict, strict regulations about their girls drinking. I got blacklisted from Stephens for keeping my dates out too late as many guys did at Missouri."

Director John Gunnell was so impressed with Scott's work, he invited him to play in the Stephens company's 1951 summer season and offered him a job as staff actor with the college's Playhouse for $15 a week during the school year. The Stephens drama department retained five male actors who would also teach courses in such topics as Western Literature. Meanwhile, despite his distaste for the personal intrusion it required, Scott continued to study journalism. He realized that acting was a tenuous way to make a living. Not surprisingly, his practical father advised him acting was not a good idea.

He was not sure which career path he should ultimately follow. His friend and fellow Stephens actor William West recalled, "Writing was very much an interest. At the time he wasn't sure which way his career would go, towards writing or acting. He was also interested in social work and criminology. He was talking about taking the FBI exam after getting his degree, or maybe going into criminal social work." Ironically, Scott would take up both professions, but as an actor. He played a social worker on the series *East Side/West Side* and portrayed policemen in numerous films and TV shows.

Although he had withdrawn from the Missouri Workshop Theatre, Scott received its highest honor, the Purple Mask, in the spring of 1951. His fiction was also finally gaining recognition. The May 24, 1951 *Columbia Missourian* stated Scott had won second prize of $25 in the Mahan Story Contest for "Carnival Near the Black." He also got honorable mention for another story, "Blessed Fruit." Both of these stories, and a third called "The Master," are available in the University of Missouri archives.

"Carnival" is a child's-eye view of a brutal Depression-era world. There are many autobiographical elements in the story—a coal-mining background, a dead mother, and, most significantly, a rough, distant father. The narrator is a young boy named Gyp who is growing up in a rowdy Kentucky coal camp called the Black.

Gyp's father, Jack, a widower coal miner, takes the boy to a carnival in nearby Virginia. Amid the strings of colored lights, freak shows, and cotton-candy booths, the father and son discover an exhibition boxing ring with a barker offering $100 to anyone who can last three rounds with the formidable Killer Myers. After a fellow miner is quickly KO'd by Myers, Gyp's father takes off his jacket and tells the boy he's about to earn two months' pay. Jack is savagely beaten by Myers in two rounds. Mary, a trapeze artist with the carnival and Myers's mistress, attempts to stop the slaughter, revealing that Myers has coated his hand wrappings in plaster of Paris so that his fists land like sledgehammers.

The hard-edged but soft-hearted Mary takes pity on the wounded Jack and his boy. She calls for a doctor and puts Jack up in her tent.

While his father recovers from broken ribs, Mary takes the motherless Gyp around the carnival and shows him its colorful, enchanting "artists." She regales him with stories of her past—dancing on Broadway, meeting famous people like Will Rogers, John Barrymore, and Al Jolson, and visiting far-off cities like San Francisco, Denver, and St. Louis. The boy is dazzled by this beautiful, maternal creature.

The brief, magical interlude is smashed by Killer Myers, who tears into Mary's tent and accuses her of cheating on him with Jack. Mary begs him to have some sense. Jack has been mostly unconscious since the fight. She's just taking care of him and the kid. Myers ignores her protestations of innocence and viciously stomps on Jack's stomach. Mary screams and Gyp falls to his knees. Myers roughly hustles Mary out of the tent, presumably to teach her a lesson in the same manner. The story ends with Gyp and his father, who is close to death, looking up at the top of the tent.

"Carnival" is touching without being overly sentimental. It displays a strong sense of place and brings the hardscrabble mining community and the tawdry midway vividly alive. One of the contest judges commented, "I selected this story as the best entry in my first group. It has great color and vitality. Every minor action contributes to the final climax."

The story also conveys Scott's ambivalent emotions toward both his parents. The father, presented with admiration, anger, and fear, is based on Scott's own, with his muscular vitality and dogged determination to overcome difficult odds. Scott builds up the father as a hero and then destroys him. The maternal figures—Gyp's mother and Mary, the substitute—are both remote, like Scott's real mother. Each offered love and comfort, only to be taken away—Gyp's mother by death and Mary by Killer Myers. Mary briefly shows Gyp the dazzling, artistic world of the carnival and her Broadway past, just as Helena Scott showed young George the wonders contained in fiction and poetry.

While "Carnival" is precise and economical, Scott's honorably mentioned "Blessed Fruit" is floridly melodramatic. A well-dressed young girl climbs the shabby steps of a run-down building to keep a mysterious doctor's appointment. The sordidness of the hallway and the doctor's office are laid out in graphic detail. Cockroaches scamper across the walls. The smell of cigarettes and booze hangs heavy in the air. It's gradually—and unsurprisingly—revealed that Dr. Brady, the alcoholic physician, is an abortionist and the girl, Diane, is "in trouble" and in need of his services. Her boyfriend, Johnny, has not given her enough money for the operation, and the doctor, who is having an attack of conscience about his profession, refuses to provide his service for less than the customary fee. After Diane explains her predicament—her religious, intolerant family; no means of support for the baby—Brady attempts to persuade her to have the child. She remains firm and Brady relents, agreeing to perform the illegal procedure.

The point of view shifts from an omniscient narrator to Diane's stream-of-consciousness interior monologue describing her pain and anger as she alternately recites the Hail Mary prayer and curses Johnny. Like "Carnival Near the Black," the story ends in tragedy when Brady exits his operating room and picks up the phone to inform Johnny that Diane has not survived.

Scott employs film noir-ish clichés to establish the grimy atmosphere, and indulges in overwrought prose, yet there is a strong subtext to both characters' actions. One of the judges commented, "Characterizations are developed so that the story provides an interplay of motives rather than a flat series of stereotyped personality clashes."

The University of Missouri Archives also yielded up "The Master," a brief tale set in the world Scott hoped to inhabit soon—Broadway. James Langley Brighton is a once-famous playwright now on the skids. He's written what he believes will be his comeback vehicle. But Mac, his agent, arrives at Brighton's country home with the news that George Hines, his producer, will not touch the script.

The agent leaves, meeting Hines on the way out. The producer is accompanied by two men. As Mac pulls out of the driveway, he looks down at the title page of Brighton's manuscript: "The Tragedy of Hamlet, Prince of Denmark." We realize Hines and his two cohorts have arrived to cart the pathetic dramatist off to an insane asylum. "The Master" isn't particularly original, but it does effectively encapsulate the rocket-like rise of a dazzling theatrical career and the deadening boom when it crashes to earth.

The three stories serve as ironic commentary on different aspects of Scott's life. "Carnival Near the Black" provides an extreme version of his emotionally barren childhood. "Blessed Fruit" can be seen as a prophetic view of some of his unhappy romantic relationships. "The Master" is a short glimpse, however jaundiced, into the professional theatre scene he longed to join.

Scott was making strides in his acting and writing. He had done well in the Mahan Short Story contest and he had a steady though low-paying job, appearing in the Stephens Playhouse summer 1951 productions of such lighter-than-air fare as *The Happiest Years*; *Personal Appearance*; *The Linden Tree*; *Yes, My Darling Daughter*; *The Bees and the Flowers*; and *Claudia*. He took another step toward adulthood by falling in love and getting married.

He first saw Carolyn Hughes on the Stephens stage in Jean Anouilh's modern-dress version of *Antigone*. She was a tall, willowy beauty originally from Belfast, Ireland, who had emigrated to Toledo, Ohio, in 1943 with her American mother and two brothers when her father, an Irish linen salesman, died. "He loved how she spoke," Victoria Lewis, the daughter of Carolyn and George C., said of her parents' early courting. "She had an Irish lilt to her voice, plus she had wanted to be an actress so she was very articulate. He always told the story that he felt in love with her when he asked her how old she was. She said she was twenty and the way she said it, he just loved it."

Over Easter vacation 1951, Carolyn went home to Toledo, and while visiting her, Scott proposed. The July 13, 1951 *Columbia Missourian* ran a feature on Scott, stating he was appearing in the Stephens production of *The Happiest Years* and was engaged to Hughes. The formal announcement appeared in the next day's *Missourian*. They were married a month and a half later on August 31. The couple traveled to the bride's hometown of Toledo for the double-ring ceremony, which took place at St. Mark's Episcopal Church. Scott's brother-in-law, Carroll C. Hamilton of Alexandria, Virginia, served as best man. It was a rushed marriage, and one of which Scott would soon grow weary. Just as he'd been in a hurry to become a man by joining the Marines right out of high school, Scott was in a hurry to become an adult with this marriage to a girl he'd known only a few months. It was all too much, too soon.

There wasn't much of a honeymoon. The couple took a brief trip to Michigan to visit the groom's family and then returned to Columbia, moving into a cramped basement apartment with its own entrance at 1610 Wilson Avenue, a tree-lined street just a few blocks from both Stephens and the University of Missouri. Scott resumed his journalism studies and began rehearsals, with his new wife also in the cast, for the first fall Stephens production, *Night Must Fall*. Scott had a field day as Danny, the charming, sociopathic killer who flatters his way into the good graces of a selfish elderly woman and then strangles the old girl. Carolyn played Olivia, the victim's secretary, who falls in love with the charismatic strangler.

In addition to his journalism requirements at the University of Missouri and a full schedule at the Playhouse, Scott also taught a course in Mastery of Western Literature. The class was the lowest of his priorities. He didn't have time to read the required books, so he spent class time discussing *Les Misérables* with the young coeds. One of his students was Tammy Grimes, an elfin girl from Boston and the future Tony-winning, husky-voiced star of such Broadway musicals as *The Unsinkable Molly Brown* and *High Spirits*. She also played opposite him at the Playhouse. She found him very handsome, but somewhat aloof. "He had a temperament that provoked one to keep one's distance," the actress recalled. "You just didn't go up and hug him. He was a private man, but he did teach me how to make scars in makeup class." She also noticed that Scott's talent inspired the rest of the company to rise to his level: "The minute he walked into a room there was a lifting up, so to speak, and one had to do one's best."

There were ten productions in the Stephens 1951–52 season, and Scott was cast in seven of them. He followed *Night Must Fall* with such varied roles as the domineering Reverend James Morrell in Shaw's *Candida*; the duplicitous Joseph Surface in Sheridan's *School for Scandal* (with Carolyn as the coquettish Lady Teazle); a rising young English director in a forgettable comedy called *The Distaff Side*; the frantic producer Gordon Miller in the farce *Room Service* (played by Groucho Marx in the film version); a walk-on part of a bellhop in *Born Yesterday* (with Grimes in the lead); and the romantic juvenile in Christopher Fry's poetic drama *The Lady's Not for Burning*.

After *School for Scandal*, Carolyn served as stage manager or sound technician on many of the shows. She was featured on the "Woman's World" page of the October 31, 1951 *Columbia Missourian*. The article was titled "Talents Include Homemaking: Erratic Schedule Is the Lot for Actor's Wife" and was accompanied by a photo of the first Mrs. Scott looking like the prototypical, June Cleaver *hausfrau*, wearing a triple strand of pearls as she pours a cup of coffee. "We've been married only two months, so George hasn't had much time to form any favorites in my cooking," she told the reporter, "but so far, he seems to like my Irish stew."

"We would like to try New York, and then in twenty or thirty years, retire to California," Carolyn predicted at the story's finish. Her vision of a rosy future acting with her husband would prove overly optimistic.

3

The Dark Ages

KAREN TRUESDELL SAT TRANSFIXED AT the Stephens Playhouse as she watched George C. Scott strangling a wheelchair-bound old lady. He was playing the role of Danny, the delightful and devilish killer in a revival of *Night Must Fall*. The impressionable freshman was mesmerized by the young actor's raspy voice, impressive physique, and galvanic presence. Over fifty years later, she recalled:

> He just had something about him. Even when he was young, when he was twenty-six years old, if he stepped onstage—I hate the cliché 'bigger than life' but that's what he was. He was so dynamic that you couldn't keep your eyes off him. He was fierce. In this part, he could be fierce and weird. I don't know. It was just one of those things; it was love at first sight. I turned to my roommate and said "I'm going to marry that man." I had never seen him before. I didn't know anything about him before he walked onstage, but I turned to her and said, "I'm going to marry that man." That was my first reaction.

Scott was nearing the end of his second summer season at the Playhouse. He had already appeared in *Apron Strings, I Like It Here, Ladies in Retirement*, Noel Coward's *Hay Fever*, and *Oliver Oliver*. This second production of *Night* would be followed by the lightweight comedy *Brighten the Corner* and the mystery *Laura*.

Truesdell reported in her memoir that when the *Night Must Fall* company had taken its bows and the lights came up, she didn't want to leave the theatre. She was a young girl, away from her home in Seattle for the first time and taking tentative steps towards fulfilling her childhood fantasies of becoming an actress. She wanted to keep this feeling alive. This dominating man she had just watched for two hours embodied her theatrical ambitions and her romantic longings.

Scott was playing Danny for the second time. He was the star of the company, shooting on all cylinders, displaying the incredible drive he had inherited from his father. He was spending thirty hours a week rehearsing and performing. Once the fall semester began, he piled on journalism classes at Missou and continued to teach Mastery of Literature to the Stephens girls. In addition, he became a father: Carolyn bore a daughter, Helen Victoria, in December 1952. She was named for Scott's sister and the heroine of *The Red Shoes*, Carolyn's favorite movie. It was decided she would go by Vicky, since there were enough Helens in the Scott family. The young couple moved from the basement on Wilson Avenue to slightly larger accommodations at 403 North Ann Street. Carolyn had graduated and given up acting for the moment, taking the occasional stage managing, box office, or sound operator job to concentrate on raising the baby. Despite his wife's sacrifice, Scott must have felt enormous pressures. Both he and Karen Truesdell were seeking something—Scott craved a release from his growing responsibilities and Truesdell dreamed of romantic love and a career on the stage.

The first production of the 1952–53 Stephens fall season was a return engagement of *Laura*, the last show of the summer series, with Scott repeating his role of Detective Mark McPherson. While *Laura* was in production at night, he began rehearsing Arthur Miller's *Death of a Salesman* as Biff, the tormented elder son of the tragic middle-class everyman Willy Loman. Scott would play Willy to acclaim more than two decades later on Broadway. Also in the cast were Tammy Grimes as Letta, one of the girls Biff and his brother Happy pick up; Scott's friend William West as the neighbor Howard; and, in the small role of the Woman in Boston with whom Willy has a brief affair, Karen Truesdell.

By this time, Truesdell's attraction for Scott had blossomed into a full-blown crush. She began skipping classes and taking on any menial backstage chore—including scraping the gum off the bottom of theatre seats—in order to be near her idol. She confided her feelings to her roommate, who cautioned her to be careful. This was a married man with a baby and a reputation for heavy drinking. There was talk he'd beat up a bartender the previous summer. Truesdell dismissed her friend's misgivings, telling her she knew her passion wouldn't lead to anything. For now, at least, she had to be content with stolen peeks at Scott's muscular build in the common dressing room during costume changes for *Salesman*.

The drama did even better at the box office than *Night Must Fall*, setting a new attendance record. The *Columbia Missourian* ran a feature article on Scott in the November II edition, stating he was taking a "rest" from his recent leading roles by playing the bit part of a fussy butler in *The Importance of Being Earnest*. The young actor already disdained the film industry. "The motion picture business, among other things, robs an actor of his independence," he told the reporter. He went even further, stating that the idea of playing to a "dead" audience, as opposed to the breathing one the theatre affords, was enough to drive Scott from even considering a career on screen.

The vacation of *Earnest* was followed by a forgettable comedy, *Lady of Letters*, and *As You Desire Me*, Luigi Pirandello's examination of a beautiful woman suffering from amnesia. Truesdell was cast as the heroine, alternating with another Stephens actress for half of the two-week run. Here was her chance to play opposite her beloved George—but she found she could barely look at him during their scenes. The next production, *Petticoat Fever*, another bubble of a play, brought them even closer together.

Scott played Dascome Dinsmore, an eccentric telegraph operator living in remote Alaska. Truesdell was Clara Wilson, his rejected fiancée, who trails him all the way to the frozen north to win him back. The play required Truesdell not only to share the stage with her idol, but to kiss him. The director, Doug McCall, staged the scene so that Clara would burst into Dascome's room, leap into his arms, and attempt to lay a big, wet smack on him. Dascome is no longer interested in Clara, so he turns his face, accepting a peck on the cheek, and puts her down.

On the second night of performances, Truesdell paused before entering, throwing off the timing. When she jumped onto Scott, he did not turn away. Instead, he returned the kiss. In fact, the performers smooched for so long, the audience responded with cat calls and wolf whistles. The director ordered them to go back to his original blocking. A passionate embrace made no sense, because the telegraph operator was now in love with another woman. "Step back, Trues," Tammy Grimes advised her fellow student. "You don't want this. Everybody knows what's going on." The third night brought another erotic liplock between Scott and Truesdell. McCall pulled the pair aside and demanded they stop fooling around and follow directions. For the remainder of the run, they did just that, allowing only a brief peck onstage and avoiding each other behind the scenes. Truesdell knew she was playing with fire. Reminders of Scott's marital status were everywhere. Carolyn served as secretary to the Playhouse and could be seen behind the bars of the box office, selling tickets. Scott would often bring baby Victoria on for curtain calls. But Truesdell couldn't get those two kisses out of her mind.

Neither could Scott. Two weeks after *Petticoat Fever* closed, when Scott was in his second production of *Laburnum Grove*, he met Truesdell in a coffee shop off campus and confessed the attraction was mutual. "We looked at each other for a while," Truesdell recalled, "and I said, 'Maybe we ought not to see each other.'"

"That would be pretty impossible because we're cast in all these shows together," Scott observed.

"What are you going to do?" Truesdell asked.

"We'll work out something," he answered with a smile.

"That was the beginning of our sneaking around," Truesdell recalled. They met after performances of the next show, Shakespeare's *The Tempest* (Scott was Stephano, the drunken butler, and Truesdell played the tiny role of Iris, a spirit). Truesdell would slip out once the curtain had fallen, meet Scott at his car, and they'd drive to the parking lot of a closed supermarket for some heavy petting. Their smooching sessions went no further—at first. Truesdell was nineteen, and "good" girls of that age in the early 1950s didn't "put out," especially with married men.

The unconsummated affair continued until Scott got a job for the summer with the Mad Anthony Players at the Toledo Zoo Theatre in Ohio, an Equity stock company on the grounds of the city's zoo. He urged Truesdell to apply for an apprentice position so they could be together. When her application was accepted, she was deliriously happy. The only wrinkle in their perfect plan was Carolyn and the baby would be coming, too. Scott and his family would be living with Carolyn's brother and sister-in-law in Toledo.

Truesdell had to swallow her disappointment. She was growing impatient with playing the role of the other woman and only getting to reveal her true feelings for Scott onstage. The Stephens semester closed with Jean Anouilh's *Ring Round the Moon*. Once again they were cast as lovers, with Scott in dual roles of twin brothers Hugo and Frederic and Truesdell as Isabella, a ballet dancer enamored of Frederic.

The Mad Anthony Players productions included *Dark of the Moon*, *Uncle Tom's Cabin*, *Present Laughter*, *Brighten the Corner*, *Dear Ruth*, *The Great Big Doorstep*, and another production of *Petticoat Fever*. Truesdell was Scott's leading lady in *Brighten the Corner* and tempted him as the vamp Joanna Lyppiatt in *Present Laughter*.

During that summer Truesdell and Scott consummated their relationship and Scott gave her his mother's wedding ring, telling her she was his real wife. Like an omen from a romance novel, the ring was lost during their first completed tryst in a deserted park. And the pressures of carrying on an affair and caring for his marriage and a baby were taking their toll on Scott, who began drinking heavily before and after performances. The lovers missed the final dress rehearsal of *Dark of the Moon*, but Scott was letter perfect for the first performance. "When we did stock together, he was drunk most of the time," Truesdell recalled. "He would be just drunk out of his mind backstage waiting to go on, barely standing up. He would take a step onstage and come out of it immediately, run through everything perfectly with a great performance, never missing a word, and step offstage and be drunk again." This stage sobriety would be a trait he would rely on later in his career.

One night all the pressures spilled over during a post-show drive. Steering with one hand while clutching a bottle of bourbon with the other, Scott careened recklessly into a rainstorm against traffic, deliberately courting a crash. "It's the only way," he screamed to Truesdell, embracing suicide as the only alternative to their untenable situation. "His face changed," Truesdell recalled with a shudder. "His skin kind of got very taut and his lips got narrow. He looked like a demon." Truesdell hit her head against the dashboard and Scott nearly killed both of them before he finally pulled over. The Toledo season was nearing an end, and the couple had to find some kind of resolution.

The solution Scott offered was not ideal, but at least it was a change. He would focus on his acting career and quit Stephens and the University of Missouri only two hours shy of a degree in journalism. He would leave Carolyn and the baby with her brother's family in Toledo, telling her he was headed to New York to establish himself on Broadway and would send for her once he had a job. He failed to inform his wife he was taking Karen along—as well as their close friend Jake Dengal, another actor with the Toledo company, to split expenses. The lovers had allowed their passions to ride herd over common sense: Truesdell turned down a job with a theatre in Michigan in order to accompany Scott, who naively believed all three would magically win paying roles in no time. Then he could afford to tell Carolyn the painful truth and marry Karen.

It was the beginning of what Scott would later call his "dark ages"—five years of disappointment and frustration. The trio found a dismal, one-bedroom flat with peeling wallpaper near the Hayden Planetarium on Manhattan's Upper West Side for $90 a month. Scott and Truesdell shared the bedroom while Dengal slept on the pull-out sofa. Reasoning that Scott was the most talented of the three, Truesdell put her acting ambitions on hold and took a position as a dental assistant, while Dengal acquired work as an usher in a movie theatre. Scott went in search of acting jobs, but found himself in more barrooms than agents' offices. The closest he got to a theatre or movie set was on the day he hitchhiked to Hoboken, New Jersey, to watch his idol Marlon Brando filming *On the Waterfront*. The two would eventually share the screen and the distinction of being the only actors to refuse an Oscar, but that would be more than twenty years in the future. For now, the young actor's volcanic anger was vented offstage at strangers—his nose was broken again during a drunken brawl.

Dengal eventually moved out and the lovers found an even smaller abode. All they could afford was one room with a bathroom down the hall shared with another family. The miserable Truesdell continued to lie to her parents about her living arrangements. She told them she was rooming with Tammy Grimes, who had also moved to the city to pursue an acting career. She desperately needed her college friend's shoulder when she learned Carolyn was pregnant. When Scott told her the news, she quickly realized he must have had sex with his wife during the Toledo summer, when he had given her his mother's wedding ring and called her "his real wife." She felt as if she had been cheated on, but Carolyn had the power and her lover's name in marriage. Truesdell didn't even have the ring, having lost it the day Scott had given it to her. Betrayed and dejected, she was caught in a web of lies and the trap was about to get stickier.

During the Thanksgiving weekend, Scott thumbed a ride back to Ohio to be with Carolyn. While he was gone, Truesdell missed her period and discovered she, like her rival, was expecting a baby. She confided in Grimes over the lonely four-day weekend. What was she going to do? The father of her child was enjoying turkey, cranberries, and stuffing with his pregnant wife in Toledo while she was stuck alone in New York. Scott returned after the holiday bearing a gift—the wishbone from Carolyn's turkey. Truesdell sobbed herself to sleep without telling her lover her terrible news. After work that night, she came home to find him drunk and enraged at her for imagined infidelity. Just before the situation became violent, Grimes arrived. As Scott was menacingly swinging an exercise dumbbell at Truesdell, Grimes stepped between them like a heroine in an old-fashioned stage melodrama and pleaded, "Don't hit that girl! She's carrying your child!" Too blotto and angry to comprehend Grimes's words, Scott continued to advance. Truesdell grabbed a frying pan from the tiny stove and clocked him on the side of the head. He staggered but failed to fall. "Hit him again, Trues!" Grimes shouted, and the second swat did it. The towering actor dropped like a sack of potatoes. The friends scurried away to Grimes's apartment.

When her lover was finally sober and the lump on his head went down, Truesdell returned to inform Scott he was to be a father for the third time. In an eerie echo of his short story "Blessed Fruit," his first thought was to send Truesdell to an abortionist. She refused. Why did Carolyn get to keep her baby and she couldn't? Scott pleaded with her to reconsider, but she was adamant. As he did on the night of the wild rainy highway drive, the desperate Scott attempted extreme measures to escape his predicament. According to her memoir, several nights after the frying pan incident, Truesdell dreamed she was being smothered. She awoke to find it was no dream: the love of her life was covering her face with a pillow. She managed to fight him off and smelled gas. He had sealed the windows and turned on the gas, intending to kill himself as well.

It was a literal wake-up call. Truesdell decided that the man she loved and had sacrificed her dreams for was dangerous to herself and her baby. Grimes had earlier suggested she go to a home for unwed mothers in Newton, Massachusetts, not far from Grimes's hometown of Brookline. The next day she informed Scott she was having the baby whether he liked it or not. After she had earned a few more weeks' pay at the dentist's office, she would stay with Grimes's family in Massachusetts and spend the rest of the time until her confinement at the home.

The couple spent a depressing Christmas together, a pathetic tree with few decorations the only ornamentation in their one-room apartment. Their dinner consisted of two cans of turkey soup and peanut butter sandwiches. In February 1954, Truesdell left New York and Scott to stay with the Grimes family in Brookline. At Penn Station, he promised they would be together someday.

Scott's father demanded that he return and take care of Carolyn, even offering to pay for an apartment. Carolyn lost her baby, and Truesdell delivered hers, a girl named Michelle, at the charity ward of Boston General Hospital in late August. (To protect her daughter's privacy, in her memoir Truesdell referred to her as Tracie.) Scott paid her one visit after Michelle was born. He had finally told his wife about the affair, he said, and Carolyn had agreed to a divorce. He and Karen could be married. But it was too late: Truesdell was already engaged to a Back Bay socialite who had befriended her during her stay with the Grimeses and her time at the Florence Crittenden Home for Unwed Mothers. Though she still loved Scott, she didn't have the heart to break off the upcoming wedding.

For a brief period, Scott had custody of baby Victoria in Detroit while Carolyn stayed in Toledo to sort out the complicated situation. "It was during that time that I got very sick," Victoria recalled:

> George said that he left me alone in a crib to go to the corner drug-
> store for some aspirin for my fever. On the way home, though, he

passed a bar and badly wanted a drink. But, for some reason, he decided not to go in. He returned to find me in convulsions and chok-
ing. He had a scar on his thumb from where I bit him. [Years later]
I expressed my gratitude to him for not stopping that day or else I
might not be here. George and his father had me hospitalized.

Victoria was soon returned to her mother's care in Toledo. Carolyn's family told George to stay away from his daughter, who was legally adopted by Carolyn's new husband two years later.

He now had nothing—no money, no job, no wife, no lover, no
children. New York held no promise for him. He couldn't go back to
Stephens. The story of Truesdell's pregnancy had spread and the dean
refused to rehire him as a staff actor. The only place he could go was
his father's house. The family had moved to the high-toned neighborhood of Square Lake, three miles north of Bloomfield Hills, near his
childhood home of Pontiac.

He continued to pursue an acting career, finding work at the nearby
Will-O-Way Playhouse, an Equity stock theatre specializing in comedy. "We were known as the laughing stock of Michigan, because we
did nothing but comedies," Bill Merrill, the theatre's director told biographer W. A Harbinson. Scott was "a very strong actor in a little
theater . . . our seating capacity was only 400 and the first row was very
close."

Merrill recalled Scott's first role for him was in *Affairs of State*, a politically themed Broadway hit, and that the young man was so broke
Merrill advanced him rehearsal money so he could eat. Evidently,
Scott's father was providing room but not board. Scott did so well during the summer that he suggested a winter season, when riskier material might be attempted. (Few playgoers ventured out of their warm
homes on chilly Michigan nights, so audiences would be small no matter what the programming.) Scott wanted to try producing as well.
In addition to this ambitious task, Scott played the title role in the
playhouse's first winter show, *Mister Roberts*. He followed the wartime

comedy-drama with some of his previous favorites—producing and acting in *Night Must Fall* and *Death of a Salesman*—as well as *Detective Story* and an original play, *Chris Dumonde*. The plays were considered an artistic success by the local press, but, as expected and as Scott later recalled, audiences stayed away in droves due to the lack of heat in the converted barn theatre.

"We were well aware of his ability right away," remembered Detroit-area TV personality Sonny Elliott, who augmented his weatherman duties at the local NBC affiliate with appearances at the Will-O-Way. "George played a handcuffed felon in *Detective Story* and he played it as though he really were being arrested. He had such an intensity that we were all impressed. . . . His wrists almost bled [from the handcuffs], he played the intensity so high."

According to Elliott, Scott had that intensity offstage as well. His macho image was enhanced by the knife he kept in his boot, although Elliott never saw him draw it out. "He was a most interesting man," Elliot related. "Whenever he talked, we listened. He had a compelling nature. Not an especially friendly guy. We knew his father was a big wheel with a company in Detroit." George D. was now an executive with Ex-Cell-O and determined to force his wayward son to face up to his responsibilities.

Scott Junior would later tell the *Detroit Pictorial News* he was so broke during this time, he had no place to stay and occasionally slept on the stage. But Bill Merrill claimed Scott was staying with his father, although Scott Senior would not step in to help when alimony payments were due. The young actor would occasionally find himself on the wrong side of the law for failure to comply with his divorce agreement. Bill Merrill told W. A. Harbinson, "I had to bail him out a couple of times. At least the prosecuting attorney turned him over to me. . . . Mr. Scott [senior] would kind of throw up his hands. That's why I went to get him out of jail and so forth. Because Mr. Scott would say, 'Bill, I've got other sons and George is a man and he's got to stand on his own two feet.' So, in order to have a show, I'd have to go bail him out."

Escape from his father's house would soon be possible, but this time Scott would head west. Harvey Taylor, drama critic for the *Detroit Times*, asked Bill Merrill to choose the Will-O-Way's best actor for the season. The lucky winner would be awarded a screen test for Warner Brothers in Hollywood, through Taylor's connections with the studio. Merrill chose the intense young man who rubbed his wrists raw for his art.

New York hadn't worked out, but maybe Los Angeles would. Merrill paid Scott's way to the West Coast, where the actor took up residence in a low-rent hotel on Figueroa Street. He shot the screen test at Warners, and attended a cocktail party arranged by Harvey Taylor, but no job offers materialized. For the first few weeks, he would walk the eight miles from Figueroa to agents' offices on Sunset Boulevard. "I would start out dry and fresh," he recalled, "and arrived mean and sweaty. No wonder I couldn't get a job. The agents would take one look at me, and either throw me out or offer me a dime for a cup of coffee." The hike was good exercise, but it didn't help his career. "I got a job as a short-order cook," Scott later told Rex Reed, "made some rounds, went to the studios, but mostly sat around MacArthur Park, watching the drunks."

His personal dark ages got really dark now. Scott was fed up with the artistic limits and low wages of summer theatre and the humiliation of depending on his father for a roof over his head. As he had done in Missouri and New York, when the situation got difficult, he just up and left.

For several months, Scott banged around the country. He never discussed this bleak period in any interviews, so details about his aimless sojourn are few. W.A. Harbinson conjectures the unemployed actor was living the life of a hobo. He had reached the bottom. Finally, he decided he couldn't continue this rootless existence or he'd wind up a corpse on the side of an interstate.

He couldn't go back to his father's home. Asking for help from Karen Truesdell or Carolyn Hughes was out of the question, so he turned to the only person who might show him compassion: his sister, Helen. Scott made his way to Washington, D.C., the site of his Marine days of drinking and the burial detail. Helen was living there now with her husband, Carroll Hamilton, the best man at Scott's wedding to Hughes. When he arrived in the national capital, Scott spent his last dime to call his sister and she took him in.

Hamilton gave his brother-in-law a job with his construction firm. Scott drove a truck, poured concrete, and got his health back. He also resolved to give up acting. But the glimmer of ambition hadn't faded altogether. After several months of working with his hands, he saw an ad announcing auditions for Pirandello's *Six Characters in Search of an Author* by a local community theatre. He joined the cast and continued construction by day.

A different person might have been content. Scott had a steady job, a place to live, his health, and he was acting—albeit for free in a community production, but at least he was onstage. He even had a new love interest—Pat Reed, a singer and actress who was also in the cast. He couldn't be alone. He was not a womanizer, but he did need the steadying influence of a female helpmate to fight his demons and pursue his goals. Reed herself shared those goals, and amateur theatre didn't satisfy either of their hungers. Scott knew he could be a professional actor. Pat encouraged this spark. The two soon married and Scott bet on another throw of the dice—back to New York to conquer Broadway.

4

New York Again

RICHARD III IS AMONG THE most coveted roles in the Shakespearean canon. This "hunchbacked toad" revels in his villainy, stepping over countless corpses on his ascent to the English throne. The world rejects him because of his physical deformities—a limp due to the unevenness of his legs, a withered arm, and a humpback—so he rejects the world. The character's unabashed self-interest, combined with the physical challenges of playing him, has placed Richard on the dream-role lists of most serious actors. The part had been tackled by every great male star from Richard Burbage, Shakespeare's original, to Edwin Booth to Gielgud, Richardson, and, most famously, Laurence Olivier, who directed himself in an elaborate film version, released in 1955, the same year George C. Scott returned to New York.

Richard would provide Scott with the opportunity of a lifetime, but he had to go through hell to get it. Back in New York, the actor was determined to conquer the stage. In Pat Reed, he found a fellow aspiring performer, and he was no longer hampered by the trauma of carrying on an extramarital affair and fathering an illegitimate child. However, he still tended to drown his frustrations in alcohol. Those frustrations must have been immense. The Broadway stage was entering a golden age, with playwrights like Tennessee Williams, Arthur Miller, William Inge, Horton Foote, and Lillian Hellman illuminating

the struggles of a self-deluding America and providing insightful actors like Kim Stanley, Julie Harris, Maureen Stapleton, Jason Robards,
Eli Wallach, and Anne Jackson with roles of complexity and depth.
Off-Broadway was another fertile field of dramatic promise about to
come into bloom. Yet here was Scott, a powerful actor able to penetrate to the heart of any character, praised to skies in the regions, with
over a hundred stock and college credits on his resume, unable to find
acting work.

The only steady employment he did find was in a bank, operating
a check-sorting machine during the graveyeard shift. "I'd come out
at ten in the morning after having worked ten hours," he told Julius
Novick of the *Village Voice*, "and, you know, to me it was cocktail
time. . . . I used to go to a Greek bar around the corner down on Broad
Street somewhere, and by twelve noon I was shit-faced, y'know? And
in the meantime—the reason I took the night job is so I could make
rounds in the daytime."

"To this day, G. C. despises banks," an anonymous friend was quoted by Rex Reed many years later. "He probably keeps all of his money
from *Patton* in a shoe box guarded by one of his German shepherds."

In addition to the bank job, Scott sold rugs when he wasn't making
the rounds of auditions and producer's offices. Meanwhile, Pat tried
out for singing gigs and held down a secretarial job.

Scott often expressed his frustrations with his fists. His fellow actor
Jason Robards told Percy Peterson for *Motion Picture*, "George had a lot
of fights in New York—but somehow he came out of them okay. It
was his own temper that almost destroyed him. He punched so many
walls and mirrors that it is surprising he is still able to close his fist."

Prospects for paid acting jobs weren't completely bleak. In the
summer of 1956, Scott found employment with the Sun Parlor Playhouse, a stock company in Windsor, Ontario, just across the bridge
from his hometown of Detroit. Local TV weatherman Sonny Elliott,
a fellow player from the Will-O-Way, costarred with Scott in *The
Tender Trap* at Sun Parlor: "I was more well known than George at

that time which is strange to say, but I was. I got the lead and he played the second lead."

Scott's tough guy reputation was still very evident. "He could be intimidating," Elliott remembered. "One morning we sat on the porch of the theatre. He had a fight with his wife and just pushed her off the porch. We thought that was kind of macho, you might say. It was strange for us."

This roughhouse playing carried over into his acting, even in light fare like *The Tender Trap*. Elliott got a taste of it when they were rehearsing:

> He knocks on the door in one of the scenes and opens it. There he is drooping in the doorway. I said to him, "For God's sake, George, give me someone to bounce against. Give me a little life when you open the door." . . . So the next time we had a rehearsal, he opened the door, grabbed me by the hand, he yelled, he screamed, he let me know he was playing it up as far as he could. Then without letting go of my hand, he threw me across the stage completely and knocked me onto the couch. He peered close to me as he did in *Anatomy of a Murder* and said "Is that up enough for you?"

Apart from this brief summer sojourn, there were no other acting jobs in the offing. The situation was getting desperate. Both Scott and Pat were killing themselves in boring jobs earning low wages. Neither was making any headway toward a professional performing career. Scott had alimony and child support payments. Their finances were further strained when Pat gave birth to a son, Matthew, in the fall of 1957. After seven years of banging his head against the wall of show business, Scott saw no signs a single brick would ever be dislodged.

Finally, just as the "tapocketa-tapocketa" sound of the check-sorting machine was about to send him over the edge, Scott learned the Off-Broadway New York Shakespeare Festival was holding auditions for *Richard III*. This was it. Make or break. He had to have this role. If he didn't get it, he would give up this damned crazy dream of being an actor once and for all.

Joseph Papp, head of the Festival, was similar to Scott in his determined pursuit of artistic freedom and his bucking of show-biz conventions. Beginning with the founding of the Festival in 1954, Papp's goal was to snatch the Bard off the dusty library shelf and bring him alive, bloody and sweating, into the modern age. He wanted a muscular, vital, free Shakespeare to whom anyone—not just the academically inclined or middle-class ticket buyers—could relate. The careers of many notable performers, including Roscoe Lee Browne, J. D. Cannon, and Scott's future wife Colleen Dewhurst, were launched by the Festival.

The company had been playing in the Emmanuel Church on the Lower East Side, the East River Park Amphitheater, and various outdoor locations around the city. With *Richard*, they would have a permanent venue of their own, the 650-seat Heckscher Theatre at Fifth Avenue and 104th Street. It was a new theatre, a new chance for the Festival and for Scott.

Stuart Vaughan, the director of *Richard* and stager of many Festival productions, knew of Scott without realizing it. He remembered,

> In 1952, I guess it would be, I was one of two leading men in a summer stock company in Toledo, Ohio. . . . [The previous summer], this guy named George Scott was the leading man of the same Toledo company. We had mutual friends. An actress who I had worked with was there the same season as Scott. She told me about Scott, this wonderful actor who had been playing the Witch Boy in *Dark of the Moon*. He had set up shop with a girl apprentice. They had disappeared from view the night of the dress rehearsal. My friend Greg Falls, the director, walked his role. Apparently, George and this girl had had a long, dirty weekend and a very drunken weekend. But George, I later learned, appeared on opening night, went through the thing flawlessly, astoundingly. My friend Janice told me this story, and I said, "Gee, he sounds

like a marvelous actor. But I've gotta tell you, if this S.O.B. ever crosses my path for any reason whatsoever, he's not gonna be hired by me."

Fortunately for Scott, Vaughan did not realize the actor auditioning for Richard and the irresponsible S.O.B. who had missed a crucial dress rehearsal were the same person. Scott read for the part twice and wasn't cast. "I resorted to my usual remedy for such feelings in those days—I went out and got loaded," he later told the *Saturday Evening Post*. After the bender, he woke in the garden of a friend's house with the friend's two police dogs staring at him. "They seemed disgusted, and I was disgusted with myself." He stumbled to a phone and begged Vaughan to let him audition again. Scott resolved to study the role all night. If he still failed to win the job, he would quit acting once and for all.

Vaughan has his own version of first encountering the actor and the *Richard* audition:

My friend Janice told me there was this wonderful actor—she didn't identify him—he was doing a reading of a new play in a studio Off-Off-Broadway. It was an interesting play and I knew someone else involved with it. So I came and here's this astounding actor. It was a play about Christopher Marlowe and his demise in that seaside town where the two guys stabbed him in a duel. George played one of the villains. I said, "My God, this guy has got to come in and read for Richard," not knowing that he was the hero of the *Dark of the Moon* story. Anyway, George came in to read. I guess he had a hangover. Also the person who was reading with him was a rather incompetent young actress who wasn't a help. It was not a successful reading. But at the same time, I had seen Scott be brilliant in this other reading. I said to Joe Papp, "Joe, let's have him back again." I walked up to the front of the stage and said, "George, we like very much a potential here, but we don't feel we've seen you at your best. Would you please look at the material, come back tomorrow or the next day, and read again, because we're serious."

So, he came back again. I had somebody else read with him and he was as brilliant as I'd hoped he would be. It was not until after the *Richard* had opened that my friend Janice Halliday said, "You know that story about *Dark of the Moon*, that was the guy you'd never work with." And I said, "Well, this is amazing." What was also amazing in light of the earlier story was that Scott didn't apparently have a drink during the entire rehearsal period of *Richard*. He was absolutely disciplined and was marvelous. He had some good Shakespearean training and handled the verse beautifully. His voice kind of went from drinking over the years. But that hadn't happened yet. It was a much more flexible, normal, but very usable voice at the point when *Richard* was going on. What I thought was too bad in the end, he was just as fine an actor in the *Richard III* as he ever became and I didn't feel there was any growth. He was a wonderfully talented, wonderfully gifted person with great technical skill from the beginning and he never lost that. If his emotional, personal life and the drinking—most of which I never saw because we parted company—hadn't taken its toll, he could have become an even more splendid actor. In point of fact, we're not producing great actors in the American theater and we haven't been for some time. All the potentially great actors fall by the wayside and are found on television or in second-rate movies doing villains because they're the only people who can speak well. George's General Patton was just fine. He could have done General Patton in 1957 as easily as when he did it. To see such potential and not to see its fulfillment was more an indictment of the American theatre than an indictment of George.

Vaughan also remembered the rehearsal period:

At the first dress rehearsal, there was a place where he did a som-
ersault and his wig fell off. I think we had an invited audience.
He picked the wig up, put it on his other hand, spun it around,
went on with the lines and went offstage. It was just great. Nothing threw him.

We didn't keep the wig bit, nor did we keep the great moment
when he and Bob Blackburn as Richmond are having the fight.
We had a real mace. It was quite terrifying. We had a metal shield
for Bob. George was whacking at him with the ball on the mace,
it was a genuine one from the period. The ball broke off and it
headed into the audience. Fortunately, it headed directly to two
rows of empty seats where a group apparently had not come. A
bus or something hadn't arrived. It hit the seats and would have
killed somebody. Moral: Don't use three-hundred-year-old maces
in your production of *Richard III*.

This *Richard III*, which opened November 25, 1957, was as big a
smash as that hurtling mace. "I could tell that his Richard was dead serious about everything he said. He had that kind of menace," recalled
actress Myra Carter. Stuart Vaughan analyzed the impact Scott made
in the role:

> He had all the qualities that make for a great Richard. He was be-
> lievable as a prince. He was witty. He was the most intelligent per-
> son in the constellation of the play, which Richard is. You pulled
> for him whenever he was winning because all these other people
> [in the play] are a bunch of dolts. Then he becomes king and sud-
> denly it turns to ashes in his mouth. He got all the pathos and the
> self-loathing, all the aspects of the role. I've done it several times
> since with other people. I even played it once myself. But I don't
> think anybody I've worked with, including me, ever quite ar-
> rived at all the qualities, the energy, and the intensity that George
> brought to it. He was far more interesting than Olivier in the film.

George was the black prince. He was exciting, a black hero. He was Satanic. You kind of hated Olivier all the way through; he was playing this wicked fellow. George—under my direction, I'm not modest about that—was playing a Satanic, dark angel. Richard is very witty. He's a liar. How do you play a liar? Everybody's gotta believe him.

Scott attracted all kinds of attention, including that of agent Jane Deacy, who became his professional mother. Without benefit of a formal contract, the maternal Deacy would go far beyond the duties of a normal agent or manager—she made excuses for him and cleaned up his messes when his drinking and erratic behavior held up production schedules. Scott came to depend on her and grew jealous of her other clients—even those no longer living. Deacy had been James Dean's agent, and after his tragic death, she kept a photograph of the iconic rebel on her desk with a fresh rose that was changed daily. After a few years of working together, Scott announced he no longer required her services. When she asked why, he replied he could not stand the photo of Dean. The picture and the rose went; Scott stayed. Eventually, Deacy dismissed all her other clients to devote herself solely to Scott's career.

Scott followed up his explosive New York Shakespeare Festival debut as Richard with the much smaller part of Jaques, the melancholy exiled philosopher in *As You Like It*, again directed by Stuart Vaughan. The production opened at the Hecksher on January 20, 1958.

Scott took an unusual approach to the character by playing him not as depressed, but as savoring the ironic observations of humanity's ridiculous position in the universe as articulated in the famous "Seven Ages of Man" speech. Vaughan recalled asking the unpredictable young actor about his daringly different attitude toward Jaques:

We had gotten to dress rehearsals, and I said to George, "Are you going to wear your costume that loosely?" and he said, "Yeah.

I'm playing this guy slightly drunk all the time." I said, "I've been watching rehearsals for four weeks and we've never talked about that. I'd never gotten it until now. Maybe you have to do it more clearly. It's a good idea, now I see what's happening with the costume." He said, "I wanted to do it that way because I don't want to be some English fag." And I said, "George, I don't think you could be an English fag if you tried." That was the only barbed remark between us in two plays.

Though the role was not the center of the production, Scott drew the most attention. Richard Watts in the *New York Post* opined, "There is an especially interesting interpretation of the melancholy Jaques by George C. Scott, the Richard III of the previous Hecksher production. Mr. Scott suggests that the melancholy was something of a hoax. This Jaques is a sardonic philosopher who gets great ironic fun out of his own gloom and frankly enjoys it." Walter Kerr in the *New York Herald-Tribune* found Scott "caustic, ruthlessly intellectual yet innately good-humored . . . easily the most stimulating and funniest Jaques I have ever seen."

Despite the glowing notices, Papp had run out of funds to keep the free production going. A closing notice had been posted right after the opening night, but some money dribbled in and *As You Like It* managed to eke out a two-week run.

The satanic Richard followed immediately by an unexpectedly humorous supporting turn as Jaques demonstrated Scott's versatility to casting directors. Jane Deacy took full advantage of the interest in her new client and hustled up work in the still-vital field of New York television. Before the majority of production for the small screen shifted to the West Coast in the 1960s, Gotham was the center of live video drama. In between engagements on Broadway, East Coast–based actors would receive national exposure in a series of anthology shows exploring mature themes. Television would play a vital role in Scott's career despite his ambivalence toward it. "If you happen to be lucky enough to be neurotic and can go to pieces on the spur of the moment and then pick yourself back up and do it four more times, then you should make a fairly good television actor," he later told *TV Guide*.

After appearing in two 1957 episodes of the early-Sunday-morning series *Frontiers of Faith*, Scott made his prime-time debut on March 27, 1958 in the David Susskind production of Charles Dickens's *A Tale of Two Cities* on the *DuPont Show of the Month*. He had a tiny part as a French revolutionary. Despite his growing reputation Off-Broadway, he was not included in the principal billing with the top names, Eric Portman and Agnes Moorehead.

Less then two months later, however, Susskind gave him top billing in *Kraft Theatre*'s one-hour adaptation of *The Outcasts of Poker Flat,* Bret Harte's short story set in the lawless Wild West. Scott played Oakhurst, a gambler and con artist who finds redemption by sacrificing his life to save two innocent newlyweds from starvation. It was an unmemorable production with routine direction and low-budget production values. Scott is first introduced as a fast-talking slickster—mustached, gruff, and hiding his kindness to the hick bridegroom (played by a youthful Larry Hagman). His best moments are silent. Run out of the title town by a righteous mob, Scott's Oakhurst and a pair of harlots are trapped in a snowbound cabin with Hagman and his bride. Scott's incredulous reaction to Hagman's rustic retelling of *The Iliad* to pass the time is a textbook example of comic underplaying. His tender kiss of the painted whore played by Janet Ward and his stunned, resigned acknowledgment when Hagman says, "I'm proud to know you" reveal a realization that a lifetime of card sharping and boozing have brought him to nothing.

That same year Scott returned to the French Revolution, playing Robespierre to Peter Ustinov's Danton in *The Empty Chair* (written by Ustinov) on NBC's *Omnibus*. He also starred in a mystery thriller entitled *We Haven't Seen Her Lately* on the *Kraft Mystery Theatre*. In this creaky melodrama, Scott played a menacing gardener, skulking around the English estate of a missing old lady. The hour-long potboiler was replete with stormy nights, unsolved murders, spooky séances, and creepy organ music. There are only two scenes of interest. In the first, Scott is pretending to be a medium to gain the confidence of the now-found, superstitious old dame. He elaborately grimaces and twitches, pretending to receive messages from beyond the grave, all the while shifting his eyes to the old lady's suspicious niece. It's a comic cameo of split intentions—pulling the wool over the elderly woman's eyes and monitoring the reactions of her attractive niece. Scott conveys both objectives clearly and with humor. In the second scene, Scott encounters the killer of his sister. Just by stepping into the room and looking at the man who murdered a relative he loved, Scott charges the air with menace. Something is going to happen. A mundane soap opera is suddenly alive with possibility. Scott thrashes the blighter and justice is served, but the flashes of the actor's brilliance failed to save *We Haven't Seen Her Lately* from obscurity.

While his television career was taking off and stage offers proliferated, Scott's offstage life was a disaster. Unlike Oakhurst, Scott hadn't acquired the self-knowledge that alcoholism and violence could potentially ruin him. In his memoir, Larry Hagman recalled Scott arriving at a *Poker Flat* rehearsal grimacing in pain and walking with a decided limp. When Hagman questioned his costar, Scott lifted his shirt, exposing black and blue marks from shoulder to waist on one side of his body. "George explained that he'd beaten up a cop," Hagman wrote. "Actually, he'd started with one and then taken on three or four—he couldn't remember the exact count—who then beat the crap out of him with sand-filled socks, bruising his kidneys. As a result, he came to the studio pissing blood."

"The more successful I got," Scott said, "the worse the drinking became. I'd suffer blackouts and loss of memory. Life became a sort of crazy charade."

The charade of his marriage to Pat Reed, at any rate, was about to explode. Scott was soon to meet yet another attractive actress who would prove to be a catalyst for change.

5

A "Bus Accident"
with Colleen Dewhurst

IF EVER THERE WAS A female match for George C. Scott, it was Colleen Dewhurst. He would later describe her as magnetic. She was also one of the few actresses who could hold the stage with him. When she played Shakespeare's Cleopatra, critic Frank Aston of the *New York World-Telegram* described Dewhurst as "a cat, a witch, a siren, a babe, an evil, a doll, an inspiration." All those contradictory qualities as an actress fitted her as a woman. This tall, Amazonian life-force with a laugh like a volcanic explosion of merriment was also described by her friend Maureen Stapleton as "a marshmallow, a pushover who shouldn't have been let out in public alone." She was generous to the point of the ridiculous. Stapleton quipped in her autobiography that Dewhurst would give you the shirt off her back and then offer you her back as well. Born into a Montreal family where women's intellect was respected, she was an acting natural, receiving her training onstage in summer stock. Like Scott, she never took formal theatrical classes.

She was physically like her future husband as well—tall, striking, and gravel-voiced. And, like him, she was making a name for herself Off-Broadway, principally with Joseph Papp's New York Shakespeare Festival, creating a memorable Kate in *The Taming of the Shrew* in 1956 as well as starring in Festival productions of *Macbeth* and *Titus Andronicus*.

"Jack Barrymore used to call these meetings bus accidents," Scott would later say of their initial encounter. The "bus accident" occurred when Dewhurst was in rehearsal for *Children of Darkness* by Edwin Justus Mayer at Circle in the Square, another burgeoning company ready to challenge the commercial Broadway establishment. The play was a comedy set in the living room of an eighteenth-century English prison warden. It was first produced in 1930 to positive reviews, but received a weak box-office. Part of Circle in the Square's mission was to "rehabilitate" worthy plays like Tennessee Williams's *Summer and Smoke* and Eugene O'Neill's *The Iceman Cometh*, which had been scuttled in their initial Broadway runs and forgotten for economic reasons.

A week before the opening of *Children* in February of 1958, Richard Purdy, the actor playing the small but crucial role of Lord Wainwright, dropped out. Director José Quintero asked the cast if they could think of anyone to take over on such short notice. Dewhurst made a suggestion of an actor she knew and the leading man J. D. Cannon recommended George C. Scott, with whom he had costarred in *As You Like It*.

Dewhurst had seen Scott in that production with Cannon's wife, Alice, as a theatregoing companion. "When I saw him on the stage in the show, I was immediately antagonistic even though I knew he was great," Dewhurst later wrote in a chapter for Howard Greenberger's *The Off-Broadway Experience*. She admitted resenting Scott for landing such a career-making role. Her husband at the time, James Vickery, was struggling, and she was friendly with Joe Papp. Why hadn't Papp given Vickery a break like that? Papp had cast her in *Shrew* and *Macbeth*. There was word that she and Scott were being considered as perfect casting for a possible NYSF production of *Antony and Cleopatra*. Could she have been attracted to him as well as jealous of his success at her husband's expense?

When Scott stepped onstage, Alice Cannon turned to Dewhurst and said, "There's your Antony." With all these emotions swirling inside of her, Dewhurst replied, "He's too short."

Her astonished seatmate, aware of Scott's towering height, could only utter, "What!"

So when J. D. Cannon proposed Scott, Dewhurst was resistant. Quintero made a directorial decision. He was going to call both candidates for the job and whichever one was home got the part. Scott was home.

Circle producer Theodore Mann first saw Scott lying down on a couch waiting to see Quintero and was immediately stuck by the intensity in his eyes.

"We had a dressing room upstairs with chairs and a cot where people could wait." Mann told *In Theater* magazine years later. "I walked by on my way to the office and saw this figure lying on the cot in an overcoat, unshaven, with a very prominent nose. It stopped me in my tracks. I went down and said to José Quintero, 'There's a guy upstairs that you'd better see; there's something about him.' José called him down and he got the part." Scott would make the Circle in the Square his unofficial theatrical home, participating in nine productions as actor, director, or both, on Broadway and Off.

Like Jaques in *As You Like It*, Lord Wainwright was a relatively minor role. He doesn't make an appearance until the third act. The first two acts revolve around the loves of the prison warden's daughter played by Dewhurst. Then Wainwright, a haughty aristocrat convicted of poisoning his wife, enters and proceeds to take center stage. Scott used a long cane as an extension of his imperial will and sat in a wooden chair like a monarch on a throne, dictating to everyone around him.

"J. D. and I worked like hell for two acts and in he came in the last one and took over the show," Dewhurst recalled. Once again, Scott garnered the attention of the critics. Richard Watts, Jr. of the *Post* forecast, "I do predict that in George C. Scott . . . the Off-Broadway stage has given us an actor destined for fame."

At the end of the season, this new king of the theatre was crowned with every possible award. He won the Theatre World and Clarence Derwent Awards for most promising newcomer for *Richard III* as well

as the Vernon Rice Award for *Children of Darkness*, and an Obie from
the *Village Voice* for those two performances and *As You Like It*. Though
he would later become famous for rejecting an Academy Award for his
starring role in *Patton*, Scott accepted all of these honors without a
fuss.

For the first four months of *Children*'s run, Dewhurst and Scott
were formal in their offstage relations, addressing each other by their
last names. In her memoir, Dewhurst would describe Scott as being
very much a loner during this time. Then one night after the show,
she realized she had forgotten her apartment keys. She went into Jack
Delaney's bar near the Circle in the Square theatre on Sheridan Square
in order to phone her husband, but there was no answer. Not knowing
what to do or where Vickery was, she came out of the phone booth
and noticed her costar Scott sitting at the bar. They talked for the first
time outside of the theatre. In between drinks, she continued to phone
Vickery to no avail. They stayed until the bar closed at 4 A.M. Scott
walked her home to try the door. It was still locked and there was
no husband at home. They went to the Cannons, who generously offered to put her up for the night. When they saw Scott and Dewhurst
together at their door, a click of recognition for romantic attraction
went off in the Cannons' minds. The leading players who had been
so distant were now laughing and joking in the middle of the night.
After Dewhurst was settled in and Scott had gone home, Alice Cannon
turned to her husband in bed and said, "I think that's dangerous."

"She had serious regard of him as an actor. That doesn't happen very
often. There was a very strong sexual attraction," said actress Myra
Carter, who knew them both. The barroom conversation led to an
offstage romance. Once again, Scott was falling in love with his leading
lady while his real wife waited at home.

That summer, Quintero cast Dewhurst in Eugene O'Neill's *A Moon
for the Misbegotten* for the first Spoleto Festival in Italy. She was simultaneously shooting her first film, *The Nun's Story*, in Rome. At roughly
the same time, Scott would also be making his motion picture debut

in *The Hanging Tree*, filmed on location in Yakima, Washington. When Dewhurst was separated from Scott, she realized they were in love and had to be together. She later wrote, "Since both of us were married, it was like murdering everyone around us, but we had no choice."

Indeed, Vickery had been married to Dewhurst since 1946 and had struggled by her side for more than ten years of bit parts and summer stock. They were still living in a cold-water flat with the toilet down the hall and she was just beginning to gain recognition. Scott's union with Pat Reed had been shorter, but she had encouraged him to return to acting, had borne him a son, and was now pregnant for the second time. "She was a very charming girl, a very sweet girl," said cabaret entertainer and songwriter John Wallowitch, Pat's singing coach. "Pat was the last one to know. She was brutalized by the whole thing. It was very hard for her to handle. She was a very sensitive woman. She adored him. It was a killer for her."

The Dewhurst-Scott affair had grown into something more than a romantic backstage interlude. When she returned from Italy and he had finished filming in Washington, they moved in together.

After the run of *Children*, Scott was scheduled to star as Othello with the New York Shakespeare Festival opposite Frank Silvera as Iago, but he forsook the Bard to heed the call of Hollywood. His first film, *The Hanging Tree*, was a Warner Brothers western detailing a romantic triangle in a Montana gold rush boomtown. Gary Cooper starred as a prairie doctor deceptively named Frail, a variation on the tight-lipped, nonconformist hero he had played in dozens of films, most notably *High Noon*. Karl Malden provided support as a randy prospector with the colorful monicker of Frenchy. Maria Schell, sister of Maximilian and a German beauty who proved herself a capable actress in the Hollywood adaptation of *The Brothers Karamazov*, was the feminine prize over whom Frail and Frenchy battle. Ben Piazza, a handsome newcomer in the James Dean tradition of laconic, doe-eyed rebels, played Frail's surrogate son, an aimless drifter the doc takes in and attempts to

teach his trade and morality. Based on his stage reputation for vivify-
ing black-hearted cads, Scott was cast as a secondary villain, Grub, a
drunken faith healer who challenges Frail's medical skills. He was paid
the then-princely sum of $4,960.43 for four weeks' work, quite a step
up from $50 a week for playing Richard III Off-Broadway.

Grub is seen only briefly in the finished film. We first encounter him
emerging from his makeshift place of business, a dirty tent festooned
with crudely made signs, advertising miraculous cures for all ailments.
Soon thereafter, Scott has his biggest scene—a fire-breathing sermon,
decrying Frail (Cooper) as a butcher and exhorting the doctor's pa-
tients to try the faith healer's brand of hands-on, spiritual medicine.
The noble Cooper grabs a flask of whiskey out of Grub's back pocket,
exposing him as a drunken fraud, and manhandles him away from the
decent folk seeking the doctor's help. Not quite used to the subtle-
ties of film performance versus the necessities of stage acting, which
requires larger-than-life emoting, Scott is so melodramatic he may as
well be twirling his moustache.

For the rest of the feature, we only see Grub in crowd scenes, ut-
tering the occasional juicy line of dialogue. "Is she loose-moraled?" he
asks of Schell's character after she is rescued from a stagecoach hold-
up and brought to town. He did get the honor of wrapping a noose
around Cooper's neck and vengefully smiling in the star's face in the
final scene. Schell offers the mob the deed to her successful mine if
they will spare the doctor. The couple—along with Piazza—ride off
into the proverbial sunset while Scott as Grub and the money-hungry
horde scrap over the deed.

It was a relatively tiny role—he received fifth billing—but it did
get him noticed. The *Variety* critic gave him an encouraging sentence,
although he misspelled the actor's middle initial: "Another pic bow is
that of George S. Scott, a saturnine fellow playing a burning zealot,
and very interestingly."

Grub was not a breakthrough role—that would come soon enough.
But Scott had gained a foothold in the cinema, an arena that would

provide him with a fabulous living, but one that would not satisfy his artistic needs. He would come to regard the filmmaking process as antithetical to the actor's craft. "In film you're always at the mercy of mechanical things," he later complained to Marion Simon, "which is never conducive to opening up." He found waiting for the crew and director to set up the shots interminable and shooting out of sequence harmful to his performances. "It's essential to be on stage if you're going to continue to be an actor," he would proclaim.

Just as his Off-Broadway debut had made a sensation, Scott's Broadway bow would be earth-shattering. After returning from the *Hanging Tree* location and setting up housekeeping with Dewhurst, he was cast in *Comes a Day*, adapted by first-time playwright Speed Lamkin, a Louisiana-born Harvard graduate, from his O. Henry Award–winning short story. Similar to William Inge's *Picnic* and *Come Back, Little Sheba*, the play is a drama of middle-class disillusion set in the contemporary Midwest. The plot centers on a dysfunctional, formerly wealthy family headed by a domineering mother and an ineffectual, alcoholic father.

Once again, Scott's part was not the leading one, but it afforded an actor's dream of potential histrionics. His role was Tydings Glen, a successful businessman and psychopathic sadist. Prior to the action of the play, Glen makes a quick profit with the purchase of a thousand toilets during a shortage after World War II and parlays that into a real-estate fortune—he makes his money on other people's waste. The play was suffused with similar not-so-subtle symbolism. The central character is the greedy mother of the once well-to-do family who betroths her daughter to Glen. Gradually, it's revealed he's a nut case. Glen's ex-wife shows up and displays the bruises she received at his hands. Scott would get to decapitate a pet bird, deliver a harrowing monologue revealing how he strangled his childhood dog, and have an epileptic fit all over the lawn furniture. To accentuate Glen's eerie menace, Scott would play an old parlor trick—cracking his knuckles without touching his hands.

Judith Anderson, the Australian-born grand dame who won a Tony
Award for her brooding Medea and an Oscar nomination for her menacing Mrs. Danvers in Alfred Hitchcock's *Rebecca*, was miscast as a disappointed Midwestern *hausfrau*. Despite her inappropriateness in the
role, Anderson's name on the marquee afforded cultural cachet.

The cast also included veteran character actor Arthur O'Connell; the
now-teenaged Brandon De Wilde, the heartbreaking child star of *Shane*
and *The Member of the Wedding;* the quirky Michael J. Pollard, later Oscar-nominated for *Bonnie and Clyde*; and Larry Hagman, Scott's costar
from the TV *Outcasts of Poker Flat*, also making his Broadway debut.

While *Comes a Day* was trying out in Boston, Scott encountered
Karen Truesdell again. Now married, Truesdell still had deep feelings
for her former lover and the father of her child. She attended a matinee
of the show and met him for a drink afterwards. Though she was dying
of unrequited longing, Truesdell kept the conversation light. Scott expressed mild interest in her marriage and informed her he had moved
in with Dewhurst. Truesdell showed him a picture of their daughter,
Michelle. Scott gave her Jane Deacy's number if "she should ever need
anything." Then Truesdell's husband, Phillip, joined them. "They
shook hands," she wrote in her memoir, "civil with no pleasantries.
After a few meaningless words were exchanged all around, George excused himself with a simple 'Goodbye.'" Scott had closed that chapter
of his life and another was about to be written.

In his book, fellow cast member Larry Hagman recalls a slightly
different version of the meeting with Truesdell. He places the event in
Philadelphia during the *Day* try-outs and adds Michelle to the group
meeting Scott in a coffee shop rather than a bar. In addition, the future *Dallas* star writes that he was sent by Scott to pick up a pregnant
Pat Reed at the airport and take her to the company's hotel while the
encounter with Truesdell's family occurred. To add another layer of
farcical confusion to the anecdote and make it sound like an episode of
his sitcom *I Dream of Jeannie*, Hagman has Colleen Dewhurst also arriving on the scene. After depositing Reed at the hotel, he kept Dewhurst

occupied until Scott could finish up with Truesdell. Dewhurst is also pregnant in Hagman's version, which is not correct. She was not expecting their first son, Alex, until a year and a half later.

Despite the messiness of his personal life—only slightly exaggerated by Hagman—Scott maintained his composure onstage. Hagman marveled at his ability to immediately sober up whenever he hit the stage.

Critic David Finkle remembered seeing the play and being stunned by Scott's performance. Then at the curtain call, Anderson, as the star, took the final call and the curtain fell. But the audience continued applauding wildly and calling out "Tydings," the name of Scott's character. "I've never seen that before or since," Finkle said. Fritz Weaver, who had appeared with Scott on television in *A Tale of Two Cities*, also attended an early performance. He remembered, "After five minutes on the stage, he was all you looked at and Judith Anderson knew it. She told somebody that I knew, 'You must come and see this young man. He's just remarkable. I don't know where he gets what he's doing.' That was from one of the first ladies of the theatre. She spotted him right away." There were reports that Scott's epileptic fit scene was so realistic, audience members in the first few rows fled up the aisle for safety.

Opening night on Broadway for *Day* was November 9, 1958. The critics summarily dismissed the play, but hailed it as a vehicle for the honored son of Off-Broadway to make his electric debut on the Main Stem. John McClain's notice in the *New York Journal-American* was typical: "*Comes a Day*, a new play by Speed Lampkin, is really a bundle of dried shaving lather, but it serves a certain purpose: it gives George C. Scott an opportunity to reveal one of the great bravura, flamboyant performances in recent memory."

Walter Kerr in the *New York Herald-Tribune* gave more details of Scott's performance:

> Rubbing his eyes as though they were constantly burning, tossing
> a rose to the crow he is going to kill, holding himself rigid and

silent while his knuckles crack rhythmically, he is a clear, alarming, brilliantly convincing case from a Freudian textbook. The figure is stunningly designed—watch the fumbling, inarticulate gestures of his childhood violence turn into a dazzlingly graphic, almost musical pattern in mid-air—and it expands in venom as the evidence closes in. Mr. Scott's work is fascinating.

His onstage violence was matched offstage. "He was terrifying in those days," a friend later told writer Marion Simon in the *National Observer*. "You would sit in his living room and know that any minute he might bust you in the nose. He was absolutely uncontrolled."

Hagman recalled Scott striking a bar patron with a plateful of canapés in mid-conversation, drawing blood and nearly cutting off the man's ear. "From then on, I made it a rule always to sit real close to him," Hagman wrote, "so he couldn't wind up and punch me." In another frightening incident, Hagman reported that during a rooftop barbecue, Scott dangled Brandon De Wilde by his ankles over the parapet for stepping on one of Scott's lines. After promising never to commit such an offense again, a terrified De Wilde was pulled back to safety by Scott, who then calmly sat down and cut into his steak.

During intermission one night, Scott punched a mirror in his dressing room and had to go onstage wearing a rubber glove to keep the blood from dripping on the set. He later explained to Stu Schreiberg in *USA Weekend*, "I had a few pops of booze and before I went out for the third act, I looked at myself in the mirror. I hated what I saw. Whammo! I smashed the mirror with my hand. I'm now bleeding like a hog and the stage manager is frantic. I still have to go back onstage, so he ran to the nearby drugstore and returned with a rubber glove. When the play ended, I went immediately to the hospital for twenty-two stitches. I still have the scars."

There are so many different versions of the glass-smashing story that the event has become apocryphal. Different sources place the mirror-punching backstage during *Children of Darkness*, while others state the target of Scott's fist was a window. Larry Hagman gives the most dramatic version by placing it on opening night of *Day*. According to him, Scott entered their shared dressing room "ready to explode." After he had spent the day with Dewhurst, "who was due to give birth at any moment," Reed served him with divorce papers at the stage door. (Reed was, in fact, the wife was who due at any minute. She gave birth to a daughter, Devon, on November 29, 1958, three weeks after the opening.) In a rage, Scott smashed a window lined with chicken wire, severing several veins. With an hour before the curtain, Hagman rushed to a nearby restaurant for a bucket of ice. Scott's entire arm had been bandaged and he plunged it into the bucket. The cast rebandaged him just before he went on. "Though drunk, pissed off, and bleeding, he still gave one of the greatest performances I've ever seen on a stage," Hagman concluded his edition of the tale.

The details may vary from teller to teller, but all agree that Scott was simultaneously soaring to stardom and plunging into alcoholic chaos. All this out-of-control behavior culminated with a rude and literal wake-up call. Later during the run of *Day*, Scott woke up in a jail cell for having beaten up a man at a party the night before. He had been at a theatrical gathering and gotten into a disagreement with a press agent named Thurston. Words escalated into blows and the host was forced to call the police. Fortunately, the victim chose not to press charges and Scott was released. "But the nightmare was still there," he said. "I couldn't remember the party or the fight or anything. I realized then I had fallen into an abyss of alcoholism from which I *had* to pull myself out." As if that weren't enough, he was also mugged in the park during this year and had his nose broken yet again.

Between his onstage fits and offstage fisticuffs, Scott was in terrible physical and psychological shape. Only his incredible stamina was saving him from a complete breakdown. In a later interview, Scott said he was relieved when the play closed after twenty-eight performances. Other sources say Scott was infuriated when the *Day* closing notice was posted and that's why he punched the mirror. Nevertheless, several rewards came out of the whole debilitating experience. Scott was nominated for a Tony Award for Best Featured Actor, and a story editor for director-producer Otto Preminger saw the show, leading to his being cast in Preminger's next film, *Anatomy of a Murder*.

The night in jail and the prospect of working with Preminger, a Teutonic autocrat who would tolerate no alcoholism on his strictly controlled sets, forced Scott to consider stopping drinking. "I got scared . . . " he said. "I realized I was destroying myself and Colleen." He went to a psychiatrist, and when that didn't produce results, he consulted a friend who was a member of Alcoholics Anonymous. Scott joined and was active in the organization for two years. He described drinking not as illness, but as a habit he had to break.

To escape the rhythm of boozing, Scott returned to the manual labor he had taken up in his brother-in-law's employ. He built brick window frames, brick bookshelves, and a brick master bed. "They say Sarah Bernhardt slept in a coffin, so why shouldn't I sleep in a brick bed?" he joked. "I could never find a bed big enough or hard enough so I decided to build one myself." His landlord threatened him with eviction for fear the bricks would crash into the basement. Scott and Dewhurst were living together without benefit of wedlock in a converted carriage house on Horatio Street in Greenwich Village. He was separated, but not yet divorced from Reed at this point.

The bricklaying did not entirely replace alcohol. Scott would go through dry and wet periods for the rest of his life, never stopping altogether. As the year 1958 ended, however, there was hope for the future. He had recognized he had a drinking problem and was attempting to control it; he had made a literally smashing, although short-lived, Broadway debut; and he was about to make a major film.

Nineteen fifty-nine was a year of great promise and new beginnings for Scott. He had started living with Dewhurst, his first two films— *The Hanging Tree* and *Anatomy of a Murder*—were released, he starred in five television specials, and as the year was ending he began rehearsals for *The Andersonville Trial*, his second Broadway role and the one that would clinch his status as a star of the theatre.

The year began with a five-performance benefit concert production of *Antony and Cleopatra* opposite Dewhurst. Proceeds were to go to the New York Shakespeare Festival's summer season. There were no props or sets. The actors were dressed in modern clothes and sat on benches upstage when they were not in scenes. Scott later commented that Antony was beyond his range and joked he should have played Cleopatra.

Richard Watts, Jr. of the *New York Post* disagreed, finding much to praise in Scott's performance: "[W]hen Mr. Scott, possibly getting a touch of Richard into his Antony, goes into action, especially in the scenes where he accuses Cleopatra of disloyalty, the sheer dramatic forcefulness of his portrayal is nothing short of tremendous. There is an almost savage fascination in everything he does." Dewhurst would later play Cleopatra opposite Michael Higgins in a full-scale production at Central Park's Delacorte Theatre.

Despite his attendance at A.A. meetings, Scott was still falling off the wagon occasionally. Bette Henritze was cast as one of Cleopatra's handmaidens. As part of the informal staging, she was sitting next to Dewhurst onstage when they were not directly involved in the action. One night, Dewhurst leaned over to Henritze and asked how she thought Scott was acting. Henritze responded that he seemed to be doing very well. Dewhurst then whispered, "Seventeen martinis."

Before starting work on *Anatomy of a Murder*, Scott appeared opposite Dick Van Dyke and Teresa Wright in *Trap for a Stranger* on *The U.S. Steel Hour* (broadcast February 25). Then he and Dewhurst traveled to Salt Lake City to star as Shylock and Portia in a University of Utah production of *The Merchant of Venice*. The tragic moneylender was one of Scott's favorite roles. He would play it to great acclaim two years later in the first production at the New York Shakespeare Festival's Delacorte Theatre in Central Park. Scott had even written an adaptation of it for television and had hoped to produce it as a movie in

Venice itself. The play was eventually filmed, with another adaptation and another director, in the city of the title with Al Pacino as Shylock in 2004.

Anatomy of a Murder began filming on March 23, 1959 in Ishpeming, Michigan on the state's Upper Penisula, north of Scott's hometown of Detroit. He was initially offered a small supporting role as a bartender, but coveted the prominent part of prosecuting attorney Claude Dancer, who jousts with James Stewart's folksy defense lawyer Paul Begler. "This was the part that would explode him into the public's eye," Dewhurst wrote in her memoir. While Jane Deacy negotiated to gain the crucial role for Scott, Dewhurst was contacted about playing the ingénue, an innocent witness, in the same film. During a meeting with Preminger, Dewhurst frankly told the director she was nobody's idea of a defenseless young woman. At the end of the interview, Preminger abruptly asked her if she had ever heard of an actor named George C. Scott. The actress admitted knowing of his work.

The imperious film impresario then inquired if she thought he was right for the prosecuting attorney. Without betraying her personal interest in the matter, Dewhurst stated she thought he would be perfect. After several more days of agent-producer discussions, Scott was finally offered Dancer.

In addition to the film legend Stewart, Scott would be joined by sturdy character actors Arthur O'Connell (from *Comes a Day*) and Eve Arden as well as highly touted newcomers Ben Gazzara and Lee Remick. In a piece of stunt casting, the judge was to be played by Joseph N. Welch, the Boston lawyer famous for standing up to red-baiting Senator Joseph McCarthy during televised Congressional hearings. The bartender role originally offered to Scott went to Murray Hamilton. Though he didn't appear until over an hour into the film, Scott did more than hold his own amid this stellar company. He stood out.

The original novel written by John D. Voelker under the pseudonym Robert Traver, was on the *New York Times* best-seller list for sixty-one weeks. Voelker was a judge on the Michigan Supreme Court and had served as a prosecuting attorney for fourteen years. He based his book, noted for its authenticity, on a real 1952 case about a Korean War vet (Gazzara) accused of murdering an innkeeper who had raped the soldier's wife (Remick). But had the woman been raped or had she led her supposed attacker on? That question transformed *Anatomy* from a routine courtroom programmer to a complex and—for its time—shockingly frank treatment of legal and sexual issues. The guilt or innocence of the soldier becomes secondary to the maneuverings of the seemingly selfless defense lawyer (Stewart) and the shifty big-city prosecutor (Scott), each bent on outdoing the other.

The dictatorial, Viennese Preminger had previously challenged Hollywood's puritan ethic with the mildly risqué (by today's standards) sex comedy *The Moon Is Blue*. The producer-director defied the Production Office by permitting the word "virgin" to be spoken in the film and released it without the Office's stamp of approval. This gave *Moon* a blue glow and drew curious audiences. *Anatomy* provided Preminger with the potential for a large picture featuring a name-heavy cast and sensational subject matter.

Wendell Mayes, who collaborated on the script for *The Hanging Tree*, wrote the *Anatomy* screenplay and added a character not present in the novel—defense witness Mary Pilant, the role Dewhurst turned down, which was eventually played by Kathryn Grant (Mrs. Bing Crosby). The inclusion of this character handed Scott a golden opportunity. In the climactic scene, Dancer interrogates Mary in the false belief she was the secret lover of the murder victim. As the questioning intensifies, he leans so closely into her, he resembles a shark about to swallow a guppy. Though audience sympathy went with folksy fisherman-lawyer James Stewart, they were riveted by the scary Scott, particularly in this scene, easily the most gripping in the film.

If Stewart had any notion that Scott was stealing the film from him, he didn't show it. Even if he did, it didn't seem to bother him. In fact, the old pro was the epitome of graciousness to the newcomer. Scott was impressed with how professionally and generously Stewart conducted himself. During his off-camera scenes when all he had to do was read lines to Scott, Stewart would be completely in costume, giving a full performance. Scott would later adopt the same courtesy for his fellow actors when he had out-of-shot scenes.

Stewart's gentlemanly demeanor must have helped make the difficult shoot and the lonely location bearable. Stewart recalled, "The region is so remote that even Detroit, Lansing, and other Michigan cities feel it is a part of the polar ice cap. I won't mention the weather, which ranged all the way from a jolly seventeen below to a sweltering thirty. It snowed as late as the middle of May."

Scott found distraction for a few days when Dewhurst visited him. Preminger had been informed by Scott of the unwed nature of their relationship—which was still a sensitive subject since they were both still married to others. The director arranged for Dewhurst's travel and accommodations and told everyone she was being flown to the set to discuss a role. Preminger's other kindnesses to Scott included advancing him money. "He lent me money on *Anatomy of a Murder* when I was broke," he later told Rex Reed. "So I like him. I was never one of his whipping boys." The director even went so far as to counsel Scott on his career, telling him not to take a job just for the money.

Preminger wanted to take advantage of the novel's hit status so he moved as quickly as possible to get his film into general release. A sneak preview was held in San Francisco in mid-June, roughly one month after filming was completed on May 16. *Anatomy* had its world premiere in Scott's hometown Detroit on July 1, 1959 and opened in New York the next day. Three weeks later, it opened in L.A. Scott and Dewhurst flew to the coast for the Hollywood premiere. Before the screening, they slipped into their seats unnoticed. Afterwards, everyone noticed him. Who was this unknown actor with the frightening glare who managed to steal a picture from Jimmy Stewart? In *The Hanging Tree*, Scott was covered by scraggly whiskers. No one in Hollywood would have seen any of Scott's stage performances and probably didn't even know there was such a place as Off-Broadway. Movieland well-wishers spotted Scott and began pumping his hand, congratulating him for his performance.

As they progressed towards the lobby, Scott and Dewhurst found themselves in a scene straight out of *The Day of the Locust*. The mob surrounded them and began pushing in their eagerness to get at the new star. For a macho guy with a fear of crowds, the first crush of celebrity must have been terrifying. Then, seemingly out of nowhere, Stewart appeared and shepherded Dewhurst to a table in the lobby bar to sit next to his wife, Gloria. He returned with Scott to face the audience and the photographers outside. Stewart was graciously protecting Dewhurst from uncomfortable questions as to her relationship with Scott. Unlike today, when no one would bat an eye if a hot new actor was living with a woman outside of wedlock, in the late 1950s, it could have hurt Scott's burgeoning career. "As flashbulbs exploded throughout that night and I watched George go from being an actor to being a star," Dewhurst wrote in her memoir, "I realized that Mr. Stewart had put me in the safe position of not having to be identified by the press or having to explain my relationship to George (which in those days was highly unacceptable)."

Fortunately, Scott and Dewhurst's highly unacceptable living arrangements were never reported. But many found *Anatomy*'s explicit script highly objectionable. Its overt references to rape prompted the Legion of Decency to call the film outside the "bounds of moral acceptability and propriety."

Despite the censorial carping, *Anatomy* was praised. *Variety* chattily summed up its appeal as a "top-notch courtroom meller. . . . Its mystery is adult, it is complex and confounding and it is laced with humor and human touches. . . . George C. Scott has the suave menace of a small-time Torquemada." It was voted the best film of the year in a poll of critics conducted by the *Film Daily* trade publication. In a nice piece of career symmetry, Dewhurst's film debut, *The Nun's Story*, ranked third.

After *Anatomy* wrapped, Scott didn't rest on his laurels. He returned to New York and filmed, in rapid succession, four television appearances. *People Kill People Sometimes*, opposite Geraldine Page and Jason Robards, aired September 20 on *Sunday Showcase*; *Target for Three*, with Ricardo Montalban and Liliane Montevecchi, was viewed by *Playhouse 90* audiences October 1; a segment of *Look Up and Live*, CBS's Sunday morning series, followed; and *Winterset*, Maxwell Anderson's 1935 verse drama for *Hallmark Hall of Fame*, was broadcast on October 26.

Like *Anatomy of a Murder*, *People Kill People Sometimes* was based on an actual case—that of a woman (Page) who shoots her millionaire husband (Robards) mistakenly believing he is a prowler. *Daily Variety* partially praised Scott's performance: "George Scott, the psychiatrist, had one big acting scene in trying to restore sanity to the distraught Miss Page, but his earlier participation was not for the great unwashed."

The *Variety* critic was not the only one to have mixed feelings about the actor. Milton Wilson, who played a small role in *People*, recalled, "One night during rehearsals, there was a party. [Scott] was there and several of the stagehands were there. He was quite a mean drunk. He got into a fight with one of the stagehands and really did a great deal of damage. The rest of the stagehands had a little plot. When he came into the studio when they were rehearsing, they were going to drop a sandbag on his head to get even. The producers got wind of it and were able to defuse the situation and it didn't come to pass."

Target for Three revolved around an assassination plot on a fictional South American dictator. Scott, Ricardo Montalban, and H. M. Wyant starred as the trio of conspirators. Wyant is killed early in the show and the remainder of the drama focuses on the conflict between the rational man of conscious (Montalban) and the hard-driven revolutionary (Scott, once again typecast as a fanatical villain). *Variety* admired producer John Houseman's *Playhouse 90* production values, but found David Davidson's script sterile—"There was an aura of dramatic coolness about the play that made it more a study than a drama." However,

Scott and Montalban were lauded—"Both performed with strength, conviction and believability."

In *Winterset*, Scott played the tubercular gangster Trock Estrella. Anderson's poetic drama evoking the Sacco and Vanzetti case had won the New York Drama Critics Circle Award for Best Play and stirred audiences who remembered the real-life events, but its purple verse comes across as stilted today.

The play opens with Trock, covered up by a fedora and the up-turned collar of an overcoat, revealing to his sidekick Shadow he is fatally ill and been given the clichéd six months to live. Before his final ticket is punched, he intends to get revenge on those who put him in prison. The story is then taken over by Don Murray and Piper Laurie as Mio and Miriamne, young lovers menaced by Trock.

Scott is quiet in his menace, saving his power. The turgid melodrama only comes alive when Murray gets the drop on Trock by drawing a gun on him. Scott's eyes radiate fear. Murray is prattling on with high moral authority about the ghosts of all the men Trock has murdered returning to haunt him. Scott is backed up against the wall, his hat has fallen off and his protective overcoat has opened. He's exposed, metaphorically naked. You can almost smell Trock's sweat. His cowardice is more alive and interesting than Mio's decency. Suddenly, Anderson's esoteric poetry takes on a gritty texture. After an hour of talk, something is about to happen. Someone is about to be shot. It's real.

Echoing Larry Hagman, Piper Laurie recalled, "He used to show up every morning late, battered, bruised, with Band-Aids. The word was he'd been in a brawl the night before over a woman or something. He was a terrifically attractive-looking man, except I was terrified of him. I didn't want to get near him. He had this reputation of being this ferocious wild man."

Not long after the broadcast of *Winterset*—on November 13, to be precise—Scott went into rehearsals for his next Broadway venture, *The Andersonville Trial*. As in *Anatomy*, he would be playing a prosecuting attorney. But unlike Claude Dancer, Lieutenant Colonel N. P. Chipman has more at stake in his case than courtroom glory. Based on historic events, the trial is set soon after the Civil War and determines the fate of Captain Henry Wirz, the Confederate Commandant of Andersonville, a prisoner-of-war camp where over 14,000 Union soldiers perished under appalling conditions. Chipman argues Wirz, the only Southerner to be tried as a war criminal, was morally responsible for those deaths. The defense counters he was obeying orders and cannot be held personally accountable for the tragedy. As Wirz's lawyer gains ground with this point and Chipman's case appears to weaken, the prosecutor treads dangerous ground by suggesting that a man's ethical obligations exceed the necessity for military obedience. Much like *Anatomy*, the play reaches an emotional peak with Scott relentlessly grilling a witness—Wirz himself, who passionately justifies his actions and pleads for his life.

Andersonville Trial opened at the Henry Miller Theatre on December 29, 1959 after tryouts in New Haven and Philadelphia. In a lengthy review in the *Herald-Tribune*, Walter Kerr highlighted Scott's performance, describing his "ecstatic smile whenever he loses a point," a memorable small delight of director José Ferrer's production. Kerr continued,

> Here is what Mr. Scott does: having paced the courtroom like an exceedingly thirsty cougar, lashed out at a witness, bullied the judge, and built the tension to the point where one feels that justice is about to dissolve into hysteria, he stops abruptly as if his windpipe had been cut, and pauses.
>
> The minute things go wrong, the actor's eyes open wide. His face lights up, however fleetingly, in a sunburst of sheer glee, a spasm of rapture. Someone else has got the better of Mr. Scott, and the fact floods him with admiration.

After the psychotic Tydings Glenn in *Comes a Day*, the ruthless Claude Dancer in *Anatomy*, and the unsympathetic Chipman in *Andersonville*,

Scott was now fixed in the public mind as a dangerous villain. "The ironic thing is that in stock I played lots of comedies," he complained to *Newsweek*. "But now I'm typed as a heavy. I can't get a comedy to save my life. But, I hope to master the situation ultimately."

This pigeonholing as a bad guy had an impact on the actor. Despite his morally ambiguous position, Wirz was reaping the audience's sympathy, and Scott was gaining their enmity. He told critic-interviewer Leonard Probst of his difficulties during the *Andersonville* run:

> The character [Chipman] was one of a man who's extremely righteous, not self-righteous, but on the side of right, a moral man who had to prosecute an immoral man who deserved prosecution and hanging, which is what he got. At the end of the evening the weight of empathy and compassion for the poor man who was being prosecuted was so preponderant that everyone on the side of right was despised literally. When the curtain went up, you could feel the waves of hatred coming at you across the footlights. It began to get on my nerves after a while. It was very difficult. I recall suffering badly from it. José Ferrer was the director and he wrote me a wonderful letter one time, because he could see that I was undergoing a considerable amount of strain because of this. He said, you must continue to do what you're doing because you're doing it very well and you must not allow this feeling, this hatred, to stop the kind of work you're doing. I never forgot it and I never conquered it either, never. It was agony every night to go on stage, literally agony.

At one point, the agony spilled over during a cab ride. "Herbert Berghof [who played Wirz] told me that once he had been in a taxi with George," Fritz Weaver related. "They had just done *The Andersonville Trial*. Herbert said to George, 'You should stop trying to play good people. You're a natural villain,' and George got out of the cab. Just left, he was so hurt by this remark. I mean George admired

Herbert very much. Herbert made it up to him afterwards. He said, 'I'm just talking about the pure force that you bring. Nobody else has it. Why should you want to come down from that?'"

While the pain of playing an onstage villain was making him miserable, alcohol was not significantly contributing to his moods. He occasionally strayed into a barroom but continued to attend A.A. meetings. He missed one performance of *Andersonville*, realizing he was too drunk to go on. There would be no repeat of the seventeen-martini night at *Antony and Cleopatra*. Though he may still have been bending the elbow now and then, Scott was able to recognize when not to go onstage. He seemed to be gaining control in both his career and his personal life. "You suddenly know how blind you've been," he told columnist Sidney Fields of his change in perspective. "It's like looking at the grass for the first time. It's green and it's growing."

6

A Third Marriage, *The Hustler*, and the Theatre of Michigan

THOUGH IT MAY NOT HAVE been legal yet, Scott's live-in arrangement with Colleen Dewhurst was for all intents and purposes a marriage. They combined their finances, asking their close friend Circle in the Square producer Theodore Mann to withhold half of their salaries (at Circle they each received $75 a week) and give them the rest for pocket money. They often ran short; Scott loved to gamble at the race track and usually picked the wrong horse. Mann was trying to get them in the habit of saving money and would advance them funds of his own. "How could I refuse these glorious human beings anything?" he wrote in his memoir, *Journeys in the Night*. As their movie and TV salaries increased, Mann acknowledged he was not expert enough to handle their rapidly growing income and advised they hire professional investors to do the job.

Despite the financial arrangement and cohabitation, many friends had believed it was a transitional love affair, releasing Scott and Dewhurst from their respective unhappy unions with Pat Reed Scott and James Vickery. These friends would never have thought the two highly emotional personalities would take the permanent step of officially tying the knot. It would be like two tornadoes coming together. Even Dewhurst had her doubts, but there was a slight complication. She was pregnant. Actress Myra Carter recalled receiving a phone call from

Dewhurst who told her she had "a bun in the oven. Me being so British, I didn't know what it meant. Even so, she didn't know that it [the relationship] would last."

With a baby on the way, the couple pushed aside their trepidations and continued living together without the benefit of wedlock until Scott's divorce was final. Dewhurst began the new decade of the 1960s headlining on Broadway in *Caligula* opposite Kenneth Haigh, who had to strangle his pregnant costar every night.

Scott received a tremendous career boost by earning an Academy Award nomination for Best Supporting Actor for *Anatomy of a Murder*. Hollywood columnist Hedda Hopper predicted he would win. He was pitted against Arthur O'Connell for the same film, Hugh Griffith in *Ben-Hur*, Robert Vaughn in *The Young Philadelphians*, and Ed Wynn in *The Diary of Anne Frank*. To gain Oscar recognition for his second film thrilled the young actor, but he was trampled under the wheels of a *Ben-Hur* stampede. The spectacle won a record-breaking eleven Oscars, including one for Griffith for his performance as an Arab chieftain. Scott was crushed. The defeat gave birth to a relationship with Oscar as stormy as any of his marriages. In an interview three years later, Scott revealed his ambivalent emotions about his losing the Academy Award, "I was disappointed. And then after thinking it over, I was disappointed over being disappointed. I determined never to be placed in such a position again."

The prospects of a new baby as well as hobbies, reading, pets, and work helped distract Scott from the Oscar letdown. He continued to act in TV specials, including George Bernard Shaw's *Don Juan in Hell* for the syndicated *Play of the Week* series and *The Burning Court* for NBC's *Great Mysteries*. *Don Juan* is a four-character philosophical debate set in the underworld between the title romantic figure of legend, the woman for whom he was murdered in a duel, her father (now transformed into a statue), and the Devil. Scott played Lucifer as an effete, almost effeminate sensualist, using a pair of dark glasses to accentuate his moral ambiguity—a device Scott would later employ to devastating effect in *The Hustler*. This Satan is attractive and charming. He's like a host at a garden party, gleefully arranging the social hierarchy in the afterlife. While Siobhan McKenna is highly theatrical as Dona Ana, Don Juan's former lover, Scott had learned to scale down his acting for the small screen and gave a contained, fascinating performance. The *Play of the Week* series was produced by David Susskind, who had previously employed Scott in *A Tale of Two Cities* and *The Outcasts of Poker Flats* and would later figure prominently in the actor's television career.

An interview in the June 1960 issue of *Theatre Arts* offered a glimpse of the Scott-Dewhurst Greenwich Village carriage house and the domestic side of their hectic lives. Half-open books—the Bible, Will Durant's *Caesar and Christ*, a biography of Hitler—were scattered everywhere. A chessboard was set up, recreating a famous game between Morphy and Anderson around the time of the Civil War, in which Scott was playing both the black and white sides. Two cats roamed about. One was named Zorro (nicknamed George Raft for the furry white handkerchief in the area where a breast pocket would be), and the other was called Tiger (nicknamed Ladybird for her gender).

By the summer his divorce from Pat Reed Scott was final, and he married Dewhurst in a small, unpublicized ceremony. Pat kept her married name and continued her singing career. She eventually got into television production and became New York City's Film Commissioner under three different mayors. Scott and Reed's children, Devon and Matthew, would visit their father and continue to be part of his new life.

In another sign of permanence, Scott and Dewhurst acquired the services of a combination housekeeper and nanny, a necessity if the actress was to continue her career. Christine Davis, who would affectionately become known to the Scott family and their friends as Nana, came into the household as her former employers, the actor John Marley and his wife, were moving from New York to Hollywood. In her

job interview with Dewhurst, she displayed her eagerness for the position by asking for a broom and sweeping up.

New life was beginning for Scott, but death was close as well. Ian
Keith, a castmate from *The Andersonville Trial*, passed away in March.
In his memory, Scott founded the Ian Keith Award, an annual accolade
to be presented to a performer at the New York Shakespeare Festival
"most deserving of aid and encouragement toward a career in the theatre." The prize was a silver chess knight and a check for $1,000. In an
even closer tragedy, Scott's half-brother Bob drowned in Gilbert Lake,
Bloomfield Township on July 18. Less than a month later on August 1,
1960, Dewhurst gave birth to her first son, Alex.

Three weeks later—barely enough time to get the new baby settled—Scott commenced rehearsals for a Broadway production of *The
Wall*, Millard Lampell's stage version of John Hersey's novel about the
Warsaw Ghetto uprising against Nazi occupiers. British actress Yvonne
Mitchell was making her American stage debut as Rachel Apt, who
embarks on a doomed romance with Scott's character, a cynical lout
named Dolek Berson.

Reviews were mixed, with most of the critics faulting Lampell's
adaptation. John McClain's headline in the *New York Journal-American*
was typical: "Major Novel, Minor Play."

"[I]n spite of a resplendent cast and opulent settings, the drama . . .
is a big bloody bore," McClain moaned. He went on to chastise Scott,
who was either "miscast, hopelessly, or misdirected by Morton Da
Costa or just not trying—for I never for a minute thought he came to
life." Richard Watts, Jr. of the *New York Post* was slightly kinder, calling Scott "less comfortable than usual."

Another loose brick in *The Wall*'s shaky foundation was the lack of
empathy between Mitchell and Scott. "It sprang from their approaches
to acting," observed cast member Marian Seldes. "Yvonne was precise,
George impulsive. I think Yvonne was afraid of him. He was like a
wild animal and she was a tame one." He was so mad at Mitchell at

one rehearsal two months after the show had opened, he punched the scenery and broke his hand.

Mitchell had a stipulation in her contract that she could withdraw from the show if her costar, Scott, missed a significant number of performances. The actor failed to appear from Monday to Friday due to his injured hand. She quit that Saturday.

Seldes, who had been playing the supporting role of Symka, Dolek's invalid wife, and standing by for Rachel, took over for the departing Mitchell. "Having the chance to play two parts with George was fascinating," Seldes wrote in her memoir. "He is an unusually sensitive actor. You receive an entirely different set of vibrations from him the instant you bring him a new impulse, a look, a thought." During one performance Seldes came close to receiving more than a set of vibrations from Scott when both tried something new. She recalled,

> There is a moment where she [Rachel] is talking to him, really commanding his attention. He's not agreeing with her. In one performance, George put his hand over his face. He'd never done it before. Then I went for his hand and what I saw in his face was so terrifying. Afterwards, he said to me, "It's a good thing I love you, because I'm a prizefighter and you don't touch a prizefighter. I don't mean you did the wrong thing. I just mean my reaction [when touched] is to sock someone." That's what I saw in his face.

Seldes also saw "gentle worldiness" and "humanity" in Scott. Despite his penchant for violence and persisting bouts with alcoholism, his fellow actors respected and enjoyed him. "We all felt lucky to be working with him," Seldes said. "We knew his drinking was an illness." She fondly recalled his restaging of the climactic love scene between Dolek and Rachel after she had taken over the part. He called her to his dressing room and suggested different blocking for the moment the two embrace in a bunker. "What would you think if I just climbed on top of you?" he said. Seldes liked the idea and the new, more intimate staging remained.

But Scott did not. According to Seldes's date book, the star gave his notice on January 23, 1961 after a closing notice had been posted and then new funds had been raised to continue the run. Despite the infusion of cash, Scott left the production on February 4. His understudy, Robert Burr, took over while the show limped on for another month. Production costs were too high and the cast too large to keep it running after mixed notices and the loss of both of its stars. *The Wall* collapsed after 176 performances.

Meanwhile, Dewhurst met with more success in another stage version of a hit novel. She played Mary Follet, the young widow in *All the Way Home*, Tad Mosel's adaptation of James Agee's Pulitzer Prize–winning novel *A Death in the Family*. This sensitive study of a Knoxville, Tennessee, family's adjustment to the death of the father won the Tony Award and was Dewhurst's first hit Broadway show. She won a Tony for Best Supporting Actress, a strange choice of category since she was onstage constantly and the story centered on her. Because she was billed below the title on the marquee, the Tony Awards considered her a supporting performer. It turned out she was supporting something equally precious as the play during the *All the Way Home* rehearsals and tryouts. Producers had begged her not to visit with Scott during the pre-Broadway run in Boston for fear of her getting pregnant again. Their fears were realized when Dewhurst announced she was in fact expecting a second child. Fortunately, her character was also in the family way and she remained in the company. All that was required was a slight change of dialogue from "You don't show, Mary" to "You show, Mary." Campbell was born July 19, 1961, less than a year after his brother, Alex.

While their shows were playing at the Billy Rose and Belasco theatres respectively, Dewhurst would visit her husband. "Colleen came backstage several times," Seldes recalled. "She also helped look for

George when the stage manager couldn't find him. *The Wall* company loved her, too."

During the run of *The Wall*, Scott received a backstage visit from actress Piper Laurie and director Robert Rossen to discuss his playing Bert Gordon, a ruthless gambler, in Rossen's new film set in a gloomy world of dank pool rooms, half-empty bus stations, and shadowy bars. Its cast of desperate characters holds on to life by their fingernails while scratching out their own versions of the American Dream. The film was called *The Hustler*.

The Twentieth Century-Fox feature was based on an obscure novel by Walter Tevis derived from his experiences working in a pool hall when he was a college student. There he met a real-life hustler named Eddie Parker who would serve as the model for the role eventually played by Paul Newman. Parker used several aliases including Eddie Felsen, the name employed in the novel. Parker would say that a number of incidents in the movie were based on his life, including having his finger broken and challenging "New York Fats," a rotund yet elegant pool champion.

Rossen was intimately acquainted with the story's grimy milieu. A teenage pool hustler himself, he had begun a play on the subject called *Corner Pocket*. Rossen made his first big impact in 1947 with the boxing drama *Body and Soul*, another sports film about an athlete challenging corrupt forces. He went on to win an Oscar for directing *All the King's Men* in 1949. In the 1950s, he was a blacklist victim for failing to testify before the House Un-American Activities Committee. He later cooperated and confessed to previous membership in the Communist Party. Despite this admission, Rossen was unable to find work in Hollywood and went into self-imposed exile in Europe. When he returned to America, his film career continued on a downward spiral with mediocre features like *Islands in the Sun* and *They Came to Cordura*. He saw *The Hustler* as a chance for a comeback.

Sidney Carroll penned the screenplay, which Rossen rewrote. The completed script was sent to Newman, who was shooting *Paris Blues* on location in the French capital. Newman got through half of the script and agreed to shoot pool as Fast Eddie. Jackie Gleason, best known for his comedy variety series, applied his considerable skill with the cue and his underused dramatic talents to playing Minnesota Fats, the nattily attired champion Eddie challenges.

Piper Laurie was disenchanted with the costume dramas she had been relegated to in Hollywood and eagerly accepted the role of Sarah, Eddie's alcoholic, suicidal lover. Laurie had worked with Scott on the TV production of *Winterset*, and perhaps Rossen took her along to the meeting after the performance of *The Wall* to put him at his ease.

The three went to the bar around the corner from the Billy Rose Theatre. They sat at a small table with Rossen and Laurie facing Scott and ordered beers. Laurie later recalled to Michael Sragow, "I had never been that close to him. I was always on the other side of the room [during *Winterset*]. And I don't think we said two words to each other that night. Then, when we started the movie weeks later, we never spoke to each other except when we did our scenes. I was still very uneasy with him—and I decided not to worry about it because that was useful for my performance, and for the movie."

Rossen wanted to shoot on location in New York. Fox executives balked at the expense, citing the growing budget of their mammoth *Cleopatra*, then filming in Europe and draining the studio's coffers. They eventually agreed to Gotham locations, reasoning that this little pool-hall drama couldn't possibly present as many problems as the gargantuan Elizabeth Taylor–Richard Burton epic. The main scenes were shot in Ames Pool Hall just off 47th Street and Broadway in Times Square—not exactly ancient Egypt or imperial Rome.

Nevertheless, the studio was full of demands. They were eager to push the film into release to raise capital for *Cleopatra*. Rossen and his editor, Dede Allen, were pressured to have a final release cut ready in record time. Fox executives also had fears that women wouldn't understand the finer aspects of the pool games. They wanted as much of those scenes cut as possible, including the entire pre-credits sequence in which Eddie pulls a scam on a barroom full of suckers and his amoral character is established. Outmaneuvering his corporate overseers, Rossen arranged for a midnight showing of the uncut film in New York City for the casts of all the Broadway shows. The actors admired the subtle and distinctive work of their fellow thespians and positive word of mouth spread. Fox dared not tamper with the finished product then.

The Hustler premiered in September 1961 in Washington, D.C. Newsreel footage displayed Scott and Piper Laurie shaking hands with attending congressmen and senators. Scott's character, Bert Gordon, is like the stereotype of a corrupt politician, manipulating those around him to gain maximum advantage. Scott conveys Bert's craven nature, his cowardice and disregard for any sort of human attachment, through eloquent body language and careful use of props like Bert's signature sunglasses—worn even indoors and at night. The glasses hide Bert's eyes, the windows to the soul as Stanislavski described them. He removes them only at strategic moments. Bert shields his whole body as well as his eyes. He hides in the shadows, then gradually takes over the whole film.

Scott is a definite presence in the early scenes, even though he doesn't have much dialogue. We first see him in the back room of the pool hall, playing poker. When a hanger-on whispers silently in his ear, we can tell by Scott's interested expression that he's getting wind of the new hustler in front. The gambler cashes in his chips and slinks into a corner of the main pool hall, observing. Like a snake in a garden, he's waiting for his chance to strike. He sees Eddie has a special talent and is finding the best angle to exploit it. He eventually takes a prominent position to watch the match between Eddie and Minnesota Fats, sitting in a raised chair like a king. You can see the wheels turning in Bert's head as he assesses Eddie's skill and then judges his character (or lack thereof) as the young player blows his lead and falls apart. Bert later takes over Eddie's career and his life, eventually coming between the young pool shark and his depressive lover, Sarah.

The tension between Eddie, Sarah, and Bert reaches the bursting point when the trio travels to Kentucky to pick up some hustling action during Derby Week. At a party, Sarah gets drunk and Bert whispers obscenities to her. She flings her drink in his face and collapses.

"Years later, I asked him what it was he'd said to me," Laurie later recalled, "because a lot of people would ask me that. He said, 'You know, I never really said anything. I figured anything that I said would not be as powerful as what your imagination could bring.'"

The final sequence, in which Eddie returns to Ames Pool Hall for a rematch with Fats after Sarah has committed suicide, is worthy of examination. As in *Anatomy of a Murder* and *Comes a Day,* Scott is playing the villain. Bert has caused Sarah to kill herself by seducing her while she was drunk. But Scott makes that villain's thoughts and actions so intense that we are as engaged with him as we are with the hero.

As Eddie walks into the pool hall, Bert is afraid. He's basically a coward. He sees he can no longer control Eddie and, even with his thugs in full attendance, he's scared that the younger man may take a whack at him. Like a lone gunfighter in a town full of baddies, Eddie is walking into Bert's territory. Bert has control over everyone, even Minnesota Fats. During the game Rossen's montage of shots—expertly cut together by Allen—include reactions from Bert. You can read every move of the game in Scott's progressively anxious expressions. Finally Eddie has beaten Fats his way and Bert will not allow it. He explodes with the unexpected and volcanic "Eddie, you owe me MONEY!!!!!"

Rossen and Scott argued for two days over the reading of that line. Rossen wanted it conventional with the emphasis on "owe." He found Scott's preference of screaming the last word too over the top. Scott felt the scene was flat and needed an unexpected charge. He insisted on doing it his way and that this was how he was going to deliver the line. If Rossen wanted to cut it, Scott told him, it was his prerogative, he was the director. When the cameras rolled, Scott erupted on the final word. It stayed.

Eddie has won the game against Minnesota Fats, but Bert still controls the pool hall and every other big pool hall in the country. Bert's body language of confidence is back. Eddie walks out with his dignity, leaving the sinister gambler to reign in his kingdom of dusty felt-covered tables and cues.

When he utters the line about money, Rossen has him in the extreme right of the shot while Newman is in the center. Though this sequence should belong to Newman, Scott holds sway.

Critical reaction was enthusiastic for both Newman and Scott, with the entire principal cast racking up high points. Bosley Crowther of the *New York Times* singled out Scott: "The real power is packed into the character of an evil gambler whom George C. Scott plays as though the devil himself had donned dark glasses and taken up residence in a rancid billiard hall. Mr. Scott is magnificently malefic. When he lifts those glasses and squints, it's as though somebody has suddenly put a knife between your ribs."

Despite the critics' praise, Fox was worried that *The Hustler* was too small to make a big profit. The studio was still being depleted by *Cleopatra* and they needed as much cash as quickly as possible. *Hustler* should have been platformed—given a limited release in major cities and then a wider distribution after the reviews had a chance to sink in. Instead, Fox dumped the picture in saturation bookings for a fast payoff. To their surprise, it took in high grosses and they kept it running longer than expected.

Scott continued to earn quick cash doing television work, occasionally enacting a role worthy of his talents. In May 1961, he starred opposite Laurence Olivier in an adaptation of Graham Greene's *The Power and the Glory*, shot in a Brooklyn television studio. The British knight, then appearing on Broadway in *Becket*, headlined a stellar cast that also included Julie Harris, Keenan Wynn, Roddy McDowall, Fritz Weaver, Martin Gable, and fourteen-year-old Patty Duke. Once again, Scott was cast as a villain—a relentless police lieutenant in an unnamed socialist South American state not unlike Castro's Cuba. His objective is to capture and execute Olivier's whiskey priest in a purge of all religion. He could have been played like a one-dimensional, anti-Catholic cad. His entrances are accompanied by trumpets and snare drums, but Scott gives the lieutenant more than the conventional military cold-bloodedness. The passion in his voice reveals he believes he is doing the right thing in ridding his homeland of hypocritical religious practitioners. In a typical scene, he has threatened to shoot an innocent villager unless the townspeople reveal which of them is the runaway priest whose face he does not know. "You're my people," Scott shouts when they refuse to comply, "I want to give you everything. All you have to do is look at him." There is anger, but you can also hear the love he has for his countrymen and frustration that Olivier has more power over them than he does.

The drama concludes with Scott finally capturing Olivier. The night before the priest is to be set before a firing squad, the lieutenant visits his cell. He asks the condemned man about dying. The priest tells his captor, "You are a good man. You have nothing to be afraid of." A flicker of doubt crosses over Scott's eyes. In that brief moment, the actor conveys the lieutenant's fear of mortality. You can read his thoughts in Scott's eyes: "Is the priest right after all? Is there a God outside the state? Am I damned for what I've done?" Then he reverts back to his official status and off-handedly says, "You have such odd ideas." Two great actors found what was underneath the lines and turned what could have been weepy soap opera into a drama of human connection between ideological opposites.

But not all small-screen offers were on a par with *The Power and the Glory*. Another 1961 TV job was an uncharacteristic turn as the elegant, depraved Lord Henry Wooten in a TV version of Oscar Wilde's *The Picture of Dorian Gray* for CBS's *Breck Golden Showcase*. The Wilde adaptation was produced by Scott's frequent employer David Susskind and, though his role was essentially a supporting one, he received top billing. Like the Devil in *Don Juan in Hell*, Lord Henry is a charming cad, flouting conventional morality in pursuit of his own pleasure—a man not unlike the original author. The program was a rather bland interpretation of Wilde's novel centering on a Victorian gentleman who commits numberless immoral acts. He retains his youthful beauty while his portrait, hidden in an attic, ages into the image of a craven monster. The production proceeds at a pedestrian pace, punctuated by narrative passages from the book read in a dry monotone by Sir Cedric Hardwicke.

Scott made a feast of Wilde's epigrams, chowing down on them with relish. One of Sir Harry's better *bon mots*, expertly delivered, was "To get back my youth, I would do anything in the world, except take exercise, get up early, or be respectable."

In the final scene, Scott overcame the fear of appearing like "an English fag," stated to Stuart Vaughan during *As You Like It*. As Sir Henry, he laughs hysterically at Dorian's declarations of reformation and then stands behind the young man and asks, "Why is it that we have all had to pay the piper and you have gotten off scot-free?" referring to the handsome man's ageless appearance. Sir Henry's hands are about to touch Dorian's shoulders. We see Scott in a mirror and his hands hesitate a moment before comforting his friend. Scott's face displays a mixture of lust, envy, regret, and anger. He is clearly stopping before indulging in a potentially homoerotic embrace. The hands finally caress Dorian's shaking shoulders and Sir Henry briefly gives way to his attraction for Dorian. He then retrieves his cloak and cane, ready to depart. Here Scott delivers an ordinary exit line—"I'll see you . . . at the club"—showing an aching desperation that combines his homosexual yearning for Dorian with a need for the object of his desire to remain as corrupt as Sir Henry.

That same year, he and Dewhurst packed up the kids, flew to the West Coast, rented a house in Malibu, and took whatever offers their agents could drum up. They both landed guest shots on the popular

Ben Casey medical series in an episode called "I Remember a Lemon Tree." In the *Casey* segment, Scott was afforded an actor's dream—he was cast as a morphine-addicted surgeon. He got to play a withdrawal fit, and then a tear-jerking deathbed scene after revealing he was taking the drug in order to deal with a painful terminal disease. Despite the conventions of the script, Scott was brilliant. He was perfectly balanced between Vince Edwards's hairy-chested blank slate as the chiseled Ben Casey and Sam Jaffe's hysterical overplaying of the kindly chief of staff, Dr. Zorba. Scott's face is like an X-ray, revealing everything going on inside, and there is so much happening. In stark contrast, Edwards has nothing and Jaffe has nothing real.

In one roller coaster of a scene, Scott as Dr. Karl Anders goes through the proverbial gauntlet of emotions while Edwards, the star of the series, stands like a post. When Casey discovers Anders with a needle, Scott's whole body and face slump. He collapses into a chair. His relief is visible. Now that he's been found out, he doesn't have to pretend anymore. While Edwards delivers a moralistic lecture on the evils of addiction, Scott's eyes are working, subtly broadcasting his thoughts—"How can I get out of this? What can I say to this asshole to keep my career?" Then, he literally throws himself on Edwards's mercy, weeping into his tunic. He draws back and his face twists with agony as he begs Edwards to keep silent.

The episode concludes with an absurd scene of Scott about to expire and Dewhurst as his pregnant wife going into labor almost simultaneously. Scott utters a sappy line of dialogue—"Don't think about yesterday; think about tomorrow"—and she leaves to have their baby. By the end of the hour, a totally different character for 1961 prime time—a nasty-tempered drug addict—is just another of Ben Casey's saintly sufferers, ascending to heaven just in time for the final commercial. Scott was nominated for an Emmy Award.

While laughing all the way to the bank with the money he was making from TV appearances, Scott was preparing to risk his savings for a dream of artistic fulfillment. Having worked on Broadway in three productions and observed its financial workings, the actor had come to believe plays could be developed with greater artistic freedom and more efficiently bankrolled if they originated outside of the hit-or-flop pressure cooker of New York. Anticipating the regional theatre movement of the late 1960s, Scott and Theodore Mann of Circle in the Square set up the Theatre of Michigan. The goal was to produce plays in Scott's hometown of Detroit and then bring them to Broadway if they were successful. This would theoretically lead to theatres springing up all across the country. "Imagine a prosperous Broadway supported some day by the Theater of Michigan, the Theater of Kentucky and so on. Then we'll have the Theater of the U.S.A." Scott predicted to *Time* magazine. A film and television production unit was also planned.

Scott and Mann's general vision did come true years later, although neither would be involved. Resident theatres like the Arena Stage of Washington, D.C., the Seattle Repertory Theatre, the Actors Theatre of Louisville, and the Yale Repertory Theatre did emerge to send their hits like *The Great White Hope, I'm Not Rappaport, Crimes of the Heart,* and *Fences* to a drama-starved Broadway. But the Theatre of Michigan would not survive its initial productions.

The first two stage projects of the company were *General Seegar*, a military drama by Ira Levin, directed by Scott, and *Great Day in the Morning,* by Alice Cannon (J. D. Cannon's wife), a memory play about a family in Depression-era St. Louis to star Dewhurst and staged by José Quintero. Mann and Scott convinced theatre owner David Nederlander to rent them the Shubert without an initial deposit. When asked where the capital would eventually come from, Scott dramatically slapped his hand down on the Shubert's orchestra rail and cried, "We'll get the money!"

Scott and Dewhurst, along with one-and-a-half-year-old Alex and six-month-old Campbell, moved to a hotel in Detroit and took on the difficult task of fund raising. "There we were stuck in an expensive hotel while our money was running out," Dewhurst wrote in *The Off-*

Broadway Experience. "In order to arouse interest, we performed scenes in the homes of the so-called elite of Detroit. They turned out to be the local *La Dolce Vita* crowd. It was not until we were booked into the Jewish homes that we were treated with respect. Ready for us, they listened without a drink in their hands. They understood what we were there for and showed their approval by writing checks. Unfortunately, however, there were not enough of them."

With cash running low, Mann and the Scotts threw a lavish party for dignitaries of Detroit in the hotel's ballroom and charged it to their bill. The turnout was less than spectacular. The mayor did show up, but there were only about fifteen local bigwigs in attendance. Enraged by the lack of enthusiasm for his pet project, Scott proceeded to get drunk, cursed his hometown's lack of cultural acumen, and began smashing the mirrors which lined the ballroom. His producer and his wife managed to get the enraged actor-entrepreneur under control and upstairs. The dejected couple went to bed, sure the dream was over. Their sleep was interrupted by a suddenly enthusiastic Mann, bursting into their room and asking for fund-raising brochures. "His hysteria overwhelmed us," Dewhurst wrote. "Then the next morning the one thing we knew was that we had to get out without facing the hotel management. We put on all the clothes we had, even overdressing the two children, and made our escape." In his memoir, *Journeys in the Night*, Mann records a slightly different version with Scott being put to bed, no late-night visit from himself, Dewhurst calmly buttering toast and pouring coffee the next morning, and no clandestine getaway.

Overdressed kids making a quick exit or not, the Theatre of Michigan was still practically broke. With the company about to crash before it even got started, Scott came up with the idea of selling stock to the public at a low price. The standard practice for mounting a Broadway show was and is to create a partnership with the investors as limited partners and the producers as general partners. Showmen had been talking about a stock-sales approach for years, but no one had ever tried it. The Theatre of Michigan became the first stage production company to sell shares directly to the public. Its first offering was 125,000 shares at $3 apiece. Advertisements were placed in the local newspapers and a small office was rented to provide a Detroit mailing address. A few days after the first announcement of the stock offer, Scott and Mann walked to their closet-sized office to find it bursting with mail sacks. Each was bulging with checks in denominations of $2, $4, $8, and $10—drips of cash, but put together it was a strong beginning. To complete the company bankroll, Scott turned to a previous savior—television. CBS and United Artists Television agreed to put $75,000 into the Theatre of Michigan as part of the $125,000 they paid to get a contract from Scott for a new series. "They wanted me and I needed them, so we got into bed together," Scott explained to *Time* magazine.

Now rehearsals and production could start. Scott was juggling producing and directing while living with his family out of suitcases. A photo spread in the *Detroit News Pictorial Magazine* showed the actor-director-producer in his hotel suite with both small sons in his lap and his bare feet propped on a coffee table while reading a script.

A typical day consisted of a breakfast of pastry in the hotel; rehearsals of *General Seegar* in the morning, followed by lunch consisting of a candy bar and some coffee; answering mail and phone messages until Dewhurst finished rehearsals for *Great Day in the Morning*; and then a quick dinner together followed by another rehearsal. Afterwards, Scott and Dewhurst would play cards with the cast and chat with Mann, who had just flown in from New York where he was still tending to Circle in the Square business.

By now, the growing Scott family had moved from Greenwich Village to a penthouse apartment in Manhattan on West 56th Street with a terrace and a park a block away for the boys to play in. Scott spoke to an interviewer of moving back to Detroit to live and setting up a movie production company.

His goal of creating his art and enjoying his family far from the commercial grind of Broadway and Hollywood seemed attainable. But financial realities set a roadblock in his path. A few weeks into rehearsal, the Securities and Exchange Commission demanded the company halt its stock sales because of a technicality. The theatre was a Michigan-based entity and only had the right to sell stocks in that state. The money from CBS, a New-York based company, exceeded that mandate. The SEC allowed them to keep the funds from the $2 and $4 investors, but because of CBS's investment, they could not sell any more shares. Scott poured in an additional $75,000 of his own, but it would prove to be lost money.

General Seegar opened in Detroit to mixed notices. The play starred William Bendix, best known for playing good-hearted lugs in films like *Detective Story* and *Lifeboat* and on the TV series *The Life of Reilly*. The melodramatic plot centered on the titular general, who drives his non-conformist son into the military. The boy is killed in what appears to be an accident during a training session. On the day of a ceremony to honor him, young Seegar's wife reveals that the boy committed suicide. The disillusioned general attempts to stop the sham event. But the Army needs a gallant fallen hero for public relations and the hollow commemoration proceeds with Seegar ordered to shut up or be drilled out of his beloved military. The play was written by Ira Levin, who had had Broadway hits with *No Time for Sergeants*, a merrier view of service life that made a star of Andy Griffith, and *Critic's Choice,* an equally lighthearted comedy.

Before the production ended its week of performances in Detroit, Bendix was fired and Scott replaced him. He had only five days to rehearse before going to Broadway, but, as the director, he already had the script memorized. Mann told the *New York Post*, "We've had a difference of interpretation, shall we say, between Mr. Bendix and ourselves, but we were fortunate to have one of the best actors in the country ready to go on and what more could a producer want?" Scott initially thought he was too young at thirty-five to play a sixty-year-old general. But the age difference was the least of the play's problems. *Seegar* made the move to Broadway, was roundly panned, and closed after two performances. As usual, Scott was praised. Walter Kerr in the *Herald-Tribune* cheered, "Bully or braggart, dictator or inconsiderate dad, we like him fine. Mr. Scott is simply so much more interesting than the other people on stage, including the virtuous ones, that we secretly hope he gets the better of this scene and the next scene and the one after that."

Not long after *Seegar*'s rapid demise, *Great Day in the Morning* played only ten performances on Broadway and shuttered. The Scotts lost $75,000 of their own savings. Dewhurst's Tony nomination for her performance was small consolation. "You've got to learn one thing as a producer, George," director Harold Clurman advised him, "no more of your own money."

"We spent all the money we'd raised, and all of my own, too," Scott later told the *New York Post*. "It was a stunning body blow. I still believe in the idea, but it needs a lot of hard educating first. People outside of New York have a great fear of being provincial. They don't accept a play unless Broadway has OK'd it. And neither production had enough critical approval here to run without a lot more money than we had."

Rather than declare bankruptcy, Scott hoped to get the company back on its feet in 1964. Meanwhile, he was concentrating on an equally important activity. Despite the failure of both plays, the Theatre of Michigan softball team with Scott pitching finished the season in the Broadway Show League. Dewhurst told *Look* magazine, "When he was casting his play *General Seegar*, he put a good ballplayer in every walk-on role." The team went on to win the championship and Scott was chosen most valuable player. Scott loved playing softball. In his pre-*Richard III* days, he had played on a pickup team of actors, taking on all comers, on weekends on Central Park's diamond number three. Other players included Bruce Dern, Robert Loggia, Charlie Dierkop, and Paul Newman. They played for $100 a game, splitting the winnings to $11 each, and held the diamond until they lost, sometimes from 9:30 A.M. to 9:00 at night.

The Theatre of Michigan established Scott's penchant for bucking the establishment, trying to control the product and have it done his way.

While *Seegar* was in rehearsals and Scott was defying the Broadway system, he was presented with the opportunity to go against the Hollywood status quo as well. For his performance in *The Hustler*, Scott received his second Oscar nomination. This time he was up against Jackie Gleason from the same film, George Chakiris (*West Side Story*), Montgomery Clift (*Judgment at Nuremberg*), and Peter Falk (*Pocketful of Miracles*).

Still stinging from his defeat for *Anatomy of a Murder,* embarrassed by his need to win, and unwilling to participate in what he regarded as a tawdry process having more to do with advertising than excellence in acting, he sent a telegram to the Academy refusing the nomination. "I take the position that actors shouldn't be forced to outadvertise and outstab each other," he told the *New York Post*.

Wendell Corey, the President of the Academy, responded in a letter, "You were nominated by a vote of your fellow actors and the Academy cannot remove your name from the list of nominated performances. The Academy nominates and votes awards for performances and achievements as they appear on the screen. Therefore, any one person responsible for such a performance or achievement cannot decline the nomination after it is voted."

Ironically, Scott's father, George D. Scott, was also in the running for an Oscar, if indirectly. He was vice president of the Ex-Cell-O Corporation, which had sponsored an industrial documentary called *Project Hope*. It had received a nomination for Best Documentary Short Subject.

On Oscar night, April 9, 1962, host Bob Hope cracked wise, "How 'bout that George C. Scott? He's sitting at home with his back to the television set." Scott was not alone in missing the ceremony. Of his fellow nominees, only Falk and Chakiris were present. Just as Scott had been defeated in 1959 by a sweep for a blockbuster, he lost again to an overwhelming favorite. Previously he had been trampled by the chariots of *Ben-Hur*; this time he was stomped by the dancing feet of the Sharks and the Jets. The film version of the revolutionary Broadway musical *West Side Story* claimed a total of ten Oscars (one shy of *Ben-Hur*'s record eleven) including the Supporting Actor prize for Chakiris as the doomed Shark gang leader, Bernardo. Again, Scott lost to a less deserving winner. While the handsome young dancer-actor was certainly dynamic executing Jerome Robbins's spicy choreography, he was no match for Scott's fire-and-ice Bert Gordon. Perhaps if he hadn't withdrawn his name, Scott would have won.

The Scott family was not entirely unrewarded. *Project Hope*, the Ex-Cell-O-sponsored short triumphed in its category. George C. sent a good-natured wire to his father: IF ONE OF US HAD TO WIN, I'M GLAD IT WAS YOU. Though Scott Senior was not directly involved in the film (the award went to producer Frank P. Bibas), it must have felt like a scene from his childhood for Scott Junior to see his father's project honored while he was passed over. *The Hustler* had been nominated for nine Oscars and won two in the technical categories of art direction and cinematography.

To regain his financial footing and pay off his debts after the Theatre of Michigan wipeout, Scott abandoned directing and producing to focus on acting. He could have declared bankruptcy, but he felt that wouldn't have been honorable. In order to get the backing for his theatre, he had committed himself to an artistic straitjacket: a three-year contract for a series with CBS to start shooting in 1963. It was a heavy commitment of thirty-two segments the first year and twenty-four the next. But Scott was determined to make the straitjacket as comfortable as possible. He had signed on to play an international newspaperman in a different exotic location each week. Here was an echo of his college ambition to be a journalist. The projected series would be filmed abroad in numerous exotic locations. Not a bad gig. However, the final result would be entirely different. Scott, who had a say in the development of the show, later opted for more realism. Instead of romantic European cities, the series would take place in the slums of New York.

He was also in talks to film the romantic comedy *They Might Be Giants* for United Artists, with Harold Prince directing and Dewhurst playing opposite him. *Giants* would not be committed to film for eight years, and Joanne Woodward would eventually play the role intended for Dewhurst.

Before submitting to the grind of a weekly television series, Scott took on a soul-feeding assignment. He would play Shylock in *The Merchant of Venice*, the New York Shakespeare Festival's inaugural production at the outdoor Delacorte Theatre in Central Park. It only paid $100 a week, a fraction of what he could command for a guest shot on TV. He did it out of love for the role and for Joe Papp, who had given him his first break as Richard III. Papp was presenting the kind of theatre Scott had hoped to achieve with the Theatre of Michigan. The Shakespeare Festival was offering the classics for free to theatergoers from every stratum of society, and after eight years the company finally had a permanent theatre of it own.

Papp, who was directing as well as producing, thought Shylock should be in the throes of a "magisterial, biblical rage." He told Scott, "Never turn the other cheek. You want to hurt these people that have hurt you. Don't softsell it. People will understand your anger."

The actor's anger matched the character's. While he was playing one of the most challenging roles in the Bard's canon, Scott still made noises about getting out of acting altogether. He told the press he would rather direct and produce as he had done with the Theatre of Michigan company. He was angry at the demise of the ambitious enterprise and the indifference of Broadway audiences. "It's like playing to a bustling vacuum," he railed. "I hate audiences by the nature of the beast: hot ladies in fur capes, waving their programs and coughing, and hot perfume swelling up over the footlights at you. . . . Sometimes I think I am losing my stamina, my strength to fight these terrible ladies . . . And sometimes I think I will try again. You see, ours is a love-hate relationship."

Though rage was his specialty, the highlight of *Merchant* was a quiet moment. In one of the final scenes, Scott as Shylock held a handkerchief belonging to his daughter, Jessica, who has eloped with a Gentile. He would allow the gentle breeze blowing off the nearby lake to carry off the token of his departed daughter.

What led to this simple but stunningly effective piece of stagecraft? He explained to Lewis Funke,

> At the loss of the daughter what I did was try to kill her. I tried to murder her by trying to tear the handkerchief, but he couldn't tear the handkerchief, but I could have. How can he separate himself from her? It's impossible to separate yourself from your child, no matter what, and not being able to tear her, literally to kill her, he had to be a big enough man to let her go and be free. That was the whole feeling behind the hankie bit. And so I can't murder you, I can't stop you from doing what you've done, I can't make you pay for hurting me, so I'm going to be a large enough soul to let you be free. All I did was open my hand and the wind did the rest. It's a memorable thing because it's a kind of a piece of business that's damn near foolproof. And it worked.

Indeed it did, as did the entire performance. Fritz Weaver called it "the best American Shakespeare I have ever seen." Weaver did find Scott was having vocal problems projecting to fill the new 2,300-seat amphitheatre:

> It took away from my enjoyment of what he was doing. I kept thinking, "George, calm down, stop shrieking right on the chords." So the second act opened and he just proceeded to lift the play up to the stars. It was so powerful. You forgot all about the voice. You forgot about everything. You were in the presence of a very great performance. I was no longer aware of the voice. I was aware of a suffering human being. I'll never forget it.

The Delacorte opened on June 18, 1962 and began a tradition of New Yorkers picnicking in Central Park while waiting for free tickets to productions under starlit skies. Papp read a congratulatory telegram from First Lady Jacqueline Kennedy. Mayor Wagner gave a speech. *Merchant* was broadcast live with no commercial breaks by local station WCBS-TV and seen in 800,000 homes. The viewing audience was estimated to be two million, probably the most for any of Shakespeare's plays at a single sitting up to that point. Sadly the tape has been lost to the ages. Not everyone was enchanted by Papp's choice and its television airing. The New York Board of Rabbis protested the broadcast, calling the play anti-Semitic and inflammatory, and the Jewish War Veterans sent a delegation to picket the CBS offices.

Bruce Minnix, director of the television broadcast, recalled bold acting choices by Scott that might have alleviated the rabbis' concerns: "I thought he did the 'Does not a Jew have eyes' section with a whole new read on it. It was genuinely moving, but it was also demanding, which is an interesting combination. Most [actors performing the speech] will say it like, 'Oooooh, poor me, don't I bleed, too.' Scott was saying that and getting your sympathy. But, at the same time, he was saying, 'That shouldn't be.'"

Among the thousands attending the live production was director Stanley Kubrick, who cast Scott as the war-happy General Buck Turgidson for his next project, a comedy on the unlikely topic of nuclear holocaust with the unwieldy title of *Dr. Strangelove or: How I Learned to Stop Worrying and Love the Bomb*.

Before *Strangelove* and his new television series began filming, Scott undertook a change-of-pace role and his first film lead in *The List of Adrian Messenger*. It also provided a switch from the usual for its director, the legendary John Huston. Scott would play a leading hero after a string of supporting villain roles, and Huston got to romp through England with an escapist thriller after dealing with the neurotic shenanigans of Marilyn Monroe in *The Misfits* and Montgomery Clift in *Freud*. Based on Philip MacDonald's novel, *Adrian Messenger* was supposed to be a cunning party game featuring major stars like Kirk Douglas (also the film's producer), Burt Lancaster, Tony Curtis, Robert Mitchum, and Frank Sinatra playing cameo roles in heavy disguise. They wouldn't remove their makeup until the final reel. Moviegoers would supposedly get a thrill from guessing who was who. This charade was wrapped around a murder mystery with Scott as stiff-upper-lip British sleuth Anthony Gethryn on the trial of a serial killer.

Producer Douglas had seen Scott in *The Andersonville Trial*, later recalling him as "magnificent in the leading role, slim as a razor." Douglas labeled director Huston "certainly one of the most talented men in the industry. But John could also be a bit of a charlatan. If he wanted to slough something off, he could slough it off. I don't think he really felt the spirit of it."

Huston put himself into the spirit of *Messenger* by inserting a fox hunt—one of his favorite activities—into the script and insisting it be filmed in Ireland, where he was living for tax purposes. He also cast himself as the leader of the hunt, several of his titled friends as extras, and his young son Tony in the small part of the killer's intended last victim. Despite the blandness of his role, Scott infused his detective with a clipped vitality. Scott admired Huston, the director of such classics as *The Maltese Falcon* and *The Treasure of Sierra Madre*, later calling him "a remarkable creature. He wrote in several fox hunts. I had never ridden a horse, but I lied and told him, sure I could ride. I was thrown off that damn horse three times in one afternoon and cracked three ribs. I didn't do much riding after that."

When the film opened in May 1963, Scott was overshadowed by the movie-star guessing game. Even the film's main conceit didn't work. Douglas, Lancaster, and company were all so obviously covered up with wigs and rubber facial applications that it didn't take a Sherlock Holmes to figure out they were not who they seemed. *Time* magazine called this cinematic costume party "only a tribute to the art of makeup man Bud Westmore." Scott did receive some good notices. The

New York Mirror said he made the film: "Without him it would have been very little, but his performance as a British pip-pipper puts it up there among the better suspense stories." *Films and Filming* praised his "sharply etched performance. . . . One of the best scenes simply shows [Scott] muttering eccentrically to himself while racking his brains over a recalcitrant clue."

Scott soon took another departure from his usual run of tough guys and nasty villains. On October 17, 1962, ABC broadcast the "Brazen Bell" episode of its high-class, in-color western series *The Virginian*, starring the original Willy Loman, Lee J. Cobb, as a former judge and father figure to a makeshift family of cowboys. Scott guest-starred as a meek schoolteacher saddled with a domineering wife (played by Anne Meacham). This assignment, though otherwise unrewarding, offered Scott an opportunity to stretch his acting muscles by playing an unlikely role. Even the character's name, Arthur Lilly, is unconvincing, a ridiculously obvious play on "lily-livered coward." The episode turned on the hackneyed plot device of a pair of vicious escaped convicts holding captive the schoolchildren in Lilly's care.

The usually macho actor was totally convincing as the soft-spoken academic. From the moment he steps off the train and inquires about lodgings in a voice full of trepidation, responding with a quavering "Yes, dear" to his shrewish spouse's demands, Arthur Lilly is a vibrant, flawed man. Scott takes the meager scraps of the script and creates a believable character. There is a subtext to his timidity. He has a secret—a school where he previously worked burned down due to his negligence—and he's terrified anyone will find him out. Scott's every action is informed by this fear. He nearly jumps out of his skin and reacts with rage when a student frightens him with a snake. But Lilly finally finds his resolve. After his wife has been fatally shot by the captors, he movingly recites Oscar Wilde's "The Ballad of Reading Gaol" to distract the killers and allow Cobb and the good guys a clear shot at the gang leader. That same year Scott was also on the boob tube in the "Strike a Statue" segment of *Naked City* and "I Don't Belong in a White Painted House" in *The Eleventh Hour* series.

As if to prove his versatility, Scott followed the refined British investigator of *Adrian Messenger* and the mild-mannered coward of *The Virginian* with a rough-hewn tiller of the soil. Dewhurst was cast as Abby Putnam in Eugene O'Neill's *Desire Under the Elms* for Circle in the Square, to be staged by José Quintero, her *Children of Darkness* director. Franchot Tone, a Hollywood star of the 1930s, was set to play Ephraim Cabot, Abby's elderly but strong-willed farmer husband. After a few days of rehearsals Tone withdrew, explaining he was not up to the physical and emotional demands of the role. Dewhurst called her real-life spouse, who was in California filming a TV role, about stepping in. Scott was at first reluctant to take on the demands of O'Neill, but threw himself into the part. Perhaps he was hesitant to explore the father-son rivalry central to the plot with its echoes of his own relationship to his dad. Ephraim and his son, Eben, played by Rip Torn in this production, battle not only over the family farm (which belonged to Eben's mother who died young), but also over the love of Abby. During rehearsals Scott observed to Dewhurst that she and Quintero worked spontaneously, while Scott methodically planned his performances beforehand. "When he takes a role he applies all his heart, mind and soul until he captures the complete and total concept of the role," Quintero wrote in his memoir. "With George it has to be a big concept such as the George Washington Bridge or the Golden Gate Bridge. I don't know why I always liken his concepts to bridges, but I do. Maybe it's because he then begins to work on this concept like a magnificent theatrical engineer."

As he did in *General Seegar*, Scott was playing a much older man. He arrived three hours before curtain to apply the makeup and whiskers to transform himself into the seventy-eight-year-old Putnam. But this was a vigorous septuagenarian. In a clever piece of staging, Ephraim and Eben hauled unequal weights of farm equipment onstage, and

Scott would lug the heavier one, demonstrating not only Ephraim's strength, but his rivalry with his son.

That rivalry bled into real life. Scott became convinced Torn's on-stage flirtations with Dewhurst were a little too convincing and threatened to wrap a metal pole used as a prop around his neck, unless Torn left his wife alone. When Circle producer Theodore Mann told Dewhurst of the incident, she burst out laughing and then catching her breath said, "Oh, the poor baby."

Scott infused Ephraim with the kind of raw energy and drive that had propelled George Dewey Scott to leave the coal mines and rise to corporate success. Howard Taubman in the *New York Times* wrote, "Mr. Scott brings the required harshness and cruelty to the character of Ephraim Cabot, the fierce, flinty septuagenarian who has forced the grudging New England soil to yield fruit, but who has not been softened by age or man." The *Village Voice* admired his dedication: "[He] commits his whole being as an actor to animating this elemental character. He succeeds superbly. It is Ephraim who speaks to us here, who stands against these assaults, who stands and survives like the trees and rocks. More valuable even than Mr. Scott's range of talent as an actor is his devotion to the real work of acting, to bringing us everything of the character and the play."

Despite the plaudits, Scott would only stay with *Desire* for a month before leaving for England to star in Stanley Kubrick's wacko comedy with the long-winded title.

7

Dr. Strangelove and
East Side/West Side

A MONTH AFTER *Desire Under the Elms* opened, Scott left the cast and re-turned to England to begin filming *Dr. Strangelove*. The dark, nuclear-holocaust comedy was based on a straight thriller novel by ex-R.A.F. navigator Peter George, published as *Two Hours to Doom* in Britain and *Red Alert* in the U.S. The story contained the same basic plot upon which *Strangelove* pivoted—a renegade general authorizes an Ameri-can strike against the Soviet Union, setting in motion the possible end of civilization. Maverick director-producer Stanley Kubrick and his coproducer James B. Harris purchased the rights for $3,500 with the intention of making a dramatic adaptation for Seven Arts. Sterling Hayden, Scott, and his *Merchant of Venice* costar James Earl Jones were hired to play serious versions of their eventually comic *Strangelove* char-acters. Initially, the director envisaged Scott as the screw-loose general who launches the attack. "Kubrick first offered him the part Sterling Hayden played and he turned it down. He said, 'I'll play the other part,'" recalled Scott's close friend Clifton James, meaning the war-happy General Buck Turgidson, the Chief of Staff who is not entirely unopposed to destroying the Russians.

Kubrick and Harris's partnership and their deal with Seven Arts dis-solved, forcing the director to find a new distributor for the film. Co-lumbia Pictures stepped into the breach, but only if Peter Sellers would star and play multiple roles as he had in Kubrick's *Lolita*. Meanwhile, Peter George had initiated a lawsuit against Harvey Wheeler and Eugene Burdick for similarities between *Red Alert* and their novel *Fail-Safe,* another end-of-the-world thriller. George won an out-of-court settlement, but that did not affect the *Fail-Safe* United Artists film version, which conceivably could have been released before Kubrick's movie. To avoid confusion with *Fail-Safe* and to fully employ Sellers's comedic talents, the serious *Doom* became the raucous *Strangelove*. According to Kubrick, the transformation was a result of the inherently absurd nature of the content rather than legal or casting necessities. The destruction of civilization by intelligent nations could only be treated as a cosmic joke, the auteur told Terry Southern, the author of the comic cult novels *Candy* and *The Magic Christian*, when he asked Southern to collaborate on a satiric treatment of the material.

Thus what could have been a standard evocation of the day's nuclear paranoia became a timeless cartoon on the madness of war—a comic companion to Kubrick's earlier pacifist drama *Paths of Glory*. *Strangelove* ushered in a decade of politically tinged black humor, influencing television, books, and movies with its we're-all-going-to-hell-so-we-might-as-well-laugh-it-up attitude.

To satisfy Columbia and get his money's worth out of Sellers—who was being paid $1 million, half of the film's total budget—Kubrick cast his hot star in four roles: properly British Group Captain Lionel Mandrake, cringing U.S. President Merkin Muffley, former Nazi and maniacal presidential advisor Dr. Strangelove, and Major T. J. "King" Kong, the Texan pilot who rides the fatal bomb like a bucking bronco as it drops on Russian soil. Eventually, Sellers dropped the last role, claiming discomfort with the Texas accent, and former rodeo clown Slim Pickens took it on. Early in preproduction, the director was even considering having Sellers play a fifth role—Turgidson.

Fortunately for Scott, three roles were enough for Sellers, and Scott turned in a brilliantly exaggerated performance, exactly right for the satiric tone of the film. Kubrick, who had hustled chess games in

Greenwich Village to finance his first movie, played chess with Scott in between shots, often beating him and gaining his respect. "This gave me a certain edge with him on everything else," Kubrick told writer Michel Ciment. "If you fancy yourself a good chess player, you have an inordinate respect for people who can beat you."

Many film commentators have conjectured Buck Turgidson was inspired by real-life hawkish General Curtis LeMay, the head of Strategic Air Command in the 1950s and the Air Force Chief of Staff in the early 1960s. Scott told Professor Richard Brown his characterization was based on a business colleague of his father's in Detroit.

Whether LeMay or the businessman was the principal source of inspiration, Buck Turgidson is a walking political cartoon, so intent on advancing his right-wing view of the world he doesn't realize its logical endgame is Armageddon. Like Claude Dancer in *Anatomy of a Murder* and Bert Gordon in *The Hustler*, Turgidson enters after the central action has been established—in this case, General Jack D. Ripper (Sterling Hayden) has gone off his nut and launched an unauthorized attack on Russia. We find Buck in a tryst with his bikini-clad secretary, Miss Scott (Tracy Reed, the daughter of director Carol Reed), as the phone rings to alert him to the potential disaster. Wearing shorts and an open sport shirt, Turgidson slaps his bare belly like an ape beating his chest as he assesses the nightmare situation and affects a swaggering, casual front. The scene focuses on the general's sexual and military obsessions. "I'm sorry, baby," he coos to Miss Scott as he leaves to save the world. "Start your countdown without me, and I'll be back before you can say 'Blast off!'" Even his name suggests a priapic stud (Buck) and an erect sexual organ (Turgidson, derived from turgid, defined as "swollen, distended abnormally, or bombastic").

The funniest scenes are the ones between the ineffectual President (Sellers) and Turgidson as the latter attempts to convince his commander-in-chief a nuclear nightmare wouldn't be so bad. Scott is like a used-car salesman, pushing his horrifying proposal with a smile, "I'm not saying we won't get our hair mussed. I'm saying ten to twenty million people killed—tops—depending on the breaks." That last "tops" is thrown in as if he were describing a faulty fan belt, nothing to be worried about.

In another high point, Turgidson transforms himself into an enthusiastic boy describing the skill of American B-52 pilots. All but one of the fighters has been successfully recalled before reaching Soviet air space. President Muffley asks Turgidson if the lone plane could conceivably reach its objective and plunge the world into a nuclear abyss. Not thinking of the consequences of the question, Scott launches into a rhapsodic revelry on the beauty of aeronautics. He stretches his arms out and giggles in pure macho appreciation of flying skill, Yankee know-how, and gleaming hardware. Suddenly the realization of what he's saying spreads across Scott's face and he is stopped like a wounded eagle, his arms frozen in mid-flight.

Scott claimed to have contributed a great deal to the dialogue as well as the performance, joking that he should have gotten a screen credit. Explaining the fluid nature of the shooting script (credited to Kubrick, Southern, and Peter George), Scott said of the director, "He's a perfectionist and he's always unhappy with anything that's set. Every morning we would all meet and practically rewrite the day's work."

Singular in his vision, Kubrick was most concerned with the grand sweep of his overall design. A staff photographer for *Look* magazine at sixteen years old, the director was most intrigued with the look of his films, and not as focused on the acting, music or script. Kubrick didn't like naturalism and encouraged the cast, Scott in particular, to give farcical performances.

"The irresistible force met the immovable object when Stanley asked George to do over-the-top performances of his lines," James Earl Jones wrote in an essay for the *Wall Street Journal* on the occasion of *Strangelove*'s fortieth anniversary, adding,

> He said it would help George warm up for his satiric takes. George hated this idea. He said it was unprofessional and made him feel

silly. George eventually agreed to do his scenes over-the-top when Stanley promised that his performance would never be seen by anyone but himself and the cast and crew. But Kubrick ultimately used many of these 'warm-ups' in the final cut. George felt used and manipulated by Stanley and swore he would never work with him again.

But in a 1996 *Chicago Sun-Times* retrospective of great cinema, critic Roger Ebert wrote of Scott's work, "I found myself paying special attention to tics and twitches, the grimaces and eyebrow archings, the sardonic smiles and gum-chewing, and I enjoyed the way Scott approached the role as a duet for voice and facial expression."

The original ending was intended to be more raucous than the final ironic climax of mushroom clouds erupting as a World War II recording of the sentimental "We'll Meet Again" plays. After Major Kong has ridden the fatal bomb and annihilated a healthy chunk of the Russian population, a pie fight erupts in the war room as Turgidson discovers hidden cameras on the person of Soviet Ambassador De Sadesky (Peter Bull). "We threw a thousand pies a day for five days, and Stanley wouldn't let us clean them up," Scott told Harry Haun of the *New York Daily News* almost thirty years later. He continued,

> Every day, we'd walk into the war room set, and rancid sugar and cream would be everywhere. . . . Peter Bull, playing the Russian ambassador, threw a pie at me. I ducked and it hit Peter Sellers, who swooned into my arms. Then I had the line 'Our beloved President has been cut down in the prime of life by a pie.' When Jack Kennedy was assassinated, the whole sequence went. Had to. It was a helluvah scene, but it was untenable because of the situation.

President Kennedy's assassination in November 1963 not only altered *Strangelove*'s ending, but pushed back its release date to January 1964. A dark comedy about the end of the world would not have been well received by an America recovering from the brutal murder of its beloved young leader.

When it was finally released, Kubrick was praised for balancing the film's outlandish and serious elements. The picture also sparked a debate on the possibility of accidental nuclear war. There was a small, conservative, anti-*Strangelove* backlash with right-wing commentators claiming the comedy was un-American. But the controversy sparked box-office interest. *Strangelove* was nominated for four Oscars, including Best Picture, Director, Actor (Sellers), and Screenplay Based on Material from Another Medium, losing in the first three categories to the more comforting charms of *My Fair Lady* and the fourth to the historical drama *Becket*. If not for his refusal of the nomination for *The Hustler*, Scott might have received a third Oscar nod for the buffoonish Turgidson. Scott nearly steals the picture, fighting a duel with the three creations of Peter Sellers to a draw. *Strangelove* also displayed Scott's comic ability and freed him from being typecast as a villain.

Filming on *Strangelove* wrapped up on April 23, 1963. Not long after Scott's return to the States, on May 30, he and Dewhurst were named Best Actor and Actress of the Off-Broadway season for *Desire Under the Elms* by the *Village Voice* Obie Awards, which were held at the Village Gate. Dewhurst was taking a break from rehearsals for *Antony and Cleopatra* for the New York Shakespeare Festival. She graciously accepted her award from presenter Uta Hagen. Then Hagen announced Scott had won Best Actor and could not be there because he was stuck in the Bronx at a script conference for *East Side/West Side*, his new television series. Dewhurst returned to the stage to accept Scott's Obie.

To pay off his Theatre of Michigan debts, Scott had now plunged into the demanding world of weekly television. He was not just the star. Producers David Susskind and Daniel Melnick gave him veto power over the storylines and casting. Between the initial announcements and the start of production, the premise of the entire enterprise shifted from an adventure show following the exciting assignments of a foreign correspondent to a gritty drama focusing on the depressing casework of Neil Brock, a New York social worker. Instead of romantic European cities, the series would be shot in the slums of Harlem and the Bronx. As he had hoped the Theatre of Michigan would shake up the standard practices of Broadway producing, Scott wanted his first series to challenge the staid formulae of TV, then commonly referred to as the idiot box or a vast wasteland.

As *East Side/West Side* began production, the live East Coast–based drama anthology shows on which Scott had gained fame were giving way to West Coast series with continuing characters. In dramas, cowboys, cops and lawyers predominated, but no other shows about social workers dealing with such issues as prostitution, racial discrimination, and juvenile delinquency had been attempted. Not only would the focus of *East Side* be unusually realistic, Scott didn't want the same old situations week after week. "Three years from now, I don't want to be the same old Matt Dillon shooting the same old six gun at the same old heavy while Chester drags around the same old game leg," he told *TV Guide*, referring the standard plotline of every episode of the popular CBS series *Gunsmoke*. "I want this character to change organically, professionally, and even physically."

Joining Brock on his crusade to heal New York's social ills were his supervisor, Frieda Hechlinger (nicknamed Hecky), played by Elizabeth Wilson, and Jane Foster, the office secretary, played by Cicely Tyson.

Elizabeth Wilson, a close friend of both Scott and Dewhurst, remembered how she won the coveted role:

> George was responsible for me being in *East Side/West Side*. I auditioned for the role and David Susskind or a CBS executive said to George, "She's not pretty enough. We want someone really pretty to play this part." And George said, "I don't care. I want her anyway." So I got to play that part and that was a trip and a half. For many reasons. One, because we filmed it in the Bronx. Every week it was another two or three wonderful stage actors. I

became kind of like a hostess in my dressing room to make all these
people feel comfortable. It was just wild. We went out on location
a lot. I can remember that in those days Harlem was a little iffy for
white people which I can understand. We filmed six days a week.
George got upset with the way the writing was going so we took
two weeks off.

While Scott was fighting to maintain the integrity and social rel-
evance of his new series, Dewhurst was taking another whack at
Shakespeare's Cleopatra at the Delacorte Theatre in Central Park opposite Michael Higgins's Marc Antony. She was earning $100 a week
for her Queen of the Nile while Elizabeth Taylor raked in close to
$10,000,000 for Joseph Mankiewicz's gargantuan film version released
during Dewhurst's run. But the Scotts were financially recovering
from their recent Theatre of Michigan debacle. "I got $750 a week
and I think George got $10,000. He had that kind of position," re-
called Elizabeth Wilson.

The couple had moved from the apartment on West 56th Street
in Manhattan to a ten-room house in the quasi-suburban Riverdale
section of the Bronx. Their new home was close to the old Biograph
studios where *East Side* was filmed and accessible to Broadway and Off-
Broadway theatres for Dewhurst. A photo in the June 9, 1963 edition
of the *New York Times* displays Scott and Dewhurst sitting with the
two boys on their leaf-strewn terrace. Scott sips from a coffee cup as
he and Dewhurst watch two-year-old Campbell playing with blocks
and three-year-old Alex happily sitting astride a toy truck. They're
the perfect picture of a happy family. Scott could be a middle-class
businessman enjoying a restful weekend. The demons of alcohol and
frustrated ambition appear to have been banished.

But the demands of a weekly television series limited Scott's time
with his family. The actor had stripped his life of all extraneous details. There was occasional relaxation with chess, bridge, swimming,
and baseball, but Scott hardly ever ventured forth from the Riverdale

house. Even his reading was all sociological and psychological text-books, in search of inspiration for scripts and to make his performance more authentic.

As if getting the episodes in the can on a rigid, six-days-a-week schedule weren't enough, there were constant battles with the net-works, the sponsors, even the show's writing staff. As Elizabeth Wilson noted, production halted for two weeks in June when Scott was not satisfied with the level of scripts. The break was called for tempers to cool and for the writers to come up with more polished material.

The treatment of African-American characters, including office secretary Jane Foster (Cicely Tyson), was another source of controversy. Elizabeth Wilson related, "CBS would not allow Cicely to do anything but open the door and introduce people. This is so crazy when you look at television today in America. They said she can't have any dialogue."

Tyson was the first African-American performer, male or female, to hold down a recurring role on a network drama series. Though she was essentially playing a functional role with little to do other than answer the phones and file paperwork, it was an important advancement. But the idea of a black woman on an equal footing with a white man, no matter how powerless against the system, was too much for several television stations below the Mason-Dixon line, twenty-six of which would drop the show. Scott fought for Tyson to do more than open the door and introduce guest stars. In a few episodes, she did have significant dialogue but remained a minor figure. It was ten years later that she had a career breakthrough with the film *Sounder* and was nominated for an Oscar.

As the new fall season approached, CBS presented the running schedule of *East Side* shows to Scott, Susskind, and Melnick. The schedule was not in the order the creative team had intended and went against the novelistic approach Scott wanted with Neil Brock changing from week to week. If it was out of sequence, it wouldn't make sense. Here was another instance of corporate interests squashing his artistic integrity. "We've got to come to grips with controversial themes. . . ." the actor complained to Richard Schickel of *TV Guide*. "I've been just as obnoxious as humanly possible to make my associates see this."

Despite Scott's admitted obnoxiousness, network interference, and controversial subject matter, *East Side/West Side* debuted on Monday night, September 23, 1963, in the 10 P.M. slot, with a CBS lead-in of eponymous sitcoms starring Lucille Ball, Danny Thomas, and Andy Griffith. It played opposite the drama *Breaking Point* on ABC and a corny variety series, *Sing Along with Mitch,* starring bandleader Mitch Miller, on NBC. The prime time schedule was filled with witless comedies like *The Beverly Hillbillies, Petticoat Junction,* and *My Favorite Martian,* and simplistic westerns such as *The Virginian, Rawhide,* and *Gunsmoke.* Amidst these moralistic cowboys, dizzy housewives, and whimsical Martians, Neil Brock stood alone facing as near an approximation of the real world as the lowest-common-denominator-driven medium of television would allow.

The first aired episode was "The Sinner" guest starring Carol Rossen (daughter of *The Hustler* director Robert Rossen) as an unmarried mother challenged for the custody of her infant son. The controversial nature of the character's single-parent status is compounded by her line of work: prostitution. Also revolutionary was the episode's unhappy ending. After struggling with welfare agencies and courts to allow the mother to keep her baby, Brock loses. The episode ends with the child being taken by his grandmother and the defeated social worker walking out of the prostitute's depressing building and down the garbage-strewn streets.

Ratings were low during the first month on the air, but *East Side* was the best-reviewed new show of the 1963–64 season. Cleveland Amory in *TV Guide* declared it "undoubtedly the boldest, bravest and most original new series now on your screen this new season. The CBS brass, from top to bottom, deserves nothing but credit for putting this show on, and you owe it to your conscience not only to see it, but also to see that it stays on."

Notice of the show's bold venture into uncharted social territory went beyond media reviews. Senator Jacob Javits of New York, a liberal Republican, read newspaper articles from the *New York Herald-Tribune* and the *New York Times* praising the episode "Who Do You Kill?" into the congressional record. *Variety* ran a special follow-up review of the episode, stating, "For the first time, the winds of change, marking the Negro protest movement in this country, won a dramatic outing on a network."

The segment, aired on November 4, was the most harrowing and effective of *East Side*'s twenty-six episodes. James Earl Jones and Diana Sands gave scorching performances as a struggling Harlem couple coping with the death of their baby after she is bitten by a rat. Brock attempts to achieve some measure of justice and comfort for the grieving parents as well as a decent job for the bitter husband, but he can find no city agency to take responsibility for the tragedy nor any discrimination-free employment opportunities. Arnold Perl garnered the Writers Guild Award for his script. Director Tom Gries would win an Emmy and both guest actors would be nominated, but the intensity of "Who Do You Kill?" was compromised by network timidity.

"[W]e were eager to get pictures of the rat in his natural habitat, since he was the villain of the story," Scott later told *TV Guide*. "We shot some brilliant scenes of rats in action in Harlem. These were all cut out. . . . What was their reason? They thought it might be offensive to the sponsor, or to the public, or to someone; I never found out who."

Network excising of scenes and dialogue took place on an almost weekly basis. In "No Hiding Place," an episode dealing with neighborhood integration, a scene with Scott asking African-American actress Ruby Dee to dance was edited out of the script by CBS. Scott insisted it be put back in. The sequence was shot, but the network cut it out of the final broadcast.

Scott grew increasingly frustrated with CBS's restrictions and publicly criticized the network for cutting scenes. He also spent his own money to take out newspaper advertisements in several major cities, including New York, Washington, Atlanta, Dallas, and St. Louis, asking viewers to watch the episode "Go Fight City Hall," which dealt with urban renewal and its displacement of indigent tenants. The ad called for viewers to write in their thoughts on the issues raised by the program.

The series' star was not the only one agitated by *East Side*. Though the ratings were improving—they were at thirty-three by midseason, equal to those of NBC's *Sing Along with Mitch*—James Aubrey, president of the CBS network, strongly disagreed with setting so many of the segments in slums. According to producer David Susskind's account in Robert Metz's *CBS: Reflections in a Bloodshot Eye*, Aubrey called him into his office and demanded he "[g]et that fucking show out of the ghetto. I'm sick of it, the public's sick of it and it doesn't work. They've got just as big social problems on Park Avenue and that's where I want the goddamn show to be." Susskind replied that Scott would quit the show if it shifted locale. Aubrey answered, "Bring him in. I'll straighten him out." Aubrey had earned the nickname The Smiling Cobra for his cold-bloodedness and had fired beloved comedian Jack Benny after decades of service to his network with a terse "You're through." But he'd never had a confrontation with Scott.

Susskind related that when Scott did meet with the Cobra, the actor was attempting to quit smoking "for the twenty-ninth time" and was chewing on an apple to overcome his craving for nicotine. Aubrey launched into his demand that *East Side* move uptown (or at least crosstown to Park Avenue). Scott waited until Aubrey had finished and then asked if he was through. Then Scott took out a pocketknife, opened the blade ostensibly to peel his apple, and, gesturing with the open knife inches from Aubrey's nose, said, "The show is staying right where it is. Good-bye, Mr. Aubrey, we are not meeting again."

It was a dramatic moment, one worthy of *East Side*, with the principled, gutsy artist standing up to the coldhearted network executive. But power prevailed and Aubrey did get his way when Neil Brock went to work as an aide for an attractive liberal Congressman. Scott did not quit. Elizabeth Wilson and Cicely Tyson disappeared as did their squalid surroundings. The remaining episodes were set in Aubrey's preferred Park Avenue milieu. Scott was able to rationalize the upscale change to the press, stating it was in keeping with the series' "novelistic" approach. Eventually Brock would leave the congressman and run for office himself.

But Brock's continuing storyline never got that far. After five episodes of the new, tonier *East Side/West Side,* the series was canceled. Ironically on January 26, 1964, the day before the cancellation announcement, the show was named Best Film Series by the National Television Critics Association. Despite the plaudits from reviewers, America preferred to sing along with Mitch Miller rather than commiserate with Neil Brock over the problems of the poor. "I'm glad it's over," Scott would later say. "Out of twenty-six shows, we did maybe three or four good ones."

David Susskind summed up the series' insurmountable obstacles to TV historian Mary Ann Watson: "A gloomy atmosphere for commercial messages, an integrated cast, and a smaller Southern station lineup, all of these things coming together spelled doom for the show. I'm sorry television wasn't mature enough to absorb it and like it and live with it."

Friend Clifton James recalled Scott was furious with Susskind for not fighting harder to prevent *East Side*'s premature death. But Scott must not have been entirely enraged with his ex-employer. He did consent to appear on Susskind's television talk show, *Open End,* on March 1, not long after the cancellation was announced. His host and former producer asked the disappointed Scott for his views on working on a weekly television show. Scott compared the process to trash disposal:

> It isn't acting. It is a form of posturing, you know, and a form of
> garbaging lines, you shovel along, you shovel them in and back

out. You forget them right away because it is impossible—you know a television series is not acting. It is shamming. It is making it look as good as you can jolly well make it look with the restrictions and the pressures that are involved and that sounds like one gigantic cop-out, but it isn't.

Susskind shot back that despite all the restrictions, Scott did some extraordinary acting on the series. "Was it just instinct?" the host queried.

"Instinct, luck, technique," the actor answered. In addition to Scott, Susskind's guests that night were Dewhurst, Montgomery Clift, Georgia Brown, and Robert Ryan. The *Variety* review of the program noted that "except for the Scott outburst, there was little stimulus in the two hours of talk."

When the series debuted, Scott had prophetically said, "If they say we're too real, too sordid, too depressing, if we're taken off the air for those reasons, I will consider that we have not failed." *East Side* was indeed sordid and depressing. But it did open the door to a grittier, more realistic kind of TV show. Contemporary programs like *The Defenders, For the People, The Reporter*, and *The Nurses* were taking on more serious subjects.

The compassionate Neil Brock was dead, but he—along with comic General Turgidson from *Dr. Strangelove*—did break Scott's run of being typecast as a bad guy. "It [*East Side*] was a big break, which, happily, buried that fuckin' villain thing, cause otherwise I'd be stuck with it forever," he later told *Penthouse* magazine.

In an interesting postscript to the *East Side/West Side* experience, Scott received an Emmy nomination for his performance. The famous Oscar refuser hadn't attended the TV honors when he was previously cited for his *Ben Casey* guest spot. But when Jim Aubrey urged his network's personnel to boycott the ceremony due to a dispute CBS and ABC were having with NBC, the network carrying the awards, Scott said he'd be there with bells on. "I had my speech all ready," he joked, but he didn't win.

Scott later delivered his succinct view of TV to Rex Reed: "It's the most powerful communication device since the history of language and it's full of shit."

In addition to paying off the Theatre of Michigan debt, the *East Side/West Side* money enabled Scott and Dewhurst to buy Flood Farm, a rambling, ten-room, 250-year-old farmhouse and accompanying acreage in South Salem in Westchester county, fifty-five miles north of New York City. The Scott-Dewhurst family had moved twice before, not including the extended business trips to Detroit and Malibu. The boys would now have a permanent home and plenty of space to play in. For Scott, it was a realization of a dream to get out of the city and return to a bucolic setting reminiscent of his Michigan youth.

Dewhust was reluctant to move at first. Riverdale was far enough away from Broadway for her. "I had never wanted to move to the country," she later told Margaret McManus of the *St. Louis Post-Dispatch*. "George was the one who pushed us out there and I was fighting it all the way. I always thought of myself as a lady who should be in a penthouse, sweeping down the stairs in Trigere gowns, with dangling earrings. Suddenly, I've got myself a 1740 house, and thirty acres of land, and four German shepherd dogs."

Elizabeth Wilson recalled, "George bought thirty acres in South Salem, I think I heard for $89,000. Of course, today it's worth $20 million. But it was a great piece of property. Then he bought a few more acres after that. They built a couple of guest houses and the garage and the swimming pool. It became a haven."

The couple would continue to buy more surrounding land until the property expanded to thirty-three acres. They grew vegetables and kept numerous pets. The menagerie would eventually expand to include four German shepherds, two ponies, twenty chickens, two cats, three doves (a gift from Joanne Woodward after she filmed *They Might Be Giants* with Scott), and a swimming-pool bullfrog named Charlie.

"He liked to walk around the property and just enjoy the outdoors in the area," observed neighbor Scott Fowler, a teenager at the time who often babysat for Alex and Campbell. "Usually they had somebody at the house. There was always some other actor or director. The house was like a zoo half the time. It was a zoo of animals and people, very friendly people."

Fowler remembered his first encounter with his new neighbor:

> I was fourteen. We had just moved to South Salem from New York on Long Island. The house was empty next door to us. It was a big estate. Shortly after we moved in, they purchased it, Colleen and George C. Scott. It was about 1963. The first time I met them I was just walking down the road and I saw this man coming out of the driveway in a bathrobe, walking two German shepherds. The dogs ran out at me. He just started yelling, "Rusty! Gogo! Get over here!" I stopped and he came out and introduced himself and his dogs. We sort of struck up a conversation. Within a few days, my parents and brother and sister went over with me and kind of just chatted and got to know him.

The Fowlers became good friends with the Scotts; the relationship was cemented when Scott's father, Bill, acted quickly during an emergency. Bill Fowler remembered: "We were playing charades at their house one night and we smelled smoke. We ran upstairs to the bedroom with his two boys. There was flame and fire in their bathroom. I had just come in . . . and I had on a heavy denim jacket. I just came into the bathroom; I could see it was the curtains were on fire, pulled them down and beat them out with my denim jacket. For that [George] was always extremely grateful. He got very dramatic when he would tell anybody about it."

Scott enjoyed the retreat from the city, even spending time in the kitchen, cooking orange pancakes for breakfast and his special hamburgers with crumbled Roquefort cheese for lunch or dinner.

Dewhurst at first hated being away from Manhattan, but eventually grew to love the farm. Theatrical colleagues and friends in need of a place to stay were always welcome, and some stayed for years. Maureen Stapleton recalled, "Colleen collected strays, human and otherwise, and there was a revolving roster of residents at the New Salem farm. . . . You'd arrive at Colleen's, go in the house, and suddenly men, women, and children started coming out of the woodwork, or so it seemed." The Dewhurst-Scott household resembled that of the Sycamore family in Kaufman and Hart's classic comedy *You Can't Take It with You*, a raucous collection of eccentrics who did exactly as they pleased with little regard for the conventions of domesticity. Though Scott and Dewhurst both sought to create a stable, "normal" household, they were thwarted much of the time. "I have never known two people who strive so hard to be thoroughly conventional," the director José Quintero wrote, "but, guided by forces which they themselves were and are not fully aware of, fail in that task so gloriously."

Dewhurst once described a day when she tried to get organized to interviewer Rex Reed, "Well, I left a pair of wet jeans on the radiator upstairs and they nearly burned the house down and then I left the shower on and G. C. said, 'Honey, I hear a great cracking noise' and it was the roof caving in under the flood." The interview was conducted while workmen were repairing the ceiling.

Holidays were always grandly or unusually celebrated. If guests happened to be staying over during Easter, they were enlisted in writing rhyming clues for a big egg hunt. Quintero recalled a particularly riotous Thanksgiving morning. Gogo, one of the family German shepherd females, had gotten out and was copulating with a Dalmatian on the front lawn. Scott had wanted a purebred litter from her. To stop the animals' lovemaking, the entire household was awakened. Pails of hot water were thrown on the happy couple; Dewhurst shot at them with a BB gun. Nothing worked. Eventually the Thanksgiving dinner was thrown at the dogs to tempt them out of their ecstasy; four of the housekeeper Nana's pies were dropped in the confusion, and the meal was ruined. Campbell had to be taken to the hospital when Gogo bit his leg as he attempted to drag her away. A dinner of scrambled eggs and bacon was served for the guests who decided to stay.

In addition to Nana, the household included her son, Bobby, who acted as Scott's chauffeur-bodyguard, and Stuart Jensen and Tony Di Santis, a gay couple. The pair had owned an antiques store in Greenwich Village and had run into financial trouble. Dewhurst invited them to stay at the farm until they were on their feet again. They redesigned the house, stayed for about five years, became Uncle Stuart and Uncle Tony to Alex and Campbell and their school friends, then moved a few houses away for another ten years before relocating to California. For Scott, who had many gay colleagues but would make disparaging remarks about homosexuals in show business in a 1970 *Playboy* interview, sharing his home with a male couple must have been grating.

The endless parade of visitors and live-in guests made life interesting, but also more than a bit chaotic. "[E]ventually, it became too much," Alex wrote many years later, "and she drove my father out with all these lunatics, one after another, coming up or moving in."

While his current family was settling in a new home, a bizarre encounter caused a brief reunion by phone with his first wife and eldest daughter. Scott had been contacted by a girl claiming to be Victoria. The impostor said her mother would not permit her to meet with Scott; they could only communicate by phone or letters, for a year. Twelve months later, Scott found Carolyn's number through his sister, who had remained friends with his first wife. Carolyn was living in Nebraska with her second husband. "When he called he knew my mother's voice, so he knew he'd gotten the right people," the real Victoria recalled.

> Also my mom put me on so he could hear my voice. I think he had
> the courage to call because he'd been drinking. I remember he was
> incredibly, incredibly angry because he realized the full extent of
> how badly everybody had been tricked. To this day I don't know

who that person was. Sometimes it seems as if it was an aberration. I don't know if it was a stalker or somebody else. Whoever she was she had contact with everybody but George's father and everybody accepted her into the family. There were no visits, it was all by phone and letters . . . I was so delighted—I would have been about in the sixth grade then—I was so delighted for two reasons: first of all, it mattered to me that he kept a promise to whoever this was and had not tried to threaten the relationship because he kept his promise to wait the year. And also because that wasn't me, but here I am now, so like, let's talk. But he was way too angry. That phone call ended badly with my mother on the extension asking me just to hang up. He was so angry that I heard things that in sixth grade I'd never heard before. It was a really rotten intro.

Victoria would not meet her father in person until she was a freshman in college.

Free from his *East Side* commitment (the series would play in reruns through September of 1964), Scott took on two film extravaganzas emblematic of the era—a Technicolor travelogue (*The Yellow Rolls-Royce*) and a religious epic (*The Bible*). Both were designed to lure the American public into movie theatres with wide-screen wonders unavailable on their tiny black-and-white TV sets. Both roles demanded filming in Italy and were largely forgettable.

The Yellow Rolls-Royce was a multi-part potboiler, following the amorous entanglements of three owners of the titular vehicle as it travels to picturesque locations in Europe. This gooey romantic triptych was written by distinguished British playwright Terence Rattigan (author of Scott's first play, *The Winslow Boy*) and directed by Anthony Asquith. The team had had an enormous hit with the 1963 Elizabeth Taylor–Richard Burton vehicle *The VIPs*, a tale of intersecting lives at a fogbound London airport. MGM decided to follow it up with another star-heavy soap opera.

Scott appeared in the middle segment as an Italian-born gangster touring his homeland with his gum-chewing moll (Shirley MacLaine) and loyal henchman (Art Carney). When he is called to the States to assassinate a rival crime lord, MacLaine falls in love with a handsome gigolo (Alain Delon). To save her newfound amour from the returning Scott's jealousy and machine gun, she sends Delon away, tearfully claiming she doesn't love him.

Scott's role was little more than an extended cameo. The star of his segment was MacLaine, who complained he seemed more interested in playing chess than in their scenes together. Even Carney, then extremely popular due to his role as Ed Norton, Ralph Kramden's sewerworker sidekick on Jackie Gleason's *Honeymooners* TV sketches, had more screen time than Scott.

When the film was released in 1965 (with a New York premiere at Radio City Music Hall, no less), the acerbic critic Kenneth Tynan of *The Observer* aptly called *The Yellow Rolls-Royce* a "travelogue with foreground figures." Scott had to utter lines like "the stupidest, most unfeelingest broad in the world." Tynan described the dialogue as "Rattiganesque Runyonese" that "would shrivel the tongue of any self-respecting American actor who tried to speak it, so Miss MacLaine and Mr. Scott attempt to lick the script by underplaying it—in Mr. Scott's case, to the point of embarrassed inaudibility."

But the *London Sunday Telegraph* countered, "[A]nyone willing to be taken for a smooth ride could hardly find a more sumptuous vehicle, star-studded, gold-plated, shock-proof and probably critic-proof, too." This notice was more indicative of public taste than Tynan's. *Rolls-Royce* was indeed a winner for MGM, driving off with high box-office receipts.

For Scott, the film was a pleasant diversion in picture-postcard Italy, where he would soon return for another feature. The second film would wreck his marriage and send him back into the alcoholic abyss from which he had recently escaped.

8

Enter Ava

AUGUST 1964.

Rome.

George C. Scott has arrived in the Eternal City to play the patriarch Abraham in John Huston's screen version of the Bible. Scott has had setbacks both professionally and personally, but he's never been more secure. He's emerged from the wilderness of stock and community theatre to a respected position among America's finest actors. His television series was canceled after only one year, but critics praised it and he has the satisfaction of knowing he fought to keep the doomed *East Side/West Side* relevant and edgy. He imbibes occasionally, but the alcoholic rampages that lit up his "dark ages" are much less frequent. After four years, his third marriage is taking hold. He has finally found a woman strong enough to cope with him and one who is an equal partner onstage and in life. They have moved to an idyllic, isolated farmhouse, a perfect refuge from the madness of Broadway and Hollywood. Dewhurst and their sons, Alex and Campbell, have accompanied him on the shoot and are ensconced in a villa.

He is in Huston's suite at the Grand Hotel. His *Adrian Messenger* director is already bored with the assignment, having filmed the Garden of Eden; Cain and Abel; the march of the animals onto the Ark with himself as Noah; and the Tower of Babel, which erupted into a riot when the underpaid Egyptian extras started throwing rocks. On one occasion, Huston kept hundreds of cast and crew waiting while he worked out a crossword puzzle.

Now the picture will come alive again. Huston regards Scott as one of the finest actors he has ever directed. To star opposite him, the charismatic helmer has called in one of his favorite leading ladies—a great gal, maybe a trifle unsure of herself as an actress, but when the pressure is on, she delivers the goods. And she's easy on the eyes, to say the least. She loves to let her hair down and knock back a few drinks after a hard day's shoot, which is no small consideration when you're filming a complex epic. The two stars will get along famously together, Huston tells Scott. He calls the legendary beauty playing Sarah to come down to his suite to meet her Abraham. . . . And then Ava Gardner, the woman who fascinated Mickey Rooney, Artie Shaw, Frank Sinatra, Howard Hughes, the bullfighter Luis Miguel Dominguin, and arguably the entire male moviegoing public, walks in and everything—the picture, Scott's life and Gardner's—changes.

The Bible was intended as Dino De Laurentiis's epic to end all epics. The Italian mogul conceived the project in early 1961 as a means to promote the beleaguered filmmaking industry of his country. He rented a gigantic billboard in Times Square to proclaim the magnificence of his upcoming spectacular. The original concept was to film all the books of the Holy Word in two six-hour films with five world-famous *auteurs*—Huston, Orson Welles, Federico Fellini, Robert Bresson, and Luchino Visconti—filming their own segments and Huston supervising the overall production. Poet-playwright Christopher Fry was to write the screenplay. The estimated cost was $90,000,000. In the end, only the first twenty-two chapters of the Book of Genesis were committed to celluloid. Fry did pen the script, but Huston was the only director. He also played Noah (after Welles, Charlie Chaplin, Robert Morley, and Alec Guinness proved uninterested or unavailable) and provided the offscreen voice of Providence. Opera legend Maria Callas was the original choice for Sarah, but that role went to the glamorous Gardner.

Gardner, the most beautiful star to survive the Golden Age of Hollywood, flew to Rome as a favor to Huston. Exhausted from two decades of filmmaking, she had moved to Spain and worked only when she needed the money. She had enjoyed collaborating with Huston on *The Night of the Iguana* in Puerto Vallarta, but committed to his religious spectacle reluctantly. She had a case of epic-itis, having recently suffered through a mammoth turkey called *55 Days in Peking*.

The initial meeting between Scott and Gardner in Huston's hotel suite went well enough. "I liked him immediately," she wrote in her memoir. "He was over six feet tall, broad-shouldered, and powerful, with a broken nose and a quick smile. And he couldn't have been nicer." The jovial beginning carried over into the hallway where Scott suggested they get better acquainted and discuss the script over dinner.

They shared a meal and their thoughts on Fry's poetic screenplay and how to make it credible in acting terms—just two colleagues chatting over a shared difficult assignment. During their first few days of filming, they remained merely cordial and businesslike, much like Scott and Dewhurst during their initial performances of *Children of Darkness*. There was no hint of romance. Scott had his family with him and Gardner began keeping company after hours with Stephen Grimes, the film's set adviser, who had worked with her on *Iguana*.

But after a few intense scenes of playing the patriarch Abraham and his barren wife Sarah by day, Scott and Gardner were getting to know each other in the biblical sense at night. For Gardner, it was just a fling, as easily started as her liaison with Grimes, who suddenly found himself an unwelcome nocturnal visitor to the star's villa on the Via Appia Antica. The younger actor—Scott was thirty-eight, Gardner forty-two—was attentive and charming. He recited poetry, kept her laughing with sardonic jokes, and protected her from prying paparazzi. While Gardner saw Scott as a jovial temporary bedfellow, Scott had fallen in love with the ravishing screen goddess. Fred Sidewater, Dino

De Laurentiis's assistant, told biographer Charles Higham, "Scott was crazy about her from the beginning. And I mean crazy. He was hopelessly in love with her, and she was not in love with him." Scott had visions of marrying Gardner and became insanely jealous at the least mention of any of her previous lovers or husbands—particularly Sinatra.

According to Sinatra's right-hand man and valet, George Jacobs, previous to the affair with Gardner, the Voice had respected Scott, admiring his work in *The Hustler* and *Strangelove*. They had a brief encounter in 1963 on the set of *Adrian Messenger* when Sinatra filmed a one-day cameo. If Scott was jealous of Sinatra, the feelings were mutual. Sinatra would have been enraged at anyone who was with Gardner, but the fiery ex-Marine drove him especially crazy. For one thing, Scott was ten years younger than the singer. In addition, Jacobs recalled in his memoir, "Scott was threatening to Mr. S. in other ways than winning Ava and serious acting. He was a genuine tough guy, a former Marine and a brawler who actually beat up paparazzi and nosy journalists, things Mr. S. was *accused* of doing but never did."

News of the scandalous romance soon broke in the Italian and international press. One UPI shot shows the lovers casually strolling down a Roman street. Both are wearing sweaters and black-rimmed glasses. They look like a pair of college professors, engaged in a friendly intellectual debate. Dewhurst, still staying with her sons in the Roman villa, was placed in a humiliating position. At a lunch with her friends, the actor Roscoe Lee Browne and opera star Leontyne Price, she nearly burst into tears over her husband's blatant infidelity. Her sobs turned into raucous, ironic laughter when Browne pointed out their table was directly underneath a picture of Gardner.

Meanwhile, Scott wanted to make the relationship with Gardner permanent. The actress had ridden out rocky marital curves with the adolescent, inattentive Rooney, condescending bandleader Shaw, and capricious crooner Sinatra as well as insistent advances and wiretaps by wacko millionaire Howard Hughes. She had no interest in taking a trip to the altar with her tempestuous costar. He was fine for a couple of drinks and some fun in the hay while filming a tedious epic, but matrimony was definitely not in the equation.

Scott did not take this rejection well. He increased his alcohol intake and took his rage out on the object of his desire. "The problem, honey, was booze," Gardner wrote. "We both drank a fair amount, but when I drank I usually got mellow and happy. When George got drunk, he could go berserk in a way that was quite terrifying." Tipsy clinches became drunken brawls as Scott used his fists to express his frustration. Gardner's makeup calls began taking longer in order to cover up black eyes. Peter O'Toole, who was playing three angels, reportedly dropped the divine demeanor of his role and wanted to brawl with Scott to teach him a lesson.

Huston retained his high opinion of Scott as an actor. "George C. Scott was magnificent as Abraham bargaining with God in an effort to save the city of Sodom and its people," he later said. "I may not like Scott as a private person, although my admiration for him as an actor is unbounded. Christopher Fry had given Ava, Peter, and Scott very fine dialogue, and all the performances were outstanding."

But his view of Scott as a man plummeted. The director wrote in his memoir,

While we were filming in Abruzzi, the whole company stayed in a small hotel in Avezzano. One night Scott got very drunk in the bar and threatened Ava physically when she entered. In the process of trying to slow him down before he hurt someone, I climbed on his back. He's very strong and he carried me around the room, bumping into things. He couldn't see where he was going because I had my arms wrapped around his head. Ava was persuaded to leave, and we finally got Scott calmed down.

To Gardner's surprise, she got some protection in the form of three burly bruisers who materialized one evening while she and Scott were having a fight in a restaurant's parking lot. The trio simply surrounded him and walked him into a waiting car. Gardner never found out if these guardian angels actually beat up her overzealous suitor or just gave him a stern warning to keep his distance. She also never learned whether these protectors were hired by Huston or Sinatra, who was cooling out at a nearby villa while filming *Von Ryan's Express*. A contrite Scott showed up on *The Bible* set the next morning and the beatings ceased—for the moment anyway.

Sinatra never publicly commented on the violent affair between his former wife and Scott, but did tell *Photoplay* in 1965, "If there's one guy I can't tolerate, it's a guy who mistreats women. They are real bullies and what they need is a real working over by a man of their own size." Even if Scott did get a working over by someone of his own size (or bigger), the dysfunctional relationship with Gardner went on. For the sake of the film or perhaps because she was still attracted to him and the aura of danger he represented, the dinners, the strolls, and Scott's late-night visits to her room continued.

So did the punches, cursing, and hurled ashtrays. She wanted to quit the film many times, but she held on out of loyalty to Huston. She may also have found release with other lovers. Fred Sidewater told Charles Higham, "I had a taste of Ava myself. One day I took some papers to her tent in the Abruzzi for her to sign. She said, 'Oh, let's go to bed now and I'll sign the papers later.' So we did, she signed the papers and I left."

Rumors circulated that after another altercation with Gardner, Scott returned to his hotel room to discover all the sleeves of his suits, shirts, and sweaters had been cut off at the shoulder (Dewhurst and the boys would have returned to the States by this time). In another strange incident, the actor's German shepherd was mysteriously poisoned. Both events may have been less-than-subtle warnings from the burly trio of guardian angels to lay off Gardner. Scott and his bodyguard nursed the animal back to health. The actor didn't fare as well as his dog. Even after the film wrapped and Gardner left Italy, he was still sick with love for her.

As for *The Bible*, it wasn't released until 1966, when the epic to end all epics was greeted with a tremendous yawn from critics, but cheers from filmgoers. Reviews granted Huston's visual effects, including the creation of the world, were stunning, but the film—apart from Huston's winking Noah and Scott's majestic Abraham—was a reverential bore. Despite critical raspberries, the public filled cinema pews for *The Bible*, making it Huston's biggest box-officer winner up to that point.

Scott does create a multifaceted Abraham, a patriarch in communication with divine forces, but also with a human side. As he leads an army into nighttime battle with a rival tribe, his features are twisted into a mask of savagery. He slashes into the enemy with a demonic fury. Then his face softens into an almost serene beauty when the attack is won and he releases his enslaved relatives, kissing their hands with tenderness.

After Huston closed the Book of Genesis, Scott remained in Europe, pursuing his elusive siren. Gardner must have given in to his pleas. When she returned to Madrid after her Sarah scenes were finished, she told her friend, journalist Stephen Birmingham, "I've fallen for him." At time of the declaration, her arm was in a sling, a hunk of her hair had been torn out, her collarbone was broken, and she had double vision in both eyes. Birmingham observed that Gardner came from a "kind of redneck" background in North Carolina where physical abuse among lovers was common. She may have thought that was how men naturally related to women.

Birmingham's wife, Nan, recalled to Gardner biographer Lee Server that they joined Scott and the actress for Thanksgiving dinner at her Madrid apartment. It was an amiable enough evening, marred only by Gardner tossing a chicken leg over the table after informing her guests there were no fucking turkeys available anywhere in the Spanish capital. Before dinner, Gardner told Mrs. Birmingham that Scott had drunkenly smashed his head against the fireplace the previous evening. Mrs. Birmingham noticed Scott's face did look pretty bruised as he was casually chatting and munching on an apple. Mr. Birmingham described the actor's mug as looking like "raw hamburger, sort of oozing and awful." Gardner then took Nan upstairs to give her further evidence of her battles with Scott. There was a hole in the closet door where Scott had rammed his head. She had been hiding in the closet to get away from him.

After the memorable Thanksgiving dinner, there were reports that the star-crossed pair were keeping company in New York. Columnist Liz Smith recorded that while staying at the Regency in Manhattan, Gardner reported to the front desk that a man was bothering her. The house staff found the individual was Scott in his pajamas lounging on the sofa. He left without a word when asked. Clifton James recalled Gardner visited Scott at his farmhouse and actually scrubbed the floor.

Sometime after these incidents, the volatile Gardner fell out of love again, breaking it off with the brilliant but dangerous actor. Unwilling to let her go, Scott stalked Gardner across two continents, barging into her hotel suite in London and a guest bungalow in Los Angeles.

In London, Gardner was staying at the Savoy Hotel to visit her friend, the poet and novelist Robert Graves, then lecturing at Oxford. Scott was in the British capital for the premiere of *The Yellow Rolls-Royce* and stopping at the same hotel, supposedly by coincidence. He contacted her and innocently asked if they could forget the past and just have dinner together. "I agreed," Gardner wrote in her memoir. "London seemed pretty safe, the Savoy even safer." She would soon be proven wrong.

They were reportedly civil together and, according to one source, even attended the theatre—*Othello*. Shakespeare's tale of jealousy and murder was probably not the best entertainment choice, given the couple's history. Gardner detected Scott's old rages bubbling just under the surface during their evening. She quickly bid him good night in the Savoy lobby and hurried up to her suite.

Like the window-smashing incident backstage at *Comes a Day*, there are several versions of what happened next. In Gardner's memoir, the actress reports Scott banged on her door like the Big Bad Wolf. She told her maid Reenie Jordan to send the monster away as she ran into the bathroom and locked herself in. Terrified, Gardner could hear the door splintering as Scott burst into the room, demanding to see the bitch who had betrayed him. Gardner later found out Scott had held a broken bottle under Jordan's throat, screaming, "Where is she?" As Scott ransacked the suite, Gardner pulled her maid into the bathroom with her. Fortunately, there was a transom leading into the hallway. The two trapped ladies crawled out and sought asylum in a friend's suite down the corridor. Savoy security was summoned and the enraged actor was escorted to his own room. Thwarted in love and blitzed out of his mind, Scott trashed his apartment. This time, the British police took him away and he spent the night in the lockup.

Some sources claim Scott had thrown out Gardner's agent, who was going over travel plans with her for the next day. In this version of the story, the boozed-up star held the broken bottle under Gardner's throat—rather than Jordan's—and kept her hostage overnight until the authorities managed to get him away.

The January 8, 1965 edition of the *London Daily Express* reported a slightly different account, with Scott being requested to remove himself from Gardner's suite. When he refused, the bobbies were called. All accounts agree that he pleaded guilty to charges of being drunk and disorderly and was fined ten shillings (about $1.40) at the Bow Street court.

A spokesman for the Savoy told the press with traditional British reserve, "I'm afraid this incident did happen. It's quite true. But it's not the sort of thing we prefer to discuss. The police had been informed about the disturbance and were waiting outside when Mr. Scott left. They arrested him. Mr. Scott left his luggage in his room and came back the next day to check it out." When he did come back, Gardner was gone. They would not meet until Scott broke into her rooms again, this time in Los Angeles.

The marriage to Dewhurst was seriously damaged. After leaving her previous husband James Vickery, the earthy actress had tied her professional and personal fate with Scott's. She had given up city life to become a country lady, wife and mother. Now her second spouse had thrown her over for an irresistible sex symbol and he had come crawling back after said siren had had enough of him.

Dewhurst flew to Juarez, Mexico in early 1965 to file for a quickie divorce. Despite the break, the two remained close. Scott stayed at the farmhouse while Dewhurst bought a former horse farm three-quarters of a mile down the road. They frequently visited each other and several sources reported Dewhurst checked Scott into a Connecticut nursing home to recover from the alcoholic, Gardner-inspired rampages. The rest cure was not entirely effective. On March 30, 1965, Scott hit actor Patrick Desmond in the face with a mug in an apartment on West 87th Street in Manhattan, causing damage to his left eye and lacerations to his forehead and eyebrow. The *New York Times* reported Desmond filed a suit for damages of $100,000.

Not only was Scott unable to control his temper, but he was still enthralled by his dream girl. After a TV appearance in Hollywood as a conscience-stricken submarine commander in post-Hiroshima Japan for a one-hour drama, "A Time for Killing," on *Bob Hope's Chrysler Theatre* and a guest shot on *The Red Skelton Show* in New York, his next job choice was designed to reunite him with Gardner. In May 1965, Scott returned to London to play Vershinin in the Actors Studio production of Chekhov's *Three Sisters* at the Aldwych Theatre as part of the World Theatre Season. His prime motivation in accepting the role may not have been a love of the classics, but the faint prospect that he could persuade Gardner to fly in from Madrid and attend the opening night. "That was the reason he signed up. He was hung up on

Ava," recalled fellow cast member and former University of Missouri journalism major Robert Loggia.

The Actors Studio production of Chekhov's classic of the titular Russian siblings who never return to their beloved Moscow was a hit on Broadway in 1964. Director Lee Strasberg wanted to bring the entire company to London, but many were unavailable. Shirley Knight, who had played the youngest sister, Irina, got a film offer. Geraldine Page, the eldest sibling, Olga, was pregnant and unable to travel. The incandescent but highly volatile Kim Stanley, whose Masha received the most critical kudos, was willing to make the trip, but, for her own idiosyncratic reasons, she refused to act with Kevin McCarthy, the Broadway Vershinin. Her first choice for a replacement was Montgomery Clift, but because of the star's failing mental and physical health, Strasberg rejected the idea out of hand. Stanley then thought of Scott, who accepted the offer. Sandy Dennis took over for Knight and Nan Martin replaced Page. Strasberg was accompanied by his wife, Paula, and son John, who served as assistant stage manager.

But the leading lady was not on board the flight with the company. Stanley had a fear of flying and crossed the Atlantic by boat. Her sea trip delayed rehearsal time—a precious commodity with three new actors in major roles. The full cast had only eleven days to prepare. In another stroke of bad luck, because of ongoing festival performances, the Aldwych was mostly unavailable. The Studio was given an armory and an indoor tennis court for rehearsal space. The ensemble did not even set foot onstage until the day of opening night when they were allowed one dress rehearsal.

When they were finally allowed in, there were more troubles. The stage was sharply raked (Robert Loggia compared it to a "ski run") and all the props fell off the tables. Unaccustomed to the slope, actors tripped and stumbled. Tamara Daykarhanova, playing the sisters' elderly nanny, took a fall and broke her arm. The scenery had arrived only the day before and was hastily set and hung. Not all of the

costumes had been properly fitted or cleaned. Producer Cheryl Crawford was attending the final rehearsal and noticed Scott was playing a
tender love scene with Stanley in his long johns with a drooping back
flap. His uniform was being pressed. Crawford had thought the hard-
boiled, realistic Scott (whom she had hired for *Comes a Day*) was all
wrong for "dreamy, sentimental" Vershinin. She took his trouserless
state as a bad omen. But it certainly wasn't the only one.

The British crew still hadn't had a full technical run-through with
lighting, sound, and scene-shifting cues when it was time to let the audience in. The number of replacements (Robert Loggia called the London cast "a pick-up team"), the limited rehearsals, and unfamiliarity
with the Aldwych stage seriously hampered any hope of recreating the
production's New York success. The director was another problem.
Strasberg had an enormous ego and a volcanic temper, and he brooked
no disagreement. Compromise was not in his vocabulary. The teaching guru was the worst possible person to work with Scott, who could
be exactly the same way. They were like two forces of nature colliding.
The diminutive, explosive Strasberg had allied himself with the Actors
Studio in the 1950s to redefine American acting—adapting Constantin
Stanislavski's techniques to produce a more natural performing style.
The Studio approach, popularly known as "The Method," involved
long introspection, sense memory, and the actor placing himself inside the skin of the character. Scott was a natural phenomenon, hadn't
taken any formal training, and didn't like long rehearsals or bringing
his personal experiences or traumas to bear when creating a character.
He was accustomed to employing intellect and instinct, without extraneous discussion among the company or personal soul-searching.
In a later interview, he castigated any actor who "would smear their
own hang-ups over any role. I find that despicable. I can't conceive of
anyone paying money to go the theatre to look at the inner soul of
any actor who ever lived." It wasn't long before Scott began referring
to his director as "Lee-you-should-pardon-the-expression-Strasberg."
(Ironically, Scott's daughter Devon would later enroll in Strasberg's

classes.) To add to the tension, this was Strasberg's first directing job in years. It was his chance to prove himself as great a director as he was a teacher.

The high expectations, the limited preparation time, and the conflicting styles of the cast inevitably spelled disaster. The late-starting opening night performance clocked in at an agonizing four hours, almost sixty minutes over the planned running time. Stanley performed at a glacial pace. Scenery fell. Lighting cues were missed. At one point in the third act, Sandy Dennis uttered the line "It's been a terrible evening." An audience member yelled back, "It certainly has." Scott later recalled that the curtain call was worst of all, with the audience of angry Brits giving the cast a standing booing ovation.

To top it all off, Gardner did not show up on opening night. "He expected Ava to be there," Robert Loggia recalled. "But it was in the paper that she took a hike and went to her Spanish toreador boyfriend back in Spain."

Laurence Olivier came backstage and invited the entire cast to a party. According to Loggia, the rejected Scott downed a quart of gin. "George and Kim Stanley got together," he remembered. "She was consoling him, I guess, and he drank. . . . and then he wrecked his room at the Hilton and cut his hand, hitting a mirror."

The company's hangovers were not helped by the critical reaction to the ill-rehearsed, self-indulgent mishmash. The *Illustrated London News* found the production to be "one long pause, occasionally interrupted." *Punch* succinctly labeled it a "disaster."

Penelope Gilliatt lamented in *The Observer*: "The admirable World Theatre's dismal task has been to mount the suicide of the Actors' Studio—the whole endeavor is absurd and agonizing, like playing the harpsichord in boxing gloves, like filling the Spanish riding school with hippopotami."

Scott did receive some kind notices. Milton Shulman of the *Evening Standard*: "As Vershinin, the regimental colonel, George C. Scott provided a tender and sympathetic portrayal of a good, clever man destined to be miserable." Bernard Levin in the *Daily Mail* allowed that Scott, Stanley, and Luther Adler did "provide light amid the gloom. But the gloom is dark and there is a lot of it."

Strasberg added to the gloom after the damning reviews came out by gathering the company to unequivocally tell them the critics were right. John Strasberg described his father's state as "apoplectic. He began screaming, blaming the company for what they had done. It was their fault." This was more than Scott could bear. He stood in a towering rage and tightly asked, "Mr. Strasberg, you called us together to tell us the papers were right? That we're lousy actors?" The menacing ex-Marine advanced downstage and into the aisle where the bantam-weight director was railing at his cast. As the much larger Scott came toward him, Strasberg abruptly shut off his rant, turned on his heel, and swiftly left the building. John Strasberg described it as "the worst scene I've ever seen in the theatre."

Perhaps it was the ugly incident with Strasberg, perhaps it was Gardner's failure to attend the opening night—whatever the reason, Scott did not show up for the second night. Cast member Peter Masterson recalled, "The story was that he had gone nuts . . . . Maybe he tried to kill himself. Anyway he got violent. They called Kim Stanley and she went over [to his hotel] to calm him down. That was my understanding. But finally Bob [Loggia] did go on and read the part."

"Oddly enough, the audience pulled for us," Loggia said. "The British were pulling for the underdog now and we got a standing ovation for the second night. Then George came back and finished the run."

Scott continued to frequent British pubs. "He was drinking a lot," Masterson recalled. "Bob Loggia was his babysitter. He was trying to keep watch on him at night. Bob told me one day, 'I can't keep up with George. He's drinking me under the table and I can't take it any longer.'" Loggia denies any official role as male nanny for the distraught Scott.

Scott's attempt to win back Gardner was not the only plan wrecked by the terrible production. Penelope Gilliatt's comments about the suicide of the Studio Theatre proved prophetic and the unit never presented another commercial production. The plague-ridden *Three Sisters* also marked the end of Stanley's stage acting career and Strasberg's directing ventures. The Studio continued to great fame as a school with Strasberg as its lead teacher and standard bearer. Stanley later suffered a nervous breakdown, and though she would go on to appear in a few films and TV shows, she never set foot on a professional stage again.

The experience completely soured Scott on the Studio. Towards the end of the run, several of the company were interviewed by Ian Dallas for the BBC. When asked by Dallas if he would join the Studio after working on one of its productions, Scott pursed his lips and slowly shook his head. "He's a loner," joked Stanley. When asked his opinion of his director, Scott answered diplomatically, "I think Mr. Strasberg is an extremely knowledgeable man. I think he's an enormously sensitive man. I think he is a gentle man. I cannot speak about him as a teacher because, of course, I've never studied with him. I don't know particularly whether we like each other or not as director to actor. It might be interesting to explore that sometime."

Strasberg was not as generous in his assessment of Scott. He would later tell his biographer Cindy Adams, "I have more respect for George C. Scott than he has for himself. Scott has the capacity to be great, but I have never seen greatness in anything he's done. And if I really answered his slurs at me I would have to be cruel and I don't want to be."

After dissolving his marriage, Scott began examining the rest of his life and the world around him. What did it mean to be an actor? What was his function in society? Was it a valuable one? All of America was examining itself in that period. Opposing factions were tearing the country apart in a quest to redefine it. We were engaged in an unpopular war in Vietnam. African-Americans were demanding equal rights after decades of oppression. Student protests were erupting on campuses nationwide. The younger generation was rebelling in every way possible—from dress to politics—rejecting the values of their parents.

Scott attempted to examine these issues by returning to journalism, his incomplete major at the University of Missouri. He suggested to the editors of *Esquire* magazine that he travel to the center of the controversy: Vietnam. He would write the impressions of an actor, a man who makes his living facing make-believe dangers, encountering the real-life perils of a country at war.

The finished article was titled "Sorry About That," for a catchphrase used by the American military to cover everything from spilling tea to driving a jeep over a land mine. It was "the standby phrase of the American in Vietnam," Scott wrote. "It seems to epitomize his plight."

The piece begins with the author questioning the verities supplied by the entertainment industry and implying that America can no longer tell the difference between the artificial emotions offered by Hollywood and the real ones our soldiers were experiencing ("Is courage really John Wayne? Is sentiment no deeper than a commercial ballad by Frank Sinatra?") He then turns the probing on himself, asking if his profession and its association with fantasy have rendered him unable to recognize truth. The trip to Vietnam is a quest to find out. On the flight from New York to Saigon he examines his fears of venturing into unknown, perilous territory alone and explains the credo by which he has lived his life: "Never hurt a man whom you respect or a woman whom you do not deeply love." According to Scott, it was apparently all right to hurt a man you did not respect or a woman you did deeply love.

There follows a collage of vivid impressions and observations: flying abroad a cargo ship making a "controlled-crash" landing on an impossibly narrow airstrip ripped out of the mountainous wilderness at Gia Vuc; participating in an aboriginal ritual in the village of Pleiku, centering on the roasting of a whole water buffalo and drinking rice wine through long reeds from ceramic pots; allowing the girls in a village whorehouse to stroke his beard recently grown for an upcoming role; watching a team of Vietnamese doctors simultaneously cast a soldier's left arm and amputate his left leg.

As an ex-Marine, Scott probably felt more than a twinge of guilt seeing young servicemen on extended tours of duty while he would soon go back to play-acting. In the article, he confesses to discomfort with his role of representative of the folks back home and understands when he senses resentment from a few recruits.

He concludes with his personal musings on the war, explaining that is not the kind of a traditional conflict Americans are used to, with clearly defined victories. Yet, he claims, it is necessary for us to be there as part of the fight against encroaching international Communism. Ironically, he cites Patton in his argument: "Americans are impatient people. We are used to winning. We are used to getting in or getting out. . . . We must, at home, realize just a little of the fantastic complexities of this effort. This war is not Patton rushing across France to the Rhine."

It was a well-written piece, colorfully describing its locale and carefully laying out arguments for supporting the American presence in Vietnam. Scott continued to harbor writing ambitions. He would later begin, but never finish, a historical novel and a play. In 1988 he wrote a satiric piece on the demise of his sitcom *Mr. President* for the *Los Angeles Times*. Apart from that, "Sorry About That" would be his only published work of journalism or fiction.

Scott would continue to advocate for the American military in South Asia. But his view on Vietnam would shift with the increased American involvement, subsequent soaring casualty rate, and lack of solid victories. "I don't approve of the war effort necessarily," he said in 1966. "I don't think any American wants to be in Vietnam—unless he's out of his mind. . . . We're trying to get them to organize their country along democratic lines as we did 200 years ago, but they couldn't care less. They're too tired and too hungry to give a damn."

He and Dewhurst campaigned for Eugene McCarthy in the 1968 presidential election, even going so far as to spearhead a fundraiser for the antiwar Democratic candidate at Marymount College in Tarrytown, New York.

In 1980, he amended his position again and told *Playboy*, "I don't believe in fighting wars that you don't want to win. I didn't believe in Korea and I didn't believe in Vietnam . . . I would have attacked North Vietnam and I really would have *attacked* it!"

Scott left the war-scarred landscape of Vietnam for the most glamorous city in the world. On August 17, 1965, director William Wyler threw Scott a dinner party to welcome him to Paris. He had arrived in the City of Light to film *How to Steal a Million*. It was one of those fast, funny caper comedies with exotic European settings that were all the rage (*Charade*, *Topkapi*, etc.) The stars were Peter O'Toole (presumably over his fury at Scott's treatment of Ava Gardner on *The Bible*) and Audrey Hepburn with Hugh Griffith, the Welsh actor who defeated Scott in the 1959 Academy Awards sweepstakes, as Hepburn's father. Scott was assigned the supporting role of an American art collector, first offered to Walter Matthau. Matthau had demanded $200,000 (double what Twentieth Century-Fox had been willing to pay) and billing above the title in type the same size as that for O'Toole and Hepburn. Darryl Zanuck turned Matthau down flat.

The picture was on the "French schedule"—instead of the usual Hollywood dawn-to-dusk hours, filming commenced at noon and went straight through to seven. It was a relaxed, convivial atmosphere, unlike the murdering pace of American film production.

Shooting had just begun and Scott's scenes were not scheduled for another month. At first, he wouldn't be needed except for costume fittings. He used the time to work on the *Esquire* article in his hotel suite at the Ritz, hit the bars, and pine over Ava Gardner. Ernest Anderson, *How to Steal a Million*'s unit publicist, wrote to Gladys Hill, John Huston's secretary, that Scott's traveling companion, Pat Zurica, had called asking him to find Gardner's Paris phone number. After a few unsuccessful attempts to locate the number, Anderson called back, advised him to try the Hilton in Madrid, and invited Scott and Zurica to breakfast. Zurica replied he was just getting his boss to bed. It was twelve noon.

On September 14, Scott was called to be on the set the next day at noon for his first day of work. He didn't show up. Wyler's personal assistant called. The desk informed him that Mr. Scott had not yet left the hotel. Then the production manager phoned and was informed by Scott's assistant that the actor had had "a very bad night" and was still asleep, not to be disturbed. Wyler cancelled the setup and shot around Scott. Another scene was scheduled and two hours were wasted. Twentieth producer Fred Kohlmar sent a doctor to the hotel to examine the recalcitrant performer. The French physician, Dr. Jean Dax, reported in a memo that Scott was abusive: "After I introduced myself, he became extremely uncivil. My impression is that he was suffering form the aftereffects of an excessive intake of alcoholic beverages and was still not fully responsible for his actions." According to Clifton James, who was visiting his friend while he had a few days off from shooting a picture in Spain, Scott had been up all night the previous evening playing chess and drinking. James recalled that Scott was also pissed off that he playing a supporting role, a step backward after receiving top billing in *The List of Adrian Messenger* and headlining in *The Bible*.

Scott finally arrived on the set five hours late, but Wyler had already started work on the new scene. He asked Scott to wait till the end of the work day at 7:30 P.M. and that he wanted to speak to him. Scott said he would wait in his dressing room but left before then without informing anyone.

When Wyler found that Scott was gone for the day, he immediately went into action to replace him. The director already had to deal with O'Toole and Griffith, two stars with alcoholic reputations who frequently arrived on set with hangovers. Even with the relaxed French schedule, three drinkers in major roles would be too much to handle. Darryl Zanuck and Fred Kohlmar agreed and Scott was summarily fired. Anderson reported that Audrey Hepburn was "in tears and could not perform when she got the news." Despite Hepburn's pleas to give Scott another chance, Eli Wallach was taken out of the Broadway comedy *Luv* and took over the role in a matter of days. Scott later sued Twentieth Century Fox for breach of contract and won.

The year 1965 ended with the publication of "Sorry About That" in the December issue of *Esquire* and one final, mad attempt to reconnect with Ava Gardner.

Clifton James remembered having a few drinks with Scott in New York and the beautiful star's name coming up:

> We happened to be in a bar in New York and George said, "Yeah, she's in Hollywood at the Beverly Hills. So let's give her a call." Believe it or not, I got on the phone, called the Beverly Hills Hotel, and she answered the phone, just like that. He got on the phone and they started talking. They got real angry and he hung up. The next day or the next week, I can't remember exactly, he got two bottles of vodka and a Lincoln Continental and took off, drove nonstop to L.A. Got to L.A., went to Beverly Hills. They got in a big fight. He hit her. He had an obsession with glass. He was always breaking windows, breaking mirrors, cutting himself. He was scarred all over.

Tammy Grimes also recalls receiving a visit from Scott at this time at her New York apartment. He told his friend from Stephens that he wanted to marry Gardner, had just bought a new car, and was going to drive it across the country to beg for her hand.

Gardner was visiting her sister and brother-in-law in Los Angeles. She was staying in a bungalow by the pool at the Beverly Hills Hotel. At one in the morning, she heard the sounds of smashing glass and then someone forcing his way in through the back door. It was Scott. He had driven across the country to plead his case and was well fortified with those two bottles of vodka. Before Gardner could reach for the phone, Scott grabbed her, declaring his passion for her and demanding that she marry him. According to Gardner's memoir, he proceeded to beat her furiously, alternating vows of adoration with vicious blows.

Gardner wrote that convincing Scott to allow her to call a doctor friend to come and give him a sedative was the most realistic piece of acting she had ever done. "Listen, honey, you're in bad shape," she crooned to him. "You have to have a doctor." He finally relented. She soothed the savage beast with promises of undying devotion until the doctor arrived. The exhausted, drunken actor permitted Gardner's friend to inject him with a sedative and, without a word, left through the door he had broken. That was the end of the affair and the two fiery-tempered lovers finally stopped seeing each other. Gardner reported that for years she couldn't hear Scott's voice on television without trembling.

9

Two Comedies and *Petulia*

AFTER THAT VIOLENT NIGHT IN the bungalow, Scott turned to comedy—
professionally, at least. His next two films, *Not With My Wife, You
Don't!* and *The Flim-Flam Man*, were celluloid puffballs, perhaps pur-
posefully chosen to further mitigate his image as a malevolent menace,
both onscreen and off. "I try to do something different every time,"
he told *New York Times* writer Brian St. Pierre on the set of *Flim-Flam
Man*. "And I try not to do crap. Neither is easy in this business."

He did not succeed in either category with *Not With My Wife, You
Don't!*, a limp service comedy directed by Norman Panama, who also
produced the film and wrote the original treatment with Melvin Frank.
The final script was penned by Peter Barnes and Larry Gelbart (who
would later work with Scott on *Sly Fox* and *Movie Movie*). Panama
and Frank had been a team for twenty-five years, working on the Bob
Hope and Bing Crosby *Road* picture series as well as *My Favorite Blonde*
(starring Hope), *Mr. Blandings Builds His Dream House*, *White Christmas*,
and the Broadway musical version of the comic strip *Li'l Abner*. *Wife*
was on the same adolescent humor level as *Abner* and followed the basic
template of the *Road* films with Tony Curtis and Scott standing in for
Hope and Crosby. Italian beauty Virna Lisi doubled for Dorothy Lam-
our as the object of their romantic rivalry. The slender plot turns on
Lisi as Julie, an Army nurse who's always wanted two of everything.

Her marriage to Lt. Colonel Tom Ferris (Curtis) is on shaky ground because he spends all of his time running errands for a blowhard general (Carroll O'Connor in his pre-Archie Bunker days). Enter Scott as Tank Martin, a dashing, wolfish Air Force stunt pilot, licking his chops over the voluptuous Julie. During a long flashback, we learn that Tank's out for revenge because Tom underhandedly stole Julie from him during the Korean War. After conniving to ship Ferris off to Labrador for survival training (more broad slapstick involving igloos and dogsleds), Tank develops a conscience and balks at the adulterous affair. Following an unfunny brawl, the couple are reunited and Tank continues to rise through the ranks and enjoy his bachelorhood.

Panama directed with the subtlety of a sledgehammer and loaded the fragile comedy with gimmicks—animated cartoons, a satire of foreign films, clips from *Mighty Joe Young*, an extended sequence with Curtis flying through all the capitals of Europe to catch Lisi and Scott in the act, and the obligatory-for-1966 discotheque sequence.

Despite the grade-C level of the script, Scott made a consistent, sympathetic character out of a relentless womanizer. When Curtis accuses Tank of trying to seduce his wife just to prove to himself that he's not over the hill, you can see the truth of the remark registering on Scott's face. It's one of the few quiet moments in an otherwise frenetic film. Curtis wrote in his autobiography about how he worked to develop a rapid, comic rhythm with Scott, just to keep on the same level with him:

> George is very intense. He never pretended to be a comedian. This was one of his rare comedies, and I was constantly on his case. I didn't give him a chance to breathe. I always made sure my lines were on top of his. As soon as I got an idea what he was saying or asking me in a line, I'd answer without waiting until the end. That way we created an overlap, and he had no choice but to keep up with me. He didn't have an opportunity to psych me out in long pauses, the way he did so well in dramas. The tempo had to be kept

up. George is a charming man. He wanted to direct a movie with me. I said "Well, let's find me one," but as so often happens, we never did.

Critics summarily dismissed this lame effort as no better than a sitcom, but Vincent Canby in the *New York Times* conceded "Mr. Scott compels interest no matter what he does."

The Flim-Flam Man, based on a novel by Guy Owen, an English teacher at the University of North Carolina, was more successful both as a believable comedy and as an opportunity for Scott to do "something different." Here he played Mordecai Jones, legendary con man of seventy (Scott was thirty-nine at the time) fleecing locals of the backwoods and small towns of the deep South. He's joined by young Army deserter Curly Treadaway, played by Canadian Michael Sarrazin. The two develop a smooth working relationship with Mordecai as the slippery manipulator and Curly as the innocent-appearing shill. The joy of the film comes from a town-demolishing car chase and from watching the duo con avaricious store-owners and rubes skillfully played by veteran character actors Strother Martin, Woodrow Parfrey, and Slim Pickens (*Dr. Strangelove*).

Filming took two and a half months in the bluegrass country of Kentucky. The shoot was delayed somewhat when Scott injured his knee and tore a few ligaments during a table tennis match. While recovering, he had to walk on crutches and could only film scenes where he was sitting down. Production was headquartered in Lexington and locations were spread throughout a radius of forty miles, including the towns of Lawrenceberg, Winchester, and Versailles. A sign at the "neo-pseudo-Georgian motel" where the company was staying proudly proclaimed, "Welcome George C. Scott and Twentieth Century-Fox." Despite the sign, Scott was not staying at the motel. He was renting a 100-year-old thoroughbred horse ranch called Stallions' Roost just outside of Lexington. As he did on most of his film shoots, he maintained an amiable yet distant relationship with the cast and crew. However, *Flim-Flam* marked the beginning of his closest professional relationship—with Del Acevedo, who served as Scott's principal makeup artist, chess and cribbage opponent, and general companion on over twenty films and television projects.

"We both grew up in Detroit," Acevedo explained. "We both loved the Tigers and the Lions and the Redwings. George was never a basketball fan and I wasn't either, so that cemented things. I played a little chess. I wasn't that good, but we played cribbage and we shared a drink or two now and then."

Flim-Flam also marked the creation of Scott's all-male entourage, a tiny group of macho guys who would follow him from film to film, providing companionship in the trailer between setups and sage counsel when it came to barroom behavior. Acevedo recalled the basic setup:

> In the beginning, there was the wardrobe man named Ronnie Dawson. [George also] had a friend by the name of Pat Zurica. He was a retired policeman, a detective. He would travel with George. He was a big, strapping, rough-and-tough guy. If somebody was to bother George, Zurica would step in and calm the waters. He was not a bodyguard, he was someone who kept order. George would listen to these people he had confidence in. If he was getting a little loud, they'd say, "Hey chief, let's get out of here," and he would listen, because he knew those people he cared about were caring about him.

Though he could be a rough, potentially violent customer in a barroom, Scott was also capable of great acts of kindness, as Acevedo recalled:

> There was a little secretary [working on the film] in Kentucky whose boyfriend came home on leave. He was in the Air Force. They had a car accident and she got killed. Her family was very short of funds. [Cast member] Jack Albertson went around to all

the crew, taking up a collection so they could pay for the funeral. He came to George when we were making him up and he said, "George, we're taking up this collection. Would you like to contribute something?" George said, "Better than that, send me the bill for the funeral and whatever you collect, give to the family to help them along."

There are many examples of such spontaneous generosity, both large and small. Scott Fowler remembered that Scott's letters to Dewhurst from Vietnam were always covered with stamps for the teenager to add to his collection. A woman wrote to the *New York Times* in response to an article on Scott about the time her little girl was sick to her stomach on the streets of New York after a busy day of museum-going and taking in the Easter show at Radio City Music Hall. "Suddenly, a limousine pulled up to the curb," she wrote, and Scott stepped out after spending hours rehearsing for *Uncle Vanya*. "This complete stranger took time at the end of his long day to comfort her, rescue both of us from an uncomfortable and awkward situation and then had his chauffeur take us home." Actor Stephen Young, who appeared in *Patton*, told of a TV repairman working at Scott's house complaining of eye trouble. The next instant, Scott was on the phone to his eye doctor, Dr. Ackerman, to set up an appointment. Then there was the time Scott noticed the carpet in the lobby of the Circle in the Square Theatre looked particularly threadbare. Producer Theodore Mann explained they could not afford to have it replaced. "How much would it cost you?" the actor asked. Mann answered "$10,000." Without a moment's hesitation, Scott said he would pay for it. In 1991, he gave monetary gifts to his four grandchildren by Victoria Lewis so that the family could afford a house in the foothills outside Denver.

There were also generous contributions to charitable organizations. After appearing on *The Mike Douglas Show* with David Rothenberg of The Fortune Society, an organization devoted to helping ex-cons, Scott sent the society the proceeds from an oil well he had invested in.

Scott told Rothenberg if not for the grace of God, during his early struggling days, his alcoholism could have caused him to end up in prison. "He always had a reputation as a tough guy, but I only knew him as a man who was extremely concerned about others and very kind," Rothenberg said. In 1977, Scott received the Fortune Society's Karl Menninger Award for his "behind-the-scenes commitment for substantive change and the creation of opportunities for ex-offenders." It was one award he gladly accepted.

Flim-Flam was released in August 1967 and reviews were split on Scott's performance. John Allen in the *Christian Science Monitor* was on the plus side: "Mr. Scott skillfully exposes the failings of an unctuous crook. He has the requisite glibness and savoir-faire with a telling suggestion of loneliness and desperation underneath. Both the public and private sides of the man are sensitively presented, and they are touching in their contrast." Bosley Crowther in the *New York Times* unfavorably compared Scott to W.C. Fields and other stars:

> He is a serious character actor trying to be a lovable old rogue. He is a fierce dramatic firebrand trying to be a frisky scamp. Made up with flowing hair and eyebrows to look a lot like a latter-day Frederic March, with occasional glances over his spectacles and smacking of lips to remind one of Claude Rains, he plays this cornball con man skipping about through the South with all sorts of actorish frills and flutters that haven't a shred of art in them.

Scott's evaluation of director Irvin Kershner's work was uncomplimentary, "He shot a good picture with *The Flim-Flam Man*," he later told Rex Reed. "Then he went mad in the cutting room and butchered the whole thing." With *Wife* and *Flim-Flam*, Scott had established he could play comedy. Sonny Elliott, who had criticized him for his intensity when they played light farce in summer stock together, recalled receiving a copy of the latter film from his former colleague with a note reading, "Fuck you, G. C. S."

"He sent it to prove to me he could do comedy as well as drama," laughed Elliott.

Scott was also considered for two potentially significant film roles during this period, but neither panned out. He was in the running for the showy role of the lead villain in *Wait Until Dark* to menace a blind woman played by Audrey Hepburn. He turned it down as being too unsympathetic. That part went to Alan Arkin. Scott was also up for the bigoted sheriff in *In the Heat of the Night*, which became an Academy Award–winning turn for Rod Steiger. Director Norman Jewison later said Scott was his first choice, but scheduling conflicts prevented their working together.

While he was losing out on great film roles and the ones he did book were less than demanding, Scott's television work was even slimmer. His only appearance on the small screen during 1966 was a guest shot on a two-part episode of NBC's shoot-'em-up western *The Road West*, which was later stitched together and released theatrically as *The Savage Land*.

As he had done on *Ben Casey* and *The Virginian*, Scott created a three-dimensional character out of clichés and wooden dialogue. Billed as a "special guest star," he played Captain Judd Barker, a former Confederate officer leading a band of bushwhackers out to terrorize the noble Pride family (protagonists of the series) from their Kansas land claim. Instead of a blackhearted tyrant, Scott gives us a shaded man believing in the right of his cause and the worth of his violent actions. When he gives the orders to his disheveled crew to burn the Prides off their land, he chooses to be quiet. You can detect a note of regret in his voice. He doesn't want to hurt anyone, but he must follow through on his conviction that the Federal government is unfairly parceling out the acreage of what he regards as Southern territory.

Scott displays genuine sympathy when the Pride matriarch is killed during a shoot-out in the town. Barry Sullivan, the series star and leader of the Pride clan, gazes up at Barker with his dead mother in his arms and blankly delivers the line, "You murderous, you murderous . . . "

Scott as Barker looks down on Pride from his horse, and almost compassionately says, "We'll send somethin' for the buryin'." Scott expresses Barker's genuine sympathy. You can almost read his thoughts, that he didn't want anyone killed, but he still must go ahead with his objective—to get Lawrence, Kansas, under the control of his gang of ex-rebel soldiers. The scene should belong to Sullivan, but Scott packs so much meaning into his line that he obliterates the hero.

His next film was a greater challenge to Scott's skill and was as unconventional as *The Road West* was ordinary. *Petulia* was based on the novel *Me and the Arch Kook Petulia*, by Los Angeles dentist John Haase, about a free-spirited young woman repressed by her marriage to an abusive playboy. She falls in love with disillusioned surgeon Archie Bollen, who has issues of his own, having recently gone through a painful divorce. Archie didn't feel anything in his antiseptic marriage while Petulia's nonconformist spirit appeals to him. After some madcap adventures involving Petulia heisting a tuba from a pawnshop, the flighty heroine returns to the jet-set world of her husband and the mismatched lovers sadly part company.

The director was Richard Lester, an edgy auteur who never met a jump-cut he didn't like, with the Beatles films *A Hard Day's Night* and *Help!*, and the frenetic film versions of *A Funny Thing Happened on the Way to the Forum, The Knack,* and *How I Won the War* to his name. He initially hated the *Petulia* project. The people, particularly the Holly Golightly–like title character, were too cute for his sardonic taste. But the story got under his skin. He eventually realized this could be his first mature feature. He darkened the lighthearted tone of the novel and made the story into a scathing commentary on contemporary American society from his outsider's point of view (he had been out of the country for fifteen years). Lester shifted the locale as well, transferring the action from Los Angeles to San Francisco, where the Haight-Ashbury neighborhood had become the epicenter of the counterculture movement.

Casting for the leading lady was not a problem. Who better to embody the quirky heroine than Julie Christie, the symbol of the swinging sixties from her Oscar-winning turn as a soulless party girl in *Darling*? Finding the right Archie would prove more challenging. Lester had seen Scott on stage and television and surmised he had the right strength to play the vacillating surgeon. "I absolutely adored his work," the director later told Christie's biographer Anthony Hayward. "If you're going to cast a man who is weak, you cast a strong actor. If you cast a weak actor playing a weak man, you get a boring performance. But if you get a strong, gutsy performer playing this man, you still have an underlying tension in it. George is the finest performer I've ever worked with."

But Warner Brothers wanted the audience-friendly James Garner, whom Lester rejected. When the studio countered with Paul Newman and Frank Sinatra, the director held firm for his pick and won. Filming began on April 10, 1967, and Scott drew $250,000 for ten weeks' work.

While both Scott and Archie Bollen were coping with divorces, there were more differences than similarities between actor and character. Bollen represses his emotions and violent urges, while Scott would seldom hold himself back when his temper was aroused. The only time Archie really lets loose in front of another person is when his ex-wife (played by Shirley Knight) visits his new digs and brings him a bag of homemade cookies. She is subtly critical of the apartment and, by implication, of Archie's new life. Suddenly, as he did in *The Hustler* by screaming, "Eddie, you owe me MONEY," Scott smashes the quiet of the scene by hurling the cookies at Knight's back like a deadly missile. Knight recalled,

> We had very different styles of acting. George was a real meticulous planner as an actor. He was very specific in his choices and would follow them through. He wasn't as, for want of a better word, naturalistic. So when George and I were doing the cookie scene,

Richard would play tricks on George in order to get him to just go with the moment more. For example, he would say "Action," and then while the camera was rolling, he would say, "George, would you do this instead of that?" What would happen is that George wasn't able to think about what he was going to do which is what Lester wanted. It threw him off guard. As a result, for me, it's by far his best performance in a movie. I felt that it was his richest performance in film and it's a more multilayered and more surprising performance as a result of Richard Lester's work with him because he did not allow George, in any way, to do what I call "his numbers." Certain actors find a security in not being fully vulnerable in the moment. For me, acting is "I don't know what I'm going to say. I don't know what I'm going to do. I don't know what the other person is going to say or do." It's a very dangerous world that I work in as an actor. George was a little safer as an actor. For example, a performance like Patton, it's a very not surprising performance for me, in the moment-to-moment aspect of it. The character that he creates is wonderful. I don't mean to imply that he's not a great actor at all. It's just a different taste on my part.

So we were doing the cookie scene and my character is touching things and being very critical of the space and what he's done with it. I touch this sort of weird sculpture and the next thing I know I'm being hit in the back with cookies. The line was there, "What the hell are you doing, bringing me cookies," but I didn't know he was going to throw the cookies. That was fabulous because for ages after that film came out when I was in Europe, people would just look at me and say, "Cookie! Cookie!" Because there was something about that moment. The expression on my face is really, truly surprised and stunned because I did not know that was going to happen. Richard had three cameras going during that. There was one on my hands and one on me and one on George. He was able to cut to the same take. The flow of the scene is just remarkable, I think.

Julie Christie was not as confident an actress as Knight or as willing to go into "dangerous" places. She required a few takes to get the juices flowing. Conversely, Scott was usually ready right away. Lester explained his delicate balancing between his two stars to Anthony Hayward:

> Because she is somewhat insecure, Julie needs time to build into a scene. She liked a lot of rehearsal. It's odd because George, who was a theatre actor, was the most instinctive actor I've ever seen and got very bored after three or four takes, whereas Julie began to come into her own after five or six takes. It was a very difficult balance to keep both of them happy. I would do all George's close-ups first and then come round and cover Julie later so that she had time to practice while the camera was on her back. I took George's best bits early, giving Julie time to get comfortable. By the time she was ready, we were concentrating more on her than on him.

The end result is a caustic critique of a plastic world, told in fragments. Sex is commercialized by topless restaurants and motels in parking garages. Emotions are anesthetized as constant TV news of Vietnam is ignored, just as Petulia's psychic and physical wounds are glossed over. Brief scenes speak volumes. Archie's meddling friends Barney and Wilma (Arthur Hill and Kathleen Widdoes) subject him to slides of happy moments with his ex-wife, in hopes of reconciliation, then Wilma reveals with a line she hates her marriage, too.

Petulia was the official American entry for the 1968 Cannes Film Festival. But demonstrations, strikes and riots by French citizens spread from Paris to the glamorous Riviera. After gendarmes baton-charged protesters outside the main screening theatre at Cannes, Lester withdrew his feature from the festival, as did many other filmmakers. The film encountered similar bad luck during its American release. It opened on the week of Robert Kennedy's assassination in June 1968, many critics responded negatively to its jittery structure (Kathleen

Carroll of the *New York Daily News* called it "a gaily colored patch-work quilt rather than a meaningful movie"), and audiences stayed away. Cineastes have come to appreciate its quirky storytelling methods and acidic commentary on late 1960s America, and the film has acquired cult status.

Whatever their reservations about this oddball anti-romance, reviewers praised Scott's restrained work. Carroll said he "cut through the film like a surgical knife."

Sexual and romantic tension were about to be renewed in his off-screen life as well. Just as he was wrapping up playing a man coping with a difficult divorce, Scott launched a second try at marriage with Colleen Dewhurst.

10

New Marriage,
Broadway Hits, and a Flop

A PHOTOGRAPH OF GEORGE C. SCOTT and Colleen Dewhurst taken on
their second wedding day at their upstate New York farmhouse on
July 4, 1967, shows them in bright summer clothes. Their young sons
Alex and Campbell, in little-boy formal dress of white shirts, ties, and
shorts, are standing in front of them. Everyone is smiling. Scott called
it their Independence Day.

Scott had tried independence from Dewhurst for two years and it
hadn't worked. Exhausted from pursuing the elusive siren Gardner,
this wandering Odysseus was ready to come home to his faithful Penelope. After the fire of Scott's passion was extinguished and he was
finally able to walk away from Gardner, he and Dewhurst resumed
cordial relations. Scott took up residence at the farmhouse and Dewhurst bought a former horse farm three-quarters of a mile down the
road for herself and the boys. But they frequently visited each other.
Dewhurst later reported to an interviewer, "Even when we were divorced we somehow couldn't let go that last little string. At school one
little boy said his mom and dad were divorced and he was sad about it,
and our ten-year-old, Alex, said, 'Oh, that's all right, my mom and dad
are divorced, but whenever he gets off work he comes to our house, he
lives there, they're very good friends.'"

The boys' mother and father added to the ambiguity by trying out a second marriage on stage and television. Scott still wanted to work with his former wife. On the set of *Not With My Wife, You Don't,* he told reporters he planning to costar with her in a Broadway production of a two-character play called *The Exercise,* by Lewis John Carlino, to be directed by José Quintero, but it never panned out. Significantly, when their collaborations did come to fruition, they enacted couples in conflict. They were Henry II and Eleanor of Aquitaine battling over crowns and kingdoms in a summer stock production of *The Lion in Winter* at the Bucks County Playhouse in Pennsylvania. The production ran July 11–23, 1966. Scott later told *Pageant* magazine, "Colleen is one of the best actresses alive. I never had any trouble working with her while we were married, so why should I now? She is probably the best friend I have in the world."

Bucks County technical director Jack Conant remembered, "What I recall is that they were wonderful people. One little tidbit I remember is Colleen used to call George 'Rabbit.' He was like regular people. No star stuff going on." Another highlight of the summer for Scott was the Playhouse's annual softball game against the Lambertville Music Festival, a tent theatre located across the river. Scott was the pitcher. The singer Julius LaRosa from the Music Festival tried to steal third base and Scott picked him off. When Bucks County won, the victors hoisted Scott on their shoulders and carried him off the field.

The production broke all house records. Scott still was given to rages, but he was provoked this time. The actor playing King Philip of France seemed to be drunk or high onstage. He would mumble during everyone else's lines. After a performance, Scott grabbed him by the throat and screamed he'd kill him if he ever did that again. The young man later poured gasoline on himself in Central Park, perhaps as a protest over the Vietnam War. He didn't die but was horribly disfigured, losing both of his ears.

After *The Lion in Winter,* Scott and Dewhurst fought accusations of witchcraft and wrestled with the husband's infidelity as John and

Elizabeth Proctor in a CBS-TV broadcast of Arthur Miller's *The Crucible*. By this second staged union, Scott was ready to stop the playact-
ing and attempt the real thing once more. During the rehearsal and
filming of *Crucible* in May 1967, he seriously began to court Dewhurst,
asking for a second chance.

The signs did not bode well for the couple's reclaimed happiness.
Scott was comfortable with marriage only when he knew the matri-
monial bonds extended as far as the stage door and no further. Settled
down with either the siren or Penelope, this Odysseus couldn't remain
homebound. He was never at rest in his relationships.

Dewhurst may have realized this subconsciously. She certainly did
years later when she acknowledged the second marriage was probably
a mistake and joked that she and Scott got along better during their
divorces than when they were married. She would be told by a fellow
actor with an interest in the paranormal that she and Scott had been
brother and sister in a previous life and that this explained their marital
problems. They were simply too much alike. Their titanic personalities and mutual need for the spotlight were just too big to be contained
in one marriage. There was also the contrast in their temperaments.

"Colleen was a caretaker," observed close friend Elizabeth Wilson.
"She needed to help people." Dewhurst was a den mother to an ever-
expanding pack of grown-up children. She was constantly reaching
out to friends in need. If you were short of cash, needed a bed to crash
on after a bout of substance abuse, or had just lost your direction in life,
there was always room at Colleen's. The Scott-Dewhurst farmhouse
in South Salem was constantly full of guests with no fixed checkout
time. That didn't always sit well with Scott, who could often be found
upstairs reading.

Dewhurst was Big Momma to the entire world. Scott wanted her to
himself. In addition, her talent was as great as her husband's. She commanded as large a stage as Scott did, and two titanic personalities were
too much for one marriage to contain. Nevertheless, Dewhurst had
two young sons who needed a father and Scott was a man who needed

a home after chasing an illusion of perfection named Ava Gardner. He was at the house most of the time anyway, so they decided to make it official and start a home again. "They had been through so much together. It just seemed to make sense that they get married again," recalled Wilson.

Neighbor Scott Fowler remembered a phone call to his house on a Sunday morning: "G. C. called my house and said to my mom, 'I want you all to come over for breakfast and celebrate with me. I'm getting married.' I can remember my mom saying, 'You're getting married? To who?' He just said, 'To Colleen, of course.' We all went over there for breakfast. They didn't get married that day. He just wanted us to come over and celebrate the fact that they were going to get remarried."

No sooner were the wedding vows exchanged for the second time than both partners were knee-deep in work. It appeared to be their formula for a happy marriage. Scott had just finished filming *Petulia* and was fully booked for the 1967–68 Broadway theatre season. First there was *Dr. Cook's Garden*, set to open September 25 at the Belasco Theatre, which Scott would direct. Then he was to start rehearsals for an all-star revival of Lillian Hellman's *The Little Foxes* at Lincoln Center, to be directed by the red-hot hitmaker Mike Nichols. There followed three comic roles in *Plaza Suite*, a collection of one-acts set in the eponymous hotel by the reigning king of Broadway comedy, Neil Simon, also to be directed by Nichols. The play was to open at the Plymouth Theatre in February 1968 after try-outs in New Haven and Boston. Scott was also collaborating on a book about acting with writer Tom Leith (excerpts appeared in *Life* magazine, but the volume was never published.)

As if this Broadway triple play and the book weren't enough, Scott intended to direct a production of Eugene O'Neill's rarely seen 1924 play *All God's Chillun Got Wings* Off-Broadway in April. He planned to cast his *Dr. Strangelove* colleague James Earl Jones as a young African-American who weds a white woman. (The production never materialized, but Scott did later direct a revival of the play with his fourth wife, Trish Van Devere, at Circle in the Square). As for Dewhurst, she was preparing to go into rehearsals for *More Stately Mansions*—like *All God's Chillun,* an obscure O'Neill drama. She would play opposite Ingrid Bergman, who was making her return to the American stage after an absence of twenty years. *Mansions* would play Los Angeles and then Broadway. As in their original wedding day photo, the Scotts were smiling in the garden. Personally and professionally, the future couldn't have been brighter. But it wasn't long before Odysseus would hear another enchanting siren song.

For the moment, the family was officially reunited and Scott was getting another crack at one of his longtime ambitions: directing. His only previous credits in this field had been either secretive or frustrating—whether covertly coaching Dewhurst when she was having trouble from a noncommunicative Alan Schneider in Edward Albee's unsuccessful stage adaptation of Carson McCullers's *Ballad of the Sad Café,* or staging the short-lived *General Seegar* for the doomed Theatre of Michigan. Perhaps the fact that both *General Seegar* and Scott's upcoming directorial assignment, *Dr. Cook's Garden,* were by the same author should have been a warning.

Dr. Cook's Garden was a thriller-melodrama from the fiendishly clever Ira Levin about a kindly small-town physician and his young protégé who returns home for a visit before setting up practice in the big city. The twist comes when the younger doctor discovers his old mentor has been poisoning the town's malcontents and evildoers, acting as a vigilante weeder.

The central botanical metaphor was a trifle heavy. But Levin was the author of the best-selling *Rosemary's Baby,* which was enjoying success as a film thriller that year. *Garden's* producer was Arnold Saint-Subber, an elfin, Truman Capote-like entrepreneur whose credits included *Kiss Me, Kate* and a string of such Neil Simon hits as the long-running *Barefoot in the Park* and *The Odd Couple* as well as the forthcoming *Plaza Suite.* Saint-Subber was also the producer of George's next venture, *The Little*

Foxes, to be staged initially at Lincoln Center. Presenting three productions in one season with the volatile Scott was a high-risk move. The actor's reputation for indulging in alcoholic binges had followed him from show to show. But Saint-Subber was willing to roll the dice and he won big on two out of three throws.

The cast of *Dr. Cook* was led by Burl Ives as the murderous M.D. and Keir Dullea as his young colleague and accuser. Ives was an Oscar winner and Dullea had delivered notable film performances in *The Hoodlum Priest* and *David and Lisa*. The talent was all there for *Dr. Cook's Garden* to blossom, but the project turned out to be a poisonous swamp.

The largest and most troublesome plant in this theatrical fen was Ives. Scott had not cast him. Saint-Subber had hired the folk-singer-turned-actor before signing Scott on as stager. In fact, Scott had only met Ives briefly before rehearsals began.

The burly, bearded Ives was more of a personality than an actor. He had risen to fame as a sweet-voiced folk singer, warbling of blue-tail flies and rock-candy mountains on records and in a Broadway show called *Swing Out, Sweet Land*. Elia Kazan, the master director of the postwar American theatre, had staged that tuner and later employed Ives's rascally, charming persona to advantage as the crude plantation owner Big Daddy in Tennessee Williams's Southern-fried scorcher *Cat on a Hot Tin Roof*. Ives would repeat his performance in the film version and, the same year that it was released, he would win a Supporting Actor Oscar for playing essentially the same character in the sprawling western *The Big Country*.

"He's bled into acting the last fifteen years and he has a wonderfully warm, folksy quality," Scott told William Goldman for the latter's book on Broadway, *The Season*. But Scott soon found himself in conflict with his leading man, and with the playwright, too. Scott wanted the judgment-dispensing doctor to feel some ambivalence about his seemingly benign homicides. "There's no scene in here where Cook has doubts about his killing—his gardening of the community," Scott told Goldman. "Without it we have a play about a suspicious young man who points a finger and a villain who rationalizes twenty-one years of killing. It's another Warner Brothers 1940 movie, and I don't want Sydney Greenstreet; I want Pasteur gone wrong. . . . I think Ira won't deepen the play because he's worried that it'll confuse what he's written. But how deep should we go? That's my problem."

Indeed, Levin saw his play as a simple melodrama and didn't want to tinker with it.

Scott couldn't convince his author to make changes he felt were necessary and he couldn't find a common language with his leading man. "I couldn't serve him. I refused to let him do those marvelous old vaudeville turns of his," Scott later railed to Goldman. Ives lacked the acting technique to go beyond playing cute, cuddly good ole boys, and Scott was unable to get Ives to deliver a more nuanced characterization.

The director went to his producer and demanded Ives be uprooted from this *Garden*. They had to get another mature character actor. Edward G. Robinson or Charles Boyer were floated, but Saint-Subber rejected the idea. It was too late. They were too close to opening. Why not take Ives to dinner and talk it over, the producer offered.

"Take him to dinner?" Scott told Goldman. "What the fuck am I gonna say to him? You can't work around a table drinking Bloody Marys."

Dr. Cook's Garden was scheduled to hold its first preview performance on September 11. A sign in the lobby of the Belasco proclaimed, "Preview Canceled." Four days later, Scott quit, despite Saint-Subber's threat of a lawsuit. Levin, who had never directed before, took over the staging duties. Perhaps the master communicator Kazan could have gotten a credible performance out of Ives, but he wasn't called in to tend to the ailing patient.

Reportedly, Warner Brothers and James Stewart were interested in the film version and Saint-Subber felt any financial loss on Broadway could be compensated for by the sale of the movie rights. When the play finally opened, the reviews were predictably damning. "*Dr. Cook's Garden* Is Planted With Stiffs" read the headline in the *Daily News*. The show closed after a week of performances at a loss of $100,000. Warners passed on the movie deal, and eventually the story was filmed for television starring another icon of cinematic bonhomie, Bing Crosby, as the pernicious physician.

Saint-Subber had to swallow his anger at Scott because the actor was starring in his production of *The Little Foxes*, which began rehearsals almost immediately after *Dr. Cook's Garden* withered. The next Saint-Subber production, *Plaza Suite*, was to follow thereafter without much of a pause. Nichols was set to direct both productions. Scott was a major draw and, Saint-Subber rationalized, business was business. So there was no legal retaliation for Scott's *Dr. Cook* walk-out.

The Little Foxes (1939) was Lillian Hellman's finest play. The creatures of the title are a metaphor for the covetous Hubbard clan, a family of early 1900s Southern entrepreneurs whose *modus operandi* was the duplicitous double-cross. Scott was slated to play Ben, the elder brother and leader of this gang of cutthroats in stiff collars. Ben is not above covertly appropriating safe-deposit bonds from his unwilling brother-in-law to cement a deal with a Northern developer to bring a new factory to the Hubbards' small town. The tables are turned when Ben's equally conniving sister, Regina, discovers the theft and uses the knowledge to blackmail Ben and their complicit brother Oscar into making her the principal shareholder in the factory venture. Hellman's melodrama is full of plot reversals and grand dramatic scenes, the most famous of which has Regina quietly looking on while her inconveniently scrupulous husband expires of a heart attack.

Saint-Subber and director Mike Nichols had gathered an impressive roster of stars for this limited engagement at the Vivian Beaumont Theatre. In addition to Scott, there was Anne Bancroft, fresh from her iconically seductive Mrs. Robinson in Nichols's film *The Graduate*, as the triumphant Regina; E. G. Marshall, from TV's *The Defenders* and numerous Broadway dramas, as the luckless Oscar; and the sublime

British actress Margaret Leighton as Oscar's pathetic wife, Birdie. Elizabeth Wilson, who played Scott's supervisor on the ill-fated *East Side/ West Side*, understudied Bancroft.

Unlike most directors, Nichols was a box-office draw as big as any star. After his popular comedy act with Elaine May had run its course, he crossed over to the other side of the footlights to direct. His Broadway credits as a stager read like a list of the top theatrical grossers in *Variety*. Neil Simon's smashes *Barefoot in the Park* and *The Odd Couple*, and Murray Schisgal's equally popular *Luv*, were among his back-to-back hits.

Austin Pendleton, a short, quirky character actor, was cast as Oscar's grasping son, Leo. He described working with Scott as

> electrifying. He walked into a scene and gave off the energy of what the scene was about in its most purified, potent dramatic form. He bristled with the energy of the scene. If you were playing a scene with him, he just put you there. He zapped you right there. And this was from the first day of rehearsal.
>
> About a week into the rehearsal Mike Nichols said to us, "Now what we have to do is get up to the level of George." He was [already] there three or four days in. I've never seen anything quite like it. I've never seen a performance arrived at that fast that was not superficial. It was clear and sharp and alive.

Foxes opened on November 4, 1967, to enthusiastic notices. Walter Kerr in the Sunday *New York Times* offered several specific moments to savor and provided a taste of Scott's performance (unpreserved on tape) for future generations. He cited the scene of "George C. Scott discovering he's been had and toppling backward onto a sofa in a whoop of admiring laughter, then rising to tap Anne Bancroft's marble cheek lightly as though to say he'll be back for a tasty revenge."

Dewhurst's reception in *More Stately Mansions* opposite Ingrid Bergman at the Broadhurst Theatre, which premiered October 31, was slightly more qualified. Critics hailed her performance but generally agreed that the newly unearthed O'Neill drama should have remained interred.

The accolades Scott received for *Foxes* must have been some solace for the *Dr. Cook* debacle, but they did not completely dispel his eternal self-doubts about his choice of profession. Austin Pendleton related a story of Scott's missing a performance of *Foxes*:

> In between a matinee and an evening performance, I was having dinner with my brother and his wife at The Ginger Man restaurant across the street from Lincoln Center. George was a couple of tables away from us, with some friends, and seemed very jovial. I introduced him to my brother and sister-in-law and then went to the theatre. It got to be half-hour [before curtain] and George wasn't anywhere to be found. Bob Currie, one of the stage managers, who was a big guy, went across the street to the Ginger Man. He found George still there and told him, "It's time," to which George said something like "Is that so?" Bob [understood] George wasn't coming. Bob came back and reported George was not going to make the performance that night.
>
> George's understudy, Robert Symonds, found out he had to go on when the wardrobe woman went charging past him in one of the corridors backstage and told him, "You're wearing your own shoes!" This was a Saturday evening. George came in on Sunday and apologized very graciously to the company, and we went on as if nothing had happened.

When asked why Scott had decided to remain at The Ginger Man rather than perform that night, Pendleton opined, "I think he decided, during the latter half of the meal, that acting was a stupid profession." As with any show business anecdote, the story of the prolonged meal at The Ginger Man acquired embellishments with repeated tellings. The most fantastic has Scott lifting the burly stage manager and throwing him through the window of the restaurant. This can be discounted as exaggeration. Had it been true, it would have made the tabloids.

Scott and company continued to frequent The Ginger Man during the run of *Foxes*. Pendleton related,

> Almost every night, he [Scott] would take a big, round table. And he had a bodyguard with him, a guy who had been a cop. And anyone could come in and sit with them. Colleen Dewhurst would often come and sit with us after her show had finished for the night. Different members of the cast would come over. We always had a full table. It was kind of wonderful. He wouldn't hold court. He would encourage everyone to tell a story. He would say, "Austin, tell the table about such and such." It was kind of what acting must have been like in the old days. There wasn't a single unpleasant evening.

Foxes concluded its run at the Vivian Beaumont at the end of December and later transferred to the Ethel Barrymore Theatre—but without Scott. E. G. Marshall took over the role of Ben while Scott began rehearsals for what turned out to be his first big commercial hit on Broadway, Neil Simon's *Plaza Suite*.

Flashback: Sardi's East, a short-lived satellite of the original famous theatrical eatery located several blocks east of the New York theatre district. It's a busy lunchtime with waiters rushing about and dozens of conversations, mostly about show biz, mixing together to create an unintelligible din. Caricatures of stage celebrities stare down from the walls at their three-dimensional equivalents munching on appetizers and sipping soup. Amid the clinking martini glasses and cutlery, deals are sealed for Broadway shows. Seated at one table is a bespectacled, mild-mannered man who could be mistaken for an accountant. It's Neil Simon, the most successful writer of stage comedy in America. He graduated from penning sketches for Sid Caesar's television variety laugh factory to full-length plays that packed houses and became top-grossing films. The previous season, he had four shows running at the same time (*Barefoot in the Park*, *The Odd Couple*, *Sweet Charity*, and *The Star-Spangled Girl*). Simon is dining at Sardi's East to meet George C. Scott and discuss having the actor play three leading roles in his new play, *Plaza Suite*.

Simon had a reputation for churning out easygoing chuckle-getters that delighted mostly middle-class, middle-aged playgoers. He was trying something different with *Plaza Suite*, a set of one-acts unified by their leads and locale. The central idea concerned Sam, a successful businessman going through male menopause. His needy wife, Karen, is attempting to rekindle their romance by having them spend their anniversary in the same Plaza Hotel suite where they honeymooned. After some comic business with Karen confusing the dates of their anniversary and the floor of the honeymoon suite, Sam reveals he is bored with their marriage and his business and that he has been having an affair with his secretary. The curtain falls with the audience not knowing if the conflicted couple will celebrate another anniversary. In writing a comedy of marital discord, Broadway's crown price of merriment was introducing issues heavier than the battles of neatnik Felix versus sloppy Oscar.

The grain alcohol of the grim opener would be chased down with two dessert wines in the form of a pair of lighter one-act plays. The second piece was a romantic romp featuring a trendy film producer seducing his former high-school sweetheart. The evening concluded with an out-and-out farce centering on the parents of a silent bride unsuccessfully attempting to extricate her from the locked bathroom where she has barricaded herself on her very expensive wedding day. There was a fourth piece, nearly a monologue for Scott, detailing the travails of an Ohio executive visiting the big city and falling victim to nearly every possible disaster New York has to offer. This segment unnecessarily protracted the show and was cut during early rehearsals. Never one to waste material, Simon later reworked the basic premise, and the discarded one-act became a screenplay called *The Out-of-Towners.*

For *Plaza Suite,* Simon required two stars who could convincingly play three disparate roles. The directorial hat trick was to make the evening seamless. The audience should not be aware there was a sudden shift from comedic to dramatic styles. For the female leads, Maureen Stapleton was contracted. She had worked with Scott previously on an episode of his TV series *East Side/West Side* as a golden-hearted female bum. Stapleton, a superb actress with a reputation for heavy drinking and the vocabulary of a truck driver, was also known for versatility. She had vivified dramatic Tennessee Williams heroines in *The Rose Tattoo* and *Orpheus Descending* as well as the cartoonishly overbearing mother of Dick Van Dyke in the film version of *Bye, Bye Birdie.* Scott had not starred in a hit comedy on Broadway, but he had demonstrated his comedic abilities in *Dr. Strangelove.*

In Simon's memoir *Rewrites,* he relates the encounter at Sardi's East with Scott and his agent, Jane Deacy. "He greeted me with a cordial but very quick smile, the kind that vanishes even before it is completed," Simon wrote. After pleasantries were exchanged and the playwright gave the actor of a copy of the new play, Scott instructed Simon and Deacy to have lunch without him while he went upstairs to read the script. Simon protested that this was not a final draft; it had not been cut yet and therefore it was still very long. Deacy countered by suggesting that they eat slowly; Scott was worth the wait. Two hours later, Scott returned to the table, taking his time, saying hello to friends at other tables. The smile for the friends vanished from Scott's face when he got to Simon and Deacy. He threw the script on the table and simply said, "I like it. Let's do it."

Cast member Bob Balaban recalled,

> [George] never gave less than an amazing performance. Maureen said that acting with George was like being waltzed around the ice by a champion skater. You just put your arms up and let him lead.

There are some stars that get to be stars because they only care
about themselves. George was nothing like that. He did experience
an enormous amount of pressure even though he made everything
he did look easy. He was tormented. He was acutely attuned to
everything around him, which is what made him a great actor. But
the fact that his radar was turned up to such a volume and was so
sensitive is what made him tormented.

This hypersensitivity would manifest itself during *Plaza Suite*. But
so would the laser-like certainty with which Scott cemented his characters in place early in the rehearsal process. As he had in *The Little
Foxes*, Mike Nichols felt Scott had arrived at a performance-level interpretation days after rehearsals began. Nichols joked to Mary Cronin of
Time that Scott didn't even need rehearsals but stuck around anyway.

But Scott did not stay around all the time. His finely tuned anten-
nae picked up his own insecurities and, rather than face them head on,
Scott checked out of *Plaza Suite* for a while. According to Simon's autobiography, two weeks into rehearsals in New York at the Belasco
Theatre, Scott failed to show up. He did not answer his phone, did not
return calls, and failed to report to work for a second day and then a
third. Stapleton had taken to calling him "The Pussycat" in sarcastic
reference to his reputation as a rageaholic and violent drunk. She once
told Nichols she was afraid of Scott. "The whole world is frightened
of George," was Nichols's famous reply. On the third Scott-less day,
Stapleton asked the company if "The Pussycat" was in attendance.
When the negative answer came, she took out a pack of cigarettes and
announced, "Well, then, it's a good day to smoke."

According to Simon, Scott finally showed up at rehearsals on the
afternoon of the fourth day looking like "he had just relived World
War II." Rather than demanding to know where the hell his star had
been and risking getting his head bitten off, Nichols decided to take
the "business as usual" approach. As casually as possible, Nichols said
"Hi, George. We're on Act One, Scene Two. You're on the phone."

George crossed to the set, picked up the phone and said "Line." The stage manager gave him the line and the rehearsal proceeded. Just like after the missed performance of *The Little Foxes*, everything proceeded as if nothing had happened.

No one knows where Scott was for those three days or why he vanished. But, as Bob Balaban observed, he was probably feeling the enormous pressure of carrying a major Broadway show, and a "Doc" Simon comedy at that.

Comedy is a much more difficult genre than straight drama, particularly comedy with a little bit of drama thrown in. You have to bring the audience along from the lighter moments into the heavier ones without them noticing. Scott may have been thinking, "What if I can't bring them along between those transitions? What if I can't even make them laugh?" A silent audience in a drama is acceptable, but a quiet one at a Neil Simon comedy is death for an actor. Sometimes, Scott's way of handling such extreme pressure was to escape it—maybe by vanishing into a barroom.

After the disappearance there were other flare-ups manifesting Scott's insecurities. Despite Nichols's reports of perfection to *Time*, Scott had trouble with the second segment, *Visitor from Hollywood,* in which he played a hotshot film producer seeking a quick tryst with his high-school sweetheart (Stapleton). Early in rehearsals, he suggested to Nichols that the entire act be played offstage. He and Stapleton would run across the stage, shout at each other from the wings, then run back on and finish the scene in the closet. Nichols let Scott have enough rope by staging the action per the leading man's bizarre idea. The next day, Scott came back and agreed it was impractical. During dress rehearsal of *Hollywood*, Scott stopped the action and objected to Stapleton's costume. What was the problem? "She looks like a hooker," the actor replied.

Without missing a beat, Stapleton quipped, "George, that's the sweetest thing you've ever said to me." Stapleton later agreed to change the dress to keep her costar happy.

Scott was equally distressed about his own wardrobe. For the role of Jessie Borden, the hip, cutting-edge filmmaker, Scott was made to look like a "now" kind of guy—"now" for 1968, that is, with a Beatle-length wig, a pale aqua shirt, and suede trousers. Stage manager Wisner Washam remembers Scott complaining about the getup, stating he felt it made him look "faggy," that it wouldn't be funny, and, worst of all, it would divert attention from his performance. His anger about the costume boiled over at the last run-through before the first public performance in New Haven.

While he and Stapleton were rehearsing the *Hollywood* scene, Scott complained about hearing a radio playing music somewhere in the theatre. No one else heard anything. Scott insisted he could hear music, that it was driving him crazy, and that he would not continue until it was turned off. Washam was dispatched to find the source of the offending sounds. After a thorough search of the entire theatre proved fruitless and the entire company agreed they heard nothing other than their own voices, Scott shouted he was not coming back until the radio was found and silenced. He slammed out of the theatre.

The first paying customers were going to walk through the theatre doors in a few hours, and Saint-Subber, Nichols, and Simon were more than a little nervous. What if Scott didn't come back? But he did and once again company members acted as if nothing out of the ordinary had occurred. New Haven audiences greeted a slightly more serious Neil Simon with accustomed laughter and applause.

After a week of performances in Connecticut, the show moved on to Boston, its final stop before Broadway. The Beantown reception was as enthusiastic as that in New Haven. On opening night, Scott was jubilant and invited everyone up to his hotel room. Simon remembers Stapleton and Scott hugging each other, drinking champagne, and "saying in the foulest language how much they loved each other." Scott called his wife, and Simon recalled hearing this side of the conversation: "Colleen? . . . Yeah, yeah, it was a nice show. . . . Nice, my ass, it's a hit. A great big fucking hit. I'm finally in a goddamn hit, can you imagine that?" (Simon mistakenly stated in his book that Scott and Dewhurst were divorced at this point. In fact, the couple were over six months into their second union.)

But the euphoria was short-lived. Simon received a call from Nichols at 3:45 A.M. that night to meet him in his hotel room for a matter of life and death. Once they met, Nichols told Simon the horrifying news that Scott wanted to quit the play. After the opening-night revelries had wound down and the last guest had left Scott alone in his hotel room, his old demons began to haunt him. He went to Nichols's room, and for two hours revealed his insecurities and his fear of success. He said he simply couldn't do it, that he'd never been in a hit show before. He would ruin Doc's wonderful play, Maureen's wonderful performance, and Mike's wonderful direction. He was leaving in the morning.

After the initial panic subsided, the show did go on with Scott's understudy. Meanwhile, the producer, director and playwright frantically batted names of possible star replacements back and forth like shuttlecocks. Two days later, Scott returned, and again, like the dysfunctional family of an alcoholic, the *Plaza Suite* company carried on as if the desertion had never occurred. The performance was solid again, and Scott's fears did not resurface. "When he came back, he was crystal clear," said Bob Balaban.

In spite of Scott's disappearances, it was a convivial company, with cast and crew members getting together at the hotel for drinks and word games. One could say there was far too much drinking, with legendary tipplers Scott and Stapleton leading the booze brigade. During one of the after-performance parties, Scott got mad at Stapleton for some reason that she could not remember, and stormed out of the room. The rest of the night was a blank to Stapleton. She recalled in her memoir that the next morning, as the company was assembled onstage for rehearsal, Mike Nichols came in "carrying what looked to be the swamp-infected remains of some poor, drowned animal. It turned out to be my mink coat." Scott had been so furious at Stapleton's "offense" that he attempted to flush her mink coat down the hotel toilet. Stapleton could laugh and forgive.

The play finally opened in New York on February 14, 1968, and the combination of Mike Nichols and Neil Simon continued to prove a delightful one for critics and audiences alike. The surprise was Scott's ability to handle comedy, since he had been known primarily for his intense portrayals of dark, malignant villains. "We've all known for a long time that Mr. Scott was a fascinating actor in serious roles, but in his three parts he demonstrates that he is a superb comedian, with a maniacal gift for wild, uninhibited roughhouse farce," cheered Richard Watts, Jr. in the *New York Post*. There was also a major movie sale, but Walter Matthau would play Scott's roles.

Despite the accolades from the press and laughter from the public, Scott was still haunted by his particular demons and letting them out at inopportune times. Elizabeth Wilson remembered,

> We had the opening night party for *Plaza Suite* at the Plaza. The next day when Colleen went to work on *More Stately Mansions* with Ingrid Bergman, she was all banged up. George had beaten her up. Her leading man, Arthur Hill, turned to her just before their first entrance and he was furious. He said, 'I'm going to get that guy'— meaning George. I don't know if he ever did. The story was that after the party at the Plaza, George and Colleen went up to a suite and they had a fight. George threw a bottle of vodka out the window, broke the window. Then he beat her. Crazy, crazy, crazy.

Stapleton and Dewhurst were both nominated for the Tony Award for Best Actress, for *Plaza Suite* and *More Stately Mansions*, respectively. Stapleton recalled the night of the awards at Dewhurst's memorial service several years later:

> George hired a limousine to take us and since we were certain that one of us was bound to win, we each had written acknowledgments

of the other in our acceptance speeches. We sat there smiling and ready. When they announced the nominees for best actress, Colleen and I turned to each other and smiled and got our speeches ready. And whaddya know, they gave the Tony to that cunt from Australia.

The Tony went to Australian Zoe Caldwell, a friend of both Stapleton and Dewhurst, for *The Prime of Miss Jean Brodie*. *Plaza Suite* did not go home empty-handed, though. Nichols won the prize for his direction.

There were no further reports of Scott disappearing. He did leave the company in May 1968 for eye surgery to repair a detached retina, one of his recurring medical problems. He reported a shadow over his vision in his right eye. His ophthalmologist in Westchester recommended he see Dr. Albert Ackerman, one of two eye doctors in Manhattan who specialized in a new form of surgery to repair retinas with a high rate of success. Dr. Ackerman remembered seeing Scott and Dewhurst in his Upper East Side office on a Tuesday afternoon:

> He had just opened in *Plaza Suite*. I knew who he was from the movies. I examined him and drew a map of his right eye, which takes about an hour. I said, "This is very urgent." He was very calm. I knew from my experience that I could handle this and that he would get a perfect result. I told him, "I want to get you into the hospital today and operate tomorrow." He looks at me and says, "I would like to finish out the week."

Nearly forty years later, Dr. Ackerman laughed at recalling Scott's preference to end a week of performances before tending to a threat to his eyesight.

> I thought, What is going on here? He's got an emergency. . . . I didn't want him to lose the vision. I explained the situation. The

shadow was getting close to the center of the eye. By a fraction of a millimeter, he could lose his central vision. He said, "Nevertheless, I would like to finish out the week."

I said, "Look, we do this under one condition. If there is any change in your vision, then you must call me right away. Then we'll get you into the hospital. Otherwise, we'll admit you on Sunday and operate on Monday."

Scott did finish out the week, and the five-hour operation was a success. "An absolutely perfect patient," Ackerman stated, contrary to Scott's image as irascible. "No demands. The retina was attached. He was out of the hospital within a week."

Dr. Ackerman advised Scott he would have to miss four to six weeks of performances. Saint-Subber and Simon hired British actor Nicol Williamson to take over. He and Scott would later play opposite each other in Chekhov's *Uncle Vanya* at Circle in the Square, directed by their *Plaza Suite* director, Mike Nichols.

Once he was back onstage, Scott insisted Dr. Ackerman see the show. In addition to enjoying a delightful comedy, the doctor also got to view a test of his handiwork. In the third act, Scott, as the crazed father of the bride, rammed headlong into the bathroom door behind which his daughter is locked. "If you wanted to test out the entire operation, you couldn't devise a more diabolic experiment," the doctor laughed. "My only instructions when he left the hospital were 'Don't get hit in the eye,' and here he was banging his head into a door eight times a week. I was stunned to see that, but I did examine him regularly. The eye was fine and he maintained his twenty-twenty vision."

In his memoir, Neil Simon recorded one other significant incident relating to the run of *Plaza Suite*. One day while passing Scott's dressing room, the playwright noticed the star reading a thick script. He asked what it was. The actor replied he was reading a terrific screenplay—*Patton*.

11

Patton

General George S. Patton, nicknamed "Old Blood and Guts," was a natural for the big screen and a natural for Scott. Like the actor who would eventually immortalize him, Patton was a magnificent practitioner of his chosen art form who chafed at authorities attempting to rein him in. They both strutted and fretted their hour upon their individual stages and made no compromises with their personal vision. A self-confessed prima donna, Patton daringly commanded Axis-crushing American armies in Africa, Sicily, France, and Germany. But he earned the disapproval of his superiors by slapping a soldier suffering from battle fatigue. He also sparked controversy with his open distrust of the Soviets, proposing to devastate them with an unprovoked attack immediately after the end of World War II. He said what he thought was right and had no patience for diplomacy. Ironically, he did not die in battle, but from wounds received in an automobile accident. *Patton* had been in development hell for nearly twenty years when a script of the project finally reached the hands of the one actor who would make the volatile commander spring to vivid life.

A film biography had first been proposed on October 21, 1951. Frank McCarthy, a staff producer at Twentieth Century-Fox, sent studio head Darryl F. Zanuck a cable suggesting such a project. Zanuck replied with a cable from Europe, "Get going on it." McCarthy had known Patton during World War II when he had served on the Secretary of the War Department's general staff. But he was met by a frontal assault from Patton's widow. She believed the press had tarnished his reputation and did not want further intrusions on her husband's memory. Mrs. Patton managed to prevent cameras churning until her death in 1953. Then the surviving family members resumed the offensive. The general's son and daughter persuaded the Department of Defense to block production for more than a decade.

Eventually, the U.S. government relaxed its stance and allowed Fox to proceed. In 1966, a new screenwriter with directing ambitions named Francis Ford Coppola was hired to write the script because he was young and had no preconceived notions about the complex general. In addition, he had just done work on another war flick, *Is Paris Burning?* Apart from that, the only military experience the future *Godfather* auteur had was playing the tuba in his military-school band.

McCarthy's first choice to play the rebellious general was Spencer Tracy. Through its various stages of preproduction, the role was offered to almost every macho star in Hollywood, including Burt Lancaster, Lee Marvin, Rod Steiger, Kirk Douglas, and Robert Mitchum, all of whom turned it down. John Wayne was briefly considered because of his reputation as a symbol of military invincibility in countless war pictures, but McCarthy felt the Duke lacked the acting chops to convey Patton's ambivalent attitudes toward war and his complex intellectual abilities.

The perfect candidate was finally found when Darryl Zanuck screened *The Bible* for McCarthy, and, pointing to Scott as Abraham, said, "There's your Patton." The maverick leader was lurking under all those Old Testament whiskers. Over the objections of the entire Fox board of directors, who felt he wasn't a big enough name, Zanuck contacted Scott.

Veteran helmer William Wyler was set to direct, but he disliked Coppola's script. So did many of the Fox brass, feeling its unconventional opening (with Patton addressing the audience as if they were his troops) and its acknowledgment of the general's belief in reincarnation were too edgy for a mass-market war film. A second script was written by James Webb of which Wyler approved. By this time Scott had been offered the role with which he would be forever identified. Scott preferred Coppola's version, which took in both the subject's flaws and virtues. Scott found Webb's Patton a one-dimensional war hero. "I simply refused to play George Patton as the standard cliché you get from newspaper clippings of the time," the actor told the *New York Times*. "I didn't want to play him as a hero just to please the Pentagon, and I didn't want to play him as an obvious, gung-ho bully either. I wanted to play every conceivable facet of the man." Scott told McCarthy he did not want to enact another war-crazed General Buck Turgidson from *Dr. Strangelove*.

Wyler decided not to take on *Patton* or Scott, whom he had fired from *How to Steal a Million*. The sixty-four-year-old director, who had endured ulcers on his previous two productions, claimed the six-month shoot in Spain would be too physically taxing. Instead, Wyler went on to a different battlefront, opting to direct a star whose tenacity and demands equaled Scott's: Barbra Streisand in her film debut, *Funny Girl*.

Producer McCarthy was in despair of ever getting his dream project battle-ready. "I had no director and no star," he later told the *New York Times*. "Then Scott's agent called to say he would do it if they reverted to Coppola's script."

Since Coppola had moved on to other projects, McCarthy hired Edmund North to polish Coppola's screenplay. The two shared screenwriting credit. A replacement for Wyler was still needed. Franklin J. Schaffner had just turned in a money-making hit for Fox with *Planet of the Apes*. The studio bigwigs concluded that if Schaffner could stage the battles on a futuristic Earth between gorillas and Charlton Heston (and make them believable), remounting World War II would be a piece of cake.

To prepare for the role, Scott took a leaf from Laurence Olivier's playbook and worked on the character from the outside in. He did an enormous amount of research on the general's appearance to get into his psychological makeup. He endlessly watched newsreels of Patton and read thirteen biographies several times each. When filming started, he had his dentist make a special set of caps just like the general's, shaved his head, and wore a wig of grey crew cut. The applied moles on his face were identical to Patton's. He also filled in part of his nose, and shortened it with tape and putty. One aspect of Patton he decided not to duplicate was the general's uncharacteristically high-pitched, squeaky voice. "I thought about using that," Scott later told Christina Kirk of the *New York Daily News*, "but I was afraid that it might become too distracting for the audience, so I abandoned it rather early in the study. I just used my normal, raspy voice."

Neighbor Scott Fowler recalled a morning when Scott's research for his upcoming role comically collided with the real military:

> I was probably in my senior or junior year in high school. It was a real foggy, foggy morning. All of a sudden we heard a helicopter. There was a small opening in the clouds over this field behind G. C.'s house, it was between his house and our house. This big helicopter landed and came right down into the field. Of course, we all ran out of our house. G. C., Colleen, and their kids came out of their house. It happened to be a Marine helicopter being taken from Maine down to New Jersey and there was no instrumentation in it. Officers got out of the helicopter. It was a Sunday morning. G. C. was in his bathrobe as usual. We were all in our bathrobes and pajamas. They went over to him and said, "Could we maybe use your phone to call our base?" They didn't recognize him. At the time, G. C. was studying for the movie *Patton*. He used to walk around in the fields in the morning, reciting his lines and he would be wearing the uniform. This morning he was wearing his bathrobe and pj's. He invited them in to call their base and have some breakfast. Of course, he said for us to come as well and have breakfast. Anyway, his uniform, the *Patton* uniform, was hanging in the hallway. When these

officers walked in the door and saw all the stars on the uniform, they
came to attention and they said, "Sir, may we use your phone?" It
was just so funny, they just snapped to attention. He looked at them
looking at the uniform and he started laughing and he explained
what it was all about. So when the officer in charge called his home
base, he said, "Sir, you will not believe where we landed. We landed
in General Patton's field and we're here with General Patton right
now." We could almost hear the officer at the other end of the line
saying, "Are you crazy?" That was pretty funny.

Patton began filming on February 1, 1969, outside of Segovia. According to a studio press release, the scheduled shoot would last twenty weeks and, apart from four days of location in England and one in
Morocco, would take the production all over Spain. That country was
chosen because the terrain resembled the lands where Patton fought
from North Africa to Europe and the Spanish had a wealth of weap-
onry from the 1940s. America had supplied them with airplanes and
equipment at the end of WWII and they had kept it in good working
order ever since. There were one hundred speaking parts. The Spanish
Army would be standing in as extras for U.S. troops. The final production cost would be $12,500,000.

That tremendous budget was almost put into jeopardy when Scott
experienced a recurrence of his vision problems. Dr. Albert Ackerman
recalled receiving a phone call from Colleen Dewhurst in the spring
of 1969:

> She was calling from Spain. She says, "George can't see. They've
> stopped production. What should we do? They think he has an-
> other detached retina. His eye is closed and he has pain." I gave her
> the names of a few ophthalmologists in Europe.
>
> She called me back in an hour and says, "George won't see any-
> one but you. Could you fly to Spain to see him?" I said, "Yes, I can
> fly to Spain tomorrow." I had a case in the morning, an emergency

detachment. I said I'll leave in the afternoon and I'll be there. She hangs up. Then I get a call from a Dr. Siegel, head of the medical department at Twentieth Century-Fox. "Dr. Ackerman," he says, "we'll do anything if you can go out and see Scott." So they make arrangements for me and my wife, first-class on TWA. I left the following evening and we flew to Madrid.

We met Colleen and the manager, Chico Day, I think his name was. They met us and said, "George couldn't fly up from Almaria. Would you mind flying down to see him?" I had packed instruments, medication, all sorts of things. We got everything together, sped across Madrid to this private airport and took off in a private, six-passenger plane.

During the trip, Colleen described what was going on with the picture. She said, "George has been carrying the picture. The rushes were sent to Zanuck. Zanuck thought this was the greatest performance given by an American." So we knew we were into something great. Colleen keeps talking on and on as she does in her wonderful voice. Meanwhile, my wife is getting very, very sick. After about a half hour, she says to her, "Colleen, let's not talk." Then there was a sudden silence. We finally arrived at this airport where there was a squadron of Nazi planes on the ground for the film. We get off the plane and Colleen lets out a laugh, I mean this was Mother Earth, and she says, "That's the funniest thing I ever heard"—meaning for someone to tell Colleen not to talk. Thereafter whenever she saw Lynn, my wife, she would say "Let's not talk" as a greeting.

Anyway, they took us immediately to the villa where George was staying. This was Orson Welles's villa. It was a huge mansion, huge living room filled with very depressed people. This was the cast, the producers, and so forth. Production had been stopped for a week. They all didn't know what the outcome was going to be. There was a very large, winding marble staircase about five feet across going upstairs to the second floor. I raced up, went to

A shot of Scott from the early 1960s, just as he was beginning to conquer stage, screen, and television. (PHOTOFEST)

ABOVE LEFT: A young George C. Scott with his mother, Helena Scott, nicknamed "Honey," circa 1935. The elegant Helena was an amateur poet and encouraged her son's love of stories. (COURTESY OF VICTORIA LEWIS)

ABOVE RIGHT: Young George (left) with his father and sister, not long after his mother died. (COURTESY OF VICTORIA LEWIS)

BELOW: The wedding reception of Scott and Carolyn Hughes. From left: the stepfather and mother of the bride, Carl B. Ecker and Mildred Hughes Ecker; the bride and groom; and the stepmother and father of the groom, Betty Hurd Scott and George Dewey Scott. (COURTESY OF VICTORIA LEWIS)

FAR LEFT: George with his sister, Helena, at the wedding reception. (COURTESY OF VICTORIA LEWIS)

LEFT: Carolyn and George with baby Victoria, December 1952. (COURTESY OF VICTORIA LEWIS)

BELOW: Cross-examining Lee Remick in *Anatomy of a Murder* (1959). Scott's electric performance as prosecuting attorney Claude Dancer earned him an Oscar nomination. (PHOTOFEST)

RIGHT: With Colleen Dewhurst in a publicity shot for their joint guest appearances on *Ben Casey* (1961). (PHOTOFEST)

BELOW: As the war-crazed General Buck Turgidson in *Dr. Strangelove* (1964). (PHOTOFEST)

ABOVE: One of Scott's favorite pastimes was softball. (PHOTOFEST)

BELOW: With Cicely Tyson (far right) in *East Side/West Side* (1963–64). The CBS-TV series was praised for its tackling of socially relevant issues, but it was canceled after only one season. (PHOTOFEST)

RIGHT: With Ava Gardner in Rome. While the two were starring in *The Bible* (1966), they carried on an affair. When Scott wanted to marry Gardner, she refused and he reacted violently. (PHOTOFEST)

BELOW: In the role that made him a star—General George S. Patton (1970). (PHOTOFEST)

ABOVE: The slap heard round the world. Patton's striking a soldier got him into hot water. Scott's refusal of the Oscar for the film caused an equally sensational controversy. (PHOTOFEST)

BELOW: With John Huston on the set of *The Last Run* (1971). Conflicts over Huston's rewrites led to the dismissal of the legendary director. (PHOTOFEST)

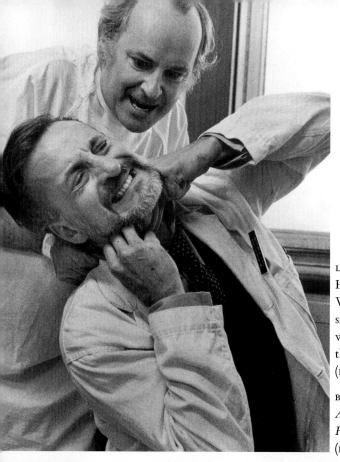

LEFT: Being strangled by Barnard Hughes in *The Hospital* (1971). While filming Paddy Chayefsky's satire, Scott was breaking up with Colleen Dewhurst for the second and final time. (PHOTOFEST)

BELOW: Directing *The Andersonville Trial* (1971) for PBS's *Hollywood Television Theatre.* (PHOTOFEST)

ABOVE: Directing *Rage* (1972) in Arizona. Scott refused to make the edits Warner Brothers wanted, and the film was quickly released without his approval. (PHOTOFEST)

BELOW: The many faces of George C. Scott (clockwise from upper left): Mordecai Jones in *The Flim-Flam Man* (1967); Patton; Harry Garmes in *The Last Run*; Abraham in *The Bible*; and the pixilated judge convinced he is Sherlock Holmes in *They Might Be Giants* (1971). (PHOTOFEST)

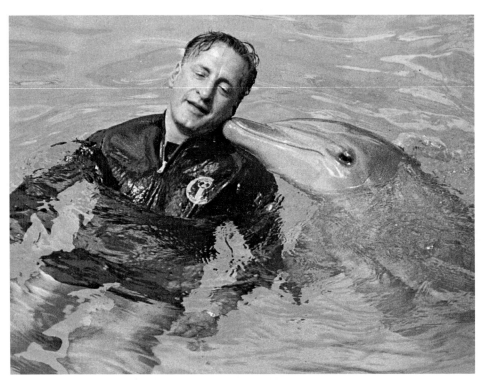

ABOVE: With an aquatic costar in *The Day of the Dolphin* (1973). (PHOTOFEST)

LEFT: Scott and Trish Van Devere leaving a Santa Monica courthouse after getting married in 1972. (PHOTOFEST)

ABOVE: With Van Devere in *The Savage Is Loose* (1974). In addition to starring, Scott directed, produced, put up his own money, and sold the film directly to theatres. After a battle with the ratings board, he lost his entire investment. (PHOTOFEST)

BELOW: With Harvey Keitel, Teresa Wright, and James Farentino in the Circle in the Square revival of *Death of a Salesman* (1975), which he also directed. (PHOTOFEST)

ABOVE: Backstage on the opening night of *Salesman* with (from left) daughter Devon, Van Devere, and son Matthew. (PHOTOFEST)

BELOW: With Mary Hemingway and David Hemmings on the set of *Islands in the Stream* (1977). Scott was playing a character based on Hemingway's late husband. (PHOTOFEST)

With Nathan Lane in Noel Coward's *Present Laughter* (1982). (PHOTOFEST)

ABOVE: With Karen Truesdell Riehl and her son, Davey, in Hong Kong while filming *China Rose* (1983). (COURTESY OF KAREN TRUESDELL RIEHL)

BELOW: At the Monterey Pro-Am golf tournament in 1983. From left: Karen Truesdell Riehl; Scott's publicist, Jim Mahoney; two unidentified friends of Scott's; GCS; Jack Lemmon; and Pat Mahoney. Scott and Riehl were attempting to rekindle their college romance. (COURTESY OF KAREN TRUESDELL RIEHL)

LEFT: With Madeline Kahn in the short-lived Fox sitcom *Mr. President* (1987–88). (PHOTOFEST)

BELOW: An all-time low. In the 1990s, Scott was nearly decapitated by Viveca Lindfors in *The Exorcist III* (1990). (PHOTOFEST)

In *Inherit the Wind* (1996) on Broadway. Despite ill health and a sexual harassment lawsuit brought by his former assistant, Scott delivered a powerful performance and was nominated for a Tony Award. (PHOTOFEST)

his room. There he was with his right eye closed. He greeted me: "Hello, Albert."

I asked what happened to him. He said, "I don't know. I can't see and I've got pain in the eye." I said, "Let's get to work." I examined him for an hour, did all the tests possible. There was no detachment. I saw some signs of inflammation or slight infection on the outside of the eye, which wouldn't account for his symptoms. I thought maybe he had some problems with his optic nerves to account for his loss of vision.

I said, "What you need is a rest and antibiotics. I'm going to give you some sedatives and we'll check you in the morning." I didn't know quite was going on except the retina was fine. I left the room. As I went down the staircase, everybody stood up and looked up at me. It was like a scene out of a movie, except I didn't have a script. I suddenly opened my mouth and said, "Mr. Scott does not have a retinal detachment. You can resume production on Monday." The background to this is when Dr. Siegel called me and said they'd do anything to get me out there, he said, "By the way, we're shooting the invasion of Anzio on Monday. We have a million dollars invested in this scene. If Mr. Scott has a detachment, could you please wait until he finishes the scene?" At that time, I said, "I'm not going through this again. I went through this with *Plaza Suite* where he delayed the operation for a show. If he has a detachment, I'm taking him home right away. I don't care about the scene. I have to save his sight."

So I made my announcement. Everyone hurrahed. The next morning, I saw him. The eye is open. The pain is gone. He still had trouble seeing with that eye, but he was well enough to film.

Even with the screenplay he had wanted and the go-ahead from his eye doctor, Scott was still not happy. There were arguments over interpretation. He told the *London Sunday Times* on April 3, 1969, "It's an unactable part and I'm not doing too well. It's an inadequate script and

it's very difficult for me. Patton was misunderstood contemporane-
ously and he's misunderstood here—and I'm ashamed of being part of
it." In the same interview, he stated, "I'm doing the best I can to load
the part with pyrotechnics, with smoke screens, with every dirty sneak
actor's trick to bring what I want to bring out, but I'm thoroughly
disgusted with the entire project."

A week later Scott was riding in a battered, chartered DC-7 from
Almaria to Crete to film the Sicilian invasion. On the flight, Scott told
reporter Carole Kass of *Variety*, "I have enormous affection for General
Patton, a feeling of amazement and respect for him. I hope the film
comes out not as an apology, but as a fair and respectful portrait of
Patton." Scott told Kass he was promised changes in the script before
he signed his contract. When they were not made, he wanted changes
in the script during shooting. McCarthy stressed that the final script
had been approved by both Zanucks at Fox (father Darryl and his son,
Richard, who was head of production), Pentagon historians, and General Omar Bradley, the film's military technical adviser. There would
be no further changes.

According to Kass's *Variety* report and Lawrence H. Suid's com-
prehensive study of military movies, Scott would demonstrate more
"dirty sneaky actor's tricks" to let filmgoers know he was not pleased
with the entire script. The map-room scene at Patton's headquarters
in Sicily when he plans to beat British commander Montgomery to
Messina—despite such a move leaving Bradley's forces to fight alone
though the center of Sicily—was one Scott wanted to scrap, because
it made Patton unsympathetic. However, by McCarthy's edict, there
would be no deletions or changes. When the time came to shoot the
scene in question, Scott indulged in "pyrotechnics" by hitting the map
and calling Montgomery an expletive (neither action was in the script).
Schaffner just shot around Scott, avoiding a confrontation.

During a later scene there was one crucial piece of dialogue for Patton to deliver to General Lucien K. Truscott, Jr. about the same ma-
neuver: "If your conscience won't let you conduct this operation I will

relieve you and let someone else do it." George wanted this line cut, believing it made Patton seem too harsh and glory-hungry. A compromise was reached between Scott and Schaffner. The star would deliver the line while lying down to indicate that this seemingly inhumane command to abandon Bradley's troops was delivered due to exhaustion. Scott later stated in Suid's book that he was lying down as a protest because Patton would never take such a physical position and it would show Scott's anger at the scene not being accurate.

Scott also disagreed over the most famous scene in the film, the brilliant opening sequence in which Patton, like a foul-mouthed Henry V on St. Crispin's Day, exhorts his troops to go through the Nazis like "crap through a goose." Scott was hesitant to have it placed at the opening of the film, according to producer David Brown, because "he thought if we started that high, we'd never get back to the peaks. Well, we did. We asked him to shoot it at the end of the picture and never told him we'd used it at the beginning." The star made filming of the sequence more difficult by insisting on repeating the entire speech every time a retake was needed rather than picking it up from where a new camera angle would start. He filmed it eight times and was letter perfect each take.

But all was not enmity between star and director. Scott also told Suid that Schaffner was "personally kind to me and tolerant of even my worst peccadilloes."

The peccadilloes were comparatively minor in relation to Scott's past drinking bouts during Broadway runs and film shoots. Karl Malden, Omar Bradley to Scott's Patton, recalled one such insignificant but revealing delay in shooting due to the star's temperament:

> We were working at Almaria in the mountains and the snow was like powder. If the wind blew, you got it all over your face. We were supposed to start work at 1 P.M. And we're working there at about 11:30, 12 noon, and the director, Franklin Schaffner, says, "Where's Scott?" They found him. He was playing Ping-Pong

with a stuntman and he was losing. He wouldn't stop playing until he beat the man. He said to the stuntman, "Don't you throw a game. I'm going to beat you." He finally did win. He was a half hour late.

Malden stated in his memoir *When Do I Start?* that it was known among the company that, despite Dr. Ackerman's warning not to, Scott was drinking heavily during shooting, but it never showed in his work. When asked how cast and crew knew about Scott's imbibing, Malden said,

> No one in the cast said anything about it. At one point, the producer Frank McCarthy came to three or four of us in the cast as we were having dinner and he said, "I want to talk to you fellows. We all know Scott is drinking heavily, and sometimes on other pictures he's gone on these binges." We all said, "Yeah." So McCarthy says, "If you're having dinner with him and he asks you to order a drink, don't ever order a drink with him. You can drink what you want, but nothing alcoholic." So I started ordering Cokes, which were very big in Europe then. We [Scott and I] never went out to dinner. But we did have midday lunches. There was never much liquor for those unless you brought it yourself. From that day on, I've never had a drink. I just don't need one. I saw what happened to a great talent when he wasn't feeling well.

"There were times when I got frightened," George later admitted to interviewer Rex Reed. "Things weren't going right so I went out and got shit-faced. That's me. Something goes wrong, I find a bottle. I don't like it about myself but I've done it before and I'll do it again."

Despite the private drinking, there was no alcoholic crimp in the action during *Patton*. "He had energy, vitality, drive," said Malden. "He was always there. There was no waiting. He would walk right in and say, 'Let's do it.' The man is in every minute of that film. We worked six days a week for five months. There was no stopping. He was in almost every scene and it was not an easy picture to make. We were all over Spain."

When the picture was released, the studio wanted it to be perceived as more than a war film. Schaffner stated that out of two hours and forty-nine minutes, only eleven minutes contain battle scenes. McCarthy wanted the film seen as an objective study of a complex figure and fought against the subtitle "Old Blood and Guts." He wanted no extra verbiage in the credits to sway viewers' opinions on the subject. It was finally released in 1970 as *Patton: A Salute to a Rebel*. In England it was called *Patton: Lust for Glory*.

Patton not only changed the perception of its title figure, but also that of its leading man. Scott had been recognized as a sturdy character actor, but he was not yet an above-the-title star. His name alone would not bring in audiences. *Patton* would change all that. It was the first hit picture Scott did in which he was the undisputed center of attention. Despite his vivid performances in *Anatomy of a Murder*, *The Hustler*, and *Dr. Strangelove*, the stars of those pictures were unquestionably James Stewart, Paul Newman, and Peter Sellers. In *The List of Adrian Messenger*, he was upstaged by John Huston's gimmick of disguised movie stars. He was in almost every scene of *Petulia* and the story was told from his character's point of view, but he shared the limelight with Julie Christie in the title role. He had a comic field day in *The Flim-Flam Man*, but Michael Sarrazin's character had the main action.

In *Patton*, Scott was the star, the sun around which every other planet revolved. From the moment he steps in front of the football-field-sized American flag in the opening to the final moments walking his dog through the fields as Jerry Goldsmith's eerie music recalling past battles plays, Scott *is* Patton. While the more famous scenes such as the slapping of the shell-shocked solider and the screaming of admiration for Rommel during the tank battle resonate with the actor's craft, it's the silent moments that add texture. Watch as he scornfully regards the sorry shape of American troops during a surprise inspection. His mouth is turned down in an exaggerated scowl so that he resembles a disappointed eagle. His eyes scorch a lieutenant attempting a smile. Then the flicker of a smile emerges as he slowly returns the salute of a gang of ragamuffin Arab boys. It's totally his show. With the exception of Karl Malden's Omar Bradley, none of the supporting cast registered beyond feeding lines to the general.

Judith Crist of *New York* called Scott's acting "one of the great performances of all time." Andrew Sarris in the *Village Voice* said he "cannot be praised highly enough for capturing both the violence and the vulnerability of the Patton personality without denigrating either into vulgar caricature or cardboard sentimentality. Scott inhabits his character without inhibiting him."

Stanley Kauffmann in the *New Republic* gave a mini-retrospective of George's career:

> George C. Scott as Patton is truly commanding, fulfilling the hard, manic streak that was apparent in him years ago when he was playing Richard III and Jaques and Shylock for Joseph Papp in New York. Scott was never shy of self-confidence and now he has brought up additional power to support it. His voice has hoarsened rather than mellowed through his career, but in the latency of explosion that lets an actor make us pleasantly nervous, he is the most remarkable star since Brando.

The comparison would soon become ironic as within two years both rebellious actors would reject Hollywood's highest honor.

Despite the critical accolades for Scott, *Patton* wasn't an immediate smash at the box office in its initial early 1970 release. It wasn't doing nearly as well as *M*A*S*H*, Fox's other, decidedly different war movie. Robert Altman's offbeat black comedy followed a crew of nonconformist surgeons through the Korean War and would later inspire a long-running, much-beloved TV series. The antiwar antics of

Hawkeye and Trapper John would have shocked Patton, though they appealed to young moviegoers disenchanted with the quagmire in Vietnam. Scott may have been motivated by the Altman film's success when he screamed at a Fox publicist, "That goddamn piece of shit is demeaning to the American military!"

Patton received a shot in the arm when President Richard Nixon stated he enjoyed the biopic. There were even rumors that the movie (which he viewed several times), inspired Nixon to order a military incursion into Cambodia—leading some political analysts to conclude the leader of the free world was drawing inspiration from the fantasy world of the movies. Nixon later denied the connection, joking he had seen *The Sound of Music* twice and it hadn't made him a writer. (Huh?)

The stamp of approval from the commander-in-chief energized more hawkish moviegoers to get to their local theatres. The film's subtitle, *Salute to a Rebel*, on the other hand, was meant to appeal to younger, anti-Vietnam viewers. The film's poster added to the entice-ment: "Patton was a rebel before it became fashionable. He rebelled against the Establishment—and its ideas of warfare." Younger audi-ences could interpret Patton's anger at his superiors and his own non-conformism as an indictment against the madness of all war, including the conflict then raging in Southeast Asia. The film benefited from this dual perspective, attracting two disparate audiences.

As *Patton* was winning the battle of the box office, its star would soon be leading his own one-man skirmish in a long-running war with his greatest foe. Like Don Quixote charging the windmill, Scott was sharpening his rhetorical lance and preparing to mount his steed to ride off against what he regarded as the gigantic golden symbol of show-biz chicanery: the Oscar.

12

Refusing to March
in the "Meat Parade"

BEFORE PICKING UP THE LANCE of Don Quixote to tilt at the giant golden windmill called Oscar, Scott donned the eccentric costume of another idealistic battler for truth and justice: the deerstalker and Inverness cape of Sherlock Holmes . . . or a man who believes he's Sherlock Holmes.

A few months after the completion of *Patton*—with a brief interlude to play a novelist with a split personality in an NBC television play called *Mirror, Mirror, Off the Wall* and cavort in a TV comedy special with Johnny Carson, Marian Mercer, and Maureen Stapleton—he shifted gears from the hard-assed, psychologically complex military genius to a lovable goofball who would not be uncomfortable in a sentimental Frank Capra comedy like *Mr. Deeds Goes to Town* or *You Can't Take It With You.* He spent January and early February of 1970 filming the romantic comedy *They Might Be Giants.* Scott would later joke on Carson's talk show that "they" had turned out to be midgets.

James Goldman's stage comedy of the same name had been presented in London at Joan Littlewood's theatre in 1964. This meringue-light whimsy concerned a daffy judge, suffering from the delusion that he is fiction's most famous detective, and his female psychiatrist, who happens to be named Dr. Watson (first name Mildred). There had been talk of Harold Prince directing Scott and Dewhurst in an American staging, but these plans never came to fruition. Joanne Woodward starred as the ironically named therapist in this film edition. It was the second feature at Universal to be produced by her husband, Paul Newman, whose production company (co-owned with John Foreman) had previously done *Winning*. Newman had briefly considered playing opposite his wife in the comedy, but he quickly realized his heartthrob image was not ideal casting for the light-headed jurist. Besides, he was filming *Sometimes a Great Notion* while *Giants* was being shot. Due to arctic winter conditions and a garbage strike in New York City, Woodward had a miserable time. But she later stated playing opposite the fiery Scott was like acting with an "erupting volcano," which presumably helped to make the freezing temperatures bearable.

Director Anthony Harvey, who had more success bringing another Goldman play (*The Lion in Winter*) to the screen, agreed that filming took place under "unbelievably severe weather conditions." But he put a more positive spin on the shoot, telling the *New York Daily News*, "It was an exciting experience in spite of the terrible winter: snow or rain or bitter cold." *Giants* was filmed entirely in New York City except for one scene in a Woodbury, New Jersey, supermarket. There were scenes all over the city: Central Park, Wall Street, Times Square, Greenwich Village, and a marvelous old movie theatre in Brooklyn called the Fox.

After initial screenings, the studio made drastic changes. Universal execs were worried audiences wouldn't understand the basic premise, so they spelled it out for them. The final scene of Justin (Scott's pixilated judge) and Mildred (Woodard's smitten psychologist) urging their eccentric friends to fight off police and hospital attendants in the New Jersey supermarket was cut, and a clumsily written voice-over prologue about all great men having their adversaries (such as Holmes and Moriarty) was added. Anthony Harvey denounced the final film. Most critics objected to the studio's mangling and found much to dislike in the final, truncated version.

Giants was released—or, more accurately, dribbled out—by Universal in several screenings from March through June of 1971. The notice from Molly Haskell of the *Village Voice* was typical of critics' re-action: "The wit turns to Christmas card cuteness, and the film winds up . . . in a veritable miasma of mush." *Saturday Review*'s Hollis Alpert found that the "fanciful mixture of the comedic and the philosophical doesn't jell." But "there is Scott, and he is almost reason enough to see the movie."

There were too many cutesy-poo weirdos as Justin and Mildred ran a wild-goose chase through the city searching for clues leading to the fiendish Professor Moriarty, Holmes's literary nemesis and a figment of Justin's addled imagination. In addition to Scott's mad judge outfitted in a Victorian deerstalker and puffing on a Holmesian pipe, there was an elderly couple sculpting outlandish shrubbery and a librarian (played by the adorable Jack Gilford) who imagines himself to be the Scarlet Pimpernel. Scott was trying for light romantic comedy, an aspect of his talent not usually shown. Haskell in the *Voice* conceded that despite *Giants'* shortcomings, the star was equipped to tackle the genre: "Charm is not a quality Scott is noted for, but here he has it in abundance, making his irresistibility to Miss Woodward quite credible."

After wrapping *Giants*, Scott flew to Los Angeles to begin rehearsals of a television production of *The Andersonville Trial*. But this time he would be behind the camera, making his first attempt at directing after the *Dr. Cook* debacle and his first staging of a film or television project. *Andersonville* was to be the pilot for a new PBS series ambitiously titled *Hollywood Television Theatre*, a program harkening back to the days of live TV drama, when viewers could enjoy original dramas and adapted versions of Broadway hits in their living rooms. Unlike those hectic early days of broadcasting, this production would be taped, not performed live. This would be familiar material for Scott, since he had starred in the 1959 Broadway production of the play.

Rehearsals began on March 18. Scott would be directing William Shatner in his own original role of Chipman, the prosecutor trying the government's case against a Confederate commandant of the titular notorious prisoner-of-war camp. The cast was stuffed with actors best known for their TV work. In addition to Shatner (beloved by sci-fi fans as *Star Trek*'s Captain Kirk), there were Richard Basehart (*Voyage to the Bottom of the Sea*), Buddy Ebsen (*The Beverly Hillbillies*), and other TV veterans like Jack Cassidy, Cameron Mitchell, Albert Salmi, and Martin Sheen. Even the Skipper from *Gilligan's Island*, Alan Hale, Jr., had a silent bit part. Producer Lewis Freedman freely admitted to using Scott's name to lure these top players to work for public television scale.

Also in the cast, playing the tiny role of the soldier who swears in the witnesses, was a much smaller name, Ray Stricklyn, a formerly promising and handsome young actor now dealing with alcoholism. Although he had only a few lines—the administering of the oath repeated for each witness—Stricklyn continually muffed them and shook visibly.

Scott was in a dry phase, having recently spent time in a rehab center, and a burly "watcher" was on the set with him to make sure he didn't take a drink. After a few blown takes, Scott took Stricklyn aside, put an arm on his shoulder, walked down a corridor and reassured the actor. "I think he sensed from his own downfall, that I was suffering and that my shakes weren't just from nerves," Stricklyn later wrote in his memoir. "He knew an alcoholic when he saw one."

Scott's own history with alcoholism and abstinence was haphazard, veering from sober periods to oblivious binges. His attempts to control his drinking were all over the map. He had been active in Alcoholics Anonymous for two years after his night in jail in 1958. He would occasionally try "ten-cent therapy," i.e., telephoning fellow alcoholics who were on the wagon for moral support. Art Carney, his costar from *The Yellow Rolls-Royce*, told a *Playboy* interviewer: "One drinker understands another. He was in bum shape, so he called and we had a long chat."

Scott preferred this ad hoc form of peer treatment rather than the formalized program of Alcoholics Anonymous. One of the basic tenets of the organization is that an alcoholic, as opposed to a heavy drinker, has no control of himself once he takes a shot. The prayer that opens every gathering has the members ask God (or their higher power) to help them "accept the things I cannot change, change the things I can, and the wisdom to know the difference." Buying into the A.A. ethic would mean admitting he had no control over alcohol, that for his sanity's sake he could not take one drop, and it appears Scott was incapable of admitting that.

The Andersonville Trial aired nationally on PBS on Thursday, May 14, 1970. Scott introduced the show with a brief improvised prologue. The telecast received raves from critics. Viewed today, Andersonville comes across as a filmed theatre presentation rather than an intimate television special. Shatner as the prosecutor, Cassidy as the defense attorney, and Basehart as the defendant give broad, stagey performances, raising their voices and gesturing melodramatically as if they were trying to reach the back row of the balcony rather communicating with each other in a confined court chamber. Cameron Mitchell as the chief judge has moments of power and presence without going over the top, but eventually joins in the shouting matches. Only Buddy Ebsen in the cameo role of a Confederate doctor has the requisite small scale necessary for the intimate medium of TV. Scott emphasized this by choosing a tight shot of Ebsen's hands as he haltingly describes the horrors of the camp. There is diverse work with the camera, with a variety of shots and cuts within the small studio set, but the theatricality of the major performances blunts the potentially devastating impact of the tragedy. Still, Scott demonstrated the ability to communicate with actors and effectively use the camera to tell a story.

Scott was not only branching out as a director, he was also testing the waters as a producer. The August 12, 1970 edition of Variety reported that he had bought the rights to Harrow Alley, an unproduced screenplay about the Great Plague of London, for $150,000. The script was written by Walter Brown Newman, an Oscar nominee for Cat Ballou and Ace in the Hole, eight years earlier and passed over by every major Hollywood studio at least twice. Scott first learned of the script on the set of *The List of Adrian Messenger*. He was playing catch with Tony Huston when Newman was visiting the boy's father, and the actor overheard the screenwriter describing the story to John Huston. There was talk of Huston directing the project with Peter O'Toole and Scott, but nothing ever came of these plans. Scott later phoned Newman and told him he could not get *Harrow Alley* out of his mind. When he had enough money, he wanted to option it. After options purchased by Huston and producer Ingo Preminger (Otto's brother) expired, Scott took one in 1968 for $15,000, and then another for the same price in 1969. When Scott couldn't get the film produced after the second option ran out, Newman's agent wanted to move on to other offers. The actor took a risk and bought the film outright.

Scott planned to produce, direct, and star in the film. "I suddenly got a check through Western Union for $150,000," Newman recalled to the *Los Angeles Times*. "I have to respect Scott for that—he put his money where his mouth is. So it became his, and I don't think I've ever heard from him again."

News of the project would crop up in gossip columns over the next twenty-five years. Some Hollywood insiders would hail the script as brilliant. Copies of it turned up in screenwriting workshops. "*Harrow Alley* is one of the best screenplays I've ever read," said Dorothy Wilde, story editor at Twentieth Century Fox. "It's an amazing piece of work." But its dark subject matter, large budget, and Scott's insistence on filming it himself without cuts proved to be insurmountable deal-breakers. "One of the most brilliant comedies I have ever read is a comedy, believe it or not, about the Black Death, written by Walter Newman," writer-director Frank Pierson observed. "The rights to it were bought by George C. Scott, who wants to direct it. But nobody wants him to direct this particular project and he won't release it. So it will never get made." Pierson's prediction was accurate.

Though nary a foot of film was shot on *Harrow Alley*, Scott never let go of it. This impossible-dream-impractical-project theme would recur a few years later when Scott got a hold of *The Savage Is Loose* and, like a dog with a blanket in its mouth, would only release it after it had been torn to shreds.

Back from directing, Scott returned to acting where he could earn more. For his next gig in front of the cameras, he made the transition from the whimsical would-be Sherlock Holmes to the brooding Rochester in the most Gothic of all Gothic romances, *Jane Eyre*. Charlotte Brontë's classic novel had been filmed by Hollywood before with Joan Fontaine and Orson Welles.

Susannah York, the vivacious British actress who had made a specialty of psychologically damaged heroines in such films as *Freud*, *The Killing of Sister George*, *They Shoot Horses, Don't They?*, and *Images*, would add the sturdier Jane to her gallery of case studies.

In June of 1970, Scott flew to Pinewood Studios, England, and then to Muker, a small village in Yorkshire where the majority of the filming would take place. He resided at a hotel in Harrogate, was driven to the location in a black Rolls-Royce, and, like the reclusive Rochester, would remain aloof from his castmates.

York was complimentary in her recollections on working with Scott, but, like most of his leading ladies, she found him somewhat distant: "He was very courteous, always prepared and professional. Quite laconic. He didn't like to rehearse. He had his Winnebago on the set and would play cards between takes. He had two or three men friends with him. Very discreet. Kept to himself."

York was not alone among Scott's leading ladies to comment on his reluctance and trepidation before shooting romantic scenes. Claire Bloom, Shirley MacLaine, Faye Dunaway, and Carlin Glynn would all report Scott's discomfort during their filmed love affairs. York recalled,

> One day we were doing a love scene and he was being rather avuncular, paternal, and I said to him, "No, no, George. You are my one

true love and I am yours. Don't be paternal. Don't act like my father." He found that rather amusing. I would tease him a little bit.
But he didn't seem to be a person who would take very much teas-
ing. British actors tend to rehearse more. He was nice and courteous. He didn't involve himself and didn't want to rehearse.

A taciturn man, very private. Some American actors like Montgomery Clift like to rehearse, but George didn't want to. He didn't
like to rehearse. I felt I knew where Jane was in the story and could
work on it on my own. I thought, "Okay, I can manage on my
own." That was cool.

"Cool" is probably the best adjective to describe the chemistry between Scott and York. As the actress recollected, Scott did not give
himself over to romantic passion. Despite her pleas to be treated as
the object of adoration rather than affection, her Jane is more like a
daughter or niece to Scott's gruff teddy bear of a Rochester. The only
fiery moments occur when Rochester rages at Jane early in their ac-
quaintance. *Variety* characterized his Rochester as "rather like Patton
on a well deserved leave" and that he failed to "bring out the smoldering romanticism, mixed with tyranny and selfishness" of the master of
Thornfield.

Jane Eyre didn't get a wide (or, in fact, any) theatrical distribution
in the U.S., but it was quite popular in Europe. The film was aired
on NBC's blue-ribbon outlet, the *Hallmark Hall of Fame*, in 1971. Both
Scott and York would receive Emmy nominations.

By now *Patton* was in wide release, and Scott was highly in demand.
Among those seeking his services was the trailblazing screenwriter
Paddy Chayefsky, one of the few scribes to have any clout in pictures.
A standard movie business joke of the day (which still holds true) was
the one about the starlet so dumb she slept with the writer to further
her career. A veteran of the Golden Age of Television and the win-
ner of an Oscar for *Marty*, his sensitive character study of a lonely
Bronx butcher, Chayefsky had about as much power as a director or

producer when it came to getting his movies made his way. He wanted Scott for his drama-comedy *The Hospital*. The role in question was Dr. Herbert Bock, a disillusioned physician not unlike Dr. Archie Bollen in *Petulia*, attempting to hold together a big city hospital against the crashing waves of bureaucracy, urban decay and indifference. Just as his beloved medical institution is crumbling, so is his personal life, with his wife kicking him out of the house and both of his children disowning him.

United Artists wanted the conventional likes of Burt Lancaster or Walter Matthau. But Chayefsky held firm for Scott. As he had done with *Patton*, the actor refused at first and then accepted, but he wanted $300,000. This was a high sum for its time and both the writer and the studio balked. Rod Steiger was considered, but he wanted even more. So Scott was hired.

Production was set to begin in March of 1971 after Scott was scheduled to complete *The Last Run*, a thriller that would reunite him with John Huston, who had directed him in *The List of Adrian Messenger* and *The Bible*. There would be ironic parallels between Scott's personal conflicts and the fictional crises facing the characters he would play in *Run* and *Hospital*.

Between *Jane Eyre* and *The Last Run*, Scott squeezed in a television production of Arthur Miller's *The Price,* filmed in London. Once again, through his roles the actor was facing father issues. Scott was playing Victor Franz, a middle-aged policeman who gave up a promising career in medicine in order to support his selfish father during the Depression. He is brought together with his long-estranged brother (Barry Sullivan), an established doctor, when their father dies and his belongings must be sold off. Dewhurst costarred as Esther, Victor's long-suffering wife. The finished production was considered by many to be superior to the original Broadway staging. Cecil Smith of the *Los Angeles Times* called it "magnificent" and went on to state that if Patton weren't his first pick as Scott's finest performance, "then this would be my choice. It is filled with a kind of massive acceptance, a pitiless understanding that despite his hatred for every day he has spent on the cops, it was the thing he had to do."

Nineteen seventy-one was a year of great change for Scott. He would become an international superstar reaching the zenith of his acclaim, landing fifth on Quigley Publications' poll of film exhibitors of top ten box office stars behind John Wayne, Clint Eastwood, Paul Newman, and Steve McQueen. He would also meet the woman for whom he would leave Dewhurst for the second and final time.

The year began full of professional promise. On January 4, Scott returned to Spain, the locale of *Patton*, to begin filming *The Last Run* for MGM. He chose this chase thriller because it reminded him of the Humphrey Bogart pictures he had loved as a kid in Michigan. (Several of those films were directed by John Huston.) Scott was cast as Harry Garmes, a retired criminal living in a Spanish coastal town. He is called into action one last time to drive the getaway car, a 1957 BMW 503, for a safecracker busting out of prison. While transporting the ex-con and his girlfriend across the Pyrenees and into France, Harry falls in love with the latter. For reasons that never become entirely clear in the final convoluted version of Scottish novelist Alan Sharpe's screenplay, the trio are pursued by a gang who are somehow connected to Garmes's escapee passenger. After several car chases and explosions, Harry is double-crossed by everyone he trusted and lies bleeding on a beach.

Ironically, Scott had asked for Huston as a director. He realized he had behaved like a maniac over Ava Gardner during the filming of *The Bible* and was grateful to Huston for his indulgence. Conditions seemed palsy-walsy on Huston's end as well. He appeared to be pleased with the script. He read it in one night after producer Carter DeHaven brought it to him at the Connaught Hotel in London and said, "It's a natural. I don't want to change a word, I love it." The caveat that followed—"There may be a couple of areas we should discuss when we get into it"— should have rung a few bells in the producer's head, but the great man had consented to direct and why stir up trouble?

For the long shots, Musante's Spanish stand-in was used. For the close-ups, the actor, a native of Bridgeport, Connecticut, with no experience with bulls, was uncertain to say the least. He was given some brief instructions by a local expert and then spoke to his director.

"All right, I've got one problem," Musante informed Huston. "I'm scared stiff. Now tell me what I'm supposed to do about that."

Huston laughed. Then, to get his reluctant actor to perform, the sixty-five-year-old legend lowered himself into the ring with his Cuban cigar still in his mouth. A dozen extras and townspeople held the bull in position. Huston moved to the spot he wanted Musante to assume and took the *muleta*, the red cape. At his signal, the bull was released and Huston made a pass over the charging mass of black flesh and sharp horns. The animal might have gored the gallant director, and Huston knew this. It was a singularly brave act, but a foolhardy one. The ballsy auteur was flaunting his machismo—but neither Musante nor Scott was watching. Both actors walked away from the location as the director was flashing his cape. The entire day's shooting was scrapped and Huston's beloved bullfight was cut from the script.

Over thirty years later, Tony Musante spoke of his dissatisfaction with the fluid state of the script:

> I said to Jane [my wife], "This is really terrible. I said yes because of George and John Huston. I read the script and fell in love with it. Now I'm reading something that's completely different. We go to wardrobe and makeup tomorrow. What am I supposed to do?" Then I thought, "Hey, come one, you're in Spain. Go to wardrobe. Everything is going to work out." About three or four days into shooting, George and I are sitting in the car used in the film, and he says to me, "Have you read the new script?" I said yes, and he asked me, "Do you like it?" I said no. He said, "We gotta do something about this." The new script wasn't even finished yet. To shorten the story, over the next couple of weeks, every day we would be shooting a different scene, sometimes from the old

script, sometimes from the new script. The basic thing was we weren't shooting the script that we started out with.

As I understand it, John and his son Tony were rewriting the script. George was furious. This went on for three weeks.

Scott missed two days of filming, claiming he was sick, but word on the set was he was sitting out in protest over Huston's script alterations.

"Sure there were script problems," unit publicist Bayley Silleck told Backes. "Huston and some of the other members of the company didn't see eye-to-eye on a couple of character interpretations, and he decided to stand on his integrity. We'll have it all straightened out in a couple of days."

Silleck's optimism was not borne out. Scott continued to complain about the script rewrites and the unsuitability of the leading lady, French actress Tina Aumont, the daughter of Jean-Pierre Aumont and the late Maria Montez. Scott claimed her eyes weren't working. "She couldn't act, it was as simple as that," Alan Sharpe said of Aumont.

If Tony Huston is to be believed, the conflicts were driving the actor to bizarre behavior. Young Huston claimed Scott ordered his Patton uniforms sent to the set and began parading around in them. *Time* magazine reported shouting matches in the early hours of the morning between the fiery star and the producers.

Tony Huston theorized to Huston family biographer Lawrence Grobel about the roots of the friction between his father and Scott: "I'd seen Scott and Dad over the years . . . there was some sort of strange chemistry there. I didn't think it was the script; there was something else cooking between them. Dad said he thought George C. Scott was a coward. To Dad, this was like seeing a flaw going right through the spirit of a man. And for this reason, Scott drinks. Whenever Scott was around Dad on a picture, you would end up with Scott drinking and trouble."

Scott may have been intimidated by the powerful older man, or perhaps Huston reminded the actor of his father. Scott wanted Huston's approval and may have resented him for this. "Huston's the greatest man who ever lived," Scott told his driver at one point during the production. The admiration was not mutual. Huston saw the actor as weak, a drunkard, a womanizer, a victim of his passion for Ava Gardner. All of these emotions were boiling beneath the surface as the battle for control of the picture raged on. Huston had been hired to make a John Huston picture and he was going to make one, goddamn it. Scott and DeHaven thought such a film would not sell in the 1970s market. The actor's conflicted emotions about the director prevented Scott from directly confronting him about his dissatisfaction with the script. On January 22, a drunken Scott called Gladys Hill at 4 A.M. to discuss his complaints. When she told him it was too late, the star roused DeHaven and they both met with Huston. The director later remembered that the only caveat Scott expressed during this late-night confab was over one scene that he wasn't even in. The meeting ended at ten o'clock that morning with the actor declaring to Huston, "You're the boss and anything you say goes and that's all there is to it!" Despite a long nap, Scott did not sleep off the previous night's alcohol intake and was unable to work that day.

A few days after his last delay of production, Scott went to DeHaven at two-thirty in the morning—the wee hours being his favorite time for confronting the creative team—and delivered an ultimatum to the producer. This was not the script he had agreed to do. He had chartered a plane to take him to Madrid and he was going home. DeHaven then summoned Huston, who insisted that the changes he'd made were right. In the end, the star won out over the director.

On January 28, Huston, Aumont, and several members of the crew left the set due to "artistic differences." The crew was gathered a few miles outside of Granada where they were shooting. Scott and DeHaven drove up. The producer informed them that Huston had been replaced. Both he and Scott expressed their admiration for the legendary director, but they believed the original script would make a better picture. DeHaven went on to say that he hoped everyone would stay with the film and that he had spoken with Huston, who had expressed a similar wish. "God help me, I had to make a decision," Scott said softly. "I want to make a good picture. I dumped John Huston." He repeated the last phrase. DeHaven asked if anyone had any questions or comments. Continuity girl Lucy Lichtig recalled that everyone was too stunned to reply. Scott and De Haven got back in their car and drove back to town.

Not surprisingly, Huston left the set with bitter feelings toward Scott. The director stated, "Scott is one of the best actors alive. But my opinion of him as an actor is much higher than my opinion of him as a man." He went even further in an interview for *Rolling Stone*, calling Scott a "shitheel." The whole *Run* experience was so negative for Huston that he never even mentioned it in his memoir, *An Open Book*. (Although, according to makeup man Del Acevedo, Scott insisted that the director be paid his full salary, this gesture apparently did little to sweeten the experience for Huston.)

MGM had Carter DeHaven shut down production for a few days. In a twist of fate common in the small world of show business, MGM was now run by James Aubrey, the former "Smiling Cobra" of CBS and Scott's nemesis during *East Side/West Side*. He dispatched Robert Littman, the walrus-mustached director of European production for the studio, to Granada from London. It was Littman's job to hold *Run* together and convince Aubrey not to shelve the picture altogether.

Littman managed to recruit Richard Fleischer, who had just finished filming *See No Evil*, a thriller starring Mia Farrow, in England, to take over the direction. Here was a journeyman director whose credits ranged from science-fiction fantasy like *Fantastic Voyage* to the overblown musical *Doctor Doolittle* to the fascinating docudrama *The Boston Strangler*. This was a reliable guy who, while not a legend like Huston, could get the job done on time and within budget and could handle Scott. Fleischer took a look at the current shooting screenplay, which was labeled "Third Draft Script." He later told David Lewin in *Today's Cinema*,

I asked, "Where's the first script and why didn't you want to do it?" On Saturday night I read the original script and liked it very much. I told DeHaven I would work the whole of Sunday with the writer Alan Sharp. . . . We got out a complete new continuity script, keeping to the original story lines, the original scenes and bringing out quite clearly the reason why the gangster [Scott] comes out of retirement for his last run.

A replacement also had to be found for the departing Tina Aumont. Scott's choice was Bonnie Bedelia, who had made an impression as the pregnant dance-marathon contestant in *They Shoot Horses, Don't They?* She had just wrapped another picture in Almaria, less than a hundred miles from Granada. Scott sent her the script and called her three times, begging her to take the part, but she wasn't interested.

When Bedelia demurred, Aumont was replaced by American actress Trish Van Devere, a decision that created several parallels between Scott's latest screen role and real life. In the *Last Run*, Dewhurst, who was visiting the set with Alex, Campbell, and her father-in-law, was cast in the cameo role of a prostitute friend of Harry Garmes. They have one extended scene together. On the surface, it appears these two, the retired gangster and the earth-mother hooker, have no emotional ties. It's strictly a business relationship. But it seems she does have feelings for him. She offers to make him dinner before he goes off on his last job. Harry declines the meal, but he trusts her to hold onto his life savings before he leaves, possibly never to return.

Then he meets the new woman with whom he becomes involved. Life imitated art as Scott would later leave the woman playing his old reliable bedmate (Dewhurst) and take up with the actress cast as his new romantic interest (Van Devere). Then, to add to a double dose of irony, in his next film *The Hospital* he would play a doctor going through male menopause whose wife has left him.

Scott was repeating the pattern of his love relationships by running away from intimacy and responsibility. As each of his marriages became weighted down with offspring and mortgages, he ran into the arms of another woman. Dewhurst represented a home with bills to pay and children to support. Van Devere was a beautiful young woman offering adulation and excitement rather than repair estimates and report cards.

Van Devere had made a hit in Carl Reiner's bizarre comedy *Where's Poppa?* and was just starting to get some recognition. She was born Patricia Dressel in Tenafly, New Jersey, and was raised in nearby Norwood. She graduated from Ohio Wesleyan in 1965 and soon thereafter began her theatrical career by touring with the Free Southern Theatre. This was an integrated company that presented plays tackling controversial racial topics like *In White America* and *The Death of Bessie Smith*, in Mississippi and South Carolina. Three years later, after working with the Poor People's Campaign for Martin Luther King, she and Scott Cunningham, a black actor who costarred with her in the Free Southern Theatre, came to New York and formed the Poor People's Theatre. The company also launched a drama school for ghetto youth. The group was supported by Van Devere's salary for the soap opera *One Life to Live*. At twenty, she had married Grant Van Devere at Wesleyan, but the union lasted less than a year.

Trish described her first meeting with Scott to Kay Gardella of the *New York Daily News*: "For a moment or two I didn't give the poor man the benefit of the doubt. When I met him he was wearing a gangster costume—black turtleneck and dark glasses. This was an actor whom I always thought of as absolutely exquisite. . . . At first I was disillusioned, then I realized it was the costume. But I was convinced he was a gangster. Actually, though, we were lucky enough to be smitten right away."

Van Devere and Dewhurst met briefly on the day the former arrived on the set. "Colleen had arrived with the two boys for about a week's vacation," Musante recalled. "There was this role open. This was the point at which Huston was being replaced by Fleischer. He said to her, 'There's this role.'"

"Colleen indicated to me that Trish was going to be a problem for her," Musante remembered. "In retrospect, you can say, 'Oh, yeah, I saw this coming.' But Colleen did indicate in a subtle way that Trish was going to be a problem." During her stay, Musante and his wife, Jane, would have dinner with Dewhurst and Scott. Later during the shoot, after Scott's wife and sons left, Van Devere replaced Dewhurst as his dining companion with the Musantes.

While a romance was blossoming, Scott's demons were being let loose. Betty Rollin witnessed a Scott flare-up while profiling him for *Look* magazine: "Have you ever seen a killer? I haven't and Mr. Scott is not one. But for one moment, in the hotel bar in Granada, he got angry at someone, and chairs flew, and three men held him back and he looked like what I think a killer looks like." Scott later acknowledged throwing a writer's boyfriend (presumably Rollin's beau) out of the bar because the man behaved like a pig.

"George has a temper," Scott Senior told Rollin. "Trouble is, he doesn't get rid of a problem the same day. He stores things up. Then, wham." Musante joked that Dewey loved being interviewed, while his son wanted to be left alone. Musante recalled that at the end of every workweek, there was a party for the *Last Run* company. Scott would foot the bill, not MGM. But the star rarely attended.

Once Fleischer took over, *The Last Run* was off and running. The new director was able to film as much each day as Huston had planned to shoot every three days. But another storm would hit the production when the Oscar nominations came out.

After Huston was gone and before the affair with Van Devere had kindled into a full-blown romance, all of Hollywood was nervously awaiting word from Spain on a much more important matter. Would Scott refuse the Oscar nomination and, given his undeniably brilliant performance as Patton, the award itself? Five days before the nominations were scheduled to be announced and after the balloting for nominations had been closed, George made it official: he would not accept the Oscar. "The Academy Awards show is a meat parade," he told reporters. "Life isn't a race. It's a war of survival and there are many who get crippled and injured on the way. And because it's not a race, I don't consider myself in competition with my fellow actors for rewards or recognition."

Columnist Hank Grant chattily commented, "According to a wire service report outta Spain yesterday morn, George C. Scott has done it again—announced he won't accept an Oscar if he wins because he doesn't like the way the Awards are handled. This will make Scott a big hero with provincial pals in the East whose prime pastime is putting down Hollywood. But here, he's admired only for his timing in making his blast after the Oscar nominations were closed Friday."

The nominations were announced on February 22 and Scott was indeed in the final Oscar cut. His performance as Patton was nominated for Best Actor along with Melvyn Douglas (*I Never Sang for My Father*); Jack Nicholson (*Five Easy Pieces*); Ryan O'Neal (*Love Story*); and his *Dr. Strangelove* and *East Side/West Side* colleague James Earl Jones (*The Great White Hope*). As he had done in 1962, he responded with a telegram sent to the Academy, stating: "[P]eculiar as it may seem, I mean no offense to the Academy. I simply do not wish to be involved. I will not attend the awards ceremony nor will any legitimate representative of mine attend." Only one previous Oscar winner had declined the award. Screenwriter Dudley Nichols refused to accept his 1936 Oscar for *The Informer* when the Academy was seen as a front for studio union-busting among movie peons like writers, directors, and performers. He accepted it two years later. But Scott was the first acting nominee ever to outright reject the honor.

Scott was perceived by some in the Hollywood community as a bad loser. He had previously lost the Oscar to Hugh Griffith (*Ben-Hur*) and George Chakiris (*West Side Story*) for performances in *Anatomy of a Murder* and *The Hustler* that were generally considered superior to those of the winners. But he told the press that he genuinely did not like the competitive nature of the Oscars. There were plenty willing to record his opinions. The international press descended on *The Last Run* set. *Time* magazine put him on its cover. Morley Safer arrived with a *60 Minutes* film crew.

Scott told Betty Rollin, "The public process of putting actors in competition with each other, when actors are colleagues and must be colleagues in order to survive, is a cruel thing." Similarly, Musante recalled,

> He told me the Academy Awards was a meat parade. Actors are always in competition, he said. You're always competing for the role. But it's not like a football game. There are no points to be scored. It's all subjective and how can you say that this actor is better than that actor? He also said what really upset him was when Brando didn't get the Academy Award for *Streetcar*. "If Brando can't get the award for *Streetcar*, then what the hell is this all about, what good are the nominations?"

But why did he accept the awards he received from reviewers' groups? The other awards he had received for *Patton* were not decided upon by a nomination process. The critics got together and voted for their favorites. The winners were just the winners and there was no humiliating step of being nominated and losing. Scott would later win—and accept—Emmy Awards for his television work in *The Price* and *Twelve Angry Men*. He explained that the TV honors were decided upon by a panel of anonymous judges rather than the very public body of Academy Award voters, so there was no intense, Oscar-style campaigning for them. Likewise, Scott didn't reject his four Tony nominations for his Broadway performances, apparently because there was no intense campaigning for these theatre accolades. He even cohosted the Tonys the season he was appearing onstage in *Sly Fox*.

Scott did not acknowledge his nomination and win of the Hollywood Foreign Press's Golden Globe Award for *Patton*, which was unofficially accepted for him by Jane Wyman. There is no record of what happened to the award itself.

Scott considered himself a man of principle and integrity. Those were qualities he admired in Patton, and his beliefs contributed to the brilliance of his performance. With the Oscar rejection, he saw himself as living up to the ideals of carrying through what you believe in regardless of the consequences or the opinions of others. He was standing up for artistic purity in a world of shallow commercialism.

On the other hand, he was a sensitive and insecure man. Having been publicly perceived as deeply wanting to win the Oscar for *Anatomy of a Murder*, he felt humiliated by losing it. Surely he would be less vulnerable if he could act like he didn't care at all and reject his subsequent nominations for *The Hustler* and *Patton*.

Strength and integrity on one side, fear and shame on the other. Scott would alternate between these twin poles throughout his personal and professional life.

With *Patton* and the Oscar nomination refusal, Scott was the most sought-after actor in the world, but already he was making noises about quitting acting. "I have reached a point where I have to go in a different direction," he told Michael Owen of the *Evening Standard*. "I wouldn't like to become a has-been if I could avoid it. We have a name for this in America. It is called quitting while you're ahead."

The Last Run completed its schedule in eight weeks, one month later than originally planned. It opened to negative reviews and poor box office in July 1971. The *New York Times*'s Roger Greenspan sniffed that the "automobile chase sequences, for all the billowing dust and squealing tires, seem to move at thirty miles an hour." The only elements to escape critical lashing were Sven Nykvist's luscious cinematography of Spain, Dewhurst's earthy cameo, and Scott's intense performance. S. K. Oberbeck in *Newsweek* gave an analysis of what Scott brought to the broken-down Harry Garmes and how he managed to create a real person despite the dull, confusing screenplay and the offscreen battles:

He can be tough, then suddenly funny as he hangs out the girl's scant undies so he can use the sink. When she tells him finally she won't, after all, run off with him . . . he says in that pain-making fast drawl of his, 'Well, I didn't think you would,' and up jumps that famous Scott grin signaling that everything inside is splintering into a zillion pieces. There's a canny, sad Plastic Man quality Scott lends his role, as though he has been through the wringer and knows what kind of ache is coming—a Bogart of the '60s, with fewer wisecracks and more defensive footwork.

Despite the scathing notices, Scott's rejection of the Oscar nomination brought *The Last Run* scads of free publicity. Producer Carter De-Haven told gossip columnist Dorothy Manners for her April 15, 1971 column: "Getting Scott for this role was good timing in view of all the talk he's cooked up. You know he's a tough cookie and you expect problems from a guy like that, but what we get on screen far surpasses every bit of inconvenience and trouble." Manners also reported British director Tony Richardson was after Scott to appear in a film version of *I, Claudius*, Robert Graves's novel of imperial Rome, but the project was never filmed. An earlier version with Charles Laughton also aborted. It would be left for the BBC to bring Graves's fascinating epic to life in a television series a decade later. Scott was also in discussions with DeHaven for a remake of *Northwest Passage* that never completed the trial to production.

Scott and Van Devere returned to the States. Before filming commenced on *The Hospital*, Scott took a trip to Las Vegas and visited the singer Vicki Carr in her dressing room between shows. Shelby Stephens of *Photo Screen* just happened to be there, and managed to get Scott to open up for an interview over a few beers. He told Stephens that he had reunited with Dewhurst because "we were both unhappy without the other. Because we both felt that the causes of our breakup could be overcome. I don't claim that we have entirely overcome them, but we know what we want. To have one's own woman is a good and necessary thing to a man, like breathing. A man will go to enormous lengths to find the woman." At this point, he was still living with Dewhurst, but he was drawn to Van Devere.

They discreetly continued to see each other in Manhattan, where Scott was to begin filming *The Hospital*. Dewhurst may have been aware of the situation. She was starring on Broadway in Edward Albee's *All Over*—an ironic title given the circumstances. But even if she didn't know of the affair, the strain of his divided domestic life began to show in Scott's work. Shooting on *Hospital* was to commence April 12, but Scott failed to show for his first day of work. On the second and third day he appeared but, according to the producers, was too drunk to be of any use.

Amidst such personal turmoil, the impending Oscar ceremony and its international media buzz probably registered as no more than a fly droning around Scott's head. He once joked he would send his dog to the gala to accept for him should he win. The Academy Awards were presented on April 15. Production on *The Hospital* halted for the ceremony—though Scott would not be attending, the film's director, Arthur Hiller, flew out to the coast since he was nominated for *Love Story*.

It was reported that on Oscar night, Scott was watching hockey on another channel and then went to bed. Meanwhile in Hollywood, giggly presenter Goldie Hawn opened the envelope for Best Actor and screamed, "Oh my God! It's George C. Scott." *Patton* producer Frank McCarthy accepted the award, which resides unclaimed in an Academy warehouse to this day. *Behind the Oscar*, a history of the awards, claims sons Alex and Campbell woke up their dad and presented him a mock Oscar in the form of a statue of Abraham Lincoln. Dewhurst appeared on *The Dick Cavett Show* a few days later and said the boys had presented Scott with the hood ornament from one of the family cars—a Lincoln. In addition to Scott's controversial win, *Patton* ran over the competition like a tank and took home a total of seven awards, including Best Picture, Director, and Screenplay.

Ironically, Scott's snub wound up improving Oscar's image. The Academy Awards were approaching forty, looking middle-aged and tired. The middlebrow Bob Hope was almost always the host, doling out the same old jokes about these kids today with their long hair, free love, and protest marches. The winning stars were frequently filming in far-flung locations, failed to collect their trophy in person, diminishing the excitement and glamour of the event. Scott's rejection spiced up the proceedings, and Oscar looked better because the prize was given to someone who had spat upon the whole process. It proved, at least in this case, that the honor really was for the best performance, not the best ad campaign, the highest-grossing picture, or a sentimental favorite.

Scott reported to the *Hospital* set the next day, sober and ready to work. Cast member Barnard Hughes recalled,

> He hadn't been there for the past two days. Word filtered back that he was here. Everybody was running around because George could be pretty ferocious when he wanted to be. I remember hearing all the turmoil out in the hall and I came out of my dressing room. George was coming down the hall in riding boots with two big police dogs on one chain. He had a baton, too. I threw myself up against the wall. George came by, saluted me with his baton, and kept on going.

Scott told reporters he had no feelings about the Oscar outcome one way or another. The Academy Award hoopla had been a sideshow to the main drama of his crumbling marriage and ongoing romance with Trish Van Devere.

13

Trish Takes Over

TRISH VAN DEVERE WAS NOW part of Scott's life—but she wasn't going to play the role of quiet girlfriend to the star. After returning to New York from filming *The Last Run* together in Spain, she spearheaded a feminist protest against the movie her new lover was headlining.

Van Devere and some friends from the Actors Studio formed a group called Women in Theatre (WIT) to increase the number of positive, non-stereotypical portrayals of women in all media. Their first planned protest was against *The Hospital* because the screenplay featured no female physicians. Scott was enraged. Van Devere later explained to the *New York Times*, "I told him 'It's not me, it's not you, it's not the fact that you have the lead in the movie. It's the *issue*.' Finally, we met with the producer and Paddy Chayefsky and pointed out there were no women doctors in the film. Paddy said, 'It never occurred to me. I could have made one of them a woman doctor and it wouldn't have changed the plot.'" To appease the protestors, two female background players were given stethoscopes.

His friction with Van Devere over the lack of women doctors in *The Hospital* was the least of Scott's worries. While continuing to see her in the city, he was still going home to Dewhurst and the boys, maintaining a front of wedded happiness. In her guest shot on Dick Cavett's chatfest a few days after the Oscars, Dewhurst painted a picture of domestic serenity at the South Salem farmhouse. The single-monikered gossip reporter Suzy reported in her May 2, 1971 column that Scott and Dewhurst had had dinner together at the Lair on Third Avenue in Manhattan with friend Jean Shepard. Suzy elaborated on the couple's plans to mount a new play by Shepard and John O'Leary on Broadway that summer with Scott directing Dewhurst in the lead. Ironically, the title reflected their marital status—*A Definite Maybe*. Five days later, Earl Wilson stated in his column Dewhurst and Scott had separated, but their plans for *A Definite Maybe* were still definitely on. Both the production and the marriage ended.

On May 9, another awards ceremony brought Scott attention. The Emmys were presented in Hollywood, and he and Dewhurst were both nominated for *The Price*. His production of *The Andersonville Trial* for *Hollywood Television Theatre* was also up in a number of categories. He declined to attend, but made no noises about declining the honor if he should win. Host Johnny Carson quipped, "Did it ever occur to you the reason George C. Scott doesn't come is because he doesn't own a tuxedo?" Presenter Suzanne Pleshette echoed Goldie Hawn's cry of "Oh my God, it's George C. Scott" when she tore open the envelope for Best Actor in a Single Performance. Jack Cassidy, who played the defense lawyer under Scott's direction in *Andersonville Trial* and was nominated against him, accepted the award for the absent winner. Dewhurst lost her Best Actress race to Lee Grant for *The Neon Ceiling*. Cassidy later told *Variety* columnist Army Archerd, "I really was surprised George won. I thought Hal Holbrook would win [for *A Clear and Present Danger*]. I didn't have a speech prepared." *Andersonville* also won for Best Single Program.

Scott sent Cassidy a telegram the next day: "Dear Jack: As I stood there holding my Emmy and looking at myself on the monitor, I said, 'George, you never looked so beautiful, neither have you spoken so eloquently. No wonder you won.' But seriously, I thank you and I love you the best. Assuredly, George C."

Because of his absence at the ceremony, many reporters assumed Scott had refused his TV honor along with the movie prize. But his

main objection to the "meat parade" film awards was the blatant campaigning nominees routinely indulged in and were expected to wage
in order to win. The TV awards were less about advertising campaigns
in the trades and more about honoring outstanding work. (The rules
of the Emmys have changed many times since and are now as subject
to "For Your Consideration" advertisements as the Oscars.) Though
he had rejected the Oscar, Scott accepted his Emmy.

Meanwhile, the romance with Van Devere was advancing, his second union with Dewhurst was crumbling, and *The Hospital* shoot
dragged on. "It's Only a Movie. All Services Continuing as Usual,"
read a sign posted at Metropolitan Hospital in Manhattan. After his
initial absence, Scott's services to Arthur Hiller, Paddy Chayefsky,
and Howard Gottfried also continued as usual. The day after the Oscars, the star was on set and prepared for his first scene—a three-page
monologue in which Dr. Bock confesses to the staff psychiatrist his
near-suicidal depression and marital disintegration. As with many of
his roles, there were parallels to his offstage life. "Along with the matter of the Oscars, George was going through his own private hell over
his marriage to Colleen," recalled actor Donald Harron, who played
the psychiatrist, to biographer Shaun Considine. "So he was literally
living the character Paddy wrote in the film. He was drinking heavily
and falling asleep in front of the television."

Despite his chaotic home life, Scott focused on Dr. Herbert Bock
with laser-like intensity. He was required to deliver long, meaty dialogue, often peppered with polysyllabic medical terms, during Hiller's
complicated shots. One sequence involved continuously shooting six
and a half pages of script. Normally such a scene would be broken up
into fifteen to twenty segments. "It was complicated," Hiller later said
in an appreciation of Scott for the book *Close-Ups*:

> Scott came off the elevator in the hospital, crossed to the nurses'
> station, where he was told there was a problem in Room 806,
> walked around the nurses' desk, where he related to two crying

people, headed down the lengthy corridor, was stopped to discuss
a problem with a young doctor, entered Room 806, where he com-
forted a crying nurse and dealt with the problem (a dead doctor
on a patient's bed), moved back out to the corridor, where he continued his discussion walking with the head nurse who had joined
him, then stopped and turned away from a group of oncoming
interns so they couldn't hear what he was saying, and proceeded
to make decisions and give orders, before heading off to another
elevator. Complicated? We had to do this one take seventeen times
before I felt it was right. Not one of those repeats had to be remade
because of George's flawed performance. On a few of the takes he
was very good and on all the others he was brilliant.

Perhaps the most complex and demanding scene in the entire film
involves Bock explaining his frustrations with the overwhelming medical bureaucracy to Barbara Drummond (Diana Rigg), the daughter
of a patient who is almost murdered by the incompetence of his staff.
He finally explodes in a paroxysm of rage and impotence: "We cure
nothing! We heal NOTHING!" The scene consisted of six pages of dialogue, three minutes and thirty-two seconds, an eternity in film time.
It was shot in a small office in the nurses' dorm in three takes on May 4,
two days before Scott officially announced his marriage was over.

Hiller recalled that three minutes into the shot Scott paraphrased
a vital word. The line was supposed to read "We have assembled the
most enormous medical establishment and people are sicker than ever."
Scott said "We have established the most enormous. . ." The actor remained in character, paused for a split second realizing he couldn't say
"establishment" or he'd be repeating himself, and finished the sentence
with "the most enormous medical entity."

"It's just remarkable that an actor could stay in character," the director wrote, "and at the same time go through that outside thinking
process and come up with not just another word, but a perfectly suitable one. Not only that, but because of his searching, it felt even more

as if he had pulled it up from his gut (which indeed he did). It gave one more dimension to the performance."

Early in the production, Chayefsky wanted Scott to play Bock as more of a comic figure than a tragic one. He complained to Gottfried, who responded he would speak to the star if they went together and Chayefsky did the talking since the film was his vision. Apprehensively, the screenwriter and producer entered Scott's dressing room. After Chayefsky made his point, Scott, who had had a difficult day, rose to his full height, pointed at the author, and bellowed, "You do your fucking writing! And I'll do the fucking acting!" Gottfried recalled to Shaun Considine that on the words "fucking acting," Scott hit himself on the chest for emphasis so hard, "I was sure he had put his hand through his chest. So we scooted out of there real fast. And I don't believe Paddy ever approached him again."

Filming on *The Hospital* finished on June 15 and it was released in New York on December 14. Critical reaction was mostly favorable with a few caveats. *Newsday*'s Joseph Gelmis felt "the good moments outweigh the bad." He admired the "grittiness of the dialogue" and the "tight and punchy staging" but opined that the black comedy ending was too absurd with the insane Dr. Drummond (Barnard Hughes), Barbara's father, posing as a staff physician and murdering doctors and nurses left and right.

Once again, Scott's performance was universally praised. Judith Crist in *New York* magazine labeled it "perhaps the finest of his career." Stanley Kauffmann in the *New Republic* concurred, calling Scott "a tornado, creating his own 3-D as he goes. An authentic actor-star." Kauffmann even went so far as to posit Scott should be considered one of the co-creators of the film. "Most of what is valid in *The Hospital* comes from Scott," he wrote.

Scott doesn't play it for laughs as Chayefsky wanted. Instead, he's deadly serious, and this makes for a deeper characterization. In one scene, Bock discovers a patient has been given the wrong treatment and died as a result. He screams at an administrator, played by

Nancy Marchand, "Where do you train your nurses, Mrs. Christie? . . . Dachau?!" If Chayefsky had had his way, Scott would have given the line a lighter reading and the impact would have been lessened. The humor comes from the absurdity of the situation, rather than the actor's calling attention to it. Scott's choice made the scene both real and comic at the same time.

The tragedy of Vietnam and the anti-establishment rebellion of the '60s prepped the public for the dark, satiric vision of a society falling apart. While they were confused by the jumbled alienation of *Petulia* in 1968, *The Hospital* finished high in box-office receipts among United Artists' features for January 1972 when it went into national release, ranking third behind such popular fare as *Diamonds Are Forever* and *Fiddler on the Roof*. At Oscar time, the film received two major nominations—Best Original Screenplay and Best Actor. All of Hollywood was abuzz. After refusing the Oscar for *Patton*, would Scott show up this time? "We're going to deliver George C. Scott, if we have to drag him ourselves," Chayefsky claimed. While Scott did not attend the ceremony, he didn't refuse the nomination, either. After the international press storm generated by the *Patton* rejection, Scott figured it would be less bother for him if he just kept his mouth shut. On Oscar night, Chayefsky won for his script, but Gene Hackman took the Best Actor award for *The French Connection*. It was Scott's last Oscar nomination.

His personal life was still a tangle. He had left the New Salem farmhouse and moved in with Trish Van Devere, but where they were staying was a mystery. An item in the July 6, 1971 *Los Angeles Herald Examiner* reported that MGM was searching for the actress to make personal appearances for *The Last Run*, but that she was unavailable. Rumor had it she and Scott were cohabitating on a houseboat somewhere along the Hudson River. Other sources cited Brooklyn Heights as their place of residence. When *Life* magazine reporter Joan Barthel asked Scott's agent Jane Deacy where the actor was living, she replied, "No particular place."

In September 1971, Scott flew from "no particular place" on the East Coast to Lizardville (his pet name for Los Angeles) to work with his *Last Run* director Richard Fleischer on the film version of Joseph Wambaugh's best-selling novel *The New Centurions*, a slice-of-lifer following the transformation of three typical, nonglamorous policemen from rookies to experienced officers. Wambaugh was writing from his own experience as a LAPD sergeant. Before filming, Scott did research on his character, old-time patrolman Andy Kilvinsky, riding around with two Los Angeles police officers, going through the booking process, speaking with the arrestees, etc.

Erik Estrada was cast as the one of the three protagonists of the novel, but his role was significantly reduced for the film. The future *CHiPs* star was still happy to be working with Scott. "A gentleman," he later wrote of his costar, "a true professional, and, most important, a man who knew what it was like to struggle for a chance to work and work hard to keep that chance alive, George was a pure joy to be around. He never hogged the scenes we shared and never seemed to take his star status all that seriously." Scott advised the newcomer not to believe his own hype, but to take the Hollywood game as just that, a game.

Though Stacy Keach's Roy Fehler is the main character and his career provides the story arc (Scott Wilson played the third officer), Kilvinsky is the film's emotional core. *New Centurions* had the potential to be an insightful record of the lives of average cops, but Fleischer directed it like a standard police procedural. Scott breathes life into several routine sequences. He simmers with a burning anger over the appalling living conditions of a group of illegal immigrants, lashing out at their greedy landlord. He brings a feisty humor to a pickup patrol of black prostitutes. "I got so much soul, I can't keep it under control," he tells them with a wicked laugh, relishing the rhyme of his quip and the sass of the hookers.

Two-thirds of the way through the picture, Andy retires and is unable to cope with the pace of ordinary life. He tries living with his daughter but is bored out of his mind. In the most moving scene of the film, Kilvinsky calls Roy just to say hi and launches into a shaggy dog story about an old man who would call the station every day to complain about an imagined prowler. The young Andy would go to his house and chase the imaginary intruder. The event became a ritual between the two. Despite the light tone and the occasional chuckle in the telling, you can see by Scott's eyes that Kilvinsky fears becoming that old man—so desperate for companionship and action that he invents a reason to call the police. After he hangs up and walks out of the frame, we hear a gunshot.

David Thomson praised the scene in his voluminous *New Biographical Dictionary of Film* and conjectured the actor contributed to the direction as well as the performance:

> Scott has one magnificent scene, where his retiring cop commits suicide, that completely exceeds Fleischer's half-hearted approach. The scene comes unexpectedly in a ramshackle apartment on a hot afternoon as traffic drones along a freeway outside. It is easier to believe that Scott was in charge of the sequence, so totally is it a matter of the way he reveals the desperation of a man retired from a relentless job.

According to columnist Sydney Skolsky, a preview audience of tough teenagers in West Hollywood stood and cheered after Scott's suicide scene.

Fleischer reported a similar reaction from the crew. During one scene in a topless restaurant, all eyes were focused on Scott rather than the bare-breasted ladies undulating in the background. The presence of this superstar is so blazing that the rest of the picture suffers when he departs it. After Andy's death, Keach's Roy gives up his law studies to focus on police work. His wife leaves him, and he takes to drink and is killed in the line of duty—a different ending than the novel, in which Roy finds contentment with his new girlfriend. A vibrant performer on stage in such roles as Hamlet, a parody of President Lyndon

Johnson in *MacBird*, and Buffalo Bill in Arthur Kopit's *Indians*, Keach is bland onscreen and the picture loses its focus. Despite this imbalance among the leads and indifferent reviews, *Centurions* was one of the top twenty grossing films of 1972.

Scott was now red hot and had more film offers than he knew what to do with. Fleischer wanted him to star in a film version of John Osborne's play *Luther* about the Protestant revolutionary. (In the end, it would be brought to the screen much later with a different director and Keach in the lead.) There were rumors Scott would direct and star in the movie of Wambaugh's next novel, *The Blue Knight* (this became a TV miniseries with William Holden). He told Army Archerd of *Variety* he was planning to headline a father-daughter story called *Lew's Girl* as well as two comedies, *Money's Tight* and *Norman, Is That You?* None of these reached completion with Scott; the latter was finally made with Redd Foxx in a totally different concept.

But what he really wanted to do was direct. As soon as his *New Centurions* scenes were completed, Scott traveled to Arizona to be in control as helmer and star of *Rage*, an explosive melodrama centering on Dan Logan, a sheep rancher who turns into an avenging killer after his son is lethally exposed to an experimental nerve gas by an errant Army test plane. The story, brought to him by his lawyer, appealed to Scott's anti-establishment streak. Once Logan learns his boy has died from exposure to the MX3 gas and he will also eventually succumb to its deadly effects, he launches an orgy of violence against the military and the manufacturing chemical company.

The screenplay by Phil Friedman and Dan Kleinman, a pair of former Princeton math majors, was loosely based on an actual incident in Utah when poison gas was leaked from an Army testing site and 4,000 sheep were killed. Producer Fred Weintraub had supervised their work in a writers' workshop. Originally a Warner Brothers project, the feature was now the property of an independent production company headed by J. Roland Getty (the oilman's son) and Leon Fromkess, a former agent and studio head. Warner Brothers would

keep its hand in by distributing the picture. After *Rage*, Scott planned
to finally direct the long-delayed *Harrow Alley* with Dirk Bogarde and
Rod Taylor.

For his first big-screen directing job, Scott surrounded himself with
familiar faces. The cast included Richard Basehart, Martin Sheen (he
had directed both in *The Andersonville Trial*), Barnard Hughes (*The Hospital*), Bette Henritze (*The Merchant of Venice, Antony and Cleopatra*), and
Stephen Young (*Patton*). Scott personally chose the key crew members,
including cinematographer Fred Koenekamp, an Oscar nominee for
Patton. In addition, he was accompanied by an extensive entourage
consisting of Van Devere; his agent, Jane Deacy; her son, Bill; his
lawyer; his makeup man, Del Acevedo; his stunt man; his wardrobe
man and driver; his biographer Tom Leith; and his German shepherd,
Torch. His father and his eighty-seven-year-old grandmother also visited the set and braved icy night shoots along with the crew. "We were
shooting in Benson, Arizona and it was cold," said Acevedo. "We were
shooting at night. George was concerned about her and she said, 'Oh,
I'm okay.' I said, 'I have a pair of wind pants that you could put under
your skirt. You could go into George's trailer there and put them on
and it'll keep the wind off your legs. Because with a skirt, you're going
to get the wind.' She wore them. She was a dear lady."

Another lady from Scott's past was also in the vicinity of the *Rage*
location. Ava Gardner was nearby filming a cameo as legendary beauty
Lillie Langtry in John Huston's *The Life and Times of Judge Roy Bean*.
Fearing a repeat of the romantic roughhousing of *The Bible*, Huston
posted a twenty-four-hour guard at Gardner's door. There were claims
in gossip columns she snuck away from Huston's watchdogs to visit
her former lover. This doesn't seem likely, since Gardner stated in her
autobiography that after he broke into her bungalow in the Beverly
Hills Hotel, she was so scared of Scott she couldn't even stand to hear
his voice on TV. In addition, Van Devere was in residence at his Tuscon
hotel suite. It is possible the former lovers met briefly to reminisce
about drunken battles and broken closet doors, but the reunion was

most likely a concoction of juicy gossip-column copy based on Scott and Gardner's proximity for a few days.

Scott was probably too busy to rekindle any fires with Gardner. After his previous impatience with directors, he wanted his first helming job on a feature to be fast and efficient. So he prepared meticulously, choosing his setups beforehand, eliminating the necessity for "coverage" or multiple shots of the same scene from different angles. "George knew exactly what he wanted, which most directors only come to after years of experience with a camera," Basehart said. "He did his cutting beforehand and avoided the old hackneyed practice of doing long shots, medium shots, and close shots on every scene, which is nauseating for everyone concerned."

Even in scenes involving multiple characters and pages of dialogue, Scott minimized the number of takes. "We work fast and we work hard, and hopefully it shows on the screen," he told Joan Barthel of *Life*, adding, "I have resented for so many years as an actor the incredible tedium of waiting for somebody to do something, making up their mind and then getting it arranged, then doing it twenty-three times, just because the director can't make up his mind whether he liked Take 3 better than Take 12. Well, unless there's some glaring technical mistake, I defy any director to tell Take 3 from Take 12."

Rage was shot from November 19, 1971 to January 11, 1972, under budget and seven days ahead of schedule, despite one of the worst snowstorms to hit Tuscon in fifteen years. Scott would give personal instructions not only to the cameramen, but also to the set dresser, wardrober, hairdresser, makeup people, prop man, and stunt drivers. Most directors would delegate these chores to assistants.

Fromkess said the only problems were that Scott would sometimes forget to say "Cut," and that the city of Benson, Arizona, would only allow filming on their highway between one and four in the morning.

The shoot may have been harmonious, quick and economical, but the film was self-conscious and simplistic. *Rage* relies too heavily on the title emotion. All we know about Dan Logan is he's a widower, he's lost his son, and he's pissed. Once he goes on his spree of violence, Logan becomes as brutal and unfeeling as the military-industrial machine he's attacking, draining all audience sympathy. Perhaps because he was concentrating on his direction, Scott's performance lacks his usual nuance. It's one note: a screaming high one typified by the central image on the movie's poster—an inhumanly furious Logan, his mouth open in a bellow of anger, about to deliver a crushing blow with a rifle butt. Granted, nobody does rage better than Scott, but here that's all he does. "Inevitably, my personal acting suffered," he admitted. "There simply was too much to do. Being a director means a twenty-five-hour day. There's no way that you can pay enough attention to your own acting as well." On most shots, his stand-in and bodyguard Pat Zurica rehearsed the scene until just before the camera began rolling.

As for Scott's direction, it's artsy and obvious. In the opening scenes, Logan and his son are so blissfully enjoying each other and the great outdoors, underscored by a schmaltzy harmonica, they could be in a commercial for camping equipment. This is obvious foreshadowing of the oncoming tragedy. In addition, Scott was overly fond of trick photography and slow-motion shots, particularly those involving pouring liquids. Coffee and tobacco juice flowed in graceful, unnecessary abundance.

Once filming was completed, Scott took off for a week's vacation on a boat rented from an unlikely source. "When we finished *Rage*, [George] got his agent to get us a boat and we got Sinatra's boat *The Tina* and took it out for a week," Del Acevedo recalled. Evidently, Sinatra's anger at Scott over his treatment of Ava Gardner did not prevent him from renting his boat to him. "He took his wife, his father, his secretary and three of his buddies. We had a week. He was waiting for them to get the film ready for him to start cutting." (Acevedo was referring to Van Devere, who was not Scott's wife yet.) But Warner Brothers, Getty and Fromkess were unhappy with the final product and demanded additional editing. Scott's contract only allowed him first cut; the final one belonged to the studio. He refused to make any further deletions and walked away from the project, never even seeing the final film. After preview audiences responded negatively, Warners re-edited the film, rendering it a jumbled mess.

Warners executive David Brown, who was at Twentieth Century-Fox at the time of *Patton*, later related he and his partner Richard Zanuck offered to allow Scott to make his own cuts, but he would not even attend the screening of the rough first version, forcing the studio to make its own editing choices. The studio dumped *Rage* in saturation bookings for a quick payoff despite Scott's protests. His reaction to the treatment of his first film as a director was similar to Dan Logan's. His baby had been eviscerated by studio hacks. Critics gave it a universal thumbs down. "Sluggish, tired, and tiring," whined *Variety*. *Newsday* characterized Scott's direction as "self-conscious and pointless." The *Village Voice* summed it up as one of "the great bombs of the last ten years." Audiences concurred and *Rage* burned away after playing a few weeks, leaving only ashes. Those ashes left a bitter taste in Scott's mouth. The next time he went behind a camera, he was determined to would be in control of everything—not only would he have the final cut, but he'd have the final authority on the advertising, the distribution, even the rating if he had anything to say about it.

After starring in four films in a row in 1971, one of which he also directed, Scott caught his breath in early 1972. He not only took a break from work, he broke off his second marriage to Colleen Dewhurst. In February, Dewhurst was in divorce court again, this time in Santo Domingo. Scott was not present, but was represented by a lawyer who informed the judge Dewhurst would receive a separation allowance of $9,165 and that Scott would pay alimony of $4,165 a month in addition to a yearly payment of $55,000. The South Salem farmhouse, valued at $750,000, was given to Dewhurst. Another clause in the divorce settlement stated that if Scott made more than $170,000 a year, his ex-wife would receive $20,000 of it. "The Dominican lawyers were very nice and entertained me," Dewhurst said. "There were troubadours singing. Oh my dear, I'm very happy. I think it's always quite a relief for both of us when George and I get a divorce."

It may have been a relief to Scott, but his relationship with Trish Van Devere was still unsettled. They were living together, but marriage was a maybe. Van Devere confessed to friends she didn't know which way the union would go. Scott had just ended his fourth marriage, a fact of which he later confessed to being ashamed, and wanted to step carefully before embarking on a fifth attempt. Then, on June 13, Van Devere told United Artists she had to withdraw from her role in *Harry Never Holds* (later released as *Harry in Your Pocket*) because she was pregnant with Scott's child. On June 20, she informed the studio the pregnancy had been a false alarm and she could return to work. She later admitted to having miscarried. Wracked with guilt, Van Devere developed psychosomatic symptoms of losing the feeling in her legs. Scott was taking her to doctors three times a week. Finally, a friend told her to take two aspirins and shut up. She heeded the terse advice and the visits stopped. On July 12, Van Devere told gossip columnist Marilyn Beck she and Scott were upset she wasn't with child but that they were hoping "that it isn't too long before I bear George's baby. No, we're not planning to marry. We don't see any reason why we should."

That same month, Scott reconnected with his eldest daughter, Victoria, who was a freshman at Fort Collins, Colorado:

> After *Patton*, I wrote him a letter in care of Twentieth Century Fox. . . . I know it was February because I mailed it with a Valentine stamp on it which was really sweet for a college freshman to do. I didn't hear from him until that summer. I didn't hear until quite a number of years later . . . how he'd actually come by the letter. Twentieth Century Fox forwarded it to his office in New York City. I think that was his business manager Jane Deacy's office. He came in early one time and he had bags of mail. Everybody was gone and he was just putzing around, trying to find something

to do. So he grabbed a couple letters off the top; one of them was mine. . . . I basically just said, "I would love to have a chance to meet you, but I don't want anything, I'm not after anything, I'm not trying to harm anybody." I didn't know if this would ever get to him. He found it and he knew it was me. He called me one day. I was working in Fort Collins at a job after school and he contacted me there. After I sat down really hard, he said, "I'd like you to come and visit."

Scott sent a Lear jet to Colorado to fly the overwhelmed young girl to California. She remembers,

I met him on the tarmac at Burbank. Trish at that point was wonderful; all through the years that they were together, we got along very well because she wasn't the ugly stepmother that ruined my mother's marriage with him. She was later than that. So we were more like sisters. She was about twelve years older than I was. She was always very welcoming. She smoothed out so many wrinkles in us getting together. . . . I spent probably about a week. They had rented a house north of Malibu, on the beach.

Victoria remained in contact with her father from then on, and described their relationship as that of "respectful, adult friends."

On September 14, 1972 at twelve noon in a Santa Monica county courthouse, Scott, forty-five, and Van Devere, twenty-nine, were legally joined by Judge Laurence J. Rittenband, as witnessed by the actor's attorney Paul S. Berger. The ceremony took all of ten minutes. When she put the ring on her husband's finger, the bride said the vows so softly Scott protested he didn't know if she meant them. She replied she had wanted to say them so that only he could hear.

Scott and his bride did not stay in the building to obtain their marriage certificate. They slipped out a back stairway to avoid publicity, and the license was brought to them by a clerk. A short report in the *Los Angeles Herald-Examiner* stated the new couple would make their home in Malibu.

The honeymoon was brief. Four days later, Scott reported to Stockton, California to begin filming *Oklahoma Crude* for Stanley Kramer and Columbia Pictures, opposite Faye Dunaway. The location was the ranch of a Basque sheep farmer. The owner's father had bought the 5,000-acre lot from the railroad before 1900. It was chosen for its resemblance to the film's time (1910) and locale (a windswept Tulsa oilfield). Dunaway starred as Lena Doyle, a proto-feminist operating a wildcat oil rig while fending off the Pan-Oklahoma Oil Company, represented by the despicable Jack Palance. John Mills as her alcoholic father shows up for a handout and to lend a hand in her struggle. After Lena rejects his offer, he hires Mase Mason (Scott), an itinerant drifter, to help out. The three form an unlikely team, united by their passion to defeat the oil monopoly. Palance eventually wrests the well from them. After vicious gun battles with the company's thugs, the father is shot, Mase and Lena have a brief tryst, and they take back the well by force. Ironically, the well runs dry. Mase announces he is pushing off for Mexico. The film ends with Lena asking him to stay.

Scott told Gregg Kilday of the *Los Angeles Times* he chose the picture because he liked the characters: "They're totally disparate people who become affectionate and needful. I get to play a ne'er-do-well, a no-account bum who becomes somewhat reclaimed." He denied there was any common thread in his recent choice of roles ("[E]ach has been reasonably distinctive. One doesn't repeat oneself.") But there is a similar theme: the little guy striking at monolithic authority, either in the form of inefficient bureaucracy (*The Hospital*), the military-industrial complex (*Rage*), or unfettered business interests (*Oklahoma Crude*). This can also be applied to Scott's offscreen approach to his work in his battle with television networks (*East Side/West Side*) and standard Broadway production techniques (the Theatre of Michigan).

Dunaway reported in her autobiography that the Stockton locals assured the company the weather would be mild and temperate, perfect for filming. "The only thing we were spared was snow. And earthquakes," she wrote. The first few days of shooting, the temperature soared to 110 degrees. The Forest Service demanded the set be closed to all visitors to lessen the danger of flash fires. Two weeks later the temperature dropped into the fifties and winds picked up speed, pushing clouds across the sky. This ruined the lighting for most of the shots. Fog covered the set for two days in November. Then it got so cold the actors had to put ice cubes in their mouth just before the cameras rolled so their breath would not be visible since the action took place in summer. Scott also remembered that it rained for nineteen consecutive days. Scott, Dunaway, Mills, and Palance had to wear rubber scuba diver's outfits under their early 1900s duds to keep from freezing. Scott carried a flask of Courvoisier for added warmth. "The cast really suffered and they were all splendid about it," Kramer said.

The director had more praise for Scott, comparing him to another film great he had worked with:

> I hate to make the comparison, but George almost totally reminds me of Spencer Tracy. He is a thoroughly professional actor, no questions asked. If I tell George to walk to that mark, turn and walk back off camera, that's what he does. Only he adds the reactive, and that's what Spence did. Someone once said that Tracy reacted better than most actors act. George is the same way. I guess it stems from confidence and experience.

Van Devere was on location, having completing a leading role in *One Is a Lonely Number*. Scott had concluded one of the biggest sources of strife in his previous marriages—and in all show-business unions—was the long separations required by film shoots. He had visited Van Devere on her *Lonely Number* sets in San Francisco and British Columbia, but only on weekends.

Kilday reported the perception on the set was that marriage had mellowed Scott. Dunaway, however, had a different impression. She recalled Scott would come in every day to watch the rushes with two big dogs on a leash beside him. "When he walked in, there was an invisible wall around him," she wrote. "It gave new meaning to the word 'boundary.' He walked into those rushes, he sat down with his wife and his dogs, he watched the screen, and he left again. That was it."

Crude may have been an attempt to revive the opposites-attract, Tracy-Hepburn romantic comedies of Hollywood's heyday, but it also turned out to be well named, with the sort of now-permissible bawdy humor the makers of those classics would have eschewed. Scatological and sexual references are numerous. To show his contempt, Scott pisses on Palance's boots. Blood splatters across an oil company henchman's bare ass after he's been shot there. Dunaway explains to Scott she hates both genders and wishes she had the sex organs of each so she could screw herself.

Richard Schickel of *Time* compared Kramer to "a college chaplain deliberately swearing in order to seem like one of the boys." Most reviewers were disappointed, finding the film as big a bust as Lena's dry oil well. There were appreciative analyses of Scott's rare stab at romance. Roger Ebert of the *Chicago Sun-Times* said, "George C. Scott just continues to grow as an actor; he's been so good recently in so many different kinds of roles that I suspect we still don't have his measure. This time he's got to be strong but a little shy; a gentleman too proud to reveal his feelings—and sometimes even scared to feel them."

In an interesting footnote, *Crude* was a hit in the Soviet Union, with the Russians perceiving it as an attack on the evils of capitalism. The film won the gold medal at the 1973 Moscow Film Festival. Kramer was cited for "for his humanist contribution to the development of the world cinema, and for his new film, which shows how two persons win a moral victory over the despotism of business and force."

14

Swimming with Dolphins and Drinking with Russians

IN KEEPING WITH SCOTT'S DETERMINATION to avoid long separations from Van Devere, his next project, *The Day of the Dolphin*, directed by Mike Nichols for Avco Embassy, would be the first of many starring both of them. They would play married scientists studying the titular bottle-nosed mammals. Jake Terrell and his wife Maggie have succeeded in teaching a dolphin, Fa (short for Alpha), rudimentary human speech. This scientific breakthrough is exploited when Fa and his mate, Be (short for Beta), are kidnapped in order to train them to place a mine under the President's yacht. Somehow, these wonder animals manage to escape, blow up the conspirators, and return to the Terrells. Jake and Maggie tearfully release them to the wild ocean, commanding them to never trust humans again, lest their intelligence be put to evil uses. The plot was more than a bit treacly, but it meant three months in the Bahamas with plenty of sun and frolicking with the dolphins. It would be the honeymoon the Scotts had missed in oven-hot-then-freezer-cold Stockton.

Working with Mike Nichols was an added bonus. Since collaborating with Scott on *The Little Foxes* and *Plaza Suite*, Nichols had followed up his Broadway triumphs with innovative films on adult themes like *Catch-22* and *Carnal Knowledge*. But here he was directing what was essentially an action picture starring cute sea creatures. Why the switch to thriller fare? Nichols had to finish his contract to producer Joseph E. Levine before he could move on to other projects. The *Dolphin* property had become available after earlier attempts by Roman Polanski and Franklin J. Schaffner hadn't set sail. The director thought it might be fun and a challenge, and Levine was certainly high on the project. "I've collected or have guarantees for $8.5 million for *Day of the Dolphin* . . ." he later bragged to columnist Earl Wilson, "It's all sight unseen! They're taking my word for it and Mike Nichols's word and because George C. Scott is the star. Mike Nichols says it's the best picture he ever made. But I'm not that pessimistic. It's the best picture anybody ever made. It's clean and international. And when George C. Scott tells the dolphin to go out to the open sea, there won't be a dry eye."

Nichols enlisted Buck Henry, his screenwriter on *The Graduate* and *Catch-22*, to adapt Robert Merle's original science-fiction novel, which had been inspired by the efforts of real-life oceanographer Dr. John C. Lilly to get dolphins to talk. Henry streamlined the plot, eliminating dolphin-human debates over the existence of God and changing a Chinese aircraft carrier to the President's vessel. But the script still suffered from schizophrenia—it didn't know whether it wanted to be a scientific study of animal intelligence or a conventional thriller.

Scott and Van Devere were intrigued by the possibilities of interspecies communications and met with Nichols in Hollywood to see if there was any way to beef up these elements and tone down the action stuff. Nichols responded there was no time for significant rewrites and asked if they were in or out. They both assented, and on December 20 they left for Miami to begin shooting. After Christmas, Scott would return to Stockton to finish up *Oklahoma Crude* while Van Devere went East to do some house-hunting. They were planning to buy a permanent residence in or around Westport, Connecticut.

Around this time, Scott was offered the starring role in *Kill the Dutchman*, based on the novel by Paul Sann about the assassination of gangster Dutch Schultz. Robert Aldrich (*What Ever Happened to Baby Jane?*, *The Dirty Dozen*) was set to direct for MCA-Universal, but Scott wanted too much creative control. According to Aldrich, the actor's demands included that he "produce as well as star and I was even willing to let him produce except that he wanted to take that literally. In other words, he wanted to control who I wanted to use as cameraman, cutter, assistant ad infinitum. Figuring that heart attacks are easy enough to come by without seeking them out, I declined to go forward under those conditions."

Though he had ascended to the number two slot on the list of top-grossing movie stars, outranked only by Clint Eastwood, Scott was getting bored with acting and had made noises about retiring from it to take up producing and directing. There was still the lingering *Harrow Alley* project, but he was unable to raise the financing. He would soon get his wish of total control with *The Savage Is Loose*.

For now it was back to the trenches—lush, tropical trenches, granted—but Scott saw acting in films as labor. In early 1973, *Dolphin* shooting continued on the isolated island of Abaco in the Bahamas. A few days into the production, he vanished. "We were filming about three days when he completely disappeared and he was on one of his long drunks," cast member Fritz Weaver recalled. "He came back looking much the worse for wear. I don't know where he had been. We were in the Bahamas and he may have taken off for the mainland. They told me that he been violent."

Perhaps Scott had been spooked by his friend Jason Robards's recent near-fatal automobile accident. Elizabeth Wilson, who played a small role, explained: "*Dolphin* was a very strange experience because Jason Robards, who was a great friend, had had that terrible automobile accident. He'd been drunk and drove off a cliff in California. Fritz Weaver replaced him. That sort of colored the beginning of the filming because we didn't know if Jason would be around anymore." Robards recovered and later joined Alcoholics Anonymous, managing his alcohol problem.

Levine was outraged at Scott for causing an expensive delay. Before *Dolphin* was in release, the producer kept his anger to himself, lest it damage his product. When Earl Wilson asked the mogul if he got along with Scott, Levine literally put his hand over his mouth and then replied, "He had the flu for a few days. But he made the picture."

The producer later expressed his true feelings at a fall meeting of the Screen Actors Guild in November 1974, castigating Scott for keeping 109 people waiting for three days while on a $750,000 salary. "He's a jerk," Levine fumed. The producer further complained that his star had never lifted a finger to promote *Dolphin* but had shot his own picture, *The Savage Is Loose*, under budget and ahead of schedule and publicized the hell out of it. Scott later responded by calling Levine an "old cunt" and an "asshole." The actor went on to blame the weather for production delays of *Dolphin*.

As with *Oklahoma Crude*, weather was indeed a factor in the three-month shoot with storms erupting off and on for two months, forcing the postponement of essential outdoor filming. And when they needed rain, of course nature refused to comply. An expensive rain machine was called into service.

Though he was newly married, Scott still had trouble keeping his demons at bay. There was the by-now obligatory bender and, to keep his violent urges in check, he still maintained a retinue of bouncer types. Fritz Weaver recalled,

> He was living on a boat with his wife Trish. He was living on a great ship that he had rented. It was preposterous, this ship. It was like a cruise ship for Aristotle Onassis or something. It was sitting out there in the bay near where we were filming. He had a party out there one Sunday. Some of us were invited out. He was pretty well oiled on that day. I noticed that he had several really tough-looking guys hanging around off the aft rail of the back end of the ship. They sort of leaned on their knuckles. They were pretty rough. You sort of avoided them. I finally said to George when we were sitting together, "Who are these guys? What are they doing here?" And he said, "Those are bodyguards." And I said,

"Bodyguards? Who's attacking you?" And he said, "No, you don't understand. They're protecting other people from me."

Scott still had the capacity to scare everyone around him. Buck Henry recalled playing chess with the star between shots. Scott's two dogs were fidgety and disturbing the game. Their master said "SIT DOWN!" The crew and cast, over a hundred people, all sat down.

Though he could command an entire film company with a single phrase, he felt contained and frustrated. Leslie Charleson, cast as part of Terrell's young research team, recalled another party on the star's yacht. Scott told his guests show business stories, getting drunker and angrier over the petty aspects of the industry. As they were leaving at about four in the morning, Charleson asked her host why stayed in the business if he hated it so much. He angrily replied it was the only job he knew how to do.

Dolphin's lack of dramatic opportunities may have added to his anger. Scott was spending hundreds of hours in the water and learning to be a pretty fair scuba diver. But you can't really sink your teeth into a role when your main scene partner has fins and Buck Henry is just off-camera, reading lines like "Pa stay; Fa want Pa stay now." The only time in the film Scott displays any passion is in an opening monologue, describing what it feels like to be a dolphin with every pore of your skin feeding your brain ecstatic sensations. The way he makes it sound, dolphins must be living in paradise. For the rest of the film, he and Van Devere (whose role is basically a throwaway) are upstaged by the gorgeous tropical island setting and the scene-stealing aquatic thespians. Henry's muddled screenplay fails to make sense of Merle's sprawling novel. Pluses are few. There's an effective cameo by Elizabeth Wilson as a smug secretary for the foundation that supports Terrell's research, and Georges Delerue's poetic score received an Oscar nomination. But overall, *Dolphin* is a beautifully photographed jumble. The critical brethren registered astonishment over heavyweight talents like Scott, Nichols, and Henry wasting their time with an animal picture suitable only for kiddie matinees. Pauline Kael called it a Rin-Tin-Tin movie and *Play-boy* compared Scott to "Moby Dick thrashing in a minnow pond."

The metaphor was an apt one. Scott was like a powerful giant, burning to fully express his abilities—not just in acting, which was growing stale for him, but in directing, writing, and producing. On the last day of shooting, Buck and Ginger, the dolphins playing Fa and Be, swam out to sea after the final shot and never returned. Scott must have envied them. They were free now, all "instinct and energy," as Jake Terrell described them, unencumbered by studio execs, the press, wives, ex-wives, children, booze, or the need for money.

If *Dolphin* was an artistic minnow pond, for his next project Mike Nichols provided Scott with a vast ocean in which to swim. The director asked Scott to play Astrov, the disaffected doctor, in an all-star revival of Anton Chekhov's *Uncle Vanya* for Circle in the Square, the company that presented *Children of Darkness* and *Desire Under the Elms*. Like *The Three Sisters*, the play is a character study of melancholy Russians, lamenting their unrealized selves between sips from the samovar. Helena, a beautiful young woman married to a pompous, much older professor, turns the household upside down as both Astrov and his friend Vanya fall in love with her. This would be Scott's first time on stage in six years and his first appearance at the Circle's new Broadway home, a huge, oval-shaped stage surrounded on all sides by the audience. Ironically, the space had been endowed by *Dolphin*'s "asshole" producer Joseph E. Levine and bore his name. *Vanya* would be the final presentation in Circle's first uptown season. Scott was reluctant to return to the stage and was particularly resistant to playing matinees. "I won't play for those fucking blue-haired ladies," he told Circle producer Theodore Mann. Scott had just attended a midday performance and was infuriated by the talking and candy-wrapper rattling of the predominantly matronly female audience. Mann promised any bluehairs would be stopped at the theatre door. "If I see one fucking bluehaired lady, I'm walking," Scott responded.

In addition to Nichols, the cast was full of former collaborators. Julie Christie from *Petulia* was the bewitching Helena; Barnard Hughes from *The Hospital* and *Rage* played Serbrayakov, her insufferable husband; and Elizabeth Wilson from *East Side/West Side* was Sonya, Serbrayakov's daughter, who has an unrequited crush on Astrov. The company also included Conrad Bain as Waffles, a gregarious tenant; Cathleen Nesbitt as Vanya's judgmental mother; and the legendary silent film star Lillian Gish as the elderly nanny. For Vanya, Astrov's friend and fellow depressive, Nichols cast the British equivalent of Scott: Nicol Williamson, a fiercely talented and independent actor given to bending the elbow. He had replaced Scott in *Plaza Suite* while the latter was recovering from his operation to repair a detached retina. Eleven years younger than Scott, Williamson had recently had an international triumph as Hamlet and was planning a one-man late-night cabaret show to be performed Off-Broadway after performances of *Vanya*. Scott may have been envious of the younger actor's energy and ambition. The two similarly tempered stars clashed during the early rehearsal period. Elizabeth Wilson recalled,

> Nicol Williamson was a wonderful actor. George was jealous. I can remember when Lillian Gish, Cathleen Nesbitt, and I came in for our first dress rehearsal. We were told it had been postponed because George had gone into Nicol's room—bless his heart—and said, "What do you think you're playing? Hamlet? Come on, what's the matter with you?" Of course, everyone was intimidated by George because of his gifts as an actor. Nicol Williamson said after that he never really got back on track because he was so intimidated. I remember about that same incident, Mike [Nichols] said to me, "I've got to talk to George." He arranged for George to come to his apartment. He lived on 81st and Central Park West in one of those towers. Mike had a triplex. I just remember Mike saying, "Oh God, I hope he doesn't push me through the window."

Nichols did not suffer a fatal fall and must have convinced Scott to tone down his competitiveness with Williamson. A collegial atmosphere was a trademark of a Nichols production and a necessity for *Vanya*. Despite this production's "all-star" status, Chekhov's work is a starless play in which the entire cast needs to perform as an ensemble. To achieve this, the director attempted unusual rehearsal techniques, including having the company read the script while lying on cots in order to relax them.

Scott and Nicholson came to a truce and enjoyed meals and drinks together outside the theatre. "My wife and I see him constantly," Williamson told interviewer Christopher Sharp once the show had opened. "We have dinner with him twice a week. He gets pleasure out of making wry comments about his audiences. Last week, he was terrific. He stopped three guys who were taking pictures right in front of him. He stopped the whole show at the second act. 'Stop that or I'll come and take those [cameras] away from you.' The audience applauded."

During another performance, Elizabeth Wilson related, Scott went a step further to halt an impolite shutterbug.

> One matinee of *Uncle Vanya*, a lady started taking pictures in the middle of the show. Well, honey, he charged up the aisle after her. An usher knew to grab the woman and get her out of the way. It turns out the woman had just gotten off a plane from Ohio and she didn't know better. So George didn't grab her or grab her camera. He came back down on stage. I've never forgotten this. He turned to me and said, "Now what do we do?" I said, "Well, let's start the scene again." We went offstage and started it again. That was the kind of anger he was capable of.

Scott had buried the hatchet with Williamson, but there were still occasional sparks of rivalry. All the Circle dressing rooms were equipped with speakers so the actors could hear their cues. Scott had been getting very little laughter for what he regarded as Astrov's comic moments, while Williamson was getting more than his share of guffaws, particularly when he was clownishly pining over Julie Christie. One night the resentment boiled over and Scott smashed the speaker during Williamson's scene. The speaker was not replaced and he could concentrate on his performance.

During an offstage incident, Scott took on the unusual role of preventing a confrontation and saving his British castmate from serious trouble. Elizabeth Wilson said,

> I used to have lunch between shows with George. This one time, Barnard Hughes, George, Nicol, and I went out. Nicol was pretty plotzed. He saw this police car came by and he did this [making an obscene gesture] to the car. "Screw you." They stopped the car. They got out. They were going to arrest him. George had just done *Patton*. He just moved around and said to them, "Excuse me. Do you know who I am?" And the policemen saluted him, said, "Yes, sir," and walked away.

Williamson later reported his views of his costar to columnist Joyce Haber: "He's the most lauded actor in America, and the most highly paid, and he's a tortured man, given to outbursts of rage and extraordinary behavior. I enjoyed *Vanya*. Probably because it was such an experience working with [Scott]. But it wasn't easy. It's quite staggering, the degree of his self-loathing." In fact, while hoisting a few after a performance, Scott turned to Nicholson and asked, "How does it feel to be working beside a drunken, aging actor?"

The question was probably meant as a joke, but it revealed Scott's basic insecurity. His fears proved to be unfounded, at least as far as this limited engagement went. Chekhov was as big a hit as the top-drawing Broadway musicals. The entire run sold out. As he left the Circle theatre each night, Barnard Hughes recalled seeing dozens of eager theatergoers lining up at the box office, preparing to camp out in hopes of cancellations for the next performance.

The *New York Times* reported ten favorable reviews and only one mixed. Many critics compared Williamson and Scott to pugilists, scoring who had gotten in the most devastating punches, as if the play were a boxing match. The *New Yorker*'s Brendan Gill thought Scott was a "match" for Williamson while Martin Gottfried of *Women's Wear Daily* found that Williamson "simply acts circles around Scott" and "blows him right off the stage." Ted Kalem in *Time* continued the sports metaphors, the two actors' scenes had "the charged intensity of *mano a mano* contests between bullfighters." The acerbic John Simon of *New York* magazine found Scott better than a melodramatic Williamson and on a par with Laurence Olivier's Astrov from a filmed British version of the play from the early 1960s. "Scott radiates controlled strength," Simon wrote, "boundless energy kept within bounds by a supreme feat of self-discipline, so that a whisper, a smile, a look will emerge as a harnessed lightning bolt."

Critic David Finkle specifically recalled Astrov's scene with Helena in which he shows her his maps of the local district, displaying the eroding effects of industrialization. Helena is the only person to have shown the slightest interest in the doctor's fascination with conservation, and he is wildly in love with her. But he knows nothing will come of this adoration. "The turmoil within him was deep," Finkle said, "What was going on with Astrov was his love for Helena. Here was this brilliant doctor, stuck in this backwater. The anguish was palpable. He just came on like a raw nerve."

As he had done with the handkerchief in *The Merchant of Venice*, Scott made ingenious use of props to express his character's emotions. In the final act, Helena and the professor have left for good and Astrov has agreed never to return to the estate because his presence would hurt Sonia too much. As he is preparing to depart for the last time, Scott slowly puts on a pair of gloves, knowing that once they are on, Astrov has no reason to stay and his friendly refuge from his lonely medical practice will be gone forever. "He's lost," the actor explained to Lewis Funke. "Not only with the girl [Helena] leaving, but he's also lost the whole atmosphere he had even before she came. There's a great empty space in his life now, and he doesn't have a poolroom to hang out in anymore."

Like Astrov, Scott was losing his own poolroom—the South Salem farmhouse. It was now totally Dewhurst's and he had purchased a new home for his new life: a 6,500-square-foot fieldstone Georgian colonial situated on fourteen and a half acres on Rock Ridge Road in Greenwich, Connecticut. Built in 1917, the house had high ceilings and five bedrooms, plus three for staff. The cost was a little under $500,000.

He was really committed to Van Devere now, but he had trouble cutting the last cord from Dewhurst. Elizabeth Wilson was visiting Dewhurst when Scott displayed his ambivalent feelings towards his former wife. Wilson recalled, "This was the summer we were doing *Uncle Vanya*. He came into the driveway at South Salem. He was drunk. Colleen and I were a little nervous about him because we were afraid of him physically. I was sitting down and Colleen was sitting down. He came over. He started to strangle me. Colleen said, 'George, that's Elizabeth.' He looked kind of bewildered, as if he had meant to strangle Colleen, and he got up and left."

Over thirty years later, Wilson laughed at the memory of the bizarre incident, but added, "It wasn't funny at the time."

Even though he no longer had any right to the property, Scott resented anyone staying in the South Salem house without his consent. "For a number of summers Colleen would rent the house in South Salem and she'd head up to Prince Edward Island," Wilson recalled.

> She had a house up there because she was Canadian and she loved it. She would go away for the summer and on a couple of occasions, she would rent the house for practically nothing. I believe it was the summer of *Vanya*. I was there and I would invite people

for the weekend. I remember Julie Christie was there and she became a good friend. There were a whole bunch of people there.
George was angry that people were staying in his house. George
came in, drunk. We were all having dinner and he said, "Everybody get the fuck out. Get out." We were all terrified. I remember
the two guys Colleen had hired to take care of things—Stuart and
Tony—they were there. Stuart poured the booze down the toilet
so George wouldn't have more liquor. We all got out and got into
cars and went to Chris and Susan Sarandon's house because we
were afraid of George. We were all scared of him when he was like
that. When we finally settled down, somebody said to me, "Your
sister isn't here. Where's your sister?" She was staying in the guest
house. So we somehow called her and said, "Mary, get out. Chris
Sarandon is going to pick you up." She still remembers this. She
went out to the road and lay down by the stone fences that sur-
round the house. Chris came by in a car and picked her up. To this
day, she says, "What was all that about? George wasn't going to
hurt anybody."

Scott did take some furniture from South Salem to Greenwich. Van
Devere had hired her friend and fellow actress Marta Byer-White to
decorate Scott's office in Manhattan and the new Greenwich house.
There was a field trip to South Salem to pick up certain items. Byer-
White remembered,

There was a studio over the garage that was his part of the house.
I think it had a billiard table. He had a couch that he loved, an old
dilapidated leather couch. It was funny, he was moving into this
gorgeous new house and he wanted his old couch. So we had to
take this old, beat-up, leather couch out. Nobody helped us. It was
a very informal household. The thing that I loved was they had
two young boys at the time [Alex and Campbell] and it looked like
every single window had a ball that went through it.

Indeed, the two households could not have been more unlike. The South Salem farmhouse was like a chaotic commune with the door always open and the broken windows in the studio. Dewhurst had an army of friends trooping through, staying for weeks at a time. The Greenwich mansion was orderly, secluded and private. Visitors were rare and when they did come, they had to get out of the car and open a long, wrought-iron gate bearing a sign which read "CLOSE GATE AFTER ENTERING AND *LEAVING*." There was no phone in the main house. To get a message through to either Scott or Van Devere, you had to phone Jane Deacy, who would in turn call the caretaker, who would then leave a note on the kitchen table that might not be seen and responded to until days later.

Van Devere had clearly organized the house to provide her husband a peaceful retreat. She gave him two presents to ease his tensions—a miniature organ and a bread-baking kit. She reasoned he could banish his demons by playing music or kneading dough rather than downing a fifth of scotch or punching out barroom strangers. She also put herself and her career behind her husband's needs. "George has to come first," she said. "Before, acting came first with me. But because of the nature of George and myself, that's the way it will have to be."

Though she put Scott first, Van Devere was no pushover—particularly when it came to politics, as demonstrated by her protest on the *Hospital* set. The radically liberal Van Devere and the independently conservative Scott often sparred over ideologies. She nicknamed him "Old R. and I." for Rigid and Inflexible. He called her his "collectivist." Their tempers would flare when discussing the women's movement, Watergate or Vietnam, but Van Devere seldom backed down. Her temper could be equal to his; she had had tantrums as a child, causing her to black out. Disagreements would sometimes end in physical scuffles that resembled two children playfully wrestling. But there were compromises as well. Van Devere admitted that in the 1976 presidential election, she campaigned for "the most middle-of-the-road politician," Birch Bayh.

A few weeks after *Uncle Vanya* completed its run on July 28, 1973, Scott
flew to the West Coast to film *Bank Shot*, an unfunny caper comedy
based on Donald Westlake's novel. The feature was in the style of *The
Hot Rock*, *The Gang That Couldn't Shoot Straight*, and *Who's Minding the
Mint?*, with a castful of crooked misfits pulling an unusual heist. In
this case, the scheme is to steal an entire bank housed in a trailer. Scott
played Walter Ballantine, a grizzled escaped con and leader of the gang
of kooks. To elicit laughs, he was outfitted with caterpillar-sized eye-
brows and played the part with a lisp. The same character had been enacted in a totally different vein by the devastatingly handsome Robert
Redford in *The Hot Rock*, also derived from a Westlake work. "George
was better casting than Redford for Walter Ballantine," said Bob Balaban, who played one of the gang. He continued,

> He looked beat-up; not like a leading man. It was not a very good
> movie. My character was part of his gang. One of my functions
> was to drive this Model T Ford. I did not have contact lenses and I
> did not know how to drive a stick shift. I was without glasses. I re-
> member George sitting in the back seat and saying, "Try not to get
> us killed, Balaban." I didn't want to be remembered as the young
> actor who killed George C. Scott.

This fiasco was directed by Gower Champion, a former song and
dance man turned Tony-winning stage director and choreographer.
He was no more in control of *Bank Shot* than Balaban was of the
Model T. Champion had mounted such long-running hits as *Bye, Bye
Birdie*, *Hello, Dolly!*, and *I Do! I Do!* and was tired of the backbreaking
demands of Broadway. He had just pulled a show (*Irene* with Deb-
bie Reynolds) out of the crapper during its disastrous out-of-town
tryout and he wanted to establish a film career, which he expected
to be less stressful. Champion's only previous feature credit was *My
Six Loves*, a featherweight comedy starring Reynolds released twelve
years previously.

Champion's friend Jess Gregg told biographer John Anthony Gilvey, "He made it up as he went along. . . . He didn't have any concept where it was going—no ending."

Scott called it "a dreadful film. I did it for the money and because I admired Gower Champion." Champion went back to the relative calm of Broadway and never directed another film.

Lately, Scott's career was like a bad roller coaster. Artistic highs (*The Hospital, Uncle Vanya*) were followed by too many lows (*Rage, Day of the Dolphin, Oklahoma Crude, Bank Shot*). He was ready to get off the ride and get behind the controls.

15

A Tame *Savage*

FRIENDS WOULD OFTEN JOKE THAT George C. Scott's need for control was so great that when riding in the back seat of a car, he would not let the driver lower the sun visor. "Not even when the sun is blinding me," one chum said, "because *he* has to see the road ahead." His film debut as a director, *Rage*, left him bitter over his lack of say-so on the end product. Now he had a movie, *The Savage Is Loose*, that would be totally his, "to the maddening heights of egomania," he joked. He would star in it with Van Devere, direct it, produce it, and rewrite Max Ehrlich and Frank De Felitta's script. For once, he would have the last word on every detail, right down to the goddamn poster to be hung in the lobby. *Savage* would also be his ticket out of acting. If the picture earned enough coin at the box office, he could forgo the heftier acting salaries and concentrate his energies behind the scenes.

The script came to him through United Artists. There were only four characters—botanist John, his wife, Maida, and their son, David, to be played by two actors at different ages. The family is shipwrecked on a tropical island in 1905 with no hope of rescue. Realizing his offspring will outlive him, John trains David to be a matchless hunter. When the son grows into a young man, his sexual urges drive him to challenge his father for the only available woman—his mother. David attempts to kill John, using the very skills his father has taught him. As a result of the conflict, Maida nearly loses her mind, setting their hut on fire. Finally, the warring parties reach an accommodation in their oedipal struggle. The final shot has David embracing Maida while she reaches out to John; the implication being the two men will share her. Survival trumps social taboos. The father-son conflict probably appealed to Scott with the son challenging the father, and not supplanting him in the mother's affections, but gaining equal status there.

UA backed out after a change in administration and Scott bought the script for his company, Devon Campbell Productions, named for two of his children. "Having done that, I felt that it was a rather propitious moment and a good piece to break out with because of the size of it," Scott later explained. "It wasn't a cast of eight and a half million people and we didn't have to go twelve places in the world to do it and it wasn't going to cost an awful lot of million of dollars so I was pleased with that, but mainly, it was a matter of thinking it was a distinctive piece, an original piece, and something unique. That's why we decided to pursue it to the bitter end." And bitter it was. Just as he had with the Theatre of Michigan, Scott invested his own money and lost most of it. Between his own funds and bank loans, Scott and Van Devere put in $850,000 of the film's proposed $1,600,000 production cost. "We hocked the ranch for this one," he later told *People* magazine. The other $750,000 was provided by eleven other investors. The couple took no salaries for directing and acting.

In another bold move, they planned to sell the film directly to the theatre owners and chains. Standard studio procedure was to rent copies of the film to theatres, which returned a percentage of the profits. The Scotts' lawyer advised against it, telling them it couldn't be done. Scott responded, "They told Henry Ford he couldn't make one car a day."

In addition to selling the owners the prints, Scott would supply an advertising campaign (he hated the *Rage* movie poster) and, when available, personally promote the film in the city at the time of its initial screening. It was time of change in the film industry. The studios' iron grip on every aspect of film distribution was loosening for the first time in fifty years. Francis Ford Coppola was planning to establish a company to exhibit his own films. Independent films like *Walking Tall* and *Billy Jack* were being rented directly to the individual theatres. By selling the prints rather than renting, Scott was going them one better.

To find a location, Scott's agent-manager, Jane Deacy; executive producer Bob Relyea; and Van Devere went on a scouting trip while Scott was directing Martin Balsam and Teresa Wright in *Death of a Salesman* for the Philadelphia Drama Guild—another move away from acting. Van Devere and company had to find a spot that had beach, mountains, and jungle. They passed on Hawaii and the Caribbean, but Relyea spied the perfect location from the air as they flew up the west coast of Mexico.

Van Devere explained to Pierre Cossette for the *Saturday Evening Post*: "It couldn't be too pastoral or South Sea Island–like. I found a place which was just incredible, not far from Zihuatanejo, but there was no way to get into it. The one existing road there was went out behind the mountains, and it would have meant a three-hour boat ride every morning. As it was we had to bulldoze through the jungle to get to this place. It took them nearly a week to clear a path to the sea."

While his wife was zooming over lush Mexican jungles, Scott was waging a war of "artistic differences" in wintry Philadelphia. In the March 3, 1974 *Philadelphia Inquirer*, Howard A. Coffin reported Scott had walked out of rehearsals six days before the opening. Playwright Arthur Miller took over the direction. William Ross, the Drama Guild's artistic director, told the press Scott had a "very bad cold" and that he had returned home to recuperate. Miller had arrived in Philly earlier in the week, attended a run-through, and had dinner with Scott. Ross said there were no disagreements between playwright and director that he knew of. An unnamed source informed the *Inquirer* that there was friction between the two and between Scott and his two leads. The source went on to say there was a clause in Miller's contract that allowed him to observe rehearsals and consult on the production—the first major revival of his classic work since its premiere in 1949. Scott had been unaware of this and Miller's kibitzing may have been the cause of the disagreement.

Perhaps Scott's need for control was so driving, it led him to drop out of the Philadelphia *Salesman* altogether rather than even listen to the author's suggestions. Whatever the reason, Scott did not return to the City of Brotherly Love and the production opened to positive reviews without him. He would put his own stamp on Willy Loman the following year when he staged and starred in his production at Circle in the Square.

There was still the *Savage* to prepare for. A location had been found and construction started to make it accessible. As he had done with *Rage*, Scott made up an eighty-page summary of every shot he wanted to use, a practice most directors, with the exception of the meticulous Alfred Hitchcock, eschewed. To resemble a man stuck on a desert island for fifteen years, Scott went on a strict exercise and diet regimen, eating nothing but eggs, spinach, and grapefruit. He lost twenty-two pounds, but increased his smoking to deal with hunger; he was up to two packs before noon. He called his smoking "suicidal." But he was no longer "overweight, flabby, and lethargic. . . . I was delighted at the age of forty-seven to realize I wasn't an old man yet."

Casting was not much of a problem, since he only needed two actors to play David as a boy and as a young man. "I tried to talk him into getting Robert De Niro to do the son," close friend Clifton James recalled. "De Niro wasn't known at that time. See, George cast somebody who was no threat at all. That was his blind spot. De Niro would have been a threat." Indeed, for his son and rival Scott cast John David Carson, a white-bread TV actor who had played one of the well-scrubbed research crew in *Day of the Dolphin*. De Niro had his breakthrough in *Godfather Part II* the next year. Lee H. Montgomery, an experienced child actor, played the younger David.

Production and physique-wise, Scott was ready, but emotionally and psychologically, he was showing stress lines. What was he thinking?

He had over three-quarters of a million dollars of his own money tied up in this movie. And he was selling it directly to the theatre owners. Was he nuts? What if nobody bought it? His dreams were scenarios of panic. In one, he was acting in *Uncle Vanya* and couldn't remember his dialogue or find his necktie. In another, he was simultaneously directing seven or eight movies and all were in chaos. A third featured Scott reenlisting with his old Marine company, but all of his fellow leathernecks are as youthful as ever, while he is in his late forties: "Generally I'm standing in a supply room, with a terrible hangover, being issued a 1952 uniform."

Another echo of the past would soon haunt him, but it would be more than just a dream. Just as he had reunited with Victoria, another daughter would soon reconnect with him. Michelle, the daughter of Scott and Karen Truesdell, was now a teenager. She had grown up believing Karen's husband Peter was her father, but she had always had a feeling it was someone else. Somebody famous. Her mother had been an actress, hadn't she? And why did she keep all those photos of celebrities? Karen and Peter had divorced and Michelle was living with Peter, who told her the truth. After making calls to Tammy Grimes and others from Truesdell's past, Michelle boldly called her real father and introduced herself. Scott later told Truesdell he had known he would receive that call someday. He accepted his daughter and warmly invited her to join her half-brothers and sisters in Mexico for the *Savage* shoot. For the next four years, when she wasn't attending college, Michelle lived with Scott and Van Devere. Eventually, he legally adopted her. Deprived of his presence as a child, Michelle craved her father's attention, which would lead to tensions between him and his fifth wife.

Yet another daughter was actively re-entering his life. Devon Scott was now fifteen. With her brother Matthew, she had regularly visited her father and Colleen Dewhurst in South Salem. Now she decided to follow her dad into the acting profession. She had been cast as the rebellious middle child of Paul Sorvino on *We'll Get By*, a CBS sitcom created by Alan Alda. After the Mexican sojourn, she moved in with

Scott and Van Devere in Hollywood while filming the show. Scott was not pleased with her early career choice. "Acting is a very difficult life, very damaging," he told Aljean Harmetz of the *New York Times*. "Even if Devon does make it, the earlier you make it, the less chance you have of being a human being. I don't think it's a wholesome profession for anybody, certainly not for young people." (Devon would go on to do another TV series, *The Tony Randall Show*, and eventually moved to England to pursue an acting career there. Another Scott offspring, Campbell, found success on both stage and screen, appearing on Broadway opposite his mother in *Long Day's Journey Into Night* and starring in numerous films. Following his father's rebellious bent, Campbell whose stunning good looks could have earned him leading roles in Hollywood blockbusters, chose instead to participate in mostly independent films such as *Longtime Companion*, *The Secret Lives of Dentists*, *Big Night*, *The Impostors*, an avant-garde interpretation of *Hamlet*, and *Roger Dodger*. He won the National Board of Review Award for Best Actor for the last. Also like his dad, he branched out into directing and producing.)

Filming on *Savage* commenced April 22, 1974, and lasted eight weeks. The spot Bob Relyea saw from the air was a stretch of beach near the fishing village of Lo De Marcos, north of Puerto Vallarta, which achieved fame as the location of John Huston's *The Night of the Iguana*. Every morning, Scott and Van Devere would rise before dawn and get into a Mercedes, and Scott's driver, Al Zanone, would take them seventy kilometers along a switchback road through the jungle to a palm-ringed sliver of sand that served as the setting for the shipwrecked family's story.

Any delay causing the film to go over its strict shooting schedule would come out of Scott's pocket, at about $10,000 a day. He kept reporting to work despite attacks of stomach cramps and dysentery. The breakneck pace often led to dust-ups with his leading lady. "It was hard," Scott later said. "Trish feels that I was often inconsiderate of her needs as a performer. I felt that she wasted time by talking and intellectualizing. I'm not impressed with actors who sit around looking for so-called motivation. On a number of occasions, I made that clear to Trish—in no uncertain terms. If anything, I believe I was overly considerate—that I comforted her far too much."

"When things go wrong here," Van Devere said to Aljean Harmetz on the set, "George becomes more patient, benevolent, and generous. Because he's in *control*." She wasn't always in control, at one point raging off the set. Van Devere told Mike Douglas on the latter's talk show: "About two in the morning in the middle of the Mexican jungle, I said, 'Okay, that's that. I'm getting out of here.' I started tromping through the jungle in the middle of the night. Obviously [I] could go nowhere. When I realized how foolish I was, I just turned and went back and said, 'All right, ready to work.'" Despite Scott's best efforts to hold costs down, when advertising and the costs of the prints were added in, the final bill for *Savage* was approximately $3,000,000 (according to *Variety*). Fortunately, that was just the sum raised by direct sales to theatre chains, including the United Artists Theatre Circuit, Plitt Theatres, the Sterling Danz Circuit, and individual cinema owners. Scott would eventually just about break even on the film's first release. He still retained the rights to foreign, TV and airline sales and could realize a profit there.

Once the shooting was complete, the Scotts took a year's lease on Greta Garbo's former home in Beverly Hills. They moved in with Devon, Michelle, paintings, baskets, vases, and the mini-organ from Greenwich. They also installed an editing room in the garage for Scott to finish the post-production. Then they took a private jet on a barn-storming publicity tour to meet with the press and theatre owners in Atlanta, New Orleans, Charlotte, Dallas, Kansas City, St. Louis, and Union, Missouri, where the couple were the guests of honor at a Rotary luncheon. As Scott described *Savage*'s Freudian storyline, a few of the Union upper crust stirred uncomfortably and looked down at their chicken-fried steaks. "I think it's a tasteful film," Scott assured them, "and it will have a PG rating. If they try to give it an R, I'll fight them to the last drop of my blood."

The rating did cause a bloody battle. The movie rating system was a recent invention of Jack Valenti, president of the Motion Picture Association of America, to combat concerns of parents as general-release films of the late 1960s like *Who's Afraid of Virginia Woolf?*, *Blow Up*, *The Pawnbroker*, and *Marriage Italian Style* were taking on more adult themes and displaying more flesh. To prevent government regulation, Valenti proposed a letter-based scale determined by an MPAA-appointed board designed to inform patrons of the contents of films before they bought their tickets. G was for General Audiences, and reserved for family fare along the lines of *Bambi* and *Snow White*. PG (Parental Guidance) meant the going was a little racy but nothing unsuitable for adolescents. An R (Restricted) rating forbade anyone under seventeen from viewing the film unless accompanied by an adult. An X, usually held for outright porn with the occasional mainstream exception like *Midnight Cowboy*, upped the age limit to twenty-one, and no one younger would be permitted admittance with or without a guardian.

Although *Savage* contained no nudity or cursing, the ratings board concluded the main theme of the film was incest and slapped an R on it. Scott felt that would cut into sales of film—if it was perceived as a dirty picture, families would stay away. He launched a Patton-like offensive against the board, beginning with an appeal. He railed to Charles Champlin of the *Los Angeles Times*,

> If I had wanted to make a film about incest, I'd damn well have done it—put two people in bed in the second reel and kept 'em there for the next ten reels. . . . If the wife had stabbed herself and jumped off a cliff we could have had a PG. A nice murder would have taken the raters off the hook. That's the insanity of it. Look what you've got in PG movies. Twenty bloody guys and dead in the first five minutes, sexual titillation of every kind. It's monstrous.

Scott claimed there was no incest because the boy was raised without that taboo. He compared the screenplay to a Greek tragedy with the father teaching the boy the law of the jungle and the mother instructing him in the philosophy of compassion. The real theme of the film was the survival of the family and making difficult choices in impossible circumstances. But the board wasn't buying it; they denied his appeal and the R rating stood. "One of the members came up to me after the hearing," Van Devere said. "He apologized, said he was in a bind and had to vote the way he did. He said, 'I voted against you, but I liked the film, and I can't wait to take my four kids to see it.' These are not bad people, really not. They had no disagreements with the film, but they didn't even project their own opinions. They were too concerned with what the public will think, especially kids."

Scott counterattacked with a publicity campaign. In nine cities where *Savage* was playing, he ran newspaper coupon ads, offering a refund to any adult filmgoers who concurred with the R rating. Just send in the ticket stubs along with the coupon and Scott (not the movie theatre) would more or less cheerfully return your money. On the other hand, if you agreed with Scott that the R was unfair, fill in the coupon stating so and Scott could use it to challenge the rating. He also proposed theatres open the film without any rating and let the audiences decide if it was prurient. In another offensive, he launched a series of screenings for community leaders and hired an independent marketing firm to survey their opinion on the rating. To add gasoline to the fire, the U.S. Catholic Conference condemned *Savage* as unfit for Roman Catholics, and the National Council of Churches of Christ, a Protestant organization, upbraided Scott for suggesting the film open with no rating.

Scott and Van Devere went on every talk show you could name, including those hosted by Dinah Shore, Merv Griffin, Johnny Carson, and Mike Douglas. On Douglas's chat fest, Scott debated Valenti on the MPAA decision and accused the organization's president of invoking the threat of government censorship to justify the ratings board.

The enterprising couple even sat inside the giant tic-tac-toe board on *The Hollywood Squares,* where, before taping began, the portrayer of General Patton told the popular game show's producer he was "scared shitless."

He should have been scared of the reaction to the film. The *New Yorker*'s Pauline Kael, usually a champion of Scott, groaned, "*The Savage* crawls by in slightly under two hours, but they're about as agonizing as any two hours I've spent at the movies."

"Sometimes the worst thing you can have is total approval," said playwright Larry Gelbart, who later worked with Scott on *Sly Fox* and *Movie Movie.* "You need naysayers, not because they say nay, but because they can keep you from your less than brilliant ideas." Critically, *Savage* was a fiasco, and box office performance was mediocre. On top of the negative popular and critical reaction and the ratings controversy, Scott was having trouble collecting his fees for the direct sales of the film. The Savage Is Loose Company and Devon Campbell Productions eventually sued the United Artists Theatre Circuit for $30,000,000. Though he did collect some of the money owed, between legal fees and costs to fight the R rating, *Savage* would wind up putting Scott $2 million in the hole.

Even with the bad reviews, the rating headaches, and the financial bath he had taken, Scott would not let go of his dream project. In 1977, he rented the RKO 59th Street Theatre in Manhattan to turn the *Savage* loose again. He told the *New York Times,* "[N]ow I'm four-walling the movie—leasing the theatre for $240,000, paying for everything, including advertising, and taking whatever receipts I can get." Audiences had had their fill on its first run and attendance was scant. After a year, Scott finally ended *Savage*'s run and it disappeared, rarely to be seen on TV, video, or DVD.

While *Savage* was turning into an unintentional disaster, Scott had been working on an intentional one. On August 12, 1974, he began filming *The Hindenburg,* a fact-derived drama imagining the 1937 explosion of the German passenger dirigible as the work of anti-Nazi saboteurs. Pauline Kael described it as "*Grand Hotel* in flames in the sky. Every couple of years, the American public is said to crave something. Now it's calamity." With the success of *The Poseidon Adventure*, studio heads fought each other to see who could churn out the biggest, most star-studded disaster picture. *The Towering Inferno, Earthquake, Airport '75, Juggernaut, The Cassandra Crossing*, and numerous others treated moviegoers to big stars and bigger special effects. The *Poseidon* recipe was so easy to follow: Step 1—Hire dozen or so top names. Step 2—Get them on board a ship, plane, or train. Step 3—Mix in a tidal wave, explosion, or bomb. Step 4—Rake in the dough.

Scott and director Robert Wise (*The Sound of Music*) refused to categorize the film as part of the current trend, because it dealt with historic events. Scott frankly admitted he had taken the job because he had turned down the lead in *Poseidon* and realized he had missed out on a fat payday and a starring role in a hit. He would use his $1,000,000 salary (his first in six figures) to help pay off the *Savage* expenses and to finance a film about burn victims. He was inspired by a visit to the Institute for the Burned in Ann Arbor, Michigan. Eleanor Perry (*Diary of a Mad Housewife*) was working on a script and Van Devere was set to disfigure her patrician features to play a patient. He swore *Hindenburg* would be his last film, but he had been making noises about retiring from acting since *Oklahoma Crude* and few believed him.

Scott played a German officer assigned to ferret out the saboteur on the zeppelin's maiden transatlantic voyage. The passengers and crew each had a clichéd storyline. Anne Bancroft was a pot-smoking countess, Gig Young a fast-talking American producer, Charles Durning the stalwart captain, Burgess Meredith and Rene Auberjonois colorful card sharps, and so on and predictably so forth. As with *Day of the Dolphin*, Scott was given little chance to develop a character. Most of his scenes were expositional, with his officer interrogating suspects. Throughout the film, his usually expressive face is almost totally blank, until just before the ship blows up, when he discovers the explosive device planted inside a watch. There is a gripping intensity to Scott's features as he tries to disarm the bomb. It only lasts a few seconds before the thing goes off, but it's the only sign of life in the entire film. *Newsweek* condemned it as "the most dismal attempt yet to cash in on the disaster formula." As with most blow-'em-up flicks, the spectacular explosions and crashes were the best elements of *Hindenburg* and it won Oscars for special visual and sound effects.

To further pay down the *Savage* debt, Scott played real-life attorney Louis Nizer in *Fear on Trial*, a CBS movie on blacklisting in the TV industry. Nizer represented radio personality John Henry Faulk in his suit against a right-wing publication for branding him a Communist during the McCarthy red-baiting era of the 1950s. According to director Lamont Johnson, the star was paid a near-record fee for a video appearance. *Film and Filming* said Scott "dominates the film [broadcast on October 2, 1975] and a fair proportion of its $700,000 budget. The money has been well spent. Scott brings a towering presence to the story, a determination and honesty tempered with practical cynicism."

The burn-victim film to star Van Devere never materialized. The lawsuits over collecting *Savage* fees and its dismal box office performance scared off potential investors. To make it up to his wife, Scott directed her in a revival of *All God's Chillun Got Wings*, an obscure 1924 Eugene O'Neill drama about interracial marriage he had planned to stage Off-Broadway with James Earl Jones in the late '60s. Now it would be presented at Circle in the Square and serve as Van Devere's Broadway debut. Said press agent Susan L. Schulman, who worked with both actors,

> People assumed that Trish's career was thanks to him. What they forgot was she was a very well respected actor before they got together. She had quite a lot of success. I think she'd done stage, but I know she'd done several films before they met and had been quite an accomplished actor. I think it was always a real problem that

people perceived her as only having a career because she married George C. Scott. In fact, she probably would have had a better career without him, because she was so in his shadow. I think people tended to kind of dismiss her because of it where in fact she was quite formidable. Although they never said this, I always felt that he probably did that production so that people could see that she was a good actress.

It must have been difficult to be directed by your husband, particularly when he's regarded as the finest actor in America, you're appearing for the first time on Broadway, and you've been critically lambasted in your last few films. Like the leads in *Kiss Me, Kate*, the married star and director brought their offstage conflicts into their professional lives. Judith Barcroft, Van Devere's understudy, recalled,

I thought she was very difficult to direct. He wanted her to use the maternal side of herself. There was a scene where [her character] Ella is supposed to hold a straw doll. He wanted her to hold the doll and rock it. But she didn't want to go near it.

They had a tremendous fight just before the opening and she left the theatre. So I had to go on. I didn't have any rehearsals and I'd never even been backstage before. The hairdresser led me around. But my husband was a stage manager and he had told me an understudy should always be prepared. I went on and got bravos.

Van Devere returned the day after her walkout and *All God's Chillun* opened on March 20, 1975, to decidedly mixed reviews. O'Neill was trying to be progressive in 1924 (a near-riot erupted during the original production because a white actress kissed the hand of a black actor), but over fifty years later, his histrionics came across as antiquated and melodramatic. "Although I've always wanted to do *Chillun*," Scott told a reporter for the *New York Sunday News*, "at the first reading I said this is a play that cannot be done. It was not an idle comment, but I hope I was being facetious, but I'm not sure. I could turn out to be right."

Most of the critics agreed with him. "This is a very poorly written play," Clive Barnes bluntly stated in the *New York Times*. "Its lines are like dead rocks and its dramaturgy is basic to the point of being childlike." Van Devere came in for the worst blows. Barnes found her "playing lacked energy, notably in her enervated style of madness, and was altogether too characterless." As usual, the peppery John Simon of *New York* magazine launched a frontal assault, calling the revival "a major disaster." On Scott, he asked, "Why must this absorbing actor insist on becoming a dreary director?" Van Devere was "catastrophic."

Walter Kerr in the *Sunday Times* gave his usual thoughtful review and provided a glimpse of the potential power of the production. While acknowledging the datedness of the play ("You've been white to me, Jim," the Caucasian Ella tells her black husband), he admired Scott's stage pictures:

> Faced with the play's spareness on the one hand and its uneasy ambiguity on the other, director Scott has made his own bold effort to translate the vision into a quasi-poetic dream-state, making it a thing of silences and spaces. Two children, one black, one white, walk in solitude along a brick-paved tenement street, fire-escapes dangling overhead. A wino, singing a broken melody, rummages through trash cans at his leisure, all joints loose in their sockets. . . . A young man does not see a girl until she has vanished from the stage; he then calls her back, stressing the long, lonely gallery that lies between them.

Scott had considerably more success at the Circle three months later when he directed himself in a revival of *Death of a Salesman*. Though he was constantly telling anyone who would listen that he planned to get out of acting, he continued to stretch and challenge himself. He had played the son Biff at Stephens College, but now was tackling one of the most difficult roles in American theatre—Willy Loman, Arthur Miller's archetypical little man, reaching the end of a unremarkable career with nothing to show for it. Written in the days before IRAs and Keogh accounts, Willy has no savings or retirement plans. His Brooklyn home is still mortgaged and surrounded by towering apartment buildings. Willy cherishes the illusion that if he is not a big business wheel, his sons will be. But Biff is an aimless drifter, and his brother, Happy, is more interested in sleeping around and having a good time than in climbing the corporate ladder. In an emotionally wrenching scene, Biff confronts his father on his true nature. "I'm a dime a dozen, Pop, and so are you," he cries. (Again, Scott was drawn to father-son conflict.) Unable to face the falsity of his American dream, Willy commits suicide to leave his family the insurance money, which turns out to be insignificant. The play ends with Willy's tiny funeral gathering and his wife weeping as she reveals she made the last payment on their house that morning.

This was the first Broadway revival since the play's legendary premiere starring Lee J. Cobb and directed by Elia Kazan. Unlike the Philadelphia production, Scott was determined to stage the play without Miller's opinions, insisting that the playwright stay away from rehearsals. He kept the same actress (Teresa Wright) from Philly to play Linda, Willy's loyal and long-suffering wife, but made several significant changes from the original script. He had two actresses play the Woman in Boston, the doxy with whom Willy has an affair, changing the dalliance from a plot device to a sign of Willy's weakness. There were two intermissions rather than one. For the roles of the neighbor Charlie and his nerdish but ultimately successful son, Bernard, Scott hired two African-American actors, Arthur French and Chuck Patterson. This was years before nontraditional casting was commonplace on New York and regional stages. "I was roundly criticized for that because there weren't any black people in Brooklyn at the time of the play," Scott told Michael Reidel for *Theatre Week*. "Even Arthur Miller didn't like it. But I thought it was a hell of a good idea, mainly because

I liked the actors involved." Late in the play, after losing his job of twenty years, Willy is offered a job by Charley. He responds, "I just can't work for you." With a black actor in the role, the line took on a racial charge.

For the sons, the director-star cast against type. James Farentino, an outgoing actor who played the extroverted Happy in a 1966 television version of *Salesman*, was the quiet, introspective Biff. Harvey Keitel, best known for a tough but laconic performance in Martin Scorsese's *Mean Streets*, enacted his exuberant sibling. (Keitel was filming another enigmatic Scorsese street thug in *Taxi Driver* during rehearsals.) Chuck Patterson told biographer Marshall Fine, "George wanted Harvey to be expansive as Happy and James to be moody, dark and poetic as Biff. But he was getting the opposite thing from each actor. That worked itself out in rehearsal." Director Arvin Brown found the casting an inspired stroke. "That created a kind of tension because they were playing against type," he told Fine. "That made it really interesting."

The biggest difference between Kazan's production and Scott's was his own interpretation of Willy. While Lee J. Cobb was a defeated, pathetic man, Scott managed to retain his strength as an actor while playing a weak character. This Willy would rage like an outer-borough King Lear at the injustices dealt him. He also decided to play Willy as mad from the beginning of the play. "Willy doesn't know he's defeated, you see," Scott told interviewer Margaret Croyden. "He's at the brink of total insanity in my opinion."

William Glover of the Associated Press compared Scott's Loman to "an embittered, chained Prometheus, a raging though defeated General Patton." *Time*'s T. E. Kalem said, "When his head is bowed, it is not in resignation but rather like that of a bull bloodied by the picadors yet ready to charge again."

"If there were nothing in the performance but weakness and defeat," wrote Julius Novick in the *Village Voice*, "however finely modulated, we would quickly grow tired of it. It is the tension between strength and weakness that fascinates us."

Arthur Miller, though he was excluded from the production process, was appreciative of Scott's approach:

> I think it has an enormous effect, primarily because he has a he-
> roic approach to it instead of a piddling little shoemaker's approach.
> There aren't many actors of that scope, so I appreciate that. The play
> is really one continuous poem. It has no scenes. It has no interstices.
> It's all one thing and it takes a gigantic wind to sustain it. You can't
> do that play with a petty, little strategy. It takes a man that's willing
> to fall on his sword to do it. He's eminently one of those actors. And
> I'm glad. I appreciate that. It moves me to watch him.

Audiences were also moved, awarding standing ovations every night
of the limited run—and this was before playgoers leaping to their feet
became a common occurrence on Broadway. "I've never forgotten it,"
said Bob Balaban. "I had to muffle my sobs at the end of the play. He
epitomized the towering futility of this person."

Scott hoped to bring the production to Los Angeles or London
and film it with his *Patton* cinematographer Fred Konekamp. "George
wants to do the film from the actors' point of view as well as the audience's," James Farentino told the *Los Angeles Times*. "He wants to shoot
rehearsals, actors driving from home, audiences coming into the theatre. He hopes to give the filmgoing public a feeling of what the theatre
is all about." Financing for such a film fell through and the Scott *Salesman* never traveled beyond the Circle in the Square. The only record of
Scott's extraordinary performance is a brief excerpt shown on *Camera
Three*, CBS's Sunday morning cultural program. While imploring his
boss, Howard, to let him stay on with the firm, Willy is remembering
the salesman who inspired him to go into the business—Dave Singleman, an old-style drummer who earned his living with a glad-handing
personality. Scott begins the scene like a smooth-talking pitchman, using his tale of Singleman to plead his case. Then he gets carried away
by his own story and almost tears up with nostalgia over the fellowship

now gone from his profession. "Today, it's all cut and dried, and there's no chance for bringing friendship to bear—or personality," he says with more than a hint of longing. When the boss grows impatient and brushes Willy aside, Scott switches from misty-eyed nostalgia to impotent rage. Like a frustrated child, he yells about his sales averages in 1928. Howard interrupts him and Willy abruptly stops, realizing that his career is over. Howard leaves and Willy is devastated.

While Scott was rehearsing *Salesman*, Howard Gottfried and Paddy Chayefsky, producer and writer of *The Hospital*, brought him the script for *Network* with the intention of offering him the role of Howard Beale, the crazed network anchor who delivers the most memorable line of the film and arguably of the 1970s: "I'm as mad as hell and I'm not going to take it anymore."

Gottfried and Chayefsky told him he was for perfect for Beale. But Scott turned them down without giving a reason. Director Sidney Lumet believed it was because he had done something now forgotten to offend the actor despite the fact that they had never met and that Scott refused to work with him. Scott later confessed to Richard Brown he didn't take the part because he didn't think it was big enough. Despite the relative brevity of the role, Peter Finch received a posthumous Oscar for his performance as the wild-eyed Beale and Scott did eventually work with Lumet on *Gloria*. It was his last film performance.

After *Salesman* closed, Scott suffered a near heart attack. It was kept out of the press and Van Devere demanded they take a much-needed vacation. They went as far from civilization and show business as possible, hiring a yacht and crew to sail them around the Fiji Islands for three weeks. Van Devere penned an article on the trip for *Family Weekly*, quoting letters she sent during the vacation. She relished being at sea. "Last night we were at anchor in the bay," Van Devere wrote to her mother, "George and I slept on mats atop the wheelhouse. It was wonderful snuggled under a blanket . . . brilliant stars . . . good sound sleep." They snorkeled, strolled on pristine beaches, visited tiny villages, snapped photos of fruit bats flying out of a dormant volcano, and snuggled close while watching spectacular sunsets. Van Devere collected seashells while Scott fished and played gin with his Uncle Bud, who traveled with them for five days. "George C. is a riot," Van Devere said in a letter to her brother, "he's boning up on everything from bowlines to charts, sails, weather, wind and stars. It's all for his next film, *Islands in the Stream*, the last story Ernest Hemingway wrote before his death. George plays an old sailor, so he's trying to learn how to go about *being* an old sailor. It does keep him busy!" (In fact, Scott would be playing a sculptor who is also a skilled seaman.)

They were finally getting some peace, but the marriage was hitting rough spots. They had agreed to take on projects together so they wouldn't be separated. "One of the big dangers of show biz marriages is that one person goes one way and the other goes another," Scott said. "After a year, you come together and realize you have nothing in common. We have tried to avoid that." But *The Day of the Dolphin*, *The Savage Is Loose* and *All God's Chillun*—Scott's gifts to Van Devere— were bombs. Van Devere was feeling neglected, and her individual career was going nowhere. *One Is a Lonely Number* had received good notices, but MGM had failed to promote it and the picture vanished. Who was she as an actress other than Mrs. George C. Scott? "We were making each other miserable," Scott would later tell *People* magazine, "and we decided maybe we should take action." They started going to a Santa Monica gestalt therapist named Robert Resnick, who was already treating Van Devere. "He was a good man," Scott said. "We were very lucky." The therapy helped mend the cracks in the marriage, but the fissures would reappear a few years later.

16

Papa, the Beast, and a Sly Fox

WHILE TEACHING A MARINE CORRESPONDENCE course, Scott fell in love with the works of Ernest Hemingway. "I read everything he wrote while I was teaching that class, and I still reread Hemingway," he said years later. Edgar Allan Poe and William Faulkner were also on the syllabus, but, in Scott's view, Hemingway's lean, unadorned style made him the master of the short story. "He could say the most with the least amount of words," the star opined. In addition, Hemingway's persona—hard-drinking, nonconformist, tough as nails—could have served as a template for the actor's. So it was a perfect fit for Scott to play Thomas Hudson, a fictional version of the author, in the screen edition of *Islands in the Stream,* Papa's posthumously published novel. As Andrew Sarris wrote in the *Village Voice,* "George C. Scott is the Ernest Hemingway of actors as Ernest Hemingway was the George C. Scott of novelists—both violent, bullying, talented men with an anti-analytical temperament and prodigious self-discipline."

In the screenplay by Denne Bart Petitclerc, a former reporter for the *Miami Herald* and longtime friend of Hemingway, significant changes were made. Hudson is a sculptor rather than a painter. Perhaps it was felt Scott would look more macho wielding an acetylene torch than he would with a brush and palette. Characters were eliminated, and the concluding segment had Hudson smuggling Jewish refugees into Cuba rather than chasing German submarines. He dies after a fight with the Cuban Coast Guard instead of German sailors. The Jewish refugees sequence was similar to the conclusion of another Hemingway work, *To Have and Have Not*.

This was to be the first film adaptation of a Hemingway work since *The Killers* more than a decade before and quite a risk for Paramount, the producing studio. The market was saturated with violent action films like *Jaws* and sci-fi epics. Would the jaded audiences of the mid-1970s spend their four bucks on a simple drama about family relationships and personal heroism without monsters or intergalactic laser fights?

Producers Peter Bart and Max Palevsky were convinced they would. But they needed a star to sell the story. Scott was their first choice for Hudson, but he rejected Petitclerc's first draft of the screenplay, despite the participation of his *Patton* director, Franklin Schaffner. Steve McQueen, who had just worked with Schaffner on *Papillon* expressed interest and attended several meetings, making suggestions for reshaping the last third of the film that were eventually incorporated in the final script. After three weeks, McQueen begged off, citing a contractual conflict with his company First Artists to film *An Enemy of the People*. Bart later claimed the action star was uneasy with the dramatic demands of the role.

With McQueen out of the picture, Scott was sent a revised version of the script and he accepted the part. A couple of weeks later, Bart and Palevsky got word from Scott that he would like to meet with Mary Hemingway to discuss the character of Hudson. He was in previews of *All God's Chillun* at the time. Bart and Palevsky arranged for Scott to meet the widow Hemingway backstage after a performance. Mrs. Hemingway had sent Scott a note saying how happy she was to have him appearing in the film, but Scott had not answered. The *Chillun* performance had not gone well and Scott was in a rage. The five-foot-two Mrs. Hemingway approached the rampaging director and greeted him with "When I write notes to people, I expect them to answer."

Scott turned red, smiled, and said, "You've got guts, lady. I like that." Then everybody went to a bar and had a great deal to drink. During this post-performance party, Scott asked the producers, "By the way, has anyone figured out where we can shoot this picture?" There was talk of a Bahamas location, but Scott had recently made *Day of the Dolphin* there and none of the islands looked like 1941—the era of the script.

The Hawaiian island of Kauai was finally chosen. It was the least populated of the chain, with only 30,000 residents. The location had remote, rugged terrain, warm weather, and a natural harbor that did not have to be dredged so that the large boats necessary for filming could navigate it. Bart would later say another point in Kauai's favor was its scarcity of barrooms for Scott to get plotzed in.

Scott arrived on set on September 18, 1975. He had been shaving his head for *Death of a Salesman*, so it was no problem to grow his hair in a crew cut, the style favored by Hemingway. With the growth of a short beard, the Papa look was complete. When Mary Hemingway visited the set, she was struck by the actor's resemblance to her late husband. In keeping with their policy of spending as much time together as possible, Van Devere stayed with Scott in a rented beachfront estate, but she had developed interests outside of acting. After a few weeks, she took a break in Los Angeles to supervise a photography exhibit.

More than five weeks were spent on the Pacific Ocean for the fishing and boat scenes. Filming at sea was particularly onerous. To capture the scenes aboard a replica of Hemingway's yacht, the *Pilar*, the production crew soldered pontoons together to form huge module-rafts with a platform that would hold cameras, equipment, costumes, food, and portable bathrooms. The modules were towed by the support ship, a converted WWII navy ammo boat with cots for actors, electrical equipment, more wardrobe, and a dining area. Since *Patton*, Schaffner had directed a complicated jungle escape in *Papillon* and the Russian revolution in *Nicholas and Alexandra*, and he reveled in the challenge. Bart had to practically drag the director off the ship on a particularly stormy day. The crew was standing knee-deep in Pacific water and fighting hurricane-force winds. Failing to convince Shaffner to call it quits, Bart tried to reason with Scott. The actor curtly answered he would stay out as long as his director did.

"Looking at him, I realized that the day's work had become a game of chicken between these two," wrote Bart in *Shoot Out*, a book on the intricacies of the filmmaking game he coauthored with Peter Gruber. "There was mutual respect between them, but also a distinct tension, as though each was intent on proving he was more of a man than the other. The contest probably started on *Patton* and now I had inherited the results." When a crew member was nearly washed overboard, Bart shut the location down. Schaffner packed up without a word, but Scott turned to Bart and said he finally knew what producers do on a film set. "Producers prevent you from drowning," he said.

Once again, he made noises about leaving acting. He firmly stated the only reason he was still doing *Islands* was to pay off the *Savage Is Loose* debts. After just a few more films to achieve solvency he would really quit.

He told Ray Loynd of the *Los Angeles Herald-Examiner* that one of the upcoming projects was a biopic of General Douglas MacArthur, an unexpected choice since Scott was loath to repeat himself and he had already portrayed a major military figure. But he wouldn't do it if the current producers David Brown and Richard Zanuck were attached. "They want to rehash World War II with MacArthur," he said to Loynd, "but that's not where MacArthur's at. It's Japan. With his arrogance and whatever you want to say he turned Japan around in a decade."

According to David Brown, it was more than a disagreement over story focus that caused Scott to balk at working with him and his partner again. In his memoir, Brown reports he and Zanuck were taking a meeting on *MacArthur* with Scott in the office of Sidney Sheinberg, president of MCA/Universal. Scott was taken aback by their presence. He asked Sheinberg what the two of them are doing there. Brown reports Scott as saying, "I had the most unpleasant experience of my life with these two men on two films, *Patton* and *Rage*." Zanuck countered that *Patton* was the most successful film of Scott's career. "And as for *Rage*," Zanuck went on, according to Brown, "that was your movie. . . . You refused to edit it. You wouldn't even attend the screening of the rough cut. We were left to edit it." Brown reported that he and Zanuck later encountered Scott at the Bel Air Hotel. Zanuck attempted to make peace, but Scott angrily turned him down and started a fight. Brown and Zanuck fled the lounge and later cast Gregory Peck as their general.

During down times on *Islands*, Scott was rereading Hemingway, particularly *Men at War*, his collection of battle reportage, as well as Steinbeck, Camus, and Balzac. He was also interested in history, particularly the Civil War and precolonial America with an emphasis on the French and Indian War. His recent trip to the South Pacific raised his interest in the explorations of Captain Cook. He did drink, but it did not interfere with the shooting schedule. "Scott got thoroughly swackered many nights," Peter Bart said, "but there were no bars for him to invade."

Claire Bloom, who played Hudson's ex-wife Audrey, had expected her costar to be difficult based on her experiences with other macho leading men. She was pleasantly surprised, but, like many of his previous leading ladies, she noticed his unease with women on the set. The elegant British actress wrote in her memoir,

> Scott, far from being the monstrous egomaniac I had suspected him to be, was an extremely good colleague and we played together very well. Granted, he didn't have much to say to me; we stood in silence between takes. I became quite tongue-tied and couldn't think of anything interesting to say; he, meanwhile, didn't utter a word. He did become quite jolly around 6 P.M., when he was brought a glass of what might conceivably have been water; then he could gather all the men of the crew together and laugh and tell stories.

Islands wasn't released until 1977, when it was met with mixed reviews and indifference from the public. Petitclerc's screenplay and Schaffner's direction cannot overcome the episodic nature of the original novel. The strained relations between Hudson and his sons as movingly portrayed by Scott, Hart Bochner, Brad Savage, and Michael-James Wixted form the strongest part of the film. But once the kids leave halfway through, the story loses its impact. The final sequence of Hudson nobly coming to the rescue of the Jewish refugees feels tacked on.

Scott's performance is unusually restrained and subtle. McQueen may have been intimidated by the scenes where Hudson had to silently express his complicated emotions for his sons, his estranged wife, and his alcoholic first mate (David Hemmings). But Scott's eloquent face conveys the equivalent of pages of Hemingway's prose. It isn't only his features that provide a window onto Hudson's soul. In the most moving moment of the film, Scott has his back to the camera. Hudson and Audrey are rehashing their failed marriage and he is turning to make her a drink. He suddenly realizes the reason for her visit—their son has been killed in action. There is a moment of dead silence, he brings his hand slowly to the back of his neck, and then he turns around. Shock and loss have made small cracks on his stoic visage. He simply says, "He's dead, isn't he?" The he-man façade briefly slips, but he holds it firmly in place as Audrey embraces him. It's a perfectly played scene in an uneven picture.

On June 4, 1976, Scott traveled to Budapest, Hungary, to film a cameo in *The Prince and the Pauper*, an elaborate costume drama based on Mark Twain's classic. He played Ruffler, a king of thieves and former monk, with rascally charm. Scott practically winks at the camera as he governs a kangaroo court of cutthroats judging disguised royal Mark Lester, who has intruded into their unsavory midst. He later told interviewer Paul Riordan he had done it as a favor to Richard Fleischer, his director on *The Last Run* and *The New Centurions*. Alexander Salkind produced *Prince* in the same vein as his celebrity-stuffed *The Three Musketeers* and its follow-up, *The Four Musketeers*—a galaxy of stars, lots of rough-and-tumble swordplay, plenty of low comedy. The money was good and it meant a free trip to Europe. Scott received "guest star" billing, and he was back in the States within a week.

Period pieces continued with his next project, *Beauty and the Beast*, a TV movie for the *Hallmark Hall of Fame* based on the fairy tale. Here was another opportunity for the Scotts to work together. "The script was sent to him," explained Sherman Yellen, author of the teleplay. "Trish read it. She wanted to do it. Her interest in doing it was what got him to do it. It was written for a much younger woman. They came as a package." In fact, Van Devere's initial reaction was a doubtful one. "My God! I'm too old for that," the thirty-two-year-old actress exclaimed. "That part should be played by an eighteen-year-old." Her forty-nine-year-old husband replied, "My dear, if you're too old for it, what about me?"

Age inappropriateness notwithstanding, Scott looked forward to overcoming the difficulties of creating a sympathetic character while wearing a grotesque mask. To design the Beast's hideous features, he consulted his longtime makeup man, Del Acevedo. To experiment with different ideas, Acevedo's associate and son-in-law drew images of different beasts, including a werewolf and a boar, over Scott's picture. Scott wanted masks made of each of them, but Acevedo demurred, stating that each mask would cost about $1,500. So Scott settled on the boar shape. With two assistants, Acevedo made a death mask of Scott and modeled the wild boar mask on that. Then Scott decided he needed cloven hooves for his hands to go with the wild boar look. This presented another problem. They had to really seal the hooves, otherwise the makeup would get on Van Devere's costume when they danced and embraced. Once filming started in Cheltenham, England, Scott would spend took two and a half hours every morning in Acevedo's make up chair. He had three to four inches of rubber in front of his mouth and had to consume his lunch through a straw. Even scratching his nose became a major production. "Once in a while, I'll take some

implement, thrust it up through the nostrils and scratch my nose underneath there," the actor grumbled. "You can't blow your own nose,
of course. It sounds humorous, but after ten or eleven hours it's not
quite so funny." Acevedo recalled,

> He did break out because he was allergic to spirit gum. That pre-
> sented a big problem. We had shut down for a day. The produc-
> ing company was Hallmark. The in-house producer came by and
> said, "What's going on, Del?" I said, "We're waiting for the vet to
> come." I didn't say that as a joke. It just came out because George
> was always the wild boar; he hadn't become the prince yet. We
> were waiting for the doctor from British communicative diseases
> to check out George because his face was red.

In addition to the rash, Scott caught a bad cold. Despite the trials, he
limited his alcohol intake, even waving away a Bloody Mary offered
by Van Devere during an interview. "The only one I ever saw drunk
on the set was [director] Fielder Cook," Yellen recalled. "He dozed
occasionally."

Despite ten hours a day in a sweltering mask that covered his entire
visage, Scott delivered a full range of the Beast's emotions, from his
hurt at Beauty's initial rejection to joy at her coming to love him despite his hideous appearance. "It's the eyes," he told Robert Musel of
TV Guide. "The eyes are free and they are obviously the most expressive part of the face."

All the retirement talk seemed to have faded away. The Scotts were
full of plans for costarring projects, including a limited television series
based on Will and Ariel Durant's The Age of Napoleon, two more films,
and a play that turned out to be their biggest success together.

After the tragedy of Death of a Salesman, Scott was ready for a knock-
about farce for his next stage vehicle. Larry Gelbart provided it by
transposing Ben Johnson's Volpone from Elizabethan England to San

Francisco of the Gold Rush era. The principal character, a scheming rascal, poses as a wealthy invalid to bilk hypocritical sycophants of their valuables—and in some cases their wives' sexual favors—in hopes of being mentioned in his will. The idea originated with director Arthur Penn, who wanted to stage it as a TV special to benefit the Actors Studio. Penn thought of Gelbart for the adaptation since he had an earlier hit based on classic material (the ancient Roman comedies of Plautus) with the book of *A Funny Thing Happened on the Way to the Forum* (written with Burt Shevelove). Sir Lew Grade, the British showman, commissioned the script since CBS would not foot the bill. Penn organized a reading in New York with a cast headed by Art Carney and Lee Strasberg for a small audience of industry insiders. The reaction was so strong—Penn called the script "indecently funny"—that the director and producer immediately envisioned Foxwell J. Sly romping on a Broadway stage rather than confined to a television box.

Gelbart set about expanding his work to take advantage of the freedom of movement and language the stage embraced and video would not allow. CBS declined to invest in the stage venture. Lew Grade became the principal backer with the Shubert Organization and Martin Starger assisting. The new draft was sent to Scott and, as a backup, to Walter Matthau. Both said yes, but Matthau had recently undergone open heart surgery and didn't wish to leave sunny California. Scott was cast as Sly, with Van Devere as Mrs. Truckle, the pious and beautiful wife of a greedy merchant who throws his spouse into Sly's clutches. Jack Gilford, who was the delightfully groveling slave Hysterium in *Forum*, played the ancient miser Crouch. Bob Dishy played the hypocritical Truckle, and Hector Elizondo Sly's clever servant, Able.

Rehearsals began in October 1976. At the first reading, Gelbart's heart sank. To his ears, the indecently funny play landed like a wet doughnut. "My work was, in a word, terrible," he wrote in his memoir. "It was, in two words, really terrible." The writer had taken time off from a lucrative assignment on the hit TV series *M*A*S*H* to work on the play. Through the out-of-town tryouts, he furiously revised the script.

While the cast was rehearsing new scenes on the stage of the newly restored Mechanic Theatre in Baltimore and the Wilbur Theatre in Boston by day, they would perform the old version at night.

Scott's photographic memory served him well. Gelbart recalled that the star would not even read the revised pages. The author just read them to Scott once and the actor would be letter perfect at the next performance.

One of the major changes was having Scott play both Sly and the rootin' tootin' hangin' judge for two scenes in the second act, imitating the Virginia accent of his Uncle Bud. "That was his idea," Gelbart said. "As I wrote it originally, it just said The Judge. I didn't write a cast of characters saying who was playing what. But if the actor doesn't play both characters, he hasn't got much to do in the first half of the second act. So I don't know how he cooked it up, but he said, 'Could I play both parts?' and we jumped at it."

For the Broadway opening night on December 14, 1976, at the Broadhurst Theatre, Scott was more nervous than usual. When the audience was not as responsive as in Baltimore and Boston, he told friends he was sure the reviews would be mixed to bad and *Sly Fox* would close within two weeks. A previous musical attempt at placing *Volpone* in the same era, *Foxy*, had flopped on Broadway in 1964 despite a Tony-winning performance by Bert Lahr, so there was a precedent for failure. But the critics, who attended earlier preview performances, mostly found this newer *Fox* farce hilarious. Clive Barnes of the all-important *Times* declared it dangerous to your health since "a man might die laughing." There was a line down the block from the theatre the next morning. Scott was guaranteed $8,500 a week against ten percent of the gross, plus seven and a quarter percent of the profit.

He and Van Devere stayed with the show until their contracts were up in May 1977. They even cohosted the Tony Awards at the end of the season even though neither was nominated. (Bob Dishy received a Featured Actor nod, the show's sole recognition that evening; he didn't win.) Robert Preston and later Vincent Gardenia replaced Scott and *Sly Fox* had a hit run of 495 performances. Scott and Van Devere would headline the Los Angeles production at the Shubert Theatre in the summer of 1978.

Scott was nearing fifty and reflecting on his life with mixed emotions. He told interviewer Margaret Croyden he didn't make friends easily, regretted his previous unhappy marriages, and regarded his personal life as unsuccessful. When Croyden said many men at his age had similar feelings, Scott laughed and remarked he had felt this way at thirty-five.

He was also realizing his physical limitations. He gave up softball for golf, but still had plenty of energy for passionate outbursts. Christopher Lee, the British horror film star, was a frequent fellow player and recalled Scott's demeanor on the links:

> George burned with a short fuse: I once saw him fling his driver up into a tree, and it's probably still there. With George the nineteenth hole was a test too, because you never knew if he was on or off the wagon. Primed with a beer and a stiff dose of vodka, he once told me of his dislike of acting and how he'd always wanted to be a teacher, and wondered why "people are always so alarmed when they're around me." But it was the same aura that made him such a powerful actor.

Jack Lemmon recalled Scott could take trouble on the golf course with humor as well: "Once we were in a tournament and I watching the live television broadcast while waiting to tee off. George hit a shot into what look like a jungle. As he struggled to find his ball, the camera followed him. Suddenly, he turned and said, 'Lemmon, I hope you're watching and I hope you end up here, too!'"

In early 1978, Scott had a brush with mortality. He had entered the Bing Crosby Pro-Am Golf Tournament in Monterey, California. Thinking it would be fun to sail there from Los Angeles, he chartered an eighty-five-foot yacht, *Mojo*. What started as a leisurely sailing trip turned into a near-disaster. During a turbulent storm, a huge, twenty-five-foot wave smashed into the yacht, collapsing the wheelhouse and flying bridge. "We were very lucky," Scott told the *San Francisco Chronicle*. "It was the biggest wave I've ever seen. . . . It hit us right at the mouth of the jetty and we took it full front. When that son of a gun came up, we hit the deck and the wave washed over us." The *Mojo* was towed by the Coast Guard cutter *Cape Hedge* to a mooring off Avila Beach. Scott, Van Devere, and the four-member crew checked in at the Sierra Vista Hospital in San Luis Obispo. Van Devere suffered a cut foot and bruises and two members of the crew sustained minor injuries.

Sly Fox satisfied the Scotts' need to work together and they soon reteamed with Larry Gelbart on another broad comedy, this time a hilarious tribute to the sort of old-time double features Scott had enjoyed as a boy in Pontiac, Michigan. Gelbart concocted a script in collaboration with Sheldon Keller consisting of two Depression-era spoofs—*Dynamite Hands*, a boxing drama modeled on *Body and Soul* and *Golden Boy* with an idealistic young pugilist battling the mob as well as his opponents in the ring, and *Baxter's Beauties of 1933*, a lavish, Busby Berkeley-ish musical centering on an unknown chorus girl who becomes a star by the last reel. The writer submitted his screenplay under its original title, *Double Feature*, to Universal, which rejected it, fearing it would not appeal to young audiences. Martin Starger, who was working on *Sly Fox* with Gelbart, liked it and signed on as executive producer. Both Gelbart and Starger thought it would be a natural for Scott and Van Devere. He could play Gloves Malloy, the fighter's crotchety but lovable manager, and Spats Baxter, the flashy yet golden-hearted Broadway producer. She would be the boxer's bookish girlfriend and the bitchy diva of the musical takeoff.

Lord Lew Grade (principal backer of *Sly Fox* and now a peer of the realm) put up the money and Warner Brothers distributed the film.

To direct they chose Stanley Donen, Gene Kelly's behind-the-camera collaborator on such classic musicals as *Singin' in the Rain* and *On the Town*.

Gelbart found Scott a "doll" with one slight exception. "There was only one bad day where he and [fellow cast member] Art Carney holed up in his trailer with a case of something," the screenwriter recalled, laughing. "They didn't work that day."

The single day of absence notwithstanding, Scott loved the rare opportunity to play comedy onscreen in two diverse roles. For Gloves, he adopted the brusque but endearing manner of character actors like Wallace Beery, William Demerest, and James Gleason. The diametrically opposed Spats Baxter was an elegant dandy, ever ready with a kind word or a lavish tip. Both roles afforded a hammy death scene, and Scott even got to dance in the chorus of the grand finale. "Gelbart is such a good writer," he said, "and the picture was so much fun I was almost ashamed to take the money." He reflected the film's affectionate sensibility by sincerely delivering Gelbart and Keller's outlandish lines—such as Gloves Malloy's "Joey [the boxing prodigy] has hitched his trunks to a star; his hands are a rocket to the moon" and Spats Baxter's final pronouncement after collapsing backstage on opening night of his big show: "One minute you're standing in the wings, the next, you're wearing them."

Movie Movie premiered in New York during the 1978 Thanksgiving holidays to mostly favorable reviews. It opened strongly among the Gotham film buffs, but collapsed everywhere else in its February 1979 wide release. Audiences had been inundated with parody films by Woody Allen, Mel Brooks, and numerous *Mad* magazine–level spoofs like *Murder by Death*, *The Big Bus*, and *Sherlock Holmes' Smarter Brother*. *Movie Movie* got lost in the shuffle. But Gelbart's loving rather than mocking script, Donen's solid direction, and non-caricatured performances from Scott, Van Devere, and the supporting cast—including veterans Red Buttons, Eli Wallach, Barbara Harris, and Art Carney, and newcomers Barry Bostwick, Harry Hamlin, Rebecca

York, and Ann Reinking—made it a memorable valentine to a by-gone cinematic era.

Ironically, Scott would be competing with himself when his next film was released at the same time, and the two pictures could not have been more different.

After romping through a lighthearted tribute to Hollywood in its days as an innocent dream factory, Scott descended into the modern, sleazy world of porn and exploitation. On February 6, 1978, he began filming *Hardcore*, playing Jake Van Dorn, a Midwestern businessman who journeys into the seamy smut scenes of Los Angeles, San Diego, and San Francisco to find his runaway teenage daughter. His only clue is her appearance in an adult film.

Hardcore was the second film directed by Paul Schrader, a former film critic who had made a name as a screenwriter with *Taxi Driver* and *The Yazuka*. Schrader had had a difficult time with three aggressive macho stars during his first feature as a director, *Blue Collar*. Richard Pryor, Harvey Keitel, and Yaphet Kotto indulged in name-calling and fist fights. Scott proved to be almost as difficult.

He was still ambivalent about film acting. Having announced his imminent retirement on numerous occasions, he resented having to take lucrative movie parts for financial reasons. He often took out his anger with alcohol and subsequent delaying of the production. If it was a fun part (as in *Movie Movie*), the drinking was minimal. In the case of *Hardcore*, Scott indulged frequently. Schrader was somewhat prepared. Jane Deacy warned him that he would lose five days due to the star's alcoholism. Her prediction turned out to be accurate.

"That was a very depressing film," the actor told Paul Riordan. "It was shot in horrible locations. . . . It beats the hell out of me why I did it. I had sympathy for the father, I guess, and I had sympathy for the daughter. Schrader writes dark stuff."

Schrader, however, enjoyed working with Scott, but had to make certain adjustments in his shooting technique. "It was thrilling working with George, because he is such a good actor," he said. "He works in a certain way and you have to work that way. He will give you two takes. He'll give you a third if there's an absolute need for it. With George, every take is going to be exactly like the take before." One shoot illustrated this point perfectly. Peter Boyle, who was playing the scene opposite Scott, had to go to the bathroom. Schrader wanted one more take before lunch because he knew George would not give him another one after the break. So Schrader asked Scott to do the scene alone. He complied, performing the four-minute scene without Boyle giving him the cues. Boyle returned and exclaimed, "He's simply amazing. He doesn't need me. It doesn't matter what I do. His performance is exactly the same way whether I'm there or not."

"It was always a big melodrama working with George," Schrader commented, "but it was worth it, because you were getting a performance. What's really painful is when you're having trouble with an actor and you're not getting a performance. As long as you're getting a performance, it's all worth it."

A particularly melodramatic moment occurred when Scott was not needed for three or four hours while shooting in the red light district of San Francisco. The lights were set up for a series of shots to look into a bar. When the lights were shifted for the setup with Scott coming into the bar, all he had to do was enter, say two words, and walk out. When the crew was ready, he had been kept waiting for several hours and refused to come out of his trailer. When Schrader went in, Scott was in his underwear with a bottle of vodka by his side. He greeted Schrader with "This movie is a piece of shit." Schrader tried to reason with him—he's tired, it's late, but all he has to do is get dressed, walk over to the bar set, and say two words. He told his star that sometimes in the middle of filming, you're not sure about quality of the final result, but that everything turns out okay in the end.

Scott countered, "No. No. No. I've made a lot of films. This is a piece of shit. You're a good writer but can't direct." Finally, the director had to get down on his knees and promise Scott he would never direct another movie in order to get him to put on his wardrobe and say the two words. Schrader broke his promise and went on to direct *American Gigolo, The Comfort of Strangers, Affliction*, and many others.

Hardcore is semi-autobiographical. Schrader saw it as "sort of revenge fantasy" with the Scott character standing in for his father. Locations included the First Reform Church in Grand Rapids, Michigan, where Schrader attended services as a boy, and the factory where he worked. He wanted to take a rigid, religious character like his father and place him in the seedy underworld of porn.

The final film has the washed-out, overexposed look of X-rated features of the late '70s. Schrader's script and Scott's performance create an insightful portrait of Van Dorn, a powerful, self-satisfied businessman. In the early scenes, his stubborn streak is subtly displayed when he manipulates an interior decorator in his employ into changing her design without raising his voice. His world is safe and unassailable, until he sees his daughter in an adult movie, and that world crashes down on him. Van Dorn's anguish is palpable as Scott screams and cries as though in physical torment while the offending film flickers off screen. His sojourn into the underbelly of massage parlors and smut shops offers some complex and interesting moments—such as his relationship with a prostitute played by Season Hubley—but we don't learn anything about the daughter or her relationship with the father that would drive her to sell her body. Unbelievably, Van Dorn evolves into a Charles Bronson-esque superhero, as he takes on an international snuff filmmaker-gangster and rescues his daughter in the ridiculous climax. There is a brief, funny sequence where Van Dorn disguises himself as a pornographer, donning a toupee and garish pimp outfit, to find the actor who appeared with his daughter. Scott is hilariously deadpan turning down the studs looking to act in his imaginary film. Then, when he finds the right man, he savagely beats the actor, and we're back in a humorless, dark world.

There were complaints from the U.S. Catholic Conference and the Adult Film Association of America, both stating the film had maligned their respective institutions. Critics and the public were similarly turned off. "Scott's powerful performance gives the movie a stubborn anchor, but even he can't illuminate the inner workings of this rigid, angry man," snorted *Newsweek*.

After finishing *Hardcore*, Scott returned to comedy, playing *Sly Fox* at the Shubert Theatre in Los Angeles from June 20 to September 24, 1978. The principal cast was the same as for the Broadway run, except for Jeffrey Tambor, who replaced Bob Dishy as Truckle. Despite the considerable success of the show, Gelbart and Scott were still making changes. As cast member Joe Logrippo remembered it,

> The relationship of Larry Gelbart, the author, and Scott was very amiable. The production we did in Los Angeles was a tiny bit different than the one they did in New York. Scott came to him during a rehearsal and he said he didn't think a couple of lines were working properly. That they probably could get a better laugh. They discussed it. Gelbart went off. He had a portable typewriter with him. He went off in another room and within a half hour he came up with a new couple of pages, which I thought was pretty amazing.

Scott was always looking for ways to improve the performance, even down to the announcement of understudies when a regular cast member was ill. Said Logrippo,

> I understudied all the crummy roles, all the servants and the cops. So if somebody missed a performance, then I moved up to one of the other roles. The first couple of times it happened, the stage manager would make the announcement there would be replacements and it got no reaction from the audience at all. Then Scott said to the stage manager—it just showed in my opinion that Scott cared about the show—"Let me go out and tell them because

there'll be more of a rapport between me and the audience before the show starts." What he used to do is whoever was missing, he'd say, "So-and-so is now playing the captain." Of course, I was always last on the list and he always ended it with "Playing the part of the servant or policeman number one will be an actor with the great old theatrical name of Joe Logrippo." It always got a warm response from the audience and it got them into a positive mood before the show started.

The constant cries of quitting appeared to have died away. In fact, as he told the *Los Angeles Times*, he was contemplating one of the most grueling challenges an actor can undertake—a one-man show: "Next spring I'm going to direct myself in what they're now calling a monodrama from monologue. It's *Freud* taken from his writings and very well written by Lynn Roth. I'm going to try it out at the Guthrie, then take it on to the Eisenhower Theater in Washington. Then we'll decide whether or not to take it to New York or forget it. It's well written so it should work if I do it properly."

Van Devere was also planning a solo show—her subject was Victoria Woodhull, the nineteenth-century feminist who ran for president and operated her own newspaper. Neither venture got beyond the idea stage, but Van Devere was determined to establish an identity of her own, out from under her husband's shadow. The roles she took on without him were largely undistinguished. One of her few Scott-less credits during 1978 was a guest shot on *Columbo* as a murderous television executive. But he was still in the background, making an unbilled cameo as a cameraman.

In addition to presenting a photography exhibition, she formed a production company and attempted to buy the rights to Jerzy Kosinsky's novel *Being There*. Her company also filmed *Save Me a Place at Forest Lawn,* a one-act play she had seen in San Francisco. During the L.A. run of *Sly Fox*, she asked the cast for their opinion. Logrippo related,

She produced some stage play in San Francisco. She was trying to get it to L.A. She had taped it. It was basically two old ladies in a cafeteria, you know, one of those things. She had invited us over to their apartment they had rented to watch the tape and she wanted comments. So we go over there and he's in the study. You had to go right by him in order to get to where she was gonna show the tape. And he didn't even acknowledge us. I don't know what he was doing, balancing his checkbook, some paperwork. That show ran about an hour. We discussed it for a half an hour. She gave us some tea. Then we're leaving and he's still in the study, doing his paperwork and didn't acknowledge us at all. I thought that was more than a little bizarre. On the stage he couldn't have been better. Off the stage, I think he needed some help in dealing with people on a social basis. Obviously it was her idea to show that thing to us. I'm sure he wasn't pleased that she did it, but he could have said, "Hi, I'm a little busy, enjoy the show." What would it take? Thirty seconds?

After romps with dolphins, riotous farce, and fairy-tale fantasy, the Scotts turned to horror with *The Changeling*, a routine ghost story shot mostly in British Columbia. Produced by Canadian entrepreneur Garth Drabinsky and American actor Joel B. Michaels with backing by the Minneapolis-based K-Tel Corporation, the $7.5 million film was a mild scarefest with Scott as a composer mourning the loss of his wife and daughter to an automobile accident. He moves from New York to Seattle for an academic assignment and to forget his tormenting memories. With the aide of real estate agent Van Devere, he rents an enormous Victorian mansion. (She never asks why one person would need such a big place.) Before long the house groans, doors and windows fly open, water faucets start by themselves, and a tune haunting the composer's mind is found playing on an old music box in the attic. Scott and Van Devere drop everything to investigate the house's past owners. They hold a séance, rummage through city records, and eventually discover a dark secret involving a powerful politician (Melvyn Douglas). The restless spirit inhabiting the gloomy residence finally loses its patience and blows the whole place up. In the final shot, the camera finds the music box amid the rubble. It pops open and the eerie tune plays as the credits roll.

Scott had gone on record as disparaging occult films, yet he took this job, probably for the money. Canadian laws required a public declaration of the financing. The couple would earn approximately $1.6 million for screaming and reacting to the paranormal, plus Scott would collect ten percent of the gross rentals. With K-Tel's colossal earnings from selling greatest-hits albums on annoying TV commercials (they pulled in $125 million in 1978), the company could guarantee an extremely wide release in the U.S. and Canada. So Scott's payday was potentially a big one. He was even willing to chip in his and Van Devere's own money when the film went over budget. "I decided not to sit on my ass anymore and complain about getting screwed," he told *US* magazine.

After a few days of location work in New York and Seattle, *The Changeling* set up its spooky shop from early December 1978 through March 1979 in Vancouver and Victoria, the province's capital city, where the perfect rambling, Gothic domicile was found. Art director Trevor Williams erected a $200,000 façade on the house for the fiery climax. For interiors, the eighteen rooms were reconstructed on a soundstage at Panorama Studios in West Vancouver. There were a few delays and problems. Filming ran over the schedule due to bad weather and the explosive final conflagration raged out of control, necessitating a visit from the fire department.

During the Vancouver shoot, Scott visited Karen Truesdell and their daughter, Michelle, in nearby Seattle. Since they had last met, Truesdell had divorced her second husband. Michelle had moved back with her mother after friction had developed with Van Devere. Reconciled after numerous bitter quarrels, Karen and Michelle decided to go into business together and open an antique shop. The only problem was they didn't have enough capital. Michelle proposed asking her father for a loan. Truesdell balked at the idea of taking money from her former lover, but Michelle persuaded her to give it a try. Scott generously wrote them a $25,000 check, $10,000 more than they asked for.

His appearance at the antique shop would be the first time Truesdell had seen Scott since the meeting after the matinee of *Comes a Day* over twenty years earlier. Truesdell said of the encounter,

> You know when you find something is terribly shocking in your life and you fall to the floor? It was that kind of feeling. He brought Trish to the shop to see his investment. I was going to stay away. We lived down below the shop. I closed the shop for the morning. I didn't want anyone else disturbing [Michelle] with her dad. I thought he definitely didn't want to see me, he wants to see his daughter. I heard a lot of voices upstairs. I thought, well, I guess some customers came in. I'd better go up and keep them away from Michelle and her dad. I walked up and there he was. I think subconsciously I knew it was him.
>
> He introduced me to his wife, Trish. I was about three inches taller and I was grungy. I had been scrubbing the floors. I had dirty jeans on and a dirty shirt. My hands were awful. She was totally gorgeous, little and petite and beautiful. I thought the comparison was pretty hideous.

Along with the Scotts' driver, they retired to the family's apartment below the store. Truesdell confessed she deliberately invited the chauffeur in because Michelle had told her he and Van Devere did not get along. They sat sipping coffee and making small talk about the cold weather. An awkward silence was broken by Truesdell's cockapoo bursting into the room. The animal suffered from a skin disease that caused it to scratch and smell bad. It went straight for Van Devere's mink coat and rubbed its tiny body against her leg. Suppressing a laugh, Truesdell took the dog outside. The guests soon departed.

Ten months later the shop went out of business. Truesdell attribut-
ed the failure to her lack of business experience. Michelle found work
at a bakery and her mother continued with her day job at the Head
Start program. Truesdell dreaded having to tell Scott his investment
was lost, but he only laughed and said he could take it off his taxes.

The Changeling was released in March 1980 in 500 theatres. Critics were not overly enthused. Charles F. Champlin of the *Los Angeles Times* wondered over its two eminent stars slumming in a horror
picture: "Those who admired their more serious portraiture over the
years may feel that both Scott and Douglas have tarried beneath their
talents, but their professionalism in the face of the paranormal adds
strength to a highly competent diversion." David Denby in *New York*
magazine found the film "elegant and scary . . . yet it's just another
haunted house movie in the end."

Once *The Changeling* was wrapped, Scott planned to take the rest of
1979 off after working steadily for two years, although it meant passing up a multi-million-dollar deal for *Tai-Pan,* with Steve McQueen.
There were many other projects that never came to pass or went ahead
without Scott. He was to play the retired coach in the film version of
Jason Miller's Pulitzer Prize–winning play *That Championship Season.*
Nick Nolte was also cast and William Friedkin was set to direct, but
the deal fell apart. It was later filmed with Robert Mitchum in the lead
and the playwright directing. Imagine what Scott would have been
like in that film, or any of the other pictures he didn't make for one
reason or another—*In the Heat of the Night, 2001: A Space Odyssey, The
Godfather, The Poseidon Adventure, Wait Until Dark, Network, Ragtime,
10, Dick Tracy,* or an unfilmed version of Sam Shepard's play *The Curse
of the Starving Class.* Lew Grade had proposed a movie of *Sly Fox* and a
sequel to *Movie Movie,* but these never saw the light of day.

Harrow Alley was still at the back of Scott's mind, and he had started writing a historical novel about the Mexican-American War. The
story followed two young soldiers from opposing sides—a Mexican
scholar and clerk and the American son of a wealthy New York City

family. Scott tried to write at least four pages a day in the basement of the Greenwich, Connecticut, house.

There were plenty of plans for interesting and fulfilling projects, but for the next few years, Scott wound up making bad movies. Even though one was particularly awful, it would give him a chance to share the screen with a longtime idol.

17

Patton Meets the Godfather

It could have been the bout of the century. The only two actors to have refused the Oscar matching dramatic muscle in a titanic smackdown. You could almost see a referee standing center ring, making the bellicose introductions: "In this corner, George C. Scott. As the unstoppable general Patton, he licked the Germans and won World War II practically single-handed. As an actor, he defied Broadway, the studios, the Academy Awards, and the ratings board. In this corner, Marlon Brando. The actor's actor, the defender of American Indian rights. Stanley Kowalski, Marc Antony, Terry Malloy, Don Corleone, and Superman's father, Jor-El. I want a good, clean fight; now come out slugging."

But *The Formula* lived up to its name; the film is a dry, pedestrian programmer, and the clinches between Scott and Brando have all the crackle and electricity of wet laundry.

Steven Shagan came up with the idea of a thriller about recovering a missing Nazi synthetic fuel formula while in West Berlin researching for the screenplay for *Voyage of the Damned*, a true-story drama centering on a shipful of Jewish refugees fleeing Hitler. As he was going through materials on the Nuremberg trials, he came across references to such a formula, now lost or deliberately hidden. With the energy crisis and the high cost of gas filling the daily headlines, it was a natural. He wrote the story as a novel, then adapted it for the screen and planned to produce it himself. The action centers on Barney Caine, an American policeman investigating the murder of a former friend retired from the force. Caine follows the trial across Europe to learn his dead pal was involved in covering up the secret formula for producing artificial fuel, developed by Nazi scientists in the last days of World War II. He returns to the U.S. and confronts the manipulative Adam Steffel, head of a mammoth oil cartel, who is determined to suppress the information. For the role of Barney Caine, the American cop who finds himself entangled in a web of international intrigue, Shagan wanted Gene Hackman. But his director, John Avildsen, thought Scott would bring an added dimension to the part.

Avildsen would regret his choice. "I made a big mistake in hiring George Scott, who made Burt Reynolds look like Shirley Temple," the director, who had a rough time with Reynolds on a piece of schlock called *W.W. and the Dixie Kings*, later said. Shagan confessed he should have smelled trouble when he and Avildsen meet with Scott at the latter's favorite New York restaurant, Gallagher's. The actor ordered boilermakers and damned anti-war protestors. Despite slight initial misgivings about Scott's drinking and fiery temper, they signed him. Then Avildsen came up with the idea of casting Marlon Brando as Caine's adversary, Adam Steffel. Shagan and MGM loved it. They could hype the hell out it. Patton against the Godfather. The box office would explode.

They had Patton, but getting the Godfather might be a little tougher. After a string of flops in the '60s, Brando had reemerged as one of the world's biggest cinema draws and most respected thespians with the one-two punch of *Last Tango in Paris* and Francis Ford Coppola's mafia saga. Since then the legendary star had played hard to get, consenting to the occasional cameo role for fees equivalent to the gross national product of a few small countries. He made $3.7 million for *Superman* and $2 million for *Apocalypse Now*. The combined running time of both roles was about 20 minutes. For *The Formula*, Brando would receive $3 million, also eleven percent of the gross so he could potentially make another $2 million. This for a total of three scenes to be shot in two weeks.

Brando was originally contracted for ten days, but when shooting began in December 1979, he stretched out the assignment with lengthy discussions of the dialogue. He graciously threw in another scene for free in which he rescues a frog from the chlorine in his swimming pool.

In addition to endlessly analyzing the dialogue, Brando was always ad-libbing, claiming it made his performance more spontaneous. Scott would joke, "Well, Marlon, what are you going to say today?"

"What difference does it make," his costar would reply, "You know a cue when you hear one." Brando hadn't even bothered to memorize his lines. As part of Steffel's character, he wore a hearing aid, but it was actually an earpiece for a tape recorder which contained his dialogue. "He had a pressure device inside the waist of his trousers and by flexing his stomach muscles he could turn the tape on and off," Avildsen recalled. During one scene of four or five pages, Scott and Brando were required to walk down an oil field with Adam Steffel's entourage behind them. There were no cuts, and the scene had to be done in two shots. More than halfway through the long, complicated sequence, Brando stopped the action and informed the director his tape had run out.

If it were anyone but Brando, this method of working would have driven Scott crazy. He was the ultimate by-the-script actor. If a word was out of place, he'd agonize over it. His performance never varied and he only wanted to do two or three takes at the most. Brando was the ultimate improviser, embracing spontaneity, refusing to learn his lines, and always wanting another take. But Scott had been a great admirer of Brando. During his dark ages in New York, he'd hitchhiked to Hoboken to watch his idol filming *On the Waterfront*. He'd agreed to work for scale in Brando's unrealized film of *Bury My Heart at Wounded Knee*, the best-selling book on an Indian massacre of 1876.

"I was surprised how well they got on," Shagan said. "They played chess all the time. George told Marlon that he was the best actor in the world but the worst chess player. After that, George played against his computer."

Aside from chess, they shared a disillusioned attitude towards their profession. "I sensed a loss of purpose," Shagan explained, "a sense of betrayal, a feeling that they don't want to work anymore, a sense that they have come to think of acting as playing with choo-choo trains."

After two weeks, Brando packed up his choo-choos, his multi-million-dollar fee, and left. Scott relished the opportunity to play against one of his early heroes ("He goes beyond acting. He creates like an impressionist painter," he later said). But he was glad Adam Steffel was essentially a supporting role and Brando's participation was relatively brief. "With Marlon, I wouldn't want to do an entire film with the little darling because he would drive you crazy," he told *Playboy*.

Shagan and Avildsen were rid of Brando's self-indulgence but had to cope with Scott's alcoholism once they shifted locations from Los Angeles to West Berlin and St. Mortiz, Switzerland, in February 1980. There was a minor hiccup before the European trip when Scott, as he had in *The Last Run*, insisted his French leading lady be replaced. Dominique Sanda had been cast as the German counterspy with whom Barney Caine travels and fall in love. After a reading at Avildsen's house, Scott could not penetrate her heavy accent. Sanda was replaced by Swiss actress Marthe Keller, whose command of English was better and who had played similar roles in *Black Sunday* and *Marathon Man*.

The cast switch was a slight headache compared to the anxiety caused by Scott once they were in Europe. On the first location in St. Moritz, Avildsen recalled, "I'd show up in the morning and George would come in and he'd say, 'I want to drink today, I'm not working. I'm going to be in the bar.' . . . So it was a tough experience." At this point, the director felt the entire convoluted film was a disaster and hoped MGM would pay him not to finish. No such luck, and more trouble was in store. When the company moved to Berlin, Shagan received a hysterical call from Trish Van Devere at three in the morning. She informed the writer-producer that her husband was drunk, had a gun, was threatening suicide, and was asking for him.

Shagan warily entered Scott's hotel room to find his star in a bathrobe with a bottle of vodka in one hand and a .45 in the other. He sat down, pointed the revolver to his temple and asked Shagan for one good reason not to pull the trigger. "Because you have a 6:30 call," the producer replied. Scott howled with laughter and told Shagan he had come up with the perfect answer, not that the world or his sons would miss him.

After Scott got into a hot shower and Shagan ordered some food from room service, the producer threw the gun out the window into a snowbank. For the rest of the shoot, Scott behaved himself.

The partnership between Shagan and Avildsen ended badly. Avildsen favored a shorter running time and edited the film down. Shagan and MGM hated Avildsen's version, finding it confusing. Shagan later stated to *Variety* that in Avildsen's cut, Scott's performance was "totally shredded." As producer he denied his director the final cut. In response Avildsen tried to have his name removed from the credits. He didn't succeed and had to accept at least partial responsibility for the rambling end result. The murder mystery and search for the formula are standard TV-movie-of-the-week fodder, filmed with as much excitement as a traffic report. The much-anticipated clash of titans between Scott and Brando is as dull as dishwater. Scott's boredom with the role is obvious; he's just phoning it in. Brando's porked-out, rumpled cartel president is about as menacing as Elmer Fudd. The only moment of spontaneity in their climactic face-off occurs when Adam Steffel casually asks Barney Caine if he'd care for a Milk Dud.

Brando called the finished product "a terrible piece of shit." Scott was equally disparaging about his own performance: "I think I played some washed-up son of a bitch. But don't ask. I didn't wake up until the shooting was over." The movie debuted a year after filming began on December 15, 1980, for the Christmas season. The critics put coal in the filmmakers' stockings. *Variety* declared it "a clump of sludge." *Newsweek* called it "so murkily plotted that it's damned near impossible to figure out." MGM tried the slogan "The Movie the Oil Companies Don't Want You to See." It turned out to be the movie nobody wanted to see. *The Formula* took in $3.7 million in domestic sales on a $15 million budget.

With his last few films bombing financially or artistically—sometimes both—Scott was growing more weary of acting. But he also realized that to continue his lifestyle and support the households of several ex-wives and children, he had to accept what performing gigs were offered. He wanted to return to directing and accepted an offer to helm *Don't Look Back*, a television biopic to star Louis Gossett, Jr. as baseball pitcher Satchel Paige, to be shot in Hattiesberg, Mississippi. He invited Michelle to join him. Her mother was glad to have them spend time alone together, but the reunion was cut short when Scott was fired because of "creative differences."

"I have immense respect for George's creative abilities, both as an actor and director," producer Stanley Rubin told *Variety*. "But the bottom line is we simply view this project from different perspectives."

When father and daughter returned to the Scott house in Connecticut, Van Devere was less than welcoming to Michelle. The young woman later told her mother the current Mrs. Scott had greeted her with "What's she doing here?" Michelle was soon on a plane back to Seattle.

Van Devere may have been frustrated by a lack of attention from her husband and difficulties with her career. While Scott was playing opposite Marlon Brando, she was making a forgettable horror film called *The Hearse*. She had been considered for a feature based on the life of Mother Teresa and even traveled to India to meet the famous humanitarian, but the project hadn't even gotten started. Renewing their efforts to work together whenever possible, they signed to co-star in *Tricks of the Trade*, a convoluted stage caper that had had a brief previous life in summer stock. William Shatner and Yvette Mimieux starred as a psychiatrist who is really a CIA agent and his patient who is really a counterspy. There were hoary gags about analyst's couches, double-and triple crosses, numerous costume changes, and a brief nude scene in near total darkness for Van Devere. During tryouts at the Huntington Hartford Theatre in Los Angeles and the National in Washington, critics complained this espionage comedy didn't make sense and wasn't funny. *Tricks* opened for trade at the Brooks Atkinson Theatre on Broadway November 9, 1980, and folded after a single performance. The $500,000 capitalization was almost entirely lost. "The only mystery about this play is why George C. Scott elected to star in it," sneered Frank Rich, the powerful critic of the *New York Times*.

During a grim opening night gathering at the show's advertising agency, Scott made humorous comments on the lambasting *Tricks* had gotten from Rich and his ilk. An advertising executive joined in with a joke of his own: "They seemed to have invented new adjectives for us."

"How dare you!" Scott exploded. "Do you have any idea what's involved in the creative process? I'll kill you." With that he chased the hapless adman through the agency's offices. Merle Debuskey, the show's publicist, recalled the incident:

> We decided that the company should go to Sardi's and have their party because we didn't want them to be there when the reviews came in. We were up at the [advertising] agency, waiting for the reviews. The convention was on opening nights for the producer and the press agent, minimally those two, we would go up to the advertising agency and had the job of collecting the reviews before they were in print. And if they were good we would bring them into the party. So [George] wasn't supposed be there. We had gathered and the bad news kept coming in. They had an open bar. We could hear the elevator come up and open and who trotted out but George and Trish. A little bit under the weather. There was a little embarrassment; we didn't know what to do or how to tell him or if we would tell him or how do we conceal it. He didn't ask, he

went right to the bar. He'd already had enough, but he had another very strong drink. I tried to slip a Coke in but he wouldn't take it. It led to the incident where he chased this guy—he called him "Brown Suit"—he chased him all through the halls till the guy finally locked himself in an office. It didn't make any difference to George, it was just an event. He didn't really know the guy; he didn't care. He was venting.

Scott had better luck with *Oliver Twist*, a TV-movie adaptation of Charles Dickens's classic, and *Taps*, a drama centering on cadets taking over a military academy. In the former, he played Fagin, the wily leader of a gang of boy thieves, previously essayed by Alec Guinness in an earlier film incarnation and Ron Moody in the musical version. Like Shylock, the role of Fagin had acquired the stigma of anti-Semitism through stereotyped playing and Dickens's own prejudiced depiction. Scott studiously avoided these excesses and gave the role a fatherly cast as he took up little Oliver into his nest of pickpockets. He lent the old robber a dose of magisterial rage in the scene when he is hauled away by the constables, lashing out at his fellow denizens of London's underworld as they jeer at him.

In *Taps*, Scott returned to the military, portraying General Bache, the commandant of a military academy facing financial problems. After the board of directors elects to close the school, the general accidentally shoots a local boy during a scuffle and disappears from the film. Lead by their teen commanders, the students revolt and reclaim their beloved Bunker Academy. Filmed during the summer of 1981 at the Valley Forge Military Academy and Junior College in Wayne, Pennsylvania, *Taps* provided the first starring film role for recent Oscar winner Timothy Hutton (*Ordinary People*) and launched the careers of then-unknowns Sean Penn and Tom Cruise.

Taps was released during 1981 holiday season. Despite predictions its gloomy conclusion—Cruise's character is killed—would get it lost in the Christmas shuffle, the film took in $20.5 million.

Most reviews praised Scott and only found fault with the brevity of his role. One critic compared him to Marlon Brando for getting the most money for the least amount of work. Another accused him of repeating his *Patton* performance, even down to delivering a stirring speech to his troops (in this case the graduating class of Bunker Academy rather the Third Army).

Ironically, Scott did want to return to *Patton*. He had never been satisfied with the 1970 film and felt it didn't display every aspect of the general's complex personality. Patton's personal papers had been published shortly after the film was released and the actor fervently regretted not having had access to these documents during the filming.

Ladislas Farago, author of *Patton: Ordeal and Triumph*, the biography upon which the 1970 film was partially based, had penned a sequel called *The Last Days of Patton*. Scott optioned it and hired playwright William Luce to adapt it for the screen, so the actor could get Patton on the screen his way.

Meanwhile, his marriage to Van Devere had reached an impasse. They had been married for nine years, lived together for one year before that, collaborated on six films and three plays, and were in each other's company more than most married couples. Van Devere was constantly fighting the perception that her career was largely due to her husband's insistence she be part of a package deal. It finally got to be too much. Both retreated into separate worlds. Scott began calling Karen Truesdell several times a week, alternating angry tirades about the past (Truesdell called these "dump calls") with tender promises of a reunion. His college flame had recently divorced her second husband, and her mother, a sworn enemy of Scott's for disgracing the family, had died. These developments, plus the estrangement from Van Devere, encouraged him to pursue Truesdell. In December of 1981, he flew out to visit her and Michelle in Seattle on impulse, not even bringing a toothbrush. While snuggling with her in Truesdell's modest cottage, Scott apologized for going through several fortunes while she was just barely scraping by. Though he was still married, he proposed to her.

Astonished, but still in love with the father of her daughter, Truesdell agreed to wed him—as soon as he was free. Scott explained he
was taking Van Devere on a world cruise for her birthday. He couldn't
back out; he had promised. Ninety days after they returned, he would
end the marriage. Scott made another vow. When Truesdell asked him
why he had rejected the Oscar, he replied the Academy Awards were
a sham, but that if he ever did attend the ceremony, she would be his
date.

Meanwhile, Van Devere was willing to try for reconciliation and
saw the cruise as an opportunity for the couple to reconnect. Later, she
told the *Los Angeles Times*,

> It was a terrible mistake. We went on a world cruise on the QE2
> and at the end, neither of us was speaking to the other. Out of
> nineteen ports we called at, George would get off at only two—
> and at one of them we had such a terrible row that I wouldn't come
> back on board. . . . And you know what that terrible row had been
> about? Baboons. Whether we should get out of the car or stay in
> it while trying to photograph them. It's ridiculous what you can
> fight about when you set your mind to it.

They decided on a trial separation; Van Devere took her two horses to
Los Angeles, while Scott stayed in Connecticut.

However, he did not make plans for a sixth marriage. He was too
busy directing and starring in a revival of Noel Coward's *Present
Laughter* for Circle in the Square. The role was originally to be played
by Frank Langella, who had to drop out for a film commitment. Theodore Mann and his partner, Paul Libin, had lunch with Scott and he
mentioned their dilemma. To the amazement of his dining compan-
ions, Scott began quoting Coward's dialogue and explained he had
played the role in Ohio summer stock. They immediately asked him to
replace Langella. He agreed if he could also direct. It was a deliberate
change of pace. Not only was the play a light comedy—not a genre

normally associated with Scott—but the lead, Garry Essendine, was an effete, self-absorbed, sophisticated playwright-performer. This was hardly the sort of part one would expect from the portrayer of Patton, ruthless Bert Gordon of *The Hustler*, and Thomas Hudson, the Hemingway surrogate of *Islands in the Stream*. In fact, the representative of Coward's estate balked at granting permission for the Circle production, feeling Scott was miscast, but Mann insisted.

Rehearsals were delayed when the star-director underwent surgery for a detached retina. While recovering, he had Jane Deacy contact Karen Truesdell to let her know about the operation and instruct her to send any mail to Deacy's office. She told Truesdell she'd known about her for years and was glad she was back in her client's life. Scott seemed to be inching toward making good on his promises to Truesdell, but still kept her at arm's length.

Back on his feet, he began casting for *Present Laughter* and chose several new performers who would use the production as a launching pad for major careers. Nathan Lane, a wily comic actor whose major credit up until then was a short-lived sitcom with Mickey Rooney called *One of the Boys*, played Roland Maule, the crazed fan with a crush on Essendine. Dana Ivey, a veteran of regional theatre, was the vinegar-tongued secretary Monica Reed. Christine Lahti, who played the devious vamp Joanna Lyppiatt, had three previous Broadway shows under her belt but had yet to break out in major TV and film roles. Jim Piddock, cast as the butler, would later be featured in several of Christopher Guest's spoof documentaries. Kate Burton, the daughter of Richard Burton, grabbed the ingénue role of Daphne Stillington fresh out of Yale Drama School (she began rehearsals the day after graduation). Burton had dated Scott's oldest son, Matthew, when the two attended the United Nations School in Manhattan. In another family connection, Alex Scott served as his dad's assistant stage manager. The stage manager, Michael Ritchie, later married Burton.

Rehearsals ran no more than fours hours a day. Scott found that any more time would result in a lack of concentration on the part of the cast. As with his film direction assignments, he planned his staging beforehand. "He knew exactly what he wanted," Burton remembered. "For a man whose life was such a roller coaster, in terms of his work— I think my father was very similar—he was just like a laser beam. He had an incredible work ethic. Knew his lines. Was always on time. That was my dad, too."

Scott developed a close relationship with the cast, particularly Lane and Ivey. "I was just this kid who worshipped him," Lane said. "I had the attitude, Whatever you want me to do, I'll do. I'll hang from the chandelier." But there was a slight communication problem during early rehearsals:

> For the first couple of weeks, he called me Norman. It was hard enough to adjust because Nathan isn't my real name. I'm Joe, but I'd become Nathan Lane because there was already a Joe Lane in Actors' Equity. The cast was sort of giggling every time he said, "Norman do this, Norman do that." I thought of legally changing my name to Norman to avoid having to tell him. Then I said, "George, I know you think it's Norman, but it's Nathan. My name is Nathan, and by the way, I loved you in *MacArthur*." So he laughed and said, "All right, from now on you can call me Greg."

Laughter opened July 15, 1982. Critics and audiences were delightfully surprised that the same actor who had brought the blood-and-guts Patton to life could also handle the lighter-than-air witticisms of Noel Coward. "Mr. Scott is pickled with high spirits in this play," wrote Frank Rich in the *New York Times*. "He's not just terrifically funny—he's actually having fun on stage, for the first time since *Sly Fox*, and his delight is contagious." Among those praising him was a former costar. "It just split my skull," Paul Newman said, "because he was so outrageous and delicious. He was the wrong man in the wrong part doing it absolutely *right*."

Scott had vowed not to drink during rehearsals and the entire run of the show. "I've been in plays where I've drunk, and it doesn't work very well," he told Michiko Kakutani of the *New York Times*. "You're not at your best, you're not doing your job, and I've reached the point I can take the disappointment and grief without resorting to dropping a sixth of vodka every night."

But after the first six weeks, he went on a bender and missed a week of performances. Scott had bet Mann and Libin that he could make it that long totally sober. On their way back to the dressing rooms after the duration of the bet, Scott told Lane, "That's it, I won the bet. Now I'm gonna get shit-faced." A bewildered Lane could only reply, "Okay, have a good time." Dana Ivey was disappointed because her brother was visiting and had to settle for the star's understudy. When Scott returned, Ivey asked him not to miss any more performances. "Why not?" he asked.

"It's just not the same without you," she told him. "And he never missed again after that," she later said.

Though he did not miss any further showings, Scott did drink during the course of the run, which extended beyond its original engagement to a total of 175 performances. Myra Carter, who replaced Bette Henritze as the Swedish maid, recalled seeing him stagger on several occasions prior to curtain time. As a result of the extension, the next Circle production (*The Queen and the Rebels*, starring Colleen Dewhurst) opened at the Plymouth Theatre and many of the original *Present Laughter* cast left for other projects. Dana Ivey departed for the Long Wharf Theatre's production of *Quartermaine's Terms*, which later transferred to a long Off-Broadway run. Nathan Lane took a sidekick role in *Merlin*, a musical to star illusionist Doug Henning. "I was too afraid to tell him I was going to leave," Lane said. "He was banging on the door of my dressing room and he said, 'You're leaving me to do a fucking magic show!'" Kate Burton was cast in the title role in a revival of Eva La Gallienne's 1932 version of *Alice in Wonderland*, to star and be directed by the venerable La Gallienne herself. When informed of the news, Scott exclaimed, "Eva La Gallienne! Jesus Christ, is she still alive?"

Despite his sometime gruff initial reaction ("You're rats deserting a sinking ship," he would joke), Scott generously acknowledged the contribution of each departing cast member. Lane recalled, "Every person who left that show, for our last performance he made a speech and said 'If it wasn't for this person. . . . He or she added so much to the success of the show.'"

"I'd never before or since had that kind of accolade," Ivey said of the speech Scott made at her final curtain call, "and, coming from him, of course, oh my goodness, it meant the world."

As the run was ending, Scott invited Karen Truesdell and her family (their daughter, Michelle, and Davey, Truesdell's son by her second husband) to spend Christmas and New Year's in New York. He put them up in an expensive suite at the Plaza, got them house seats to *Present Laughter* and other Broadway shows, and had them stay with him in Connecticut during his days off. Truesdell was confused by Scott's mixed signals. He treated her like a wife. They played bridge and shared a pasta dinner with a neighbor couple. They slept in the same bed in Connecticut. Yet he took several calls from Van Devere, and her photos and mementoes were everywhere in the Greenwich house. There were also signs that Scott's demons were not entirely at bay. He was still drinking heavily, and got into arguments with both Karen and Michelle. He berated Truesdell for what he perceived as flirtatious behavior with young waiters (she smiled at a server who brought Davey a banana split at Gallagher's) and for deserting him twenty-five years earlier. He yelled at Michelle for not finding a direction in life and for constantly demanding his attention.

There were further red flags. One night, Truesdell reached under Scott's pillow and found a gun. He explained it was for self defense against celebrity-mad intruders. Despite the drinking, the argumentativeness, and the firearm, she wanted him back and accepted his invitation to Monterey for the Bing Crosby Pro/Am Golf Tournament in which he was to play, and then to spend several weeks in Hong Kong while he filmed *China Rose*, a television movie.

The only problem was it meant giving up her job and retirement fund at Head Start. She had used up her vacation days and was not yet vested. "I was feeling poor because I had my child to support," she said. "I had no money and I was giving everything up. It really was a hard decision, but in the end, it wasn't. I always loved him."

She firmly believed he would leave Van Devere and intended to marry her: "He told me that he was and he told me that he was when we were in Monterey. He had neighbor friends from Connecticut that he invited to Monterey to be with us. They kind of backed that up, that he was if not legally separated, they were [physically] separated . . . Then he always said, I'm getting a divorce and it won't take long."

The erratic behavior continued at the tournament. Scott would spend most days on the links with Truesdell driving him in a golf cart, followed by dinner and bridge with the couple from Connecticut. He was affectionate and tender, telling her now that he had her back, he'd never let her go. But then Scott would get raving drunk, at one point chasing Truesdell through their rented guest house like Jack Nicholson in *The Shining* before passing out while Karen hid in a closet. The next morning he was contrite and gentle as a kitten.

It was the same in Hong Kong, only more so. Michelle and Davey had accompanied their mother at Scott's invitation, yet he resented having to share his new-found love with their adult daughter and a little boy who wasn't even his. Michelle was equally needy, yearning for her father's attention and angry with her mother for taking it away from her. After long days of shooting, Scott would get blotto and curse whoever was near him. Truesdell recalled,

> He was getting very tired and very angry. There was a lot of fuss between Michelle and me. He called it turmoil, I would refer to it as tension. . . . I had to pay a lot of attention to Davey, who was at that time nine, I think. I couldn't just leave him off, so I had

to be a mother to Davey. It just kept getting heavier and heavier. George kept getting more tired and drinking more and more and more. It was heading up to some kind of explosion. I really wasn't aware of it. I thought that maybe this is the way things always were with him these days. He finally called us in and he said, "I've had enough. Just leave. Leave in a week."

Jane Deacy, who was traveling with Scott, arranged activities for the remainder of their brief stay. The disappointed family took a day trip to Macau, visited an aquarium, a museum, and an ancient fortune-teller who predicted to Truesdell, "The man you are with now will not be your future." Before their departure, Deacy presented Truesdell with a $5,000 check from Scott. She wanted to tear it up, but remembering she had given up her job, she smiled and accepted it.

On their last day, the former lovers shared a drink. "This is not goodbye," Scott told Truesdell. But it was their last meeting. Scott severed all connection with both Michelle and her mother. There was a brief phone conversation weeks later. Truesdell had accepted an interview request from the *National Enquirer* and Michelle, still believing he would keep his promise to let her work on the *Patton* sequel, called her father to warn him. She put her mother on phone. "You don't need that pile of shit," Scott told Karen, and hung up. Truesdell and Michelle did speak with a reporter from the tabloid, but the article never ran.

In Hong Kong, Scott was enraged at being alone again. He turned to his costar, Ali MacGraw, for consolation. Critics had just savaged her lackluster performance in the TV miniseries *The Winds of War*, and she was vulnerable. But, though she respected Scott and appreciated his regard, she did not respond to his advances. When asked if the two were keeping company, *China Rose*'s screenwriter, David Epstein, replied, "They were not, but I don't think it was. . . . how do I say this judiciously . . . for want of effort on George's part, but I don't think it happened." Rumors of an on-set romance reached the tabloids and were read in Seattle by a heartbroken Truesdell. She didn't believe the gossip—she had met MacGraw, who didn't seem to be the kind of person to engage of a quickie liaison.

The finished product, a conventional melodrama with Scott as an American businessman searching for his lost son in China with the aide of MacGraw as an all-purpose guide/translator/love interest, was broadcast on CBS on October 18. John J. O'Connor's review in the *New York Times* was particularly nasty and typical of the critical reaction: "If nothing else, *China Rose* never loses the courage of its simple-mindedness. A surprisingly portly Mr. Scott walks through the picture as if he had an appointment pending elsewhere. Miss MacGraw appears sincere, but somewhat dazed."

Meanwhile, Van Devere and Scott reconciled, agreeing to a loose arrangement. She would maintain her primary residence in California while he kept his a continent away in Connecticut. They would live together when their schedules permitted. Their timetables coordinated in April 1983 when he was in Los Angeles to seek backing for the sequel to *Patton*. During this business trip, Scott rustled up a pair of last-minute tickets to the Oscar ceremony. Perhaps he was attempting to curry favor with the Hollywood community by attending their biggest night after having disparaged it so publicly over a decade earlier. He needed a big budget to get *Patton II* into production and the studios could provide it. Appearing at the Oscars couldn't hurt his public relations with the moneymen. Maybe he wanted the world to know he was back with Van Devere by escorting her to this very public event. As the infamous Oscar-refuser and his wife hurried into the Dorothy Chandler Pavilion, Army Archerd, the *Variety* columnist who traditionally interviews stars on their way into the big night, caught sight of them and shouted at Scott, "Your Oscar is waiting for you at the Academy, Wilshire and La Peer."

Once inside, they were caught by the TV cameras a few times. Viewers around the world saw the rebel actor who had called the event a "meat parade" smiling and applauding with the rest of Hollywood.

Among those watching was Truesdell in Seattle. When she saw Scott with Van Devere, after he had promised that if he ever went to the Oscars it would be with her, she knew their rekindled romance was really over.

18

"All I Get Is Junk"

In the '80s and '90s, Scott turned away from movies and found steadier and rewarding employment in a medium he had once deplored—television. "All I get is junk offered me in film," he told Stephen Farber in a 1986 *New York Times* interview. "There aren't any good scripts around for a man my age. Films are oriented toward sixteen- to twenty-five-year-olds. So television has been very helpful to me in the last few years." In the movies, he attempted to assassinate adorable Drew Barrymore in *Firestarter*, traded blows with the devil in *The Exorcist III*, dispensed grandfatherly advice in *Angus*, provided the voice for a cartoon villain in *The Rescuers Down Under*, and supported Alec Baldwin and Nicole Kidman in *Malice* and Sharon Stone in *Gloria*. But on TV, he tackled deeper roles. He revisited Patton, and fought the other side of Word War II as Mussolini. He starred in adaptations of Dickens (*Oliver Twist, A Christmas Carol*) and Poe (*Murders in the Rue Morgue*). While some of his small-screen projects were slick and shallow, at least they addressed real-life issues such as abortion (*Choices*) and AIDS (*The Ryan White Story*).

"My impression was he was doing TV movies at this time because he wanted the money," said screenwriter David Epstein, who worked with him on two such projects, "and also if the scripts were good enough and it got him to locations that were interesting to him."

The theatre was his first love, and he returned periodically, mostly to Circle in the Square and in light fare. He followed up his hit revival of *Present Laughter* with another Noel Coward comedy, *Design for Living*, which he directed but did not act in.

He began filming *Firestarter* in Wilmington, North Carolina, on September 12, 1983. This Stephen King fantasy was produced by Dino De Laurentiis, for whom he had caused many headaches during the filming of *The Bible*. In addition to Scott, the cast was loaded with big names, including fellow Oscar winners Art Carney and Louise Fletcher, Martin Sheen, and newcomers David Keith and Heather Locklear. But the real star of the film was eight-year-old Drew Barrymore, who had made a hit a year earlier as the precocious little sister of the young hero in Steven Spielberg's *E. T.* The tiny granddaughter of John Barrymore played Charlie McGee, a cuddly moppet with the telekinetic power to start conflagrations. Scott was cast as John Rainbird, a Native American hit man hired by the government to gain the little girl's trust and then eliminate her. The actor's fondness for elaborate makeup was given full play—Rainbird sported a glass eye, deeply tanned skin, and a grey-streaked ponytail.

King was at the height of his popularity. By this time, eleven of his novels had been filmed or were optioned for the big screen. Barrymore was at first intimidated by her more experienced costar. She described him in her memoir as "a big man who looks kind of rough and gruff. He looked like he could be mean." The unlikely pair bonded over a mutual love of animals. Scott had his big dog Max with him. Drew took to petting him between takes, and subsequently gave hugs to Scott. "It was never like he talked down to me, which made me feel good," she wrote, "like I had the respect of someone who was at the top of his craft. Early on, he told me, 'Drew, just forget about the camera and do your job.'"

Despite gaping holes in the plot and insipid dialogue ("Suppose lighting fires is only the tip of the iceberg"), *Firestarter* lit up the box office with a domestic gross of $15 million. Scott dismissed the film as "one of those half-assed, sci-fi, Stephen King things," but the part was "fun."

Playing Ebenezer Scrooge was another fun part. He took on the humbugging miser for a CBS special, filmed in Shrewsbury, a picturesque market town straight out of Dickens in England's West Shropshire district. Contact with the press and his castmates outside of shooting was kept to a minimum. Scott tersely informed the local *Shrewsbury Chronicle* he was nearsighted, lived in Greenwich, Connecticut, and Beverly Hills, smoked two packs of cigarettes a day, and liked vodka, poker, lager, and the crossword puzzle in the *International Herald Tribune* (The entire interview consisted of dispensing these tidbits). "I admire him from a distance as we all do," Frank Finlay, who was playing Marley's Ghost, told Joan Barthel of *TV Guide*. She was unable to obtain any direct quotes from Scott, who canceled their interview at the last minute.

In addition to these off-camera curmudgeonly qualities, his characterization incorporated a desperate need to reconnect with the human community Scrooge had long ago rejected. In the scene with the Ghost of Christmas Future, stooped by his own graveside, Scott heartrendingly emphasizes the word "sponge" as he pleads with the spirit to give him another chance at life. All of his emotions burst forth like water out of a dam as he cries, "that I may SPONGE the writing from this stone."

He also gives Scrooge a wicked sense of humor, chortling like mad at his own cleverness in coming up with the quip about imbecilic holiday revelers deserving "a stake of holly" through their own hearts.

Still, Scott wasn't sure if he was right for Dickens's skinflint. Dozens of actors, including Reginald Owen, Fredric March, Albert Finney, and particularly Alastair Sim, had already taken the iconic tightwad beyond a caricature of miserliness and made him a three-dimensional being with a complicated history. Besides, he told Tom Viola, "I think we classically view Scrooge as being spare and bony. Christ, I'm heavy and big and fat. It'll be the biggest Scrooge you'll ever see. General Porky strikes again." To differentiate his from the other Scrooges, Scott played him as exhausted: "Loneliness has exhausted him. Scrooge is just as weighed down by loneliness and all that a lack of love can do to a person as Marley is weighted down by the cash boxes and ledgers."

There was loneliness in Scott's personal life, heightened by his ambiguous relationship with Van Devere. She was not with him on the British location, and rumors circulated on the set that they were separated. They maintained their truce, cohabitating when it was convenient. For much of 1984 and '85, it wasn't. *A Christmas Carol* was followed by rehearsals for *Design for Living* for Circle in the Square. Then it was off to Yugoslavia for four months to film a seven-hour NBC miniseries on Mussolini. Scott would then cross battle lines to revisit Patton in Germany and England for CBS. After that, he planned to direct and possibly star in a new play by *The Formula*'s producer-writer, Steven Shagan, called *Africa* about a broken-down screenwriter, but this project was never realized.

In the Coward comedy, Raul Julia, Frank Langella, and Jill Clayburgh played the effervescent bohemians originated by Coward, Alfred Lunt, and Lynn Fontanne in 1933. Interior decorator Gilda romantically ricochets between artist Otto and playwright Leo. After chasing each other across Europe and to New York, they finally agree to an unconventional arrangement of sharing their affections. Scott added plenty of slapstick and staged the play at a rapid clip. Reviews were mixed, with most scribes agreeing that only Langella had the right light touch, and that Clayburgh and Julia pushed too hard for laughs. In addition, the sexual freedom espoused by Coward may have been shocking to 1930s audiences, but a *ménage a trois* was old hat to theatergoers of the 1980s. Despite critical carping *Design*, like *Laughter*, was extended beyond its original engagement, running from June 20, 1984 to January 20, 1985. Langella, Julia, and Clayburgh had other commitments once their contracts ran out and were replaced by Frank Converse, John Glover, and Anne Swift.

While *Design* was entering its final month of performances and *A Christmas Carol* was broadcast on CBS, Scott embarked on the long shoot of *Mussolini: The Untold Story* in the Istra region of Yugoslavia. Filming in Italy would have trebled the budget. Stretching from Il Duce's ascent to power in 1922 to his death in 1945, the TV movie would be shown in three parts. Thanks to the high ratings accrued by long-form projects like *Rich Man, Poor Man* and *Roots*, networks were commissioning numerous miniseries. Sterling Silliphant's script focused on the fascist leader's family and personal life over political and military history. Prominence was given to his longtime mistress, Claretta Petacci (Virginia Madsen); his daughter, Edda (Mary Elizabeth Mastrantonio); and her husband, Count Galeazzo Ciano (Raul Julia, fresh from Scott's *Design for Living*), who turns against his father-in-law and is executed.

As he had done for *Patton*, Scott did extensive research. By coincidence, he was reading a Mussolini biography while filming *A Christmas Carol*. After signing on to the project, he read another five books and watched thirteen videos of newsreel footage several times. In spite of all the research, Scott was apprehensive about playing the role, "because I don't have Latin blood. I'm an Anglo-Saxon and I didn't know whether I could do the part."

But his powers of observation served him well. By viewing those newsreels repeatedly, Scott concluded Il Duce's exaggerated poses and gestures were for effect. As he explained to *TV Guide*,

> If you watch him, the eyes are going and the chin is going, and you know the man can't possibly believe that it's for real. . . . There's a great shot of him, making a speech in German in Berlin, and, as he's leaving the lectern, he turns around and puts his hand to his breast and smiles at somebody—it had to be somebody he knew very well—and gives a huge sigh of relief as if to say, "I got away with it, didn't I?" You can tell right away, "The act is over. I can be myself now."

For the role of Mussolini's common-law wife, Rachele, Colleen Dewhurst was considered. It would have been the first time she and Scott had acted together since *The Last Run* in 1971, but she was unavailable. Lee Grant was cast instead, and the Oscar winner from *Shampoo* found her costar distant both on the set and off.

> In my experience with George, he was very clenched. He spent all of his time with his makeup man who he traveled with and who was also his friend. He spent all the time with him, playing chess. He was a very clenched person. I don't know whether this was because he was on the wagon because he certainly wasn't drinking. He was very withholding socially and he tried as an actor, but you could see. He was the perfect person to play Mussolini, and yet there was no fire. When you see the performance, there was a resistance to opening himself up, either to the part or to me as his wife. But he was restraining himself all the way around, socially and as an actor.

During an intimate scene, Grant put her arm around Scott, who responded with "Please don't do that."

Scott did loosen up somewhat when Van Devere visited the set during the last weeks of filming. "He was like a puppy," Grant recalled. "He was grateful that she was there. She was like the one calling the shots in the relationship. By that I mean, he was like a lapdog. His sweetness started to come out. He showed a need. He unclenched for her."

But Grant felt this emotional lowering of his guard came too late to aid Scott's performance or their onscreen connection. "To reach him at a time when he was closing himself down was sad for me," she said. "It was clear there was not going to be any fire going back and forth between us."

There was fire lacking in the completed film as well. It's more soap opera than docudrama. "This is history as it might have been reworked for *Dynasty*," John J. O'Connor tartly commented in his *New York Times* review.

With only a month's pause, Scott launched himself into another TV spectacular, playing one of Mussolini's wartime adversaries in *The Last Days of Patton*. He had attempted to bring Ladislas Farago's treatment of the general's later years to the big screen, but there were no takers. "I couldn't sell the damn thing to a studio or anyone else," he said. "No one would touch it. In today's movie market, you've got to have gunfire or laser beams, or they don't buy." Producer William F. Storke, who worked with Scott on *Jane Eyre*, *The Price*, and *A Christmas Carol*, acquired it as a TV special with Chrysler as the main sponsor. Chrysler chairman Lee Iacocca reportedly give the idea a standing ovation in his office. (Ironically, by the time the TV movie aired in September 1986, Scott was advertising Renaults in commercials for rival carmaker AMC.) Shooting took place mostly in England. Daughter Devon had just graduated from the Central School in London and was given a small part. The film covers the last forty days of Patton's life. During this time he served as military governor of postwar Bavaria. Eisenhower dismissed him because of a controversy over former Nazis on his staff. Shortly thereafter, the general broke his neck in a car accident and was paralyzed from the neck down. He died twelve days later. Unlike the initial film, where we never meet Patton's family, there is significant time devoted to his thirty-seven-year marriage and a reference to an affair with his wife's niece. "This is the Patton I always wanted to play," Scott told Stu Schreiberg of *USA Weekend*. "The first film was too much blood and guts—too much 'let's go over the hill with the tanks and kill everybody.' This time, we see Patton after his automobile accident, completely supine in bed. . . . I think it's some of the best work I've ever done." Eva Marie Saint, who played Mrs. Beatrice Patton, recalled,

> That was a very difficult shoot. We shot in an ex-war hospital outside of London. The scenes that I had with him were when he was

really dying from that terrible accident. So he was stretched with all kinds of gear on his head and clamps.

Delbert Mann was our director. We started the scene and all of a sudden we heard an airplane. Everybody looked at everybody else and Delbert said, "I thought this was off the flight pattern." I think they made a few calls and found out the hospital wasn't off the flight pattern. I don't know how many takes we did that scene in order to get a full, complete scene. . . . Had any one of us gotten hysterical, we never would have gotten that scene. But George was right there with Del; I was right there with George and Del. We just repeated it and repeated it until we got a full take. George was so professional. God forbid you had an actor who'd say, "What do you want from me?" No, he just did the scene and I was his wife and I just stood by him.

He may have behaved himself during the deathbed scenes, but his temper did erupt on a few occasions. He exploded at a CBS photographer and an extra. Both were snapping one too many pictures in between shots. Director Delbert Mann was another target when there were delays caused by camera troubles. "Goddamnit, Del," Scott roared, "you're wasting time with too many takes of every shot." But Scott was also more than generous with his time when 300 U.S. Air Force troops, working as background players, surrounded him after a scene. The star signed autographs, told war stories, and posed for pictures. "I figured what the hell, they're serving in the armed forces," Scott explained. "So I could be at least halfway gracious, though it's not in my nature, I grant you." When he was enjoying the day's work, it put him in a good mood. In one sequence, Patton is given a surprise sixtieth birthday party by his men. During the celebration, he delivers a raunchy ditty called "Lilly from Piccadilly," about an ugly prostitute whose business benefits from the London blackouts. He added vaudeville flourishes and dance steps to the enthusiastic cheers of the normally reserved British crew. After shooting the song, he granted an interview with a *TV Guide* reporter, exuding charm as he downed a vodka and beer chaser. But when asked if he would accept an Emmy for this Patton, he refused to answer.

He needn't have worried. *The Last Days of Patton* was not recognized at awards time. Scott may have felt the original relied too heavily on battle scenes, but the sequel was like a dull visit to the hospital, with much of the film's three hours confined to the general's bedside. Rigged up like a mackerel with hooks in his temples to simulate traction, Scott was severely limited in the expressions he could produce. *TV Guide* called the focus on Patton's final suffering "both gruesome and pointless. The movie could have—should have—handled Patton's agonies in just a few minutes."

Lying in bed for hours led the actor to reflect on his mortality. "Why hang on to eighty-five and be incapacitated, deaf and blind and have to be taken care of?" he asked Stephen Farber. He was even contemplating another TV series as a means of earning enough to retire. "I would like to do a series for a few years and make enough money to get the hell out and go fishing for the rest of my life. As I said once before, I have no desire to die on stage at the age of seventy-five. I'd just as soon die in bed."

Around the time of that interview (in the summer of 1986), Scott did reach an agreement to star in a weekly half-hour sitcom, playing the chief executive in *Mr. President* for Johnny Carson's production company to air on the new Fox network. When asked why he was returning to the grind of regular television after vowing never to return after *East Side/West Side*, Scott bluntly replied, "Retirement. If this goes well, I can retire and get out of this business."

But first he would return to Circle in the Square for *The Boys in Autumn*, a two-character play by Bernard Sabath depicting a grown-up and disillusioned Huck Finn and Tom Sawyer reflecting on how their lives have drastically altered since their idyllic boyhood depicted in Mark Twain's iconic novels. Huck has become an eccentric recluse after he helped his terminally ill wife commit suicide. Tom is a has-been vaudevillian with pederastic tendencies, kindled whenever he spies a little girl with a re-semblance to Becky Thatcher. The play had been presented in San Francisco with Burt Lancaster and Kirk Douglas. Scott had tried to persuade Marlon Brando to play Tom to his Huck, but his *Formula* costar claimed he'd never be able to remember all those lines. Besides, two weeks filming a cameo on a movie for a seven-figure salary was fun. Performing a play with only one other actor was just too much work.

Since Sabath's Tom has a song-and-dance background, Theodore Mann, Circle's producer and the play's director, hired John Cullum, a Tony winner for the musicals *On the Twentieth Century* and *Shenandoah*. Cullum found his costar

> an intimidating person because he was irascible and difficult to get along with and drinking quite a bit which didn't put me off too much. I was a pretty heavy drinker myself, but not at that particular time. We would go out and I would drink wine and he would drink vodka and beer chasers. I said to him, "How much do you drink, George?" and he said, "I have to drink a quart of vodka with beer chasers or I get sick." He would have drinks during rehearsals, which were never more than three hours, usually they were less than that. I thought, "Oh my goodness." A two-character play is a very difficult piece of material to do; it's extremely taxing on both actors and I was concerned, because we had such short rehearsal periods. But my fears were very quickly allayed because George had an ability to memorize lines that was different from most people. It was as if they were embossed in his mind somehow. He could perform when he'd had a lot to drink and the only thing you'd notice would be that he would be slow. He never missed lines. He was very gracious to his fellow actors as he was to me.

Cullum said Scott was a "pleasure to work with and instinctively right all the time," but did witness his costar's irascibility over the beard he had grown for Huck:

He came in one morning, had been drinking quite a bit, and was obviously upset. He had been up for a commercial, that car commercial he did, which was worth a million dollars at least. He had gotten in an altercation with the people because they wanted him to cut his beard off and he had refused. He was adamant. He had walked out on them that morning. Here he was angry and upset and furious over a commercial he could have been making a million dollars on and we were getting maybe $600 a week. It was a little bit strange. They eventually gave in to him.

When the play opened to mostly negative reviews (Frank Rich of the *New York Times* called it one of the worst plays of an unimpressive theatre season), Scott had plenty of cause for irritability. On the second night, Cullum noticed Scott was in a less than happy mood:

At Circle in the Square, you have walk across the set in front of the audience to get backstage. The reviews had already been done by the major critics and the second-string critics were all sitting in the audience by the time we had to come in. When I came backstage, George was absolutely in a bad mood. He said, "Did you notice all those critics out there sitting with the *Times* beside them?" They had all read the reviews and he knew it. So he gave a good performance, but he was very surly. When the curtain came down on the first act and the blackout happened, he said quite clearly and loudly, "You can laugh now." He was furious with the critics.

While recovering from the bad reviews, Scott could console himself with admission to the Theatre Hall of Fame. The induction ceremony took place a week before the *Boys in Autumn* opening at the Gershwin Theatre, where honorees had their names embedded in gold letters in the lobby. The event was cohosted by Colleen Dewhurst. The former Mrs. Scott was hugged by her successor. Van Devere was now spending more time with her husband and their loose arrangement seemed to be working out. No longer having to constantly live with his unpredictable temper or live up to being as great an actor as him, Van Devere was able to give him the attention he needed on her own terms.

He finished 1986 with three more TV movies, shot in diverse locations. *Choices*, an issue-of-the-week feature on abortion, lensed in Vancouver though it was set in Manhattan. *Murders in the Rue Morgue* sent him to the setting of Edgar Allan Poe's classic short story, Paris, while *Pals*, a silly comedy with Don Ameche and Sylvia Sydney, was filmed in Savannah, Georgia. In *Choices,* Scott played a retired judge whose anti-abortion stand comes to haunt him. Both his younger wife (Jacqueline Bisset) and daughter (Melissa Gilbert) have unwanted pregnancies. *Variety* called it "fundamentally dull stuff" and the *Hollywood Reporter* opined, "Despite some sharp performances from a distinguished cast, *Choices'* scenario is so contrived, it dances and dodges around taking a stand and thus has no effective impact." *Murders* achieves a degree of atmosphere and suspense, but Scott appears listless as Poe's inspector. He has more energy in *Pals*, but it's employed in an absurd vehicle. He and Don Ameche mug for the camera as a pair of elderly ex-army buddies who stumble on a suitcase full of stolen greenbacks. He also signed up for a second series of Renault commercials, collecting $2 million for his services.

That fat fee still wasn't enough to retire on, so he began shooting *Mr. President* in April 1987. He was now fifty-nine years old. The sitcom had an impressive pedigree and potential for quality. Co-created by Ed. Weinberger (*The Mary Tyler Moore Show* and *Taxi*) and Gene Reynolds (*Lou Grant* and *M*A*S*H*), the series cast Scott as Samuel Tresch, an ex-governor of Wisconsin and newly elected head of state. The show was meant to be a mildly amusing half-hour focusing on Tresch's domestic life as his wife and two teenaged kids adjust to highly scrutinized life in the White House. Weeks in advance of the series' start date, Scott flew from Connecticut to Los Angeles to attend story conferences, writing sessions, anything so he could contribute his ideas. Few such meetings took place. When the scripts finally appeared

Scott considered them pedestrian at best. He wrote a memo to Wein-berger and Reynolds requesting they come up with relevant topics to explore. Recent comedies such as *All in the Family, M*A*S*H, Maude, The Mary Tyler Moore Show*, and many others had covered hot-button issues like racism, abortion, and homosexuality. Why couldn't *Mr. President* be as daring?

He even came up with storyline for an episode with Tresch appoint-ing a black female vice-president. Scott developed it and hired a writer for a first draft. But the idea was rejected by Weinberger as unwork-able. The writer did pen another episode on a slightly less controver-sial theme—the president's reaction to the constantly malfunctioning White House elevator. Rehearsals for the first episode were beginning and none of Scott's progressive suggestions were implemented. His frustrations with the series were compounded when his eighty-five-year-old father died on April 15. George D. Scott had retired to Florida and was looking forward to seeing his son as the President of the Unit-ed States. Their contentious relationship had caused the younger Scott much pain over the years—from the loss of his mother to anger at his stepmother to his dad's disapproval of his profession and alcoholism—but in recent years they drew closer and often spoke on the phone, mostly about sports. Perhaps because of the pressure of headlining a new series, Scott did not mention his father's passing to the producers and did not attend the funeral.

Debuting on May 3, 1987, *Mr. President* was touted as the highlight of Fox's Sunday night lineup, but drew abysmal ratings and worse reviews. Daniel M. Kimmel in his history of the network called the show "an embarrassing and expensive mess."

Fox programming chief Garth Ancier explained the sitcom's failure to Kimmel:

> We didn't understand . . . that when you're trying to start a new
> television network, you have to aim young. *Mr. President*, despite
> the fact that we had a terrific producer in Ed. Weinberger and,

obviously, George C. Scott is a huge name to get at that time to be the lead of the show—that show was not going appeal to younger viewers. It was going to appeal to older viewers. And those viewers were simply not going to turn to a UHF station to try out a new show. Had the show been on CBS, maybe.

"It was Johnny Carson's flagship show," recalled Carlin Glynn, the Tony-winning actress who played the First Lady. "It was shot in 35 millimeter. There was a seventy percent model of the White House Oval Office and living quarters. So it was quite an expensive thing. And George, of course, was making a great deal of money. I think whenever you have a debut show, it's very nervous-making for people. Because there were so many producers and it was a new network. All of a sudden some poor hairdresser would be fired just because a head needed to roll. So it was not a relaxing or happy atmosphere."

Adding to the pressure were the conflicting goals of Weinberger and Reynolds. The former wanted to make the show broader and more sitcom-y. Reynolds favored a realistic approach. "They had a basic disagreement about the show," Glynn said.

> Gene wanted the show to evolve. . . . My character was a precursor for a Hillary Clinton, a woman who takes care of the husband and the kids, but had very strong environmental stands and had my own fish to fry as it were. Gene Reynolds really, really supported that. Weinberger wanted me to watch all these Jean Arthur movies. I said, "I'm not Jean Arthur." Finally Gene Reynolds quit. He had a younger wife and a child. He said, "I have made plenty of money. This is not worth it." There was a basic schism between Weinberger and Reynolds and Reynolds was my guy.

As the weeks progressed and Reynolds departed, Weinberger's vision dominated, with President Tresch spending most of his time like a sitcom dad rather than the leader of the free world. Typical episodes had him consoling his daughter over her crush on a secret service agent, dancing with a movie star to make the first lady jealous, and disciplining his visiting nephews for toking weed in the Lincoln bedroom.

Glynn felt Scott's persona worked against the show's premise: "I often thought that one of the problems with *Mr. President* was when George was playing frustration, which on another actor would seem funny; on George it looked like he was angry, which is not good for a show that's supposed to be warm and fuzzy and fun. I thought that at the time. This is in no way a condemnation or criticism of his acting. It's just this persona, when he was trying to be a good daddy or a loving husband, looked a little annoyed by the whole thing."

Scott was more than a little annoyed by the crazy pace of weekly television production. Unlike the *East Side/West Side* days, when he battled with everyone from the suits at the network to the producers to the writers, he didn't put up as much of a fight to realize his vision of the show. He continued strenuously objecting to the grade-Z level of the humor and banality of the plots, but got nowhere. It was all he could do just to keep up with the frantic schedule.

Despite the negative press and negligible ratings, *Mr. President* was renewed for the fall. Fearful of even smaller audiences, Weinberger dropped the humor level further. The first season had been filmed with a single camera; now, to ensure bigger and more audible laughs, the episodes would be videotaped with three cameras in front of a live audience. The scenarios got sillier and Carlin Glynn's proto-Hillary Clinton was replaced with her wacky sister, played by Madeline Kahn, the bubbly and zany comedienne best known for the Mel Brooks films *Young Frankenstein* and *Blazing Saddles*. The first lady's absence was explained by a tape-recorded message stating she couldn't take the public scrutiny anymore. The changes did not improve the ratings or reviews. *Variety* moaned, "[I]t's a little painful to watch George C. Scott trying to hold this mediocre package together—something like watching one of the world's great chefs preparing a Spaghetti-Os dinner."

The series limped along until Christmas, when Fox executives asked Carson's production company if they wanted to extend the date of the network's renewal option. The show was losing Carson $20,000 a week and the company elected not to give *Mr. President* another term.

Shooting for the final episode was canceled when Scott suffered his second heart attack while watching the NFC championship game. He later came up with the idea for an article on the whole unhappy experience in the form of a conversation in the hospital between himself and the fictional chief executive he played. The *Los Angeles Times* published it under the title "The Casual Assassination of *Mr. President*." In the imaginary dialogue, the character blames the actor for not battling harder to make him and the series more real. "The working situation was positively Byzantine," Scott argues with his creation. "We were always chronically behind. In scripts, in time, most of all in quality. Had I habitually insisted on the unreality of perfection, the whole insane Chinese fire drill would have ground to a halt. They would have sued me."

"Probably," Sam answers. "Then you could have resigned with dignity." The piece goes on to lament the impossibility of producing decent television, particularly a politically oriented sitcom. Tresch sardonically jokes that if the heart attack had killed Scott, the series might have had a shot at a comeback with a bigger star. "It wasn't a total loss," Scott tells Tresch as his car pulls away from the hospital, "We also managed to insult what audience we did have and make fools of ourselves in the bargain."

Scott left Tresch and his regrets for the TV fiasco behind and pushed on to finally film *Harrow Alley*, the long-dormant script on the Black Plague. There was renewed interest in the property due to the parallel health catastrophe caused by the AIDS crisis. Scott and Van Devere went to London to scout locations and speak with British financiers. They told columnist Marilyn Beck they would both act in the proposed film, but Scott would not direct or produce. There were also roles for Martin Sheen and Brian Dennehy.

But *Harrow Alley* was never filmed. The sticking point was Scott's insistence on not changing a word of the script. "Either do it the way it is or don't do it," he said. "You see, this is my insurance policy. I can't die before I get this movie done. The minute I do it, I'm gone, I'm outta here, I'm history."

Despite the handsome salaries for *Mr. President* and the Renault commercials, all reports of retirement ceased. There were big expenses—separate households on two coasts, a battle with the I.R.S. over an investment in a herd of dairy cattle—so whatever job was available, fit into the schedule, and wasn't too terrible was the job he took. But even by these lax standards, *The Exorcist III*, a particularly execrable horror film, was an all-time low. At least he was professionally reunited with Dewhurst. She provided the voice of the devil while Scott starred as Lieutenant Bill Kinderman, the detective played by Lee J. Cobb in the original film. This gory schlockfest is an unintentional camp delight, so bad it's enjoyable. Still, Scott manages to convey some truth amidst the bloody madness. When he is forced to examine the body of one of the demon's victims—a priest Kinderman has befriended—he pauses and utters a heartbreaking sigh before lifting the sheet. His sorrow is palpable despite the absurdity of the story.

His health was not the greatest. While filming the TV-movie *Finding the Way Home* in Dallas, Scott suffered a third heart attack. "I don't have Alzheimer's disease," he joked with *Variety*'s Army Archerd after successfully undergoing an angioplasty. "I'm working out, biking, playing tennis."

He was now spending most of his time in Malibu with Van Devere. When not acting, he was writing. After 250 pages, he had abandoned the Mexican-American War novel and started a play about two Japanese generals who had defeated MacArthur in battle. At the end of Word War II, MacArthur had the generals executed summarily. He told reporter Michael Reidel that when he felt inspired he wrote every day. The trouble was when he didn't feel inspired, he didn't write and had no mechanism to overcome his creative block.

Scott had no acting block. In 1988, he toured in the one-man play *Clarence Darrow*, and in the fall of 1991 he returned to Circle in the Square to direct and star in *On Borrowed Time*, a sentimental fantasy by Paul Osborn from 1938 he had found in the Malibu library. The gentle play is a combination of Norman Rockwell and *The Twilight Zone* with lovable old Julian Northrup, referred to as Gramps, trapping the Angel of Death, portrayed as a stuffy Englishman named Mr. Brink, in an apple tree. This inexplicable ploy is used to prevent Gramps's demise and to save his orphaned grandson from falling under the care of nasty old Aunt Demetria. "There's a sweetness about it, a gentility, and a kind of sense of hope," he explained to Michael Reidel. The play was originally set in the 1930s, but Scott pushed the time frame back to the 1910s to further add to the air of nostalgia.

For Grandma, he cast Teresa Wright, his Linda Loman from the Circle *Death of a Salesman*. Supporting roles were cast with reliable colleagues like Conrad Bain (his right-hand man in *Mr. President*) and Bette Henritze. Scott made the unusual choice of casting Nathan Lane as Brink. In the original Broadway production, the role was played by Leo G. Carroll; and on film it had been played by Sir Cedric Hardwicke—two veddy proper British character actors. Lane, who had become a star in Scott's Circle production of *Present Laughter*, had a broad American comic appeal and felt he was wrong for the part:

> I didn't know the play at all. So I got a copy of it and read it. I thought, "This is a hokey old thing, this chestnut. Why does he want to do *this*, playing lovable old Gramps?" I went to see Ted Mann and said, "I don't think I'm right for this and I don't like this play. It's so hokey in this day and age of special effects movies, this whole notion of trapping Death in a tree. It's just so old-fashioned. I don't know whether it would even hold up with an audience. Let him do *Lear*, I'll play the fool. Let's do something a little more challenging." Ted said, "Well, this is what he wants to do and he wants you to play Death. If you don't want to do it,

you have to call him. I can't call him because he'll only yell and scream at me."

With trembling fingers, Lane called Scott to inform him of his decision. He was hoping to get an answering machine, but Scott picked up after one ring. "I said, 'Look, I don't think I can do this. I don't think I'm right for it.' I came up with every excuse I could. I finally said, 'It's been played by Sir Cedric Harwicke and Leo G. Carroll and Claude Rains.' Then he raised his voice and said, 'When I go, I don't want Sir Cedric fuckin' Hardwicke to take me, I want you.' So I said, 'Okay, I'll do it.'"

Casting a little boy for the grandson, Pud, was equally difficult, Lane recalled.

The first kid he hired, they let go after the first week. The understudy [Matthew Porac] took over the role. An adorable kid who had just done commercials. George was tough with the kids. There was another boy who was in it who used to laugh very nervously whenever he was around George, and one day George screamed at him, "Hey, stay in character. Don't screw around." The little boy playing Pud had a big emotional scene at the end of the play. He just wasn't capable of reaching the emotion that was needed. . . . They did the scene over and over. They worked for about twenty-five minutes and finally he said, "Look, if you don't cry, we're all screwed. We might as well go home and not do the play." And this poor little kid looked at him and sort of nodded his head as if to say, "I'll try again." He was never able to do it, but eventually George would get emotional and the scene still worked.

Despite the creaky plot and syrupy sentimentality, the play worked as well. "Mr. Scott and his fine company of actors treat the fantasy with the air of conviction that insures its believability for even a skeptical latter-day audience," wrote John Beaufort in the *Christian Science Monitor*.

"I remember the closing night at Gallagher's," Lane said. "We had a party. I walked him out and I do remember he had this big white limo. . . . He got in the car and then he opened the door again and got out. We had all been drinking a lot at this point and he said to me, 'I know you didn't want to do this play. I know you only did it for me and I'll always love you for that.' Then he got back in the car and they went off."

Just before *On Borrowed Time* rehearsals began, on August 22, 1991, Colleen Dewhurst died of cervical cancer. Adhering to her Christian Scientist faith, Dewhurst refused to submit to an operation, but relied on prayer for treatment. Her companion of sixteen years, Broadway producer Ken Marsolais, and her sons, Alex and Campbell, opened the farmhouse at South Salem for a goodbye party the first weekend of September. Friends, colleagues, and relatives gathered to recall this Olympian talent. Scott put in a brief appearance. Elizabeth Wilson remembered, "There must have been 200 people there. Jason [Robards] was there, everybody . . . George came to the event. But he came before anybody else. I asked 'Is George coming?' And I was told, 'He's been here.'"

19

"The Most Mellow Son of a Bitch
You've Ever Seen"

AFTER SUFFERING THE THIRD HEART attack, and seeing the mother of two of his children die, Scott was toning down his hellraiser image. He told the *New York Times*'s Mervyn Rothstein,

> Mellow? I've always been mellow. I have been the most mellow son of a bitch you've ever seen. Of course, I've had some problems over the years. I've made a lot of mistakes. I stopped drinking for four and a half years. I went back to drinking on my sixty-third birthday, last October. I think I'm going to go back on the wagon, but I can't promise you I will. And furthermore, I'm not worried about it. What I am is a functional alcoholic.

His roles were mellower as well—they were men adjusting to age and mortality. In TV's *Finding the Way Home*, he was an amnesia victim starting his life over in a Latino migrant farming community. There was Patton on his deathbed, Scrooge repenting his miserliness, the grandfather facing the next world in *On Borrowed Time*, and another man dealing with his imminent death in his stage next role in *Wrong Turn at Lungfish*.

Written by television and film producer-writers Garry Marshall (*Happy Days*, *The Odd Couple*, *Laverne and Shirley*) and Lowell

Ganz (*City Slickers*, *Parenthood*, *Splash*), *Lungfish* centers on a blind, terminally ill, misanthropic literature professor and the ditzy but tenderhearted volunteer who reads to him. The title (which Scott hated) is from Darwin's theory of evolution, in which lungfish are prominently featured. In the tradition of *Pygmalion*, *Born Yesterday*, *Educating Rita*, and Marshall's film *Pretty Woman*, the comedy tracks the evolution of this unlikely friendship. He gives her some culture and self-esteem; she coaxes him out of his self-imposed exile. After a workshop and production at Chicago's Steppenwolf Theatre, Marshall wanted to stage it in Los Angeles with Scott, who was reluctant from the get-go. Marshall bypassed the agents and managers and appealed to Scott directly. He learned the actor's two favorite hobbies were the Detroit Tigers and chess. He then wrote Scott he would hire an intern whose sole responsibility would be to play chess backstage with the star. The contract would include the clause "One chess partner on hand at all times." In addition, Marshall signed all his letters with names of old Detroit players like Hank Greenberg, Rudy York, and Dizzy Trout.

Lungfish opened at the Coronet Theatre in Los Angeles with Marshall directing in May 1992. Laurie Metcalf, an Emmy winner for *Roseanne* and a veteran of Steppenwolf Theatre, recreated her role as the ill-educated but wise girl the professor befriends. Tony Danza, the lovable lug from *Taxi* and *Who's the Boss?*, was her abusive boyfriend, and Kelli Williams, star of a number of TV movies, a sarcastic nurse. The reviews were mixed to bad, comparing the play to a sitcom, and Scott skipped the first performance after opening night. Understudy Richard McKenzie went on with a bucket placed in the wings so he could throw up. Scott returned the next night, but Marshall was nervous his star might bolt again. The writer-producer started secretly rehearsing Jack Klugman for the role, just in case. After Scott heard about this, he never missed another performance.

Despite the middling notices, the producers felt Scott's name plus the video recognition factor of his costars merited a transfer to Off-

Broadway's Promenade Theatre in February 1993. (Laurie Metcalf was unavailable; Jamie Gertz, another actress with an impressive TV resume, replaced her). Again the reviews were lukewarm. *Time* magazine: "The laughs, and there are plenty, come mostly from Scott's trademark vocabulary of gestures for impatience—the wide-eyed glare, the bellow, the thundering crash of his heel for emphasis as he tells the long-winded young woman, 'Short! Short!' About two hours shorter would have been best for the whole two-hour enterprise."

Scott missed the first four performances after the opening, suffering from a bad flu and complaining of chest pains. He was still drinking. Tony Danza later told *TV Guide*, "I used to try to discourage him from drinking, but more often than not I'd end up sitting next to him at a bar just listening to him talk."

Scott's eye doctor, Albert Ackerman, his wife, and Elizabeth Wilson, a fellow patient of Ackerman's, met Scott and Danza for dinner after a *Lungfish* performance. "We met them at Ernie's on the West Side," Dr. Ackerman recalled. "I guess [George] went there every night because they set him up with three drinks to begin with. Then just before dessert, Elizabeth said, 'Albert, it's time to go.' . . . She told me afterwards, 'I know when it's time to go.'" Having spent many late nights in bars and restaurants with Scott, Wilson knew when to time an exit before his imbibing became excessive and he became abusive.

Health problems continued to plague Scott. During 1994, he was diagnosed with an aortic aneurysm, a balloon-like bulge in the major blood vessel that carries blood from the heart to the head and the legs. It measured four and a half centimeters. At five and a half centimeters, it's considered smart to do elective surgery to repair it. Scott elected to do nothing.

Rather than slowing down, he embarked on another round of the most stressful work regimen imaginable: a weekly television show. One would think he'd have had enough after the contentious experiences of

East Side/West Side and *Mr. President*, but a series could pay a lot of bills. Unfortunately, the third time was not a charm. *Traps*, a police drama from Stephen J. Cannell, creator of such hits as *The A-Team* and *The Rockford Files*, was filmed in Vancouver and starred Scott as Joe Trapchek, a retired Seattle homicide detective. Dan Cortese, best known as the host of *MTV Sports* and for a series of Burger King commercials, wore a ponytail as Chris, Trapchek's rebel-cop grandson. ("The closer they get to solving a case . . . the closer they get to each other," ran the show's ad copy.) Joe's son, another officer, has been killed in the line of duty, and Chris is determined to make his mark on his own. Grandpa offers rough wisdom, often butting heads with Chris. Piper Laurie was Scott's wife, whose Alzheimer's disease draws the bickering grandfather and grandson together.

Since they had worked together on *The Hustler*, Laurie had gotten to know Scott and was no longer intimidated by his gruff reputation. "A mutual friend invited me to go with him to dinner at his and Trish's house out in Malibu," she said. "I was nervous about it, but we went and the door was open. And he was transformed in my head. He opened his arms like a big teddy bear. He said, 'Rosie,' which he knew was my nickname, and he picked me up in his arms and threw me into the air. He was just so sweet and loving."

Laurie recalled that on the set, "it was pleasant in between the scenes. I can't really say the work was changed, but he was easy to laugh with; I didn't feel self-conscious. I just felt like he was a pal and helpful."

The formulaic series debuted on CBS as a midseason replacement on March 31, 1994. Pitted against NBC's popular *L.A. Law*, the show was treated like a minor misdemeanor by critics and audiences. *TV Guide* gave it a rating of three out of ten, and the *New York Times* declared, "There is little original in the conception and hardly a spontaneous moment in the execution." *Traps* was shut permanently after only five weeks.

Scott's run of bad luck with series television continued when he filmed three segments of *New York News*, a CBS newspaper drama with

Mary Tyler Moore miscast as a ruthless editor. He had the juicy guest-starring role of the paper's new owner, but the series was cancelled before his episodes were aired.

From November 14 to December 9, 1994 Scott filmed *Angus,* a teen problem film that would have been more appropriate for an after-school TV special. He was the cuddly yet vinegary grandfather of the title character, an overweight teenager. There are some moments of snappy wit, such as his vigorously instructing his grandson to "screw 'em" when the popular kids tease him. But most of the humor derives from Scott falling asleep at the dinner table. He was the grandfather now, no longer the menacing man of action or the general leading the third army over the top. He played a variation on the same role that year as the dastardly yet adorable Blind George in *The Whipping Boy,* a children's feature for the Disney Channel. Scott traveled to France to make cute with two kid actors.

Noticeably overweight, the aneurysm potentially growing in his heart, Scott ignored the risks to his health and continued drinking. While filming *Tyson,* an HBO telefilm on the controversial heavyweight, Michael Jai White, who was playing the title role, noted Scott had trouble climbing stairs and was easily winded.

In January 1996, Scott returned to the coal mountains (Tazewell county, Virginia, not far from Wise, the town of his birth) to film *Country Justice,* a soap-operatic TV movie. Once again, he was the elderly sage, this time a retired coal miner aiding his unwed, pregnant granddaughter. "All of sudden there was a lot of relatives on the set," Del Acevedo joked. "They all claimed to be cousins. I don't know how true it was. There were a lot of them." Also on the set was Julie Wright, a former student at Piedmont Community College, working as an intern on the production. Scott hired the twenty-six-year-old as his personal assistant to help him prepare for a return to Broadway in a revival of *Inherit the Wind,* the 1955 drama based on the Scopes monkey trial. He was to play Henry Drummond, the Clarence Darrow–like attorney defending a Tennessee school teacher's right to teach Darwin's theory of evolution. The production was mounted by Tony Randall's National Actors Theatre, an ambitious undertaking to present works of weight and importance on the commercial-driven Main Stem. The economic situation had become even harsher in the three decades since Scott had attempted a similar venture with the Theatre of Michigan. Serious dramas were rare commodities on Broadway, unless they were hits in London or Off-Broadway first. None of the NAT's previous productions had turned a profit, but *Wind*, costarring Charles Durning as Scott's legal opponent, had an advance in excess of $1 million.

Battling a bad case of the flu he'd picked up in the damp mines while filming *Country Justice*, Scott was absent from several rehearsals and spent the last few days before the first preview performance in the hospital on an IV drip. Randall, who had appeared in the original production as the cynical reporter E. K. Hornbeck, was Scott's understudy and was ready to go on, but the star got out of his hospital bed, put on his Detroit Tigers jacket and T-shirt, and made it to the Royale Theatre. He was weak, but he made it. Cast member John Griesemer told Myrna Katz Frommer and Harvey Frommer in *It Happened on Broadway*,

> It was pretty grim, really shaky, kind of like watching a corpse being reanimated. It was very difficult for him to move. He had to hold on to the steps. There were long pauses while he searched for lines. But he got through it. I think it was very important that he did. The average person wouldn't think of going to work in that condition, especially that kind of work. But George just ripped out the IV and came and did the play.

During the preview period, he was still under the weather much of the time, missing performances and losing weight—he dropped a total of twenty-five pounds by opening night, which was pushed back from March 18 to April 4. Scott was enraged over his failing health and sometimes took it out on medical professionals. According to Patrick Pacheco's *Newsday* theatre column of March 28, during a visit to St. Luke's Roosevelt Hospital, he threw the plastic bottle intended for a urine sample at a nurse, cursed her, and walked out.

As the new opening night approached, Scott was regaining some strength, but still moved with difficulty. Though he was suffering, he used his infirmity for the role, his arthritic gait making him look like an old gladiator going into combat one last time against the forces of ignorance and prejudice. From the smallest comic bit to his titanic confrontation with Durning as the fundamentalist Matthew Harrison Brady, Scott summoned all of his power to what would be his last stage performance. "See you in reality," he would say to Durning before they went on—and for Scott it wasn't just a catchphrase. He was living for the stage. When *Inherit* finally opened, he received valedictory notices, with the critics taking his infirmities into account yet lauding his art. "Scott is old, and a little weary," wrote the usually sharp-edged John Simon in *New York*. "Yet here is a great actor at his apogee—one who has elevated every trick of the trade into sublimity. The tiniest gesture, the most fleeting facial play, the least stressed syllable sports the aura of the consummate."

"Old and slightly stooped," wrote Michael Feingold in the *Village Voice*, "his hawklike face now lined with wrinkles, he can command the stage even with reduced means." Griesemer corroborates,

> There were nights when I knew he really wasn't well, when he would look really drawn and peaked. But when he would get to the climax, bearing down on Charlie, making all those points and grinding, he summoned stuff that would just come up from somewhere. It would roll to the back of the theater and roll right back. Oceanic. This was the same man I had seen a couple of hours before, shuffling in from his car service in a warm-up jacket and T-shirt. Where he got the stuff to do that, I don't know. But where he was really alive was onstage.

After the glowing reviews, Scott's ailments continued. During the April 16 performance, he stopped in the middle of a speech, told the audience, "Excuse me, I have to leave" and walked offstage. He was given oxygen backstage and went home to rest. After Scott left the stage, Randall who was sitting in the mezzanine, ran down the stairs, mounted the stage and picked up right where the play had stopped.

But Scott's bouts with illness would seem like a day at the beach compared with what was about to befall him. On April 30, Julie Wright quit her $1,500-a-week job along with free room and meals at the Parker Meridian Hotel. Two days later, she filed a $3.1 million sexual harassment suit against her former employer and his production company, Devon Campbell Productions. In papers filed with Manhattan Supreme Court, Wright claimed that after one week on the job, she had asked the actor what errands she could run for him. He allegedly answered, "I need a pack of Luckys, call up room service for eight bottles of Bud and a bottle of Smirnoff, and now, for the real question: Will you have my baby?"

Wright further stated the star groped her and pressured her to have sex with him. "Based on Scott's inappropriate sexual comments and advances, I now believe the whole purpose of my employment was to satisfy Scott's sexual whims," her suit read. She claimed his unwanted overtures made her feel she was "in danger of imminent harm." Scott dismissed her allegations in a brief statement: "I am saddened that Miss Julie Wright has chosen to attack me in this way. The charges are absurd and completely untrue." He missed the performance that night and was on a plane to Los Angeles the next day.

Wright's lawyer, Mark Alsano, had asked that Scott be forced to testify before leaving town because, according to Wright, her ex-boss had told her he was going to California for surgery to treat an unnamed illness and he expected to die during the operation.

"I am concerned he will not be in the city after this weekend," Alsano told the *New York Daily News*, "and perhaps—God forbid—he may not survive. I think it's absolutely necessary that we preserve his testimony."

Jim Mahoney, a spokesman for Scott, said there were no plans for Scott to have surgery. He was just going to L.A. to see his physician because he was still suffering from a severe case of the flu. But in court, Scott's lawyer, Daniel Markewich, presented an affidavit from the actor's Malibu doctor, Jeff Harris, stating that giving testimony could kill Scott. The aneurysm Harris had diagnosed two years earlier had grown to six centimeters, and was now a "time bomb." The stress of the case could light the fuse.

"There is a ninety to ninety-eight percent chance that Mr. Scott will survive the operation, recover and return to stage and screen," Harris stated. "Without surgery, however, his future prospects for survival are bleak. . . . If untreated such a condition is life-threatening, especially in light of its continuing growth." Judge Alice Schlesinger granted the request to excuse Scott temporarily, citing his fragile health. He could wait until after the operation to deal with the case. Outside court, a frustrated Alonso told reporters it was "obvious that he skipped town to avoid deposition." That was probably one of the reasons for Scott's hasty departure, but the aneurysm was definitely a motivating factor.

Ultimately, just as Colleen Dewhurst had refused surgery for a life-threatening illness, so did Scott. The surgery would mean giving up drinking, and that was something he just couldn't do.

The sexual harassment suit was settled out of court, with Wright receiving an undisclosed sum. Was she a genuine victim of unwelcome workplace advances or a gold-digging opportunist taking advantage of a grievously ill old man? The case never came to trial and Scott never gave his side of the events in court, so there is no way of knowing.

Soon after Scott left the production, *Inherit the Wind* received two Tony nominations—for Best Revival and Best Actor in a Play. But with no sign of his star returning and a plummeting box office, Randall, who was carrying on as Henry Drummond, had to post a closing notice. It must have been especially hard for him. If not for Scott's illness and troubles stemming from the lawsuit, this would have been the first critical and financial hit for the NAT. *Wind* lost both Tonys, but Scott did cop the Outer Critics Circle Award and a special Drama Desk Award for lifetime achievement in the theatre. Randall accepted the accolades, generously stating at both ceremonies that Scott was "America's greatest actor."

Like the character he played in Paul Osborn's play, Scott was now living on borrowed time—only this wasn't a cozy fantasy with Nathan Lane as Death ready to lead him offstage. Scott had rejected his doctor's advice and could die within months. Fearful for their father's life, four of Scott's children—Victoria, Matthew, Devon, and Alex—staged an intervention at the house in Malibu. If Scott agreed to treatment, a place at the Betty Ford Clinic was ready for him. Victoria recalled,

> There was a great deal of concern about the aneurysm. We knew that he'd had that for quite some time. In May of '96, we got together. Michelle was not part of that. Campbell couldn't come. There were four of us, plus Trish, plus some family members. We worked in California with an alcohol intervention specialist because [George] couldn't have the surgery for the aneurysm until he was off the liquor. Evidently earlier that year they had tried an intervention with other members of the family. It was unsuccessful in New York. We tried again and we spent about a week locked up in a room, talking about how we wanted to phrase what we wanted to say to him—not making it personal in terms of attacking or hurtful or crummy memories or whatever. We went through a great deal of stuff and when we got all done, the interventionist said, "Eighty percent of interventions are successful. You guys look like you're in the twenty percent. Do you still want to proceed?" And we did at that point . . . We went ahead and talked to him out at their home in Malibu. Trish decided that morning not to be a part of that. Also the friends that thought they could be a part of that weren't, so it

was the four of us that went and talked to him. He did not want the help. He didn't think that he had a problem although we'd arranged a place to go. We'd also cleared our schedules because Betty Ford requires if they take somebody, the families need to come in. So we'd all cleared our schedules so that we would be able to come— whether it was from Connecticut, or Texas where I was then, or Devon from London, we all planned to come back if he would say yes. We would do whatever, because that way if he could get clear of the drinking, then he could do the surgery. But because that never happened, that's what took his life in '99.

At that point, when we left that day, we each in our own way, said . . . "We want you to get the help. We will do anything, but if you can't, we can't sit by and watch you die anymore." And so we broke off contact at that point. He always said we divorced on that day. He never saw that was anything positive that we had done. That was the last time I saw him.

Strangely, Scott did consent to cataract surgery, perhaps rationalizing he needed his eyesight if he was to continue acting and writing his memoirs. An item in the August 8, 1996 edition of *Variety* stated Scott was working with Mel Berger of William Morris on a possible auto-biography. But there was no publisher as of yet. During the summer of 1996, Scott directed Van Devere and Martin Sheen in *The Novelist*, a romantic portrait of Jane Austen by Howard Fast, at the Malibu Stage Company at Pepperdine University's Smothers Theatre, and played the captain in *Titanic*, a CBS TV movie filmed in a water-tank in Vancouver. The feature should not be confused with the later Oscar-winning film or Tony-winning musical of the same title. It was received less enthusiastically than either of those properties. "George C. Scott, as the ship's captain, looks as if he can't wait to hit the iceberg and wrap this show up," snapped the *New York Times*.

Scott's last few TV and film projects had sunk like *Titanic*, but a Showtime remake of *Twelve Angry Men* offered him the opportunity to prove he could still electrify a screen whether it was small or big. Reginald Rose's claustrophobic jury-room dissection of the justice system had been a classic TV drama and an Oscar-nominated film starring Henry Fonda and Lee J. Cobb. A dozen nameless citizens must decide the fate of a young boy accused of murdering his father. At first, it appears to be an open-and-shut case for conviction. But a lone juror (Jack Lemmon in this update) votes "not guilty" and eventually convinces the eleven others the evidence is circumstantial, causing them to change their minds. Director William Friedkin (*The French Connection*, *The Exorcist*) got the idea of making a new version while explaining the jury system to his son during the O. J. Simpson trial. In the role of Juror #3, Scott was returning to familiar territory. As the last holdout against acquittal, #3 reveals his real resentment is against his own son. Tears well up as he rails against the others about the abusive murder victim, "I don't care what kind of man he was—he was his *father*." Once again, Scott was playing out a dysfunctional father-son relationship: now he was the dad disappointed in his offspring rather than the other way around.

"[H]e had to do a scene in which he breaks down," recalled Jack Lemmon. "He did it take after take, and the emotion was always there. It was deeply moving for all of us. It was as good as acting gets."

"I must say I had a feeling that [there] weren't going to be too many more performances left in George," Friedkin later told the *Los Angeles Times*. "But when we finished the last scene of *Twelve Angry Men* about 200 people showed up from other stages to watch him do his last scene and I felt that he had nailed it . . . He was in a lot of pain during that shoot. But he never talked about what it was."

The performance reaffirmed Scott's power after a string of flops. "Scott is explosive, angriest of the twelve angry men, a father deeply embittered over his failures with his own son, full of palpable agony and rage," wrote Tom Shales in the *Washington Post*. "Naturally Scott grits his fangs and rages and roars, but if the gestures are familiar, they still seem credible and affecting. Scott may look exactly like an Al

Hirschfeld caricature of himself at this point, but he is still capable of generating megawatts of electricity." Scott was nominated for a SAG Award and won the Emmy, Golden Globe, and Cable ACE Awards. While he did not show up at any of the ceremonies, he didn't reject the honors, either. There were no jokes from the podium about the *Patton* refusal; the Hollywood community was quietly honoring one of its greatest talents—even though he had never wanted to be a part of it.

He could still work in film and television, but its more demanding nature made the stage impossible. He withdrew from a San Francisco production of *A Certain Labor Day*, written by and costarring Carroll O'Connor. "My doctor asked me not to [do the play]," he said to *Variety*'s Army Archerd, "the strain would be too much for me." He took a cameo in Sidney Lumet's remake of *Gloria*, with Sharon Stone recreating Gena Rowlands's role of an ex-gun moll on the run with an orphaned child who has witnessed a mob rubout. Scott played Ruby Rich, an Irish gangster with romantic ties to Gloria and a weakness for the horses. The actor's infirmities were evident. In the only one of his few scenes in which he wasn't seated, he was leaning against Sharon Stone for support. Despite his lack of vigor, Scott's intense eyes and whisper of a threatening smile invoke the dangerous mob leader of Ruby's youth and the attractive figure he must have been to Gloria.

Just as his children had pulled away from him for refusing to modify his drinking habits, Van Devere was separating from him. Victoria Lewis explained,

> Trish had adopted her brother's little boy, whose name also was George. She adopted him as his sole guardian. . . . All [George and Trish] did was quarrel about how he can't do this and he can't do that in the house with a little kid there. Finally, I don't know if she sent him packing or he decided to go, but it was because of the little child, he decided to look for someplace else to live. They

were still speaking. It definitely was a separation, but it was over always quarrelling over you can't drink, smoke, or cuss in front of this baby.

Van Devere stayed in the Malibu house while Scott found a small apartment in Westlake Village, forty miles northwest of Los Angeles. Scott may have felt he was being pushed away from the woman he loved in favor of a child. With no children or wife to care for him, his day-to-day needs were met by professional staff. For companionship, there were the regular visits by his faithful makeup man. "His financial manager, Hank Levine, had offices nearby," Del Acevedo said. "[Levine's] daughter, who handled his account, used to make sure he had the cleaning lady, etc., etc. He was well taken care of. Westlake is not that far from me. Once every two or three weeks, I'd go out there and give him a haircut. He liked that. We'd sit and shoot the breeze."

Showtime had such a hit with its remake of *Twelve Angry Men*, the cable network decided to refilm another property—*Inherit the Wind*. The meaty lead roles of the larger-than-life attorneys battling over freedom of expression and religious conviction had proven irresistible to many stars. *Inherit* had been made into a film with Spencer Tracy and Frederic March in 1960, and there were two previous TV adaptations (Melvyn Douglas and Ed Begley in 1965, and Jason Robards and Kirk Douglas in 1988). For this latest edition, Showtime asked Scott to star, but not as Drummond, the role he'd played in the Broadway revival. He switched roles and took on Matthew Harrison Brady, the orator who takes the case against the teaching of evolution. His friend Jack Lemmon was cast as Drummond, and Piper Laurie reunited with him as Brady's wife five years after they had costarred in *Traps*. "We were kind of like old marrieds," she said. "We didn't have to talk, yet I was comfortable saying anything I wanted to."

Director Daniel Petrie had worked with Scott on *East Side/West Side* and noticed the rage had died down in the actor: "Now in his later years and with his illnesses . . . the gentle soul emerged. Although he still had the power, there nonetheless was a sweetness about George."

Piper Laurie recalled that neither Scott nor Lemmon was at his best physically. Scott had to use his hands to get himself on his feet and Lemmon's memory was fading. She related,

> It was quite extraordinary because both he and Jack Lemmon were not in good health. Jack had a lot of trouble with his lines. George was brilliant. Physically he was very fragile. In the scenes where we had to walk arm in arm across a street or down the sidewalk, he was extremely frail and sometimes used my body to support himself. We had to work things out so it would look like he was helping me. But his mind was absolutely brilliant. He had these long, long monologues and he was perfect. Unfortunately, Jack Lemmon was not and we would have to redo it a number of times. George was brilliant every time except by the time they got to his close-up, he'd sort of blown the performance and it was very mechanical. You know, when an actor has to repeat so many times they start to imitate themselves so the performance itself I thought was not what it could have been. It was amazing because he knew Jack's part, too. Jack was wonderful; I think he got an Emmy for it. I felt George left his performance in the courtroom on the set. It was never photographed, never used.

Indeed, in the scene where Brady is questioning a young female witness, Scott's screaming intensity comes out of nowhere and seems like an imitation of his cross-examination of Kathryn Grant in *Anatomy of a Murder*. His best moments are when he eschews the typical Scott fireworks and shows Brady's softer side—trading barbs with Lemmon's Drummond with a mild yet vaguely annoyed chuckle, or gently cajoling the town's fire-breathing preacher to be charitable with the transgressing teacher on trial.

Though he had trouble even standing up, Scott still yearned to return to the theatre. He became interested in a play called *Two Were Called* by Nicholas Nappi about the conflict between Cardinal Francis Spellman and Bishop Fulton Sheen for control of the Catholic Church. Director Tony Giordano sent him the script in hopes of getting Scott to play the staunchly anti-Communist Spellman, who had ambitions to the papacy. Scott was immediately attracted to the part and signed a contract with Giordano for a Broadway production.

Giordano encountered resistance from producers. Remembering *Inherit the Wind*, the Shubert producing organization was concerned about Scott's health and his drinking. There were further, more dire concerns. Giordano said,

> The manager contacted me . . . and privately said to me, "Be careful, George is losing the use of his legs." I said, "What?" He said, "He's getting very weak and I don't know how he can go around the stage and in and out of the set the way that play requires. I think you could get yourself into a terrible bind." . . . So I told the playwright that for the sake of our professionalism and because I had such enormous respect for George C. Scott I didn't want to tell anybody that. I didn't want anybody who we had been talking with to know that George was in trouble physically.

Giordano toyed with the idea of putting Spellman in a wheelchair to accommodate Scott's anticipated infirmity. He confessed,

> I was right and I was wrong, because I would have done it, of course, but the truth of the matter is Spellman needed to be vibrant in order for him to be totally defeated by the end of the play. He needed earlier in the play to be a man who is running back and forth to the Vatican. . . . If you have a man who is in a wheelchair, he can be effective, but it's not likely that he's running to the

airport every ten minutes. I was figuring I could get away with it, but in any case, I never got that opportunity.

Along with *Two Were Called*, Scott still had plans to produce *Harrow Alley*, this time with Mel Gibson and Kenneth Branagh in the leads. While Giordano would continue in his efforts to bring the Nappi play to the stage, the Black Plague film would never reach the screen.

On Wednesday, September 22, 1999, the aortic aneurysm that Scott had failed to have treated ruptured in his abdomen. He was alone in the Westlake Village house. According to a medical website, "Rupture of an abdominal aneurysm is a catastrophe. It is highly lethal and is usually preceded by excruciating pain in the lower abdomen and back, with tenderness of the aneurysm. Rupture of an abdominal aneurysm causes profuse bleeding and leads to shock. Death may rapidly follow." A family friend found him. An ambulance was called and he was pronounced dead by the Ventura County coroner's office at 3:15 that afternoon. In the next few days, when the obituaries began appearing on the wire services and in the papers, the cause of death was acknowledged as preventable. "He could have had it operated on," his friend and publicist Jim Mahoney told *People* magazine. "But he let nature take its course, and it cost him his life." Mahoney stated that Scott was still working on his memoirs at the time of his death.

Patton and the Oscar refusal were the lead items in many of the obits, but most of the tributes and career summations examined the contradictions between the hard-drinking brawler of his public persona and the gentle, shy loner he rarely exposed. The man who defied Hollywood and Broadway was also afraid of crowds and airplanes. The abusive lover could also be a generous friend and father. The man who baked bread and played the organ could turn into a raving monster.

Rex Reed wrote in his *New York Observer* column, "The last of the big, rugged, hard-drinking, rough-living tough guys is gone. . . . It was always said that you couldn't sit in a room with G. C. without eventually getting punched in the nose, but you couldn't prove it by me. I once spent a night in his Connecticut farmhouse, where there was nothing to punch but a bunch of chickens, and he seemed more like a friendly fertilizer salesman than a slugger."

Stephen Hunter, in an appreciation piece for the *Washington Post*, recalled spotting Scott from his car as he drove to work in Baltimore. Scott was in town for the tryout of *Sly Fox* and was walking one of his dogs along the decrepit wharves of what would later become the city's fashionable Inner Harbor. "I saw a look on his face . . . that I never saw on any screen," Hunter wrote. "His face was at utter repose. He looked completely at peace—without another human being within a hundred feet."

A small service for family and friends was held in Los Angeles. On the East Coast there were more public ceremonies to mark his passing. The lights were dimmed on Broadway for one minute and a memorial service was held on October 28 at the Eugene O'Neill Theatre. Presided over by Campbell and Alex, the service featured Kate Burton, Bette Henritze, Nathan Lane, Paul Libin, Theodore Mann, Michael Ritchie, Jason Robards, and Elizabeth Wilson as speakers. Henritze, who had appeared with him in ten productions, told of coming into his dressing room for notes while the actor was in his bare feet. "George," she remarked, "I never knew that you had such beautiful feet."

"Beautiful feet and an ugly soul," he replied with a sigh.

The audience of mourners went dead silent as Henritze paused to catch her breath at the recollection of that heartbreaking moment. Here was one of the greatest actors in the world, a man at the top of his profession, revealing with casual self-deprecation his deepest anguish along with his bare feet.

"I don't think he had an ugly soul," Henritze declared with a slight break in her voice. "I will remember him with love and respect."

Robards recalled he would have drinks with Scott at Patsy and Carl's Theatre Bar when the latter was just beginning to make a name Off-Broadway. "He liked to hang out uptown with the big boys,"

Robards said. "Little did he know, he was bigger than any of us." The service concluded with scenes from *Anatomy of a Murder*, *The Hustler*, *Dr. Strangelove*, *Patton*, *They Might Be Giants*, *The Hospital*, *Death of a Salesman,* and *A Christmas Carol*.

Scott was buried in Pierce Brothers Cemetery and Mortuary in the Westwood section of Los Angeles. He was placed next to Walter Matthau and near to Jack Lemmon, Carroll O'Connor, Robert Stack, Peggy Lee, and Billy Wilder. Fittingly, his was an unmarked grave in this cemetery of the stars. According to Scott's daughter Victoria Lewis, Trish Van Devere never decided on an epitaph.

A blank stone marked his final resting place. Even in death, Scott refused to be one of the crowd.

ACKNOWLEDGMENTS

George C. Scott was an intensely private man. His performances have been reviewed and analyzed in depth, but his offstage life was largely hidden from the public view. I particularly want to thank two women in Scott's life for revealing their stories—his eldest daughter, Victoria Lewis, and Karen Truesdell Riehl, the mother of his second eldest daughter. The following family members, friends, and colleagues were more than generous in sharing their perspectives and memories.

Del Acevedo
Dr. Albert Ackerman
Bob Balaban
Judith Barcroft
David Brown
Kate Burton
Marta Byer-White
Myra Carter
John Cullum
Adrienne Daly
Merle Debuskey
Sonny Elliott
David Epstein
David Finkle
Bill Fowler
Scott Fowler
Vi Fowler
Larry Gelbart
Tony Giordano

Carlin Glynn
Lee Grant
Tammy Grimes
Bette Henritze
Barnard Hughes
Dana Ivey
Clifton James
Manny Kladitis
Shirley Knight
Joseph Koenan
Nathan Lane
Piper Laurie
Victoria Lewis
Robert Loggia
Joe LoGrippo
Karl Malden
Theodore Mann
Peter Masterson
Bruce M. Minnix

Tony Musante

John Wallowitch

Austin Pendleton

Wisner Washam

Karen Truesdell Riehl

Fritz Weaver

Michael Ritchie

Helen Wepman

David Rothenberg

Michael Jai White

Eva Marie Saint

Elizabeth Wilson

Susan L. Schulman

Milton Wilson

Marian Seldes

Sherman Yellen

Stuart Vaughan

Susannah York

Tom Viola

Libraries and archives were immensely helpful. I am indebted to the staff of the Billy Rose Collection of the New York Public Library of the Performing Arts; Jane Klain, Richard Holbrook, and the staff of the Museum of Television and Broadcasting, New York (Jane was particularly helpful, finding Scott's early television performances and interviews as well as numerous reviews and articles in *Variety* and *TV Guide*); Daniel Berger, archivist of the Museum of Broadcast Communications in Chicago, who generously opened the museum archives to me when its doors were shut to the public in anticipation of a major move; Todd H. Christine and the staff of the Missouri State Historical Society; Kris Anstine and Gary Cox, and the staff of the University of Missouri-Columbia Archives; Alan Havig, archivist at the Stephens College Archive, and student assistant Andrea Goodwin; Charlie D. Martinez of the Oakland County Pioneer and Historical Society in Pontiac, Michigan; Christopher Raab and Michael Loer of the Franklin Schaffner Archive at Shadek-Fackenthal Library at Franklin and Marshall University in Lancaster, PA; Ned Comstock of the USC Cinema-Television Library (thanks for double-checking sources over the phone, Ned); Jenny Romero and the staff of the Academy of Motion Picture Arts and Sciences Margaret Herrick Library; Sandra Joy Lee and Taylor Nygaard of the USC Warner Brothers Archive (Sandra told me I was the first person to research *Not With My Wife, You Don't!*).

Erik Haagensen, Bruce Morris, and Diane Snyder were masters of the videotape and DVD machine, making copies of rare Scott performances. Bruce is probably the only person to have the entire run of *Traps* in his collection. Larkellen and Curt Krehbiel of Columbia, Missouri, who live in what was Scott's first apartment, graciously allowed me into their home to see it. David Kaufman and Ken Geist, both good friends and authors of biographies, provided many leads, insight from their own experiences with profiling difficult subjects, and called me every time a George C. Scott movie was on television. Michael Naylor of the Bucks County Playhouse, Jim Baldassare, Ben Frank, Robert Heide, Jon Krampner, Dany Margolies, Sam Norkin, Tom Viola, Robert Windeler, and Wayman

Wong provided information, suggestions, and invaluable leads. Thanks to Gary Manacher for being a gracious host in Los Angeles, and to Bill Schoen and Masahiro Okazaki for opening their home to me in Chicago. As always, Ron and Howard Mandelbaum of Photofest were extremely knowledgeable and helpful in gathering photos.

Marvin Conan, Dan Blume, and Alfred DePew gave me incredible insights and support in their counseling and coaching. During the writing of this book, I was fulfilling my duties as managing editor and then executive editor of *Back Stage*. I thank the staff for their encouragement and indulgence. My agent, Eric Myers, was instrumental in getting this book published. His advice and experience are greatly appreciated, as are those of editor Michael Messina of Applause Theatre and Cinema Books. Thanks also to project editor Jessica Burr and copy editor Sarah Gallogly. And, of course, my partner, Jerry Katz, who held my hand when I was going crazy, kept me sane, and gave me love and support throughout the entire project.

APPENDIX A:
MAJOR THEATRE, FILM, AND TV CREDITS

THEATRE CREDITS

Richard III (1957) by William Shakespeare; New York Shakespeare Festival, producer; Stuart Vaughan, director; Heckscher Theatre. Cast: GCS, Marcia Morris, Lester Rawlins, Dana Elcar, Paul Ballantyne, Virginia Mattis, Eulalie Noble, David Metcalf, Arthur Watson.

As You Like It (1958) by William Shakespeare; New York Shakespeare Festival, producer; Stuart Vaughan, director; Heckscher Theatre. Cast: Nancy Wickwire, Robert Blackburn, Cherry Davis, J. D. Cannon, GCS, Dana Elcar, Jerry Stiller, Anne Meara, Howard Witt.

Children of Darkness (1958) by Edwin Justus Mayer; Circle in the Square (Leigh Connell, Theodore Mann, and José Quintero), producer; José Quintero, director; Circle in the Square Theatre. Cast: Colleen Dewhurst, J. D. Cannon, GCS, Arthur Malet, Ben Hayes, Rene Zwick, John Lawrence, Tom Noel, Joseph Barr.

Comes A Day (1958) by Speed Larkin; Cheryl Crawford, Alan Pakula, producers; Robert Mulligan, director; Ambassador Theatre. Cast: Judith Anderson, GCS (Broadway debut), Brandon De Wilde, Arthur O'Connell, Larry Hagman, Diana van der Vlis, Michael J. Pollard, Ruth Hammond, Joseph Barr, Lorna Thayer, Charles White, Eileen Ryan, John Dutra.

The Andersonville Trial (1959) by Saul Levitt; William Darrid, Eleanore Saidenberg, Daniel Hollywood, producers; José Ferrer, director; Henry Miller's Theatre. Cast: GCS, Herbert Berghof, Albert Dekker, Russell Hardie, Al Henderson, Robert Carroll, James Arenton, Ian Keith, Moultrie Patten, Douglas Herrick, Frank Sutton, James Greene, Robert Gerringer, Robert Burr.

Antony and Cleopatra (1959) by William Shakespeare; benefit concert performance for the New York Shakespeare Festival; Joseph Papp, director; Hecksher Theatre. Cast: GCS, Colleen Dewhurst, Edward Sherin, John McLaim, David Hooks, George Segal, James Frawley, Thomas Barbour, Bette Henritze, John Hetherington, Robert Grace, Helena de Crespo, Anita Stober.

The Wall (1960) by Millard Lampell, based on the novel by John Hersey; Kermit Bloomgarden, Billy Rose, producers; Morton Da Costa, director; Billy Rose Theatre. Cast: GCS, Yvonne Mitchell, David Opatshu, Marian Seldes, James Ray, Muni Seroff, Robert Drivas, Leila Martin, Claudette Nevins, Joseph Buloff, Vincent Gardenia, Michael Ebert, Truman Gaige, Marketa Kimbrell, Norbert Horowitz, Paul Mace.

General Seegar (1962) by Ira Levin; Theatre of Michigan Company and Theodore Mann, producers; GCS, director; Lyceum Theatre. Cast: GCS, Ann Harding, Dolores Sutton, Roscoe Lee Browne, Gerald Richards, Paul Stevens, Lonny Chapman, John Leslie, Tim O'Connor.

Great Day in the Morning (1962) by Alice Cannon; Theatre of Michigan Company (GCS and Theodore Mann), producer; José Quintero, director; Henry Miller's Theatre. Cast: Colleen Dewhurst, J. D. Cannon, Clifton James, Lou Frizzell, Eugene Roche, David Canary, Jeff Herrod, Peggy Burke, Frances Sternhagen, Eulabelle Moore, Thomas Carlin.

The Merchant of Venice (1962) by William Shakespeare; New York Shakespeare Festival, producer; Joseph Papp, director; Delacorte Theatre (Central Park). Cast: GCS, Nan Martin, Lee Richardson, Albert Quinton, Ben Hayes, Bette Henritze, Richard Jordan, Jane McArthur, James Earl Jones, Wayne Wilson, John Call, Robert Kidd, Michael Lombard.

Desire Under the Elms (1963) by Eugene O'Neill; Circle in the Square (Theodore Mann, José Quintero), producer; José Quintero, director; Circle in the Square Theatre. Cast: GCS, Colleen Dewhurst, Rip Torn, Clifford A. Pellow, Lou Frizzell.

The Three Sisters (1965) by Anton Chekhov, English version by Randall Jarrell; Actors Studio Theatre, presented as part of the World Theatre Season by the Royal Shakespeare Company and Peter Daubney; Lee Strasberg, director; Aldwych Theatre, London. Cast: Kim Stanley, Nan Martin, Sandy Dennis, Luther Adler, GCS, James Olson, Robert Loggia, Gerald Hikin, Albert Paulsen, Barbara Baxley.

The Lion in Winter (1966) by James Goldman; Bucks County Playhouse, producer; Milton Katselas, director. Bucks Country Playhouse, New Hope, PA. Cast: GCS, Colleen Dewhurst, William Jordan, Richard Lynch, D. J. Sullivan, Jeff Siggins, Louise Sorel.

Dr. Cook's Garden (1967) by Ira Levin; GCS, director (replaced during rehearsals by Ira Levin); Arnold Saint-Subber, producer; Belasco Theatre. Cast: Burl Ives, Keir Dullea, Bette Henritze, Lee Sanders, Bo Berger.

The Little Foxes (1967) by Lillian Hellman; Repertory Theatre of Lincoln Center, producer; Mike Nichols, director; Vivian Beaumont Theatre. Cast: Anne Bancroft, GCS, E. G. Marshall, Margaret Leighton, Richard A. Dysart, Austin Pendleton, Maria Tucci, Beah Richards, Andre Womble, William Prince.

Plaza Suite (1968) by Neil Simon; Arnold Saint-Subber, producer; Mike Nichols, director; Plymouth Theatre. Cast: GCS, Maureen Stapleton, Claudette Nevins, Bob Balaban, José Ocasio.

Uncle Vanya (1973) by Anton Chekhov, adapted by Albert Todd and Mike Nichols; Circle in the Square, producer; Mike Nichols, director; Circle in the Square Theatre. Cast: Nicol Williamson, GCS, Julie Christie, Barnard Hughes, Elizabeth Wilson, Conrad Bain, Lillian Gish, Cathleen Nesbitt.

All God's Chillun Got Wings (1975) by Eugene O'Neill; Circle in the Square, producer; GCS, director; Circle in the Square Theatre. Cast: Trish Van Devere, Robert Christian, Ken Jennings, Tim Pelt, Tom Sminkey, Minnie Gentry, Vickie Thomas.

Death of a Salesman (1975) by Arthur Miller; Circle in the Square, producer; GCS, director; Circle in the Square Theatre. Cast: GCS, Teresa Wright, James Farentino, Harvey Keitel, Arthur French, Ramon Bieri, Chuck Patterson, Pirie MacDonald.

Sly Fox (1976) by Larry Gelbart, based on *Volpone* by Ben Johnson; Sir Lew Grade, Martin Starger, and the Shubert Organization, producers; Arthur Penn, director; Broadhurst Theatre. Cast: GCS, Hector Elizondo, Jack Gilford, Bob Dishy, Trish Van Devere, Gretchen Wyler, John Heffernan, Jeffrey Tambor.

Tricks of the Trade (1980) by Sidney Michaels; Gilbert Cates, producer, in association with Matthew Alexander; Gilbert Cates, director; Brooks Atkinson Theatre. Cast: GCS, Trish Van Devere, Lee Richardson, Geoffrey Pierson.

Present Laughter (1982) by Noel Coward; Circle in the Square, producer; GCS, director; Circle in the Square Theatre. Cast: GCS, Christine Lahti, Dana Ivey, Elizabeth Hubbard, Richard Woods, Edward Conery, Kate Burton, Nathan Lane, Bette Henritze, Jim Piddock, Georgine Hall.

Design for Living (1984) by Noel Coward; Circle in the Square, producer; GCS, director; Circle in the Square Theatre. Cast: Jill Clayburgh, Frank Langella, Raul Julia, Richard Woods, Helena Carroll, Lisa Kirk, Robertson Carricart, Anne Swift, Arthur French.

The Boys in Autumn (1986) by Bernard Sabath; Circle in the Square, producer; Theodore Mann, director; Circle in the Square Theatre. Cast: GCS, John Cullum.

Clarence Darrow (1988) by David W. Rintels; Mike Merrick and Don Gregory, producers; national tour. Cast and director: GCS.

On Borrowed Time (1991) by Paul Osborn, based on the novel by L. E. Watkin; Circle in the Square, producer; GCS, director; Circle in the Square Theatre.

Cast: GCS, Matthew Porac, Nathan Lane, Teresa Wright, Conrad Bain, Bette Henritze, George DiCenzo, Joseph Jamroq, Alice Haining, Allen Williams.

Wrong Turn at Lungfish (1993) by Garry Marshall and Lowell Ganz; James B. Freyberg, Jeffrey Ash, William P. Miller, producers; Garry Marshall, director; Promenade Theatre. Cast: GCS, Jami Gertz, Tony Danza, Kelli Williams.

Inherit the Wind (1996) by Jerome Lawrence and Robert E. Lee; National Actors Theatre, producer; John Tillinger, director; Royale Theatre. Cast: GCS, Charles Durning, Anthony Heald, Bette Henritze, Garrett Dillahunt, Kate Forbes, Tom Aldredge, Michael Lombard, Herndon Lackey, Tom Stechschulte.

FILMOGRAPHY

The Hanging Tree (1959), Baroda Productions, Warner Brothers; Martin Jurow and Richard Sheperd, producers; Delmar Daves, director; screenplay by Wendell Mayes and Halsted Welles, based on the novel by Dorothy M. Johnson. Cast: Gary Cooper, Maria Schell, Karl Malden, GCS, Karl Swenson, Ben Piazza, Virginia Gregg.

Anatomy of a Murder (1959), Carlyle Productions, Columbia; Otto Preminger, producer and director; screenplay by Wendell Mayes, based on the novel by Robert Traver. Cast: James Stewart, Lee Remick, Ben Gazzara, Arthur O'Connell, Eve Arden, Kathryn Grant, GCS, Orson Bean, Murray Hamilton, Joseph Welch.

The Hustler (1961), Robert Rossen Productions, Twentieth Century-Fox; Robert Rossen, producer and director; screenplay by Sidney Carroll and Robert Rossen, based on the novel by Walter Tevis. Cast: Paul Newman, Jackie Gleason, Piper Laurie, GCS, Myron McCormick, Murray Hamilton, Michael Constantine, Stefan Gierasch, Jake LaMotta, Vincent Gardenia.

The List of Adrian Messenger (1963), Universal-International Joel Productions, Inc.; Edward Lewis, producer; John Huston, director; screenplay by Anthony Veiller, based on a published short story by Philip MacDonald. Cast: GCS, Dana Wynter, Clive Brook, Herbert Marshall, Gladys Cooper, Tony Curtis, Kirk Douglas, Burt Lancaster, Robert Mitchum, Frank Sinatra, John Huston.

Dr. Strangelove or: How I Learned to Stop Worrying and Love the Bomb (1964), Hawk Films, Ltd., Columbia; Stanley Kubrick, producer and director; screenplay by Stanley Kubrick, Terry Southern, and Peter George, based on the novel *Red Alert* by Peter George. Cast: Peter Sellers, GCS, Sterling Hayden, Slim Pickens, Keenan Wynn, Peter Bull, James Earl Jones.

The Yellow Rolls-Royce (1965), MGM; Anatole de Grunwald, producer; Anthony Asquith, director; screenplay by Terence Rattigan. Cast: Rex Harrison, Shirley MacLaine, Ingrid Bergman, Jeanne Moreau, Edmund Purdom, GCS, Omar Sharif, Art Carney, Alain Delon, Roland Culver, Wally Cox.

The Bible (1966), A Thalia, A.G. Production, Twentieth Century-Fox; Dino De Laurentiis, producer; John Huston, director; screenplay by Christopher Fry. Cast: Michael Parks, Ulla Bergryd, Richard Harris, John Huston, Stephen Boyd, GCS, Ava Gardner, Peter O'Toole, Franco Nero, Zoe Sallis.

Not with My Wife, You Don't! (1966), Reynard-Fernwood Productions, Warner Brothers; Norman Panama, producer and director; screenplay by Norman Panama, Larry Gelbart, and Peter Barnes; story by Norman Panama and Melvin Frank. Cast: Tony Curtis, Virna Lisi, GCS, Carroll O'Connor, Richard Eastham, Eddie Ryder.

The Flim-Flam Man (1967), A Lawrence Turman Production, Twentieth Century-Fox; Lawrence Turman, producer; Irvin Kershner, director; screenplay by William Rose, based on the novel *The Ballad of the Flim-Flam Man* by Guy Owen. Cast: GCS, Sue Lyon, Michael Sarrazin, Harry Morgan, Jack Albertson, Alice Ghostley, Albert Salmi, Slim Pickens.

Petulia (1968), Richard Lester–Raymond Wagner Productions, Warner Brothers-Seven Arts; Raymond James Wagner, producer; Richard Lester, director; screenplay by Lawrence B. Marcus, adaptation by Barbara Turner, based on the novel *Me and the Arch Kook Petulia* by John Haase. Cast: Julie Christie, GCS, Richard Chamberlain, Shirley Knight, Arthur Hill, Joseph Cotten, Pippa Scott, Kathleen Widdoes, Roger Bowen, Richard A. Dysart, Ellen Geer, Lou Gilbert, Austin Pendleton, Rene Auberjonois, The Grateful Dead, Big Brother and the Holding Company with Janis Joplin, members of The Committee, members of the American Conservatory Theatre.

Patton (1970), Twentieth Century-Fox; Frank McCarthy, producer; Franklin J. Schaffner, director; screenplay by Francis Ford Coppola and Edmund H. North, based on *Patton: Ordeal and Triumph* by Ladislas Farago and *A Soldier's Story* by Omar Bradley. Cast: GCS, Karl Malden, Stephen Young, Michael Strong, Frank Latimore, Edward Binns, Lawrence Dobkin, Michael Bates, Tim Considine, John Doucette, Bill Hickman.

They Might Be Giants (1971), A Universal-Newman-Foreman Company Production, Universal; John Foreman, Paul Newman, producers; Anthony Harvey, director; screenplay by James Goldman, based on his stage play. Cast: Joanne Woodward, GCS, Jack Gilford, Lester Rawlins, Al Lewis, Rue McClanahan, Theresa Merritt, Eugene Roche, James Tolkan, Kitty Winn, Sudie Bond, Oliver Clark, F. Murray Abraham, Paul Benedict, M. Emmett Walsh.

The Last Run (1971), MGM; Carter De Haven, producer; Richard Fleischer, director; story and screenplay by Alan Sharp. Cast: GCS, Tony Musante, Trish Van Devere, Colleen Dewhurst.

The Hospital (1971), A Howard Gottfried–Paddy Chayefsky Production in association with Arthur Hiller, United Artists; Howard Gottfried, producer; Arthur Hiller, director; story and screenplay by Paddy Chayefsky. Cast: GCS, Diana

Rigg, Barnard Hughes, Nancy Marchand, Richard A. Dysart, Stephen Elliott, Andrew Duncan, Roberts Blossoms, Robert Walden, Lenny Baker, Frances Sternhagen, Bette Henritze, Stockard Channing.

The New Centurions (1972), Chartoff-Winkler Productions, Columbia; Irwin Winkler and Robert Chartoff, producers; Richard Fleischer, director; screenplay by Sterling Silliphant, based on the novel by Joseph Wambaugh. Cast: GCS, Stacy Keach, Jane Alexander, Rosalind Cash, Scott Wilson, Erik Estrada, Clifton James, Isabel Sanford, James B. Sikking, Ed Lauter, William Atherton, Roger E. Mosley, Dolph Sweet.

Rage (1972), A Getty-Fromkess Picture Production, Warner Brothers; Fred Weintraub, producer; GCS, director; story and screenplay by Philip Friedman and Dan Kleinman. Cast: GCS, Richard Basehart, Martin Sheen, Barnard Hughes, Nicholas Beauvy, Paul Stevens, Bette Henritze.

Oklahoma Crude (1973), Columbia; Stanley Kramer, producer and director; story and screenplay by Marc Norman. Cast: GCS, Faye Dunaway, John Mills, Jack Palance, Harvey Jason, Woodrow Parfrey, William Lucking, Ted Gehring, Cliff Osmond, Rafael Campos.

The Day of the Dolphin (1973), Icarus Productions, Avco Embassy; Robert E. Relyea, producer; Mike Nichols, director; screenplay by Buck Henry, based on the novel *Un Animal Doué de Raison* by Robert Merle. Cast: GCS, Trish Van Devere, Paul Sorvino, Fritz Weaver, Jon Korkes, Edward Herrmann, John Dehner, Severn Darden, Elizabeth Wilson.

Bank Shot (1974), A Landers-Roberts Production, United Artists; Hal Landers and Bobby Roberts, producers; Gower Champion, director; screenplay by Wendell Mayes, based on the novel by Donald E. Westlake. Cast: GCS, Joanna Cassidy, Sorrell Booke, G. Wood, Clifton James, Bob Balaban, Bibi Osterwald, Harvey Evans.

The Savage Is Loose (1974), Campbell Devon Productions, Inc.; GCS, producer and director; screenplay by Max Ehrlich and Frank De Felitta. Cast: GCS, Trish Van Devere, John David Carson, Lee H. Montgomery.

The Hindenburg (1975), A Robert Wise–Filmmakers Group Production, Universal; Robert Wise, producer and director; screenplay by Nelson Gidding. Cast: GCS, Anne Bancroft, William Atherton, Roy Thinnes, Gig Young, Burgess Meredith, Charles Durning, Richard A. Dysart, Robert Clary, Rene Auberjonois, Katherine Helmond.

Islands in the Stream (1977), Paramount; Peter Bart, Max Palevsky, producers; Franklin J. Schaffner, director; screenplay by Denne Bart Petitclerc, based on the novel by Ernest Hemingway. Cast: GCS, David Hemmings, Claire Bloom, Susan Tyrell, Gilbert Roland, Richard Evans, Julius Harris, Hart Bochner, Charles Lampkin, Hildy Brooks, Michael-James Wixted, Brad Savage, Jessica Rains.

Crossed Swords (also released as *The Prince and the Pauper*) (1978), Warner Brothers; Ilya Salkind, executive producer; Pierre Spengler, producer; Richard Fleischer, director; screenplay by George MacDonald Fraser, Berta Dominguez, Pierre Spengler, based on the novel *The Prince and the Pauper* by Mark Twain. Cast: Mark Lester, Oliver Reed, Raquel Welch, Ernest Borgnine, GCS, Rex Harrison, Charlton Heston, David Hemmings, Sybil Danning, Felicity Dean.

Movie Movie (1978), Warner Brothers; Martin Starger, executive producer; Stanley Donen, director-producer; screenplay by Larry Gelbart. Cast: GCS, Trish Van Devere, Eli Wallach, Red Buttons, Barbara Harris, Barry Bostwick, Harry Hamlin, Art Carney, Rebecca York, Ann Reinking, Kathleen Beller, Michael Kidd, Jocelyn Brando, George Burns.

Hardcore (1979), Columbia; John Milius, executive producer; Buzz Feitshans, producer; Paul Schrader, director and screenplay. Cast: GCS, Peter Boyle, Season Hubley, Dick Sargent, Leonard Gaines, David Nichols, Ilah Davis.

The Changeling (1979), Associated Film Distribution; Joel B. Michaels, Garth H. Drabinsky, producers; Peter Medak, director; screenplay by William Gray, story by Russell Hunter. Cast: GCS, Trish Van Devere, Melvyn Douglas, John Colicos, Jean Marsh, Barry Morse, Bernard Behrens, Roberta Maxwell, Chris Gampel, Madeleine Thornton-Sherwood, Helen Burns.

The Formula (1980), MGM/United Artists; Steve Shagan, producer; John G. Avildsen, director; screenplay by Steve Shagan based on his novel. Cast: GCS, Marlon Brando, Marthe Keller, John Gielgud, G. D. Spradlin, Beatrice Straight, Richard Lynch, John Van Dreelan, Calvin Jung.

Taps (1981), Twentieth Century-Fox; Stanley R. Jaffe, Howard B. Jaffe, producers; Harold Becker, director; screenplay by Darryl Ponicsan, Robert Mark Kamen, based on the novel *Father Sky* by Devery Freeman; adaptation by James Lineberger. Cast: Timothy Hutton, GCS, Ronny Cox, Sean Penn, Tom Cruise, Brendan Ward, Evan Handler, John P. Navin, Jr., Billy Van Zandt, Giancarlo Esposito, Earl Hindman, James Handy.

Firestarter (1984), Universal; Frank Capra, Jr., producer; Mark L. Lester, director; screenplay by Stanley Mann; based on the novel by Stephen King. Cast: David Keith, Drew Barrymore, GCS, Martin Sheen, Heather Locklear, Art Carney, Louise Fletcher, Moses Gunn, Freddie Jones.

The Exorcist III (1990), Twentieth Century Fox; Carter DeHaven, producer; William Peter Blatty, director; screenplay by William Peter Blatty, based on his novel *Legion*. Cast: GCS, Ed Flanders, Brad Dourif, Jason Miller, Nicol Williamson, Scott Wilson, Nancy Fish, George DiCenzo, Viveca Lindfors, Barbara Baxley, Zohra Lampert, Don Gordon, Lee Richardson, Harry Carey, Jr., Patrick Ewing, Larry King, C. Everett Koop.

The Rescuers Down Under (1990) (animated), Buena Vista/Walt Disney Pictures; Thomas Schumacher, producer; Hendel Butoy, Mike Gabriel, directors;

animation screenplay by Jim Cox, Karey Kirkpatrick, Byron Simpson, Joe Ranft, suggested by characters created by Margery Sharp. Cast (voice-overs): Bob Newhart, Eva Gabor, GCS, John Candy, Tristan Rogers, Adam Ryen, Douglas Seale, Bernard Fox, Frank Welker, Peter Firth, Billy Barty.

Malice (1993), Columbia; Rachel Pfeffer, Charles Mulvehill, Harold Becker, producers; Harold Becker, director; screenplay by Aaron Sorkin, Scott Frank, story by Aaron Sorkin, Jonas McCord. Cast: Alec Baldwin, Nicole Kidman, Bill Pullman, Bebe Neuwirth, GCS, Anne Bancroft, Peter Gallagher, Josef Sommer, Tobin Bell, Debrah Farentino, Gwyneth Paltrow.

Angus (1995), New Line Cinema; Dawn Steel, Charles Roven, producers; Patrick Read Johnson, director; screenplay by Jill Gordon, based on a short story by Chris Crutcher. Cast: Charlie Talbert, GCS, Kathy Bates, Ariana Richards, Chris Owen, James Van Der Beek, Lawrence Pressman, Rita Moreno.

Gloria (1999), Columbia; Gary Foster, Lee Rich, producers; Sidney Lumet, director; screenplay by Steven Antin. Cast: Sharon Stone, Jean-Luke Figueroa, Jeremy Northam, GCS, Cathy Moriarty, Bonnie Bedelia, Mike Starr.

MAJOR TELEVISION CREDITS

Frontiers of Faith ("Strangers in the Land," "The Massacre" episodes) (1957) (NBC).

A Tale of Two Cities (Dupont Show of the Month) (1958) (CBS): Robert Mulligan, director; Michael Dyne, adaptation. Cast: Denholm Elliott, Eric Portman, James Donald, Gracie Fields, Rosemary Harris, Walter Fitzgerald, GCS, Agnes Moorehead, Fritz Weaver, Alfred Ryder.

The Outcasts of Poker Flat (Kraft Theatre) (1958) (NBC): Paul Stanley, director. Cast: GCS, Larry Hagman, Barbara Lord, Burton Mallory, Ruth White, Janet Ward, Ford Rainey.

We Haven't Seen Her Lately (Kraft Mystery Theatre) (1958) (NBC): Paul Bogart, director; teleplay by Sumner Locke Elliot. Cast: GCS, Angela Thornton, Mary Finney, Louis Edmonds, Myra Carter, Patrick Horgan.

The Empty Chair (Omnibus) (1958) (NBC): Cast: GCS, Peter Ustinov.

Trap for a Stranger (U.S. Steel Hour) (1959) (NBC): Cast: GCS, Dick Van Dyke, Teresa Wright.

People Kill People Sometimes (Sunday Showcase) (1959) (NBC): John Frankenheimer, director; teleplay by S. Lee Pogostin. Cast: Geraldine Page, GCS, Jason Robards, Jr., Zina Bethune, Nan Martin.

Target for Three (Playhouse 90) (1959) (CBS): teleplay by David Davidson. Cast: Ricardo Montalban, GCS, Liliane Montevecchi, Marisa Pavan.

Look up and Live ("The Hipster" episode) (1959) (CBS).

Winterset (Hallmark Hall of Fame) (1959) (NBC): George Schaefer, director-producer; play by Maxwell Anderson, adapted for television by Robert Hartung.

Cast: Piper Laurie, Don Murray, GCS, Charles Bickford, Martin Balsam, George Matthews, Anatol Winogradoff.

Don Juan in Hell (Play of the Week) (1960) (Syndicated): Don Richardson, director; play by George Bernard Shaw. Cast: GCS, Dennis King, Siobhan McKenna, Hurd Hatfield.

The Burning Court (The Dow Hour of Great Mysteries) (1960) (NBC): Paul Nickell, director; William and Audry Ross, writers. Cast: Barbara Bel Geddes, GCS, Robert Lansing, Anne Seymour, Raymond Bramley, Paul Stevens.

Ben Casey ("I Remember a Lemon Tree" episode) (1961) (ABC): Series cast: Vincent Edwards, Sam Jaffe, Bettye Ackerman, Nick Dennis, Jeanne Bates, Harry Landers; guest cast: GCS, Colleen Dewhurst, John Zaremba, Barton Heyman, Alice Rodriguez.

The Power and the Glory (1961) (CBS): Marc Daniels, director; teleplay by Dale Wasserman, based on the novel by Graham Greene. Cast: Laurence Olivier, GCS, Cyril Cusack, Roddy McDowall, Patty Duke, Keenan Wynn, Fritz Weaver, Julie Harris.

The Picture of Dorian Gray (Breck Golden Showcase) (1961) (CBS): Paul Bogart, director; screenplay by Jacqueline Babbin and Audrey Gellen, based on the novel by Oscar Wilde. Cast: John Fraser, GCS, Louis Hayward, Susan Oliver, Robert Walker, Margaret Phillips, Norman Boller.

Naked City ("Strike a Statue" episode) (1962) (ABC): Series cast: Paul Burke, Horace MacMahon, Harry Bellaver, Nancy Malone; guest cast: GCS, Lois Smith.

The Virginian, episode: "The Brazen Bell" (1962) (NBC): Series cast: James Drury, Doug McClure, Lee J. Cobb; guest cast: GCS, Ann Meacham, Royal Dano, John Davis Chandler, Michael Fox.

The Eleventh Hour ("I Don't Belong in a White Painted House" episode) (1962) (NBC): Series cast: Wendell Corey; guest cast: GCS, Colleen Dewhurst, John Anderson, Michael Strong.

East Side/West Side (1963–64) (CBS): Series cast: GCS, Elizabeth Wilson, Cicely Tyson, Linden Chiles, John McMartin. Twenty-six episodes aired.

Esso World Theatre ("In What America?") (1964) (Syndicated): Bert Lawrence, director. Cast: GCS, Colleen Dewhurst, Joanna Miles, Richard Jordan, Gloria Foster, William Daniels.

The Red Skelton Hour (1965) (CBS): GCS, guest star.

A Time For Killing (Bob Hope Chrysler Theatre) (1965); Phil Karlson, director. Cast: GCS, Glenn Ford, George Hamilton, Michael Parks, Inger Stevens, Dale Evans, Tom Troupe, Ernest Anderson.

The Road West ("This Savage Land, Part I and II" episodes) (1966) (NBC): Series cast: Barry Sullivan, Andrew Prine, Brenda Scott, Charles Seel, Kelly Corcoran, Kathryn Hays, Glenn Corbett; guest cast: GCS, John Drew Barrymore, Roy Roberts, Katherine Squire, Charles Gray, Rex Holman.

The Crucible (1967) (CBS): Alex Segal, director; play by Arthur Miller. Cast: GCS, Colleen Dewhurst, Tuesday Weld, Fritz Weaver, Melvyn Douglas, Cathleen Nesbitt, Henry Jones, Catherine Burns, Clarice Blackburn, Thayer David, Will Geer.

Mirror, Mirror off the Wall (On Stage) (1969) (NBC): Cast: GCS, Maureen Stapleton, David Burns.

Johnny Carson's Repertory Company (1969) (NBC): Cast: Johnny Carson, GCS, Maureen Stapleton, Marian Mercer.

Man and His Universe ("The Scientist" and "Cosmopolis: The Big City" episodes) (1969) (ABC): GCS, narrator.

The Tony Awards (1970) (NBC): GCS, presenter.

Kraft Music Hall, "The Friars Roast Don Rickles" (1970) (NBC).

A Man Called Lombardi (1971) (NBC): GCS, narrator.

The Price (Hallmark Hall of Fame) (1971) (NBC): Fielder Cook, director; play by Arthur Miller. Cast: GCS, Colleen Dewhurst, Barry Sullivan, David Burns.

The Andersonville Trial (Hollywood Television Theatre) (1971) (PBS): GCS, director; play by Saul Levitt. Cast: Richard Basehart, Jack Cassidy, William Shatner, Cameron Mitchell, Buddy Ebsen, Martin Sheen, Albert Salmi, Michael Burns, Harry Townes, John Anderson, Whit Bissell, Wright King, Alan Hale, Jr.

Jane Eyre (1971) (NBC): Delbert Mann, director; screenplay by Jack Pullman, based on the novel by Charlotte Brontë. Cast: Susannah York, GCS, Ian Bannen, Jack Hawkins, Rachel Kempson, Jean Marsh, Nyree Dawn Porter.

Bell System Family Theatre ("The Trouble with People") (1972) (NBC): five comedy sketches by Neil Simon. Cast: GCS, Elaine Shore, Jack Weston, Gene Wilder, Valerie Harper, Alan Arkin, Renee Taylor. GCS appeared in "The Man Who Got a Ticket."

From Yellowstone to Tomorrow (Bell System Family Theatre) (1972) (NBC): GCS, narrator.

Power and the Presidency (CBS) (1974): GCS, narrator.

The American Film Institue Salute to James Cagney (CBS) (1974).

Fear on Trial (1975) (CBS): Lamont Johnson, director; screenplay by David Rintels. Cast: GCS, William Devane, Dorothy Tristan, John Houseman, Judd Hirsch, Lois Nettleton, Milt Kogan, Ben Piazza, William Redfield, John Harkins, David Susskind.

Beauty and the Beast (Hallmark Hall of Fame) (1976) (NBC): Fielder Cook, director; screenplay by Sherman Yellen. Cast: GCS, Trish Van Devere, Virginia McKenna, Bernard Lee, Patricia Quinn, Michael Harbour, William Relton.

The 30th Annual Tony Awards (1976): GCS cohosts with Eddie Albert, Richard Burton, Jane Fonda, Diana Rigg, and Trish Van Devere.

Happy Birthday, Bob (1978) (NBC): comedy special honoring Bob Hope on his 80th birthday. Cast: Bob Hope, Ronald Reagan, Lucille Ball, George Burns, GCS, Flip Wilson.

Arthur Miller on Home Ground (CBC): documentary on Arthur Miller for Canadian Broadcasting Company, GCS is interviewed.

Bob Hope's All-Star Birthday Party from West Point (NBC) (1981).

Mister Lincoln (Hallmark Hall of Fame) (1981) (PBS): GCS introduces Roy Dotrice in a solo performance.

Oliver Twist (1982) (CBS): Clive Donner, director; screenplay by James Goldman, based on the novel by Charles Dickens. Cast: GCS, Richard Charles, Tim Curry, Michael Hordern, Timothy West, Eileen Atkins, Cherie Lunghi, Martin Tempest, Lysette Anthony.

China Rose (1983) (CBS): Robert Day, director; screenplay by David Epstein. Cast: GCS, Ali McGraw, Michael Biehn, Denis Lil, David Snell, James Hong,

A Christmas Carol (1984) (CBS): Clive Donner, director; screenplay by Roger O. Hirson, based on the novel by Charles Dickens. Cast: GCS, Nigel Davenport, Frank Finlay, Edward Woodward, Lucy Gutteridge, Angela Pleasance, Roger Rees, David Warner, Susannah York, Anthony Walters, Joanne Whalley.

Mussolini—The Untold Story (1985) (NBC): William A. Graham, director; screenplay by Stirling Silliphant. Cast: GCS, Mary Elizabeth Mastrantonio, Virginia Madsen, Raul Julia, Gabriel Byrne, Lee Grant.

Choices (1986) (ABC): David Lowell Rich, director; screenplay by Judith Parker. Cast: GCS, Jacqueline Bisset, Melissa Gilbert.

The Last Days of Patton (1986) (CBS): Delbert Mann, director; screenplay by William Luce, based on the book by Ladislas Farago. Cast: GCS, Eva Marie Saint, Richard Dysart, Murray Hamilton, Ed Lauter, Kathryn Leigh Scott.

Murders in the Rue Morgue (1986) (CBS): Jeannot Swarc, director; screenplay by David Epstein, based on the short story by Edgar Allan Poe. Cast: GCS, Rebecca De Mornay, Ian McShane, Neil Dickson, Val Kilmer.

Pals (1987) (CBS): Lou Antonio, director; screenplay by Michael Norell. Cast: Don Ameche, GCS, Sylvia Sydney, Susan Rinell.

Mr. President (1987–88) (Fox): Series cast: GCS, Carlin Glynn, Conrad Bain, Madeline Kahn, Maddie Corman, Andre Gower, Susan Wheeler Duff, Daniel McDonald, Allen Williams, Earl Boen. Twenty-six episodes aired.

The Ryan White Story (1989) (ABC): John Herzfeld, director; screenplay by Phil Penngroth, John Herzfeld. Cast: Judith Light, Lukas Haas, Peter Scolari, GCS, Michael Bowen, George Dzundza, Valerie Landsburg.

Descending Angel (1990) (HBO): Jeremy Paul Kagan, director; screenplay by Robert Siegel, Grace Woodard, Alan Sharp. Cast: GCS, Diane Lane, Eric Roberts, Jan Rubes, Mark Margolis, Vyto Ruginis, Richard Jenkins.

Cartoon All-Stars to the Rescue (1990) (ABC): animated special. Cast (voice-overs): GCS, Jason Marsden, Lindsay Parker, Joey Dedio, Townsend Coleman.

Finding the Way Home (1991) (ABC): Rod Holcomb, director; screenplay by
  Scott Swanton, based on the book *Mittleman's Hardware* by George Raphael
  Small. Cast: GCS, Hector Elizondo, Julie Carmen, Beverly Garland.

Brute Force (1991) (A&E): GCS, narrator.

Deadly Currents (also released as *Curacao*) (1993) (Showtime): Carl Shultz, director.
  Cast: GCS, William Petersen, Julie Carmen, Philip Anglim, Maria Ellengsen,
  Alexei Sayle, Trish Van Devere.

Traps (1994) (CBS): Series cast: GCS, Dan Cortese, Bill Nunn, Piper Laurie, Lindsay Crouse. Five episodes aired.

The Whipping Boy (aka *Prince Brat and the Whipping Boy*) (The Disney Channel)
  (1994): Syd Macartney, director; screenplay by Max Brindle, based on the book
  by Sid Fleischman. Cast: Truan Munro, Nic Knight, Karen Salt, GCS, Andrew
  Bicknell, Kevin Conway, Vincent Schiavelli, Mathilda May, Jean Anderson.

In the Heat of the Night: A Matter of Justice (1994) (NBC): Reza Badiyi, director. Cast:
  GCS, Carroll O'Connor, Carl Weathers, Alan Autry, Hugh O'Connor.

Tyson (1995) (HBO): Uli Edel, director; screenplay by Robert Johnson, based on
  the book *Fire and Fear* by José Torres. Cast: Michael Jai White, GCS, Paul
  Winfield, James B. Sikking, Malcolm-Jamal Warner, Tony Lo Bianco, Clark
  Gregg, Holt McCallany, Kristen Wilson.

New York News ("Cost of Living" and "Yankee Glory" episodes) (1995) (CBS):
  Series cast: Mary Tyler Moore, Gregory Harrison, Madeline Kahn, Joe Morton, Kevin Chamberlin, Anthony DeSando, Melina Kanakaredes, Harold Per-
  rineau, Jr., Kelli Williams; guest cast: GCS. (Episodes never aired.)

Titanic (1996) (CBS): Robert Lieberman, director. Cast: GCS, Peter Gallagher,
  Tim Curry, Roger Rees, Catherine Zeta-Jones, Marilu Henner, Eva Marie
  Saint, Harley Jane Kozak, Kevin McNulty, Scott Hylands.

Twelve Angry Men (1997) (Showtime): William Friedkin, director; screenplay by
  Reginald Rose based on his original screenplay and teleplay. Cast: Jack Lem-
  mon, GCS, Hume Cronyn, Ossie Davis, Courtney B. Vance, Armin Mueller-
  Stahl, Dorian Harewood, Tony Danza, Mykelti Williamson, Edward James
  Olmos, William Petersen, James Gandolfini, Mary McDonnell.

Country Justice (1997): Graeme Campbell, director. Cast: GCS, Ally Sheedy, Rachel Leigh Cook, Trent McDevitt, Donald Diamont, Stan Kelly.

"Germs" spot for HBO (1998): GCS stars as a commander of an army of germs
  in a parody of *Patton*.

Rocky Marciano (1999) (Showtime): Charles Winkler, director. Cast: Jon Favreau,
  Penelope Ann Miller, Judd Hirsch, Tony Lo Bianco, Duane Davis, Rino Ro-
  mano, GCS, Rhoda Gemignani.

Inherit the Wind (1999) (Showtime): Daniel Petrie, director; based on the play by
  Jerome Lawrence and Robert E. Lee. Cast: Jack Lemmon, GCS, Piper Laurie,
  Beau Bridges, Tom Everett Scott, John Cullum, Kathryn Morris, Lane Smith.

APPENDIX B:
AWARDS AND NOMINATIONS

1958

Richard III
Theatre World Award for Promising Newcomer
Clarence Derwent Award for Promising Newcomer

Children of Darkness
Vernon Rice Award for Outstanding Performance
Obie Award for Best Actor for *Richard III*, *As You Like It*, and *Children of Darkness*

1959

Anatomy of a Murder
Academy Award nomination for Best Supporting Actor

Comes a Day
Tony Award nomination for Best Featured Actor in a Play

1961

The Hustler
Academy Award nomination for Best Supporting Actor (nomination refused)
Golden Globe Award for New Star of the Year

1962

Ben Casey episode, "I Remember a Lemon Tree"
Emmy Award nomination for Outstanding Supporting Actor

1963

Desire Under the Elms
Obie Award for Best Actor

1964

East Side/West Side
Emmy Award nomination for Outstanding Actor (Series)

1968

The Crucible
Emmy Award nomination for Outstanding Actor (Single Performance)

1970

Patton
Academy Award for Best Actor (nomination and award refused)
British Academy (BAFTA) Award for Best Actor
Golden Globe Award for Best Actor (Drama)
National Board of Review Award for Best Actor
National Society of Film Critics Award for Best Actor
New York Film Critics Circle Award for Best Actor

1971

The Hospital
Academy Award nomination for Best Actor
Golden Globe Award nomination for Best Actor (Drama)

The Price (Hallmark Hall of Fame)
Emmy Award for Outstanding Actor (Single Performance)

1972

Jane Eyre
Emmy Award nomination for Outstanding Actor (Single Performance)

1974

Uncle Vanya
Tony Award nomination for Outstanding Actor in a Play

1977

Beauty and the Beast
Emmy Award nomination for Outstanding Actor (Single Performance)

1978

Movie Movie
Golden Globe nomination for Best Actor (Musical or Comedy)

1980

The Changeling
Canadian Genie Award for Best Foreign Actor

1996

Inherit the Wind
Tony Award nomination for Best Actor in a Play
Outer Critics Circle Award for Best Actor in a Play
Drama Desk Award for Lifetime Achievement in the Theatre

1997

Twelve Angry Men
Golden Globe Award for Best Supporting Actor (TV Series, Mini-Series or
    TV-Movie)
Cable Ace Award for Best Supporting Actor
SAG Award nomination for Best Actor in a TV-Movie

1998

Twelve Angry Men
Emmy Award for Outstanding Supporting Actor (Mini-Series or TV-Movie)

NOTES

Abbreviations used: CD = Colleen Dewhurst; DS = David Sheward; GCS = George Campbell Scott; GDS = George Dewey Scott; TVD = Trish Van Devere

INTRODUCTION

x "Safe actors hold back . . ." GCS quoted in "A Risk Actor Cuts Loose: Blooming Big Year for George C. Scott," *Life,* March 8, 1968.

xi "He is always vivid . . ." Harold Clurman, *The Collected Works of Harold Clurman,* edited by Marjorie Loggia and Glenn Young. New York: Applause Theatre Books, 1994, page 849.

xi "He was a deeply felt person . . ." DS interview with Dana Ivey.

1. COAL MINER'S SON

1 "I was a very sickly child . . ." GCS quoted by Louise Sweeney, "George C. Scott and the Vanishing Ego," *Christian Science Monitor,* Nov. 12, 1980.

1 "I ran to the creek . . ." GDS quoted by Nancy Clark Brown, *Appalachian Quarterly*, December 1999.

1 "One day . . ." Ibid.

3 "I worked my ass off . . ." GDS quoted by Mary Cronin, "George C. Scott: Tempering a Terrible Fire," *Time,* March 22, 1971.

4 "But it put me off performing . . ." GCS quoted by Christina Kirk, "The Real George C. Scott Stands Up," *Sunday New York News,* March 8, 1970.

4 "I played Disaster . . ." GCS quoted by Louise Sweeney, "George C. Scott and the Vanishing Ego," *Christian Science Monitor,* Nov. 12, 1980.

5 "I was brought up on . . ." GCS quoted by Michael Billington, "Back to Bogie and the Forties," *Times of London Saturday Review*, March 27, 1971.

5 "The most fascinating film actress . . ." GCS quoted by Charles Champlin, "Will It Soon Be George C. Scott, Director?" *Los Angeles Times*, Dec. 2, 1973.

6 "With a couple of exceptions . . ." GCS quoted by Mary Cronin, "George C. Scott: Tempering a Terrible Fire," *Time,* March 22, 1971.

6 "Aunt Sally and my sister . . ." GCS quoted by Barbara Gelb, "Great Scott!" *New York Times Magazine*, Jan. 23, 1977.

6 "As a small child . . ." email from Victoria Lewis to DS.

7 "He never cried or complained . . ." Helen Scott Hamilton, quoted by Mary Cronin, "George C. Scott: Tempering a Terrible Fire," *Time,* March 22, 1971.

7 "I was in junior high school . . ." GCS quoted by Peter J. Oppenheimer, "George C. Scott: I Hope My Children Never Become Actors," *Family Weekly*, Dec. 23, 1973.

7 "In my teens, I wrote . . ." GCS quoted by Michael Billington, "Back to Bogie and the Forties," *Times of London Saturday Review*, March 27, 1971.

8 "My dad was in milk . . ." GCS quoted by John Weisman, "Penthouse Interview: George C. Scott," *Penthouse*, May 1973.

8 "Because of his efforts . . ." email from Kip Hamilton to DS.

8 ". . . a character . . ." GCS quoted by John Weisman, "Penthouse Interview: George C. Scott," *Penthouse*, May 1973.

2. GROWING UP IN A HURRY

10 "Hollywood characters . . ." Tennessee Williams, *The Glass Menagerie* in *Six Modern American Plays*. New York: The Modern Library, page 315.

10 "I was very gung-ho . . ." GCS quoted by Mary Cronin, "George C. Scott: Tempering a Terrible Fire," *Time,* March 22, 1971.

11 "I was there four years . . ." GCS quoted by Jack Balch, "George C. Scott," *Theatre Arts*, June 1960.

12 ". . . broke the bridge of Scott's nose . . ." W. A. Harbinson, *George C. Scott: The Man, the Actor, and the Legend*. New York: Pinnacle Books, 1977, page 24.

13 ". . . meet outside . . ." Bob Morrissey, "My Memories of Marine Sergeant George C. Scott," Sept. 24, 1999, www.angelfire.com/ca4/gunnyg/gcscott. html.

14 "So I was bored . . ." GCS quoted by W. H. Manville, "Mister George C. Scott," *Cosmopolitan*, October 1968.

15 "During this audition . . ." Donovan Rhynsburger interview for *University Close-up* radio program, 1970, University Archives, University of Missouri-Columbia, Box 20, FF23.

15 "I'll never forget that day . . ." GCS quoted by Cleveland Amory, "The Loves and Hates of George C. Scott," *Parade*, Oct. 27, 1985.

16 "I can only say . . ." GCS quoted by Lewis Funke, *Actors Talk About Theatre:*

12 *Interviews with Lewis Funke*. Chicago, Westport: The Dramatic Publishing Company, 1977, page 237.

16 "He was something of a figure . . ." DS interview with Joe Koenan.

16 "The lawyer finished . . ." "*Winslow Boy* Marked Debut of MU Find," undated, unspecified clipping, University Archives, University of Missouri-Columbia, Box 20, FF23.

16 "It took up . . ." GCS quoted by Rich Binsacca, "George C. Scott: Portrait of the Artist as a Young Man," *Columbia Missourian*, March 29, 1987.

17 ". . . adroit characterization . . ." Robert Skeetz, "*Traitor* Proves Timely Spy Drama," undated, unspecified clipping, University Archives, University of Missouri-Columbia, Box 20, FF23.

17 "I remember that he was rather reserved . . ." Allene Preston Jones quoted by Ashley Williams, "Prodigious Career Nurtured Locally," *Columbia Daily Tribune*, Sept. 23, 1999.

17 ". . . any seeds of genius . . ." Donovan Rhynsburger interview for *University Close-up* radio program, 1970, University Archives, University of Missouri-Columbia, Box 20, FF23.

18 "George C. Scott's portrayal . . ." "*Shadow and Substance* Given Warm Reception by Audience," undated, unspecified clipping, University Archives, University of Missouri-Columbia, Box 20, FF23.

18 ". . . a fancy girls' school . . ." DS interview with Joe Koenan.

18 "Writing was very much an interest . . ." William West quoted in W. A. Harbinson, *George C. Scott: The Man, the Actor, and the Legend*. New York: Pinnacle Books, 1977, page 25.

20 "I selected this story . . ." Evaluation: "Carnival Near the Black," University Archives, University of Missouri-Columbia, University of Missouri-Columbia, Box 20, FF23.

21 "Characterizations are developed . . ." Evaluation: "Blessed Fruit," University Archives, University of Missouri-Columbia, collection cited above.

22 "He loved how she spoke . . ." DS interview with Victoria Lewis.

23 "He had a temperament . . ." DS interview with Tammy Grimes.

24 "We've been married only . . ." "Talents Include Housekeeping: Erratic Schedule Is the Lot for Actor's Wife," *Columbia Missourian*, Oct. 31, 1951.

3. THE DARK AGES

25 "He just had something about him . . ." DS interview with Karen Truesdell Riehl.

27 "The motion picture business . . ." "Student by Day, Actor by Night, George Scott Leads Busy Life," *Columbia Missourian*, Nov. 11, 1952.

28 "Step back, Trues . . ." DS interview with Karen Truesdell Riehl.

28 "We looked at each other . . ." Ibid.

30 "When we did stock together . . ." Ibid.

30 "His face changed . . ." Ibid.

33 "It was during that time . . ." email from Victoria Lewis to DS.

34 "We were known . . ." Bill Merrill quoted in W. A. Harbinson, *George C. Scott: The Man, the Actor, and the Legend*. New York: Pinnacle Books, 1977, page 48.

34 ". . . a very strong actor . . ." Ibid.

35 "We were well aware . . ." DS interview with Sonny Elliott.

35 "He was a most interesting man . . ." Ibid.

35 "I had to bail him out . . ." Bill Merrill quoted in W. A. Harbinson, *George C. Scott: The Man, the Actor, and the Legend*. New York: Pinnacle Books, 1977, page 51.

36 "I would start out . . ." GCS quoted in "Scott Had Long Hike to Success But He Made It," *Great Bend Daily Tribune* (no author listed), Dec. 4, 1966.

36 "I got a job . . ." GCS quoted by Rex Reed, *People Are Crazy Here*. New York: Dell Publishing, Inc., 1974, page 164.

4. NEW YORK AGAIN

40 "I'd come out . . ." GCS quoted by Julius Novick, "George C. Scott: His Last Bow?" *Village Voice*, Aug. 25, 1975.

40 "To this day . . ." Rex Reed, *People Are Crazy Here*. New York: Dell Publishing, Inc. 1974, pages 164–65.

40 "George had a lot of fights . . ." Jason Robards quoted by Percy Peterson, "The Terrible Tempered George C. Scott," *Motion Picture*, May 1972.

40 "I was more well known . . ." DS interview with Sonny Elliott.

41 "He could be intimidating . . ." Ibid.

41 "He knocks on the door . . ." Ibid.

42 "In 1952 . . ." DS interview with Stuart Vaughan.

43 "I resorted to my usual . . ." GCS quoted by Bill Davidson, "Great Scott," *Saturday Evening Post*, Nov. 16, 1963.

43 "My friend Janice . . ." DS interview with Stuart Vaughan.

45 "I could tell . . ." DS interview with Myra Carter.

45 "He had all the qualities . . ." DS interview with Stuart Vaughan.

46 "We had gotten to dress rehearsals . . ." Ibid.

47 "There is an especially . . ." Richard Watts, "N.Y. Shakespeare Festival Presents *As You Like It*," *New York Post*, Jan. 21, 1958.

47 ". . . caustic, ruthlessly . . ." Walter Kerr, "Theater: Saluting Off-Broadway-ites," *New York Herald-Tribune*, April 18, 1958.

47 "If you happen . . ." "The Show Is Over, but the Actor Is Still Fuming: George C. Scott Gets Some of His Frustrations Off His Chest," *TV Guide*, July 18, 1964.

49 "George explained that he'd beaten up a cop . . ." Larry Hagman, *Hello Darlin': Tall (and Absolutely True) Tales About My Life*. New York: Simon & Schuster, 2001, page 94.

49 "The more successful . . ." GCS quoted by Bill Davidson, "Great Scott," *Saturday Evening Post*, Nov. 16, 1963.

5. A "BUS ACCIDENT" WITH COLLEEN DEWHURST

51 ". . . a cat . . ." Frank Ashton, "*Antony and Cleopatra* Opens Run at Hecksher," *New York World-Telegram,* Jan. 14, 1959.

51 ". . . a marshmallow . . ." Maureen Stapleton, with Jane Scovell, *A Hell of a Life: An Autobiography*. New York: Simon & Schuster, 1995, page 134.

52 "Jack Barrymore . . ." GCS quoted by Mary Cronin, "George C. Scott: Tempering a Terrible Fire," *Time,* March 22, 1971.

52 "When I saw him . . ." CD quoted in *The Off-Broadway Experience*, edited by Howard Greenberg. Englewood Cliffs, NJ: Prentice-Hall, Inc., 1971, page 130.

53 "We had a dressing room . . ." Theodore Mann quoted in "In Memoriam: George C. Scott," *In Theater*, Oct. 11, 1999.

53 "J. D. and I . . ." CD quoted in *The Off-Broadway Experience*, edited by Howard Greenberg. Englewood Cliffs, NJ: Prentice-Hall, Inc., 1971, page 131.

53 "I do predict . . ." Richard Watts, Jr., *Children of Darkness* review, *New York Daily News*, March 3, 1958.

54 "I think . . ." CD, written with and completed by Tom Viola, *Colleen Dewhurst: Her Autobiography*. New York: A Lisa Drew Book/Scribner, 1997, page 128.

54 "She had serious regard of him . . ." DS interview with Myra Carter.

55 "Since both of us . . ." CD quoted in *The Off-Broadway Experience,* edited by Howard Greenberg. Englewood Cliffs, NJ: Prentice-Hall, Inc., 1971, page 131.

55 "She was a very charming girl . . ." DS interview with John Wallowitch.

56 "Another pic bow . . ." *The Hanging Tree* review, *Variety*, Jan. 28, 1959.

57 "In film . . ." GCS quoted by Marion Simon, "The Wild Man of Broadway: Fear of Failure Is What Makes George Run," *National Observer*, May 27, 1968.

57 "It's essential . . ." Ibid.

58 "They shook hands . . ." Karen Truesdell Riehl, *Love and Madness: My Private Years with George C. Scott*. Alpine, California: Sands Publishing, LLC, 2003, page 159.

59 "I've never seen . . ." DS interview with David Finkle.

59 "After five minutes . . ." DS interview with Fritz Weaver.

59 "*Comes a Day* . . ." John McClain, "It's a Pleasure to Hiss a Villain," *New York Journal-American*, Nov. 7, 1958.

59 "Rubbing his eyes . . ." Walter Kerr, "First Night Report: *Comes a Day*," *New York Herald-Tribune*, Nov. 7, 1958.

60 "He was terrifying . . ." Marion Simon, "The Wild Man of Broadway: Fear of Failure Is What Makes George Run," *National Observer*, May 27, 1968.

60 "From then on, I made it a rule . . ." Larry Hagman, *Hello Darlin': Tall (and Absolutely True) Tales About My Life*. New York: Simon & Schuster, 2001, page 96.

60 "I had a few pops of booze . . ." GCS quoted by Stu Schreiberg, "He Patented Patton, but Says He's a Pussycat," *USA Weekend*, Sept. 5–7, 1986.

61 "Though drunk . . ." Larry Hagman, *Hello Darlin': Tall (and Absolutely True) Tales About My Life*. New York: Simon & Schuster, 2001, page 95.

61 "But the nightmare . . ." GCS quoted by Bill Davidson, "Great Scott," *Saturday Evening Post*, Nov. 16, 1963.

62 "I got scared . . ." Ibid.

62 "They say Sarah Bernhardt . . ." GCS quoted in "Bricks Were Stepping Stones to Stardom for George Scott," *New York World-Telegram and Sun*, Sept. 19, 1959.

63 "[W]hen Mr. Scott . . ." Richard Watts, Jr., "A Dynamic *Antony and Cleopatra*," *New York Post*, Jan. 14, 1959.

63 "Seventeen martinis . . ." DS interview with Bette Henritze.

64 "This was the part . . ." CD, written with and completed by Tom Viola, *Colleen Dewhurst: Her Autobiography*. New York: A Lisa Drew Book/Scribner, 1997, page 147.

66 "The region is so remote . . ." James Stewart quoted in Gary Fishgall, *Pieces of Time: The Life of James Stewart*. New York: A Lisa Drew Book/Scribner, 1997, page 273.

66 "He lent me money . . ." Rex Reed, *People Are Crazy Here*. New York: Dell Publishing, Inc. 1974, page 167.

67 "As flashbulbs exploded . . ." CD, written with and completed by Tom Viola, *Colleen Dewhurst: Her Autobiography*. New York: A Lisa Drew Book/Scribner, 1997, page 150.

67 ". . . top-notch courtroom meller . . ." *Anatomy of a Murder* review, *Variety*, July 1, 1959.

68 "George C. Scott, the psychiatrist . . ." *People Kill People Sometimes* review, *Daily Variety*, Sept. 21, 1959.

68 "One night during rehearsals . . ." DS interview with Milton Wilson.

68 "There was an aura . . ." *Target for Three* review, *Daily Variety*, Oct. 2, 1959.

69 "He used to show up every morning . . ." DS interview with Piper Laurie.

70 "Here is what Mr. Scott does . . ." Walter Kerr, *The Andersonville Trial* review, *New York Herald-Tribune*, Jan. 10, 1960.

71 "The ironic thing . . ." GCS quoted in "First Nights: Captain Wirz On-Stage," *Newsweek*, Jan. 11, 1960.

71 "The character [Chipman] . . ." GCS quoted by Leonard Probst, *Off Camera: Leveling About Themselves*. New York: Stein and Day, 1975, page 90.

71 "Herbert Berghof . . ." DS interview with Fritz Weaver.

72 "You suddenly . . ." GCS quoted by Sidney Fields, "Only Human: Pleasure of Success After Ten Years of Pain," *New York Mirror*, Jan. 4, 1960.

6. A THIRD MARRIAGE, *THE HUSTLER*, AND THE THEATRE OF MICHIGAN

73 "How could I refuse . . ." Theodore Mann, *Journeys in the Night: Creating a New American Theatre with Circle in the Square*. New York: Applause Theatre & Cinema Books, 2007, page 157.

74 ". . . a bun in the oven," DS interview with Myra Carter.

74 "I was disappointed . . ." GCS quoted by Ben Gross, "Great Scott!—A Star Who Pulls No Punches," *Sunday New York News*, Sept. 29, 1963.

76 "[I]n spite of . . ." John McClain, "Major Novel, Minor Play," *New York Journal-American*, Oct. 12, 1960.

76 ". . . less comfortable than usual . . ." Richard Watts, Jr., "Two on the Aisle: Revolt of the Warsaw Ghetto," *New York Post*, Oct. 12, 1960.

76 "It sprang from . . ." DS interview with Marian Seldes.

77 "Having the chance . . ." Marian Seldes, *The Bright Lights: A Theatre Life*. Boston: Houghton Mifflin Company, 1978, page 227.

77 "There is a moment . . ." DS interview with Marian Seldes.

77 "We all felt lucky . . ." Ibid.

78 "What would you think . . ." GCS quoted by Marian Seldes, *The Bright Lights: A Theatre Life*, Boston: Houghton Mifflin Company, 1978, page 228.

78 "Colleen came backstage . . ." DS interview with Marian Seldes.

80 "I had never been that close . . ." Piper Laurie quoted by Michael Sragow, "Piper Laurie Remembers the Smoldering Genius of George C. Scott," Salon.com, Sept. 30, 1999.

82 "Years later . . ." DS interview with Piper Laurie.

83 "The real power is packed . . ." Bosley Crowther, *The Hustler* review, *New York Times*, Sept. 27, 1961.

87 "Imagine a prosperous Broadway . . ." GCS quoted in "Heavy Star," *Time*, Feb. 23, 1962.

87 "There we were . . ." CD quoted in *The Off-Broadway Experience*, edited by Howard Greenberg. Englewood Cliffs, NJ: Prentice-Hall, Inc., 1971, page 137.

88 "His hysteria overwhelmed us . . ." Ibid.

89 "They wanted me . . ." GCS quoted in "Heavy Star," *Time*, Feb. 23, 1962.

90 "We've had a difference of interpretation . . ." Theodore Mann quoted by Ralph Blumenfeld, "The New Leading Man Has 5 Days, Then B'way," *New York Post*, Feb. 25, 1962.

91   "Bully or braggart . . ." Walter Kerr, "First Night Report: *General Seegar*," *New York Herald-Tribune*, March 1, 1962.

91   "You've got to learn one thing . . ." Harold Clurman quoted in *The Off-Broadway Experience*, edited by Howard Greenberg. Englewood Cliffs, NJ: Prentice-Hall, Inc., 1971, page 137.

91   "We spent all the money . . ." GCS quoted by Frances Herridge, "Across the Footlights: George C. Scott Reverts to Acting," *New York Post,* June 25, 1962.

91   "When he was casting . . ." CD quoted by Ira Mothner, "George C. Scott: Don Quixote on Broadway," *Look*, Nov. 6, 1962.

92   "I take the position . . ." GCS quoted by Stan Koven, "George C. Scott vs. the Oscars," *New York Post*, March 6, 1962.

92   "You were nominated . . ." Wendell Corey letter, quoted in *New York Times*, March 6, 1962.

94   ". . . magisterial, biblical rage . . ." Joseph Papp quoted by Helen Epstein, *Joe Papp: An American Life*. Boston: Little, Brown, and Company, 1994, page 175.

94   "Never turn the other cheek . . ." Ibid.

94   "It's like playing . . ." GCS quoted in W. A. Harbinson, *George C. Scott: The Man, the Actor, and the Legend*. New York: Pinnacle Books, 1977, page 106.

95   "At the loss of the daughter . . ." GCS quoted by Lewis Funke, *Actors Talk About Theatre: 12 Interviews with Lewis Funke*. Chicago, Westport: The Dramatic Publishing Company, 1977, page 250.

95   ". . . the best American Shakespeare . . ." DS interview with Fritz Weaver.

96   "I thought he did . . ." DS interview with Bruce Minnix.

97   ". . . magnificent in the leading role . . ." Kirk Douglas, *The Ragman's Son*. New York: Pocket Books, Simon & Schuster, 1988, 1989, page 317.

97   ". . . certainly one of the most talented . . ." Ibid.

97   ". . . a remarkable creature . . ." GCS quoted by Paul Riordan, "The Films of George C. Scott," Images website, 1997, www.imagesjournal.com/issue04/features/georgecscott2.htm.

97   ". . . only a tribute . . ." "Mummery Flummery," *Time*, June 14, 1963.

98   "Without him . . ." J. G., "Scott Tops in *Adrian's List*," *New York Mirror*, May 30, 1963.

98   ". . . sharply etched performance . . ." Raymond Durgnat, *The List of Adrian Messenger* review, *Films and Filming*, July 1963.

99   "When he takes a role . . ." José Quintero, *If You Don't Dance, They Beat You*. Boston: Little, Brown and Company, 1974, page 185.

100   "Mr. Scott brings . . ." Howard Taubman, "New *Desire*," *New York Times*, Jan. 11, 1963.

100   "[He] commits . . ." Michael Smith, "Theatre: *Desire Under the Elms*," *Village Voice*, Jan. 10, 1963.

7. *DR. STRANGELOVE* AND *EAST SIDE/WEST SIDE*

101 "Kubrick first offered him . . ." DS interview with Clifton James.

103 "This gave me a certain edge . . ." Stanley Kubrick quoted in Vincent LoBrutto, *Stanley Kubrick: A Biography*. New York: Donald I. Fine Books, 1997, page 238.

104 "He's a perfectionist . . ." GCS quoted by Lawrence Grobel, "Playboy Interview: George C. Scott," *Playboy*, December, 1980.

104 "The irresistible force . . ." James Earl Jones, "A Bombardier's Reflection on *Strangelove*," *Wall Street Journal*, Nov. 16, 2004.

105 "I found myself . . ." Roger Ebert, "Great Movies: *Dr. Strangelove*," *Chicago Sun-Times*, July 11, 1996.

105 "We threw a thousand pies . . ." GCS quoted by Harry Haun, "A Kinder, Gentler George C.," *New York Daily News*, Aug. 26, 1991.

107 "Three years from now . . ." GCS quoted by Richard Schickel, "I've Been as Obnoxious as Humanly Possible," *TV Guide,* Nov. 30, 1963.

107 "George was responsible . . ." DS interview with Elizabeth Wilson.

108 "I got $750 a week . . ." Ibid.

109 "CBS would not allow . . ." Ibid.

110 "We've got to come to grips . . ." GCS quoted by Richard Schickel, "I've Been as Obnoxious as Humanly Possible," *TV Guide,* Nov. 30, 1963.

110 ". . . undoubtedly the boldest . . ." Cleveland Amory, "Review: *East Side/West Side*," *TV Guide*, Dec. 14, 1963.

111 "For the first time . . ." *East Side/West Side* review, *Variety*, Nov. 6, 1963.

111 "[W]e were eager . . ." GCS quoted in "The Show Is Over, but the Actor Is Still Fuming: George C. Scott Gets Some of His Frustrations Off His Chest," *TV Guide*, July 18, 1964.

112 ". . . [g]et that fucking show . . ." Robert Metz, *CBS: Reflections in a Bloodshot Eye*. Chicago: Playboy Press, 1975, page 228.

112 "Bring him in . . ." Ibid.

112 "The show is staying . . ." Ibid., page 229.

113 "I'm glad it's over . . ." GCS quoted by Peter J. Oppenheimer, "The Explosive Mr. Scott," May 15, 1966.

113 "A gloomy atmosphere . . ." David Susskind quoted by Mary Ann Watson, www.museum.tv/archives/etv/E/htmlE/eastsidewest/eastsidewest.htm.

113 "It isn't acting . . ." *Variety* review of *Open End*, March 4, 1964.

114 "If they say we're too real . . ." GCS quoted by Richard Schickel, "I've Been as Obnoxious as Humanly Possible," *TV Guide,* Nov. 30, 1963.

114 "It [*East Side*] was a big break . . ." GCS quoted by John Weisman, "Penthouse Interview: George C. Scott," *Penthouse*, May 1973.

114 "I had my speech . . ." GCS quoted by Bob Thomas, "Scott Views Oscars," Associated Press, March 5, 1965.

115 "It's the most powerful . . ." GCS quoted by Rex Reed, *People Are Crazy Here*. New York: Dell Publishing, Inc., 1974, page 168.

115 "I had never wanted . . ." CD quoted by Margaret McManus, "Actors Scott and Dewhurst—Steel and Fire," *St. Louis Post-Dispatch*, Jan. 31, 1971.

115 "George bought . . ." DS interview with Elizabeth Wilson.

116 "He liked to walk around . . ." DS interview with Scott Fowler.

116 "I was fourteen . . ." Ibid.

116 "We were playing . . ." DS interview with Bill Fowler.

117 "Colleen collected strays . . ." Maureen Stapleton, with Jane Scovell, *A Hell of a Life: An Autobiography*. New York: Simon & Schuster, 1995, page 135.

117 "I have never known . . ." José Quintero, *If You Don't Dance, They Beat You*. Boston: Little, Brown and Company, 1974, page 200.

117 "Well, I left a pair of wet jeans . . ." CD quoted by Rex Reed, *Conversations in the Raw: Dialogues, Monologues, and Selected Short Subjects*. New York and Cleveland: The World Publishing Company, 1969, page 123.

118 "[E]ventually . . ." Alex Scott quoted in *Colleen Dewhurst: Her Autobiography*. New York: A Lisa Drew Book/Scribner, 1997, page 147.

118 "When he called . . ." DS interview with Victoria Lewis.

120 ". . . travelogue with foreground figures . . ." Kenneth Tynan, *Tynan Right and Left*, New York: Atheneum, 1967, page 216.

120 "[A]nyone willing . . ." *Yellow Rolls-Royce* review, *London Sunday Telegraph*, Jan. 3, 1965.

8. ENTER AVA

123 "I liked him immediately . . ." *Ava: My Story*. New York: Bantam Books, 1990, page 254.

124 "Scott was crazy about her . . ." Fred Sidewater quoted by Charles Higham, *Ava: A Life Story*. New York: Delacorte Press, 1974, page 227.

124 "Scott was threatening . . ." George Jacobs and William Stadiem, *Mr. S: My Life with Frank Sinatra*. New York: HarperCollins, 2003, page 218.

125 "The problem, honey . . ." *Ava: My Story*. New York: Bantam Books, 1990, page 254.

125 "George C. Scott was magnificent . . ." John Huston, *An Open Book*, New York: Alfred A. Knopf, 1980, page 328.

125 "While we were filming . . ." Ibid.

126 "If there's one guy I can't tolerate . . ." Frank Sinatra quoted in *Photoplay*, April 1965.

126 "I had a taste . . ." Fred Sidewater quoted by Charles Higham, *Ava: A Life Story*. New York: Delacorte Press, 1974, page 227.

127 "I've fallen for him . . ." Stephen Birmingham, quoted in *Ava: My Story*. New York: Bantam Books, 1990, page 268.

128 "... raw hamburger ..." Ibid.

128 "I agreed ..." Ava Gardner, *Ava: My Story*. New York: Bantam Books, 1990, page 257.

129 "I'm afraid this incident ..." *London Daily Express*, Jan. 8, 1965.

130 "That was the reason ..." DS interview with Robert Loggia.

132 "... would smear their own hang-ups ..." GCS quoted by Barbara Gelb, "Great Scott!" *New York Times Magazine*, Jan. 23, 1977.

133 "He expected Ava ..." DS interview with Robert Loggia.

133 "George and Kim Stanley ..." Ibid.

133 "... one long pause ..." *Three Sisters* review, *London Illustrated News*, May 29, 1965.

133 "The admirable World Theatre's ..." Penelope Gilliat quoted by Cheryl Crawford, *One Naked Individual: My Fifty Years in the Theatre*. Indianapolis/ New York: The Bobbs-Merrill Company, Inc., 1977, page 241.

133 "As Vershinin ..." Milton Shulman, "Isn't It Time to Ban the First Night Gallery?" *Evening Standard*, May 14, 1965.

134 "... provide light ..." Bernard Levin, "So Much Promise Fades into Such a Lot of Gloom," *Daily Mail*, May 14, 1965.

134 "... apoplectic ..." John Strasberg, *Accidentally on Purpose: Reflections on Life, Acting, and the Nine Natural Laws of Creativity*. New York: Applause Books, 1996, page 119.

134 "Mr. Strasberg ..." Ibid.

134 "... the worst scene ..." Ibid.

134 "The story was ..." DS interview with Peter Masterson.

134 "Oddly enough ..." DS interview with Robert Loggia.

134 "He was drinking ..." DS interview with Peter Masterson.

135 "I think Mr. Strasberg ..." GCS in BBC-2 interview with Ian Dallas, June 13, 1965.

135 "I have more respect ..." Lee Strasberg quoted by Cindy Adams, *Lee Strasberg: The Imperfect Genius of the Actors Studio*. Garden City, NY: Doubleday & Company, Inc., 1980, page 17.

136 "... the standby phrase ..." GCS, "Sorry About That," *Esquire*, December 1965.

136 "Is courage ..." Ibid.

136 "Never hurt a man ..." Ibid.

137 "Americans are impatient ..." Ibid.

137 "I don't approve ..." GCS quoted in "No One Really Cares About George C. Scott," *Pageant*, December 1966.

138 "I don't believe in fighting wars ..." GCS quoted by Lawrence Grobel, "Playboy Interview: George C. Scott," *Playboy*, December, 1980.

139 "After I introduced myself ..." Dr. Jean Dax, quoted by Jan Herman, *A Talent for Trouble: The Life of Hollywood's Most Acclaimed Director, William Wyler*. New York: G. P. Putnam's Sons, 1995, page 434.

140 "We happened to be in a bar . . ." DS interview with Clifton James.

141 "Listen, honey, you're in bad shape . . ." Ava Gardner, *Ava: My Story*. New York: Bantam Books, 1990, page 259.

9. TWO COMEDIES AND *PETULIA*

143 "I try to do something different . . ." GCS quoted by Brian St. Pierre, "After *The Bible*, a Little *Flim-Flam*," *New York Times*, Nov. 13, 1966.

144 "George is very intense . . ." Tony Curtis and Barry Paris, *Tony Curtis: The Autobiography*. New York: William Morrow and Company, Inc., 1993, page 227.

145 "Mr. Scott compels interest . . ." Vincent Canby, "Warner Farce Opens," *New York Times,* Nov. 3, 1966.

146 "We both grew up in Detroit . . ." DS interview with Del Acevedo.

146 "In the beginning . . ." Ibid.

146 "There was a little secretary . . ." Ibid.

147 "Suddenly, a limousine . . ." Anne MacDermott, "Street Theatre," letter to the *New York Times Magazine*, Feb. 20, 1977.

148 "He always had a reputation . . ." DS interview with David Rothenberg.

148 ". . . behind-the-scenes . . ." "Fortune Honors: Jerry Miller, Ed Newman, George C. Scott," *Fortune News*, March 1977.

148 "Mr. Scott skillfully exposes . . ." John Allen, "'Greed's My Line' in *Flim-Flam Man*," *Christian Science Monitor*, Oct. 14, 1967.

148 "He is a serious character actor . . ." Bosley Crowther, "Screen: *Flim-Flam Man*," *New York Times*, Aug. 23, 1967.

148 "He shot a good picture . . ." GCS quoted by Rex Reed, *People Are Crazy Here*. New York: Dell Publishing, Inc. 1974, page 167.

149 "He sent it to prove to me . . ." DS interview with Sonny Elliott.

151 "I absolutely adored his work . . ." Richard Lester quoted by Anthony Hayward, *Julie Christie*. London: Robert Hale, 2000, page 94.

151 "We had very different styles . . ." DS interview with Shirley Knight.

153 "Because she is somewhat . . ." Richard Lester quoted by Anthony Hayward, *Julie Christie*. London: Robert Hale, 2000, pages 94–95.

154 ". . . a gaily colored . . ." Kathleen Carroll, "Julie Christie Charms in Mod Film," *New York Daily News*, June 11, 1968.

10. NEW MARRIAGE, BROADWAY HITS, AND A FLOP

155 "Even when we were divorced . . ." CD quoted by Saul Braun, "Great Scott," *Playboy*, April 1971.

156 "Colleen is one of the best actresses . . ." GCS quoted in "No One Really Cares About George C. Scott," *Pageant*, December 1966.

156 "What I recall . . ." DS interview with Jack Conant.

157 "Colleen was a caretaker . . ." DS interview with Elizabeth Wilson.

158 "They had been through . . ." Ibid.

158 "G.C. called my house . . ." DS interview with Scott Fowler.

160 "He's bled into . . ." GCS quoted by William Goldman, *The Season: A Candid Look at Broadway*. New York: Harcourt, Brace & World, Inc., 1969, page 24.

160 "There's no scene . . ." Ibid., page 26.

161 "I couldn't serve him . . ." Ibid., page 27.

161 "Take him to dinner . . ." Ibid., page 27.

163 ". . . electrifying . . ." DS interview with Austin Pendleton.

163 "George C. Scott discovering . . ." Walter Kerr, "We Could Have Five *Little Foxes*," *New York Times*, Nov. 5, 1967.

164 "In between a matinee . . ." DS interview with Austin Pendleton.

165 "Almost every night . . ." Ibid.

167 "He greeted me . . ." Neil Simon, *Rewrites: A Memoir*. New York: Simon & Schuster, 1996, page 258.

167 "[George] never gave less . . ." DS interview with Bob Balaban.

168 "The whole world . . ." Mary Cronin, "George C. Scott: Tempering a Terrible Fire," *Time,* March 22, 1971.

168 "Well, then . . ." Neil Simon, *Rewrites: A Memoir*. New York: Simon & Schuster, 1996, page 267.

168 ". . . he had just relived . . ." Neil Simon, *Rewrites: A Memoir*. New York: Simon & Schuster, 1996, page 267.

169 "She looks like a hooker . . ." Maureen Stapleton, with Jane Scovell, *A Hell of a Life: An Autobiography*. New York: Simon & Schuster, 1995, page 196.

170 ". . . saying in the foulest . . ." Neil Simon, *Rewrites: A Memoir*. New York: Simon & Schuster, 1996, page 268.

170 ". . . Colleen? . . ." Ibid., page 269.

171 "When he came back . . ." DS interview with Bob Balaban.

171 ". . . carrying what looked . . ." Maureen Stapleton, with Jane Scovell, *A Hell of a Life: An Autobiography*. New York: Simon & Schuster, 1995, page 196.

172 "We've all known . . ." Richard Watts, Jr., "Two on the Aisle: Hilarity in a Hotel Suite," *New York Post*, Feb. 15, 1968.

172 "We had the opening night party . . ." DS interview with Elizabeth Wilson.

172 "George hired a limousine . . ." Maureen Stapleton, with Jane Scovell, *A Hell of a Life: An Autobiography*. New York: Simon & Schuster, 1995, page 141.

173 "He had just opened . . ." DS interview with Dr. Albert Ackerman.

174 "If you wanted to test . . ." Ibid.

11. *PATTON*

177 "I simply refused . . ." GCS quoted by *New York Times*, March 29, 1970.

177 "I had no director . . ." Frank McCarthy quoted by Mel Gussow, *"Patton* Campaign: It Took Nineteen Years," *New York Times*, April 21, 1971.

178 "I thought about using that . . ." GCS quoted by by Christina Kirk, "The Real George C. Scott Stands Up," *Sunday New York Daily News*, March 8, 1970.

178 "I was probably in my senior year . . ." DS interview with Scott Fowler.

179 "She was calling from Spain . . ." DS interview with Dr. Albert Ackerman.

181 "It's an unactable part . . ." GCS quoted by David Devine, *London Sunday Times*, April 3, 1969.

182 "I have enormous affection . . ." GCS quoted by Carole Kass, *Variety*, March 10, 1971 (article title obscured, *Patton* clipping file, Billy Rose Theatre Collection, Lincoln Center Library for the Performing Arts).

183 ". . . he thought if we started . . ." David Brown, *Let Me Entertain You*. Beverly Hills, CA: New Millennium Press, 1990, 2003, page 226.

183 ". . . personally kind to me . . ." GCS quoted by Lawrence H. Suid, *Guts and Glory: The Making of the American Military Image in Film*. Lexington, Kentucky: The University Press of Kentucky, 2002, page 269.

183 "We were working . . ." DS interview with Karl Malden.

184 "No one in the cast . . ." Ibid.

186 ". . . one of the greatest . . ." Judith Crist, *Patton* review, *New York*, Feb. 9, 1970.

186 ". . . cannot be praised highly enough . . ." Andrew Sarris, *Patton* review, *Village Voice*, Feb. 26, 1970.

186 "George C. Scott as Patton . . ." Stanley Kauffmann, *Patton* review, *New Republic*, March 7, 1970.

187 "That goddamn piece of shit . . ." GCS quoted by Stephen M. Silverman, *The Fox That Got Away: The Last Days of the Zanuck Dynasty at Twentieth Century-Fox*. Seacaucus, NJ: Lyle Stuart, Inc., 1988, page 176.

12. REFUSING TO MARCH IN THE "MEAT PARADE"

190 ". . . erupting volcano . . ." Joanne Woodward quoted by Judith Crist, *Take 22: Moviemakers on Moviemaking*, New York: Viking, 1984, page 66.

190 "It was an exciting . . ." Anthony Harvey quoted in *New York Daily News*, March 29, 1970 (untitled clipping, *They Might Be Giants* file, Billy Rose Theatre Collection, Lincoln Center Library for the Performing Arts).

191 "The wit turns . . ." Molly Haskell, *They Might Be Giants* review, *Village Voice*, June 24, 1971.

191 "... fanciful mixture ..." Hollis Alpert, "In Search of Evil," *Saturday Review*, May 8, 1971.

191 "Charm is not ..." Molly Haskell, *They Might be Giants* review, *Village Voice*, June 24, 1971.

192 "I think he sensed ..." Ray Stricklyn, *Angels and Demons: One Actor's Hollywood Journey*. Los Angeles: Belle Publishing, 1999, page 181.

192 "One drinker ..." Art Carney quoted by Saul Braun, "Great Scott," *Playboy*, April 1971.

194 "I suddenly got a check ..." Walter Brown Newman quoted by John M. Wilson, "The Script That Just Won't Die," *Los Angeles Times*, Aug. 23, 1981.

194 "*Harrow Alley* is one of the best ..." Dorothy Wilde quoted by John M. Wilson, ibid.

194 "One of the most brilliant ..." Frank Pierson quoted by Mark Litwak, *Reel Power: The Struggle for Influence and Success in the New Hollywood*. New York and Scarborough, Ontario: Silman-James Press, 1986, page 181.

195 "He was very courteous ..." DS interview with Susannah York.

195 "One day ..." Ibid.

196 "... rather like Patton ..." *Jane Eyre* review, *Variety*, March 31, 1971.

197 "... then this would be ..." Cecil Smith, "Faith Restored by Miller's *Price*," *Los Angeles Times*, Feb. 4, 1971.

198 "It's a natural ..." Carter DeHaven quoting John Huston in Lawrence Grobel, *The Hustons*. New York: Avon Books, 1989, page 627.

198 "There may be a couple of areas ..." Ibid.

199 "George thinks ..." CD quoted by Mason Wiley and Damien Bona, *Inside Oscar: The Unofficial History of the Academy Awards*. New York: Ballantine Books, 1986, 1987, page 447.

199 "It requires no imagination ..." Archer Winsten, "*The Last Run* Takes Off," *New York Post*, July 8, 1971.

200 "It was very simple for John ..." DS interview with Tony Musante.

200 "... a sort of wild free-for-all ..." Clarus Backes, "And Now, the Award for Best Actor in a Near-Disaster Filmed by Hollywood on Foreign Soil," *Chicago Tribune Magazine*, April 11, 1971.

201 "All right, I've got one problem ..." DS interview with Tony Musante.

201 "I said to Jane ..." Ibid.

202 "Sure there were script problems ..." Bayley Silleck quoted by Clarus Backes, "And Now, the Award for Best Actor in a Near-Disaster Filmed by Hollywood on Foreign Soil," *Chicago Tribune Magazine*, April 11, 1971.

202 "She couldn't act ..." Alan Sharpe quoted by Clarus Backes, ibid.

202 "I'd seen Scott and Dad ..." Tony Huston quoted by Lawrence Grobel, *The Hustons*. New York: Avon Books, 1989, page 628.

203 "... greatest man ..." letter from Gladys Hill to Paul Kohner, John Huston

collection, Academy of Motion Picture Arts and Sciences Margaret Herrick
Library.

203 "You're the boss . . ." Ibid.

204 "God help me . . ." letter from Lucy Lichtig, John Huston collection, Academy of Motion Picture Arts and Sciences Margaret Herrick
Library.

204 "Scott is one of the best actors alive . . ." John Huston, quoted in *FilmFacts*,
Vol. XIV, 1971, No. 12.

204 ". . . shitheel . . ." John Huston quoted by Peter S. Greenberg, "The Rolling
Stone Interview: Saints and Stinkers," *Rolling Stone*, Feb. 19, 1981.

205 "I asked . . ." Richard Fleischer quoted by David Lewin, "The Inside Story
of a Take-Over," *Today's Cinema*, March 9, 1971.

206 "For a moment or two . . ." TVD quoted by Kay Gardella, *New York Daily
News*, Nov. 28, 1976.

206 "Colleen had arrived . . ." DS interview with Tony Musante.

207 "Have you ever seen a killer? . . ." Betty Rollin, "George C. Scott: Nothing
Ever Really Helps," *Look*, April 20, 1971.

207 "George has a temper . . ." GDS quoted by Betty Rollin, ibid.

208 "The Academy Awards show . . ." GCS quoted in Brown, Peter H. *The Real
Oscar: The Story Behind the Academy Awards*. Westport, CT: Arlington House,
1981, page 18.

208 "According to . . ." Hank Grant quoted by Mason Wiley and Damien Bona,
Inside Oscar: The Unofficial History of the Academy Awards. New York: Ballantine Books, 1986, 1987, page 447.

208 "[P]eculiar as it may seem . . ." GCS telegram quoted in *Los Angeles Times*,
Feb. 24, 1971.

209 "The public process . . ." GCS quoted by Betty Rollin, "George C. Scott:
Nothing Ever Really Helps," *Look*, April 20, 1971.

209 "He told me the Academy Awards . . ." DS interview with Tony Musante.

210 "I have reached a point . . ." GCS quoted by Michael Owen, "I Won't Join
the Oscar Meat Parade," *Evening Standard*, Feb. 9, 1971.

210 ". . . automobile chase sequences . . ." Roger Greenspan, *The Last Run* review, *New York Times*, July 8, 1971.

211 "He can be tough . . ." S. K. Oberbeck, "Plastic Man," *Newsweek*, July 19,
1971.

211 "Getting Scott for this role . . ." Carter DeHaven quoted by Dorothy Manners, "Scott Temper Didn't Slow Up *Last Run*," *Daily Mirror*, April 15,
1971.

211 ". . . we both unhappy . . ." GCS quoted by Shelby Stephens, "George
C. Scott Talks," *Photo Screen*, May 1971.

213 "He hadn't been there . . ." DS interview with Barnard Hughes.

13. TRISH TAKES OVER

215 "I told him . . ." TVD quoted by Judy Klemesrud, "Trish? Mrs. Scott? Both?" *New York Times*, Dec. 31, 1974.

216 "I really was surprised . . ." Jack Cassidy quoted by Army Archerd, "Just for Variety," *Variety*, May 11, 1971.

216 "Dear Jack . . ." GCS quoted, ibid.

217 "Along with the matter . . ." Donald Harron quoted by Shaun Considine, *Mad as Hell: The Life and Work of Paddy Chayefsky*. New York: Random House, 1994, page 281.

217 "It was complicated . . ." Arthur Hiller quoted in Danny Peary (ed.), *Close-Ups: Intimate Profiles of Movie Stars by Their Costars, Directors, Screenwriters and Friends*. New York: Workman Publishing, 1978, page 358.

218 "It's just remarkable . . ." Ibid., page 359.

219 "You do your fucking writing . . ." Shaun Considine, *Mad as Hell: The Life and Work of Paddy Chayefsky*. New York: Random House, 1994, page 283.

219 "I was sure . . ." Howard Gottfried, quoted in Ibid., page 283.

219 ". . . the good moments . . ." Joseph Gelmis, *Newsday*, quoted in *Filmfacts*, Vol. XIV, 1971, No. 18.

219 ". . . perhaps the finest . . ." Judith Crist, *New York*, quoted in *FilmFacts*, ibid.

219 ". . . a tornado . . ." Stanley Kauffmann, "From a Star to a Czar," *New Republic*, Jan. 22, 1972.

220 "We're going to deliver . . ." Paddy Chayefsky quoted in *Mad as Hell: The Life and Work of Paddy Chayefsky*. New York: Random House, 1994, page 287.

221 "A gentleman . . ." Erik Estrada, with Davin Seay, *Erik Estrada: My Road from Harlem to Hollywood*. New York: William Morris and Company, Inc., 1997, page 77.

222 "Scott has one magnificent scene . . ." David Thomson, *The New Biographical Dictionary of Film*. New York: Knopf, 2004, page 791.

224 "We were shooting . . ." DS interview with Del Acevedo.

225 "George knew exactly what he wanted . . ." Richard Basehart quoted in "George Scott 'Fine Director,'" *Greeley, Colorado Tribune*, Dec. 15, 1972.

225 "We work fast . . ." GCS quoted by Joan Barthel, "At Grips with an Angry Vagabond; George C. Scott Takes Up Directing Movies with a Suitably Titled Film, *Rage*," *Life*, Sept. 22, 1972.

226 "Inevitably, my personal acting suffered . . ." GCS quoted in "*Rage*: George C. Scott," *Action*, January, 1973.

226 "When we finished . . ." DS interview with Del Acevedo.

227 ". . . sluggish, tired, and tiring . . ." Murf, *Rage* review, *Variety*, Nov. 8, 1972.

227 ". . . self-conscious and pointless . . ." Joseph Gelmis, "Scott's *Rage* Gutters Out," *Newsday*, Nov. 26, 1972.

227 ". . . the great bombs . . ." Stuart Byron, *Village Voice*, quoted in *FilmFacts*, Vol. XV, 1972.

227 "The Dominican lawyers . . ." CD quoted by Earl Wilson, "It Happened Last Night: Marrying Again? Great Scott . . ." *New York Post*, Feb. 4, 1972.

228 ". . . that it isn't too long . . ." TVD quoted by Marilyn Beck, "Filmland Blossoms Out After Economic Crisis" (year in review column), *Pasadena Star-News*, Jan. 2, 1973.

228 "After *Patton* . . ." DS interview with Victoria Lewis.

230 "They're totally disparate people . . ." GCS quoted by Gregg Kilday, "Guess Who's Coming to a New Film Concept," *Los Angeles Times*, Jan. 7, 1973.

230 "[E]ach has been . . ." Ibid.

231 "The only thing we were spared . . ." Faye Dunaway with Betsy Sharkey, *Looking for Gatsby: My Life*. New York: Simon & Schuster, 1995, page 221.

231 "The cast really suffered . . ." Stanley Kramer quoted by Donald Spoto, *Stanley Kramer: Film Maker*. New York: G. P. Putnam's Sons, 1978, page 317.

231 "I hate to make the comparison . . ." Ibid., page 315.

232 "When he walked in . . ." Faye Dunaway, with Betsy Sharkey, *Looking for Gatsby: My Life*. New York: Simon & Schuster, 1995, page 222.

232 ". . . a college chaplain . . ." Richard Schickel, "An Oil Slick," *Time*, Aug. 20, 1973.

232 "George C. Scott just continues . . ." Roger Ebert, *Oklahoma Crude* review, *Chicago Sun-Times*, Aug. 6, 1973.

232 ". . . for his humanist . . ." Donald Spoto, *Stanley Kramer: Film Maker*. New York: G. P. Putnam's Sons, 1978, page 318.

14. SWIMMING WITH DOLPHINS AND DRINKING WITH RUSSIANS

234 "I've collected . . ." Joseph E. Levine quoted by Earl Wilson, "It Happened Last Night: *Dolphin*: Fine Finny Fare," *New York Post*, Nov. 15, 1973.

235 ". . . produce as well as star . . ." Robert Aldrich quoted in Alain Silver and James Ursini, *Whatever Happened to Robert Aldrich? His Life and His Films*. New York: Limelight Editions, 1995, page 37.

235 "We were filming about three days . . ." DS interview with Fritz Weaver.

235 "*Dolphin* was a very strange . . ." DS interview with Elizabeth Wilson.

236 "He had the flu . . ." Joseph E. Levine quoted by Earl Wilson, "It Happened Last Night: *Dolphin*: Fine Finny Fare," *New York Post*, Nov. 15, 1973.

236 "He's a jerk . . ." Joseph E. Levine quoted in "Disrespects Paid Scott by Levine," *Variety*, Nov. 13, 1974.

236 ". . . old cunt . . ." GCS quoted by Lawrence Grobel, "Playboy Interview: George C. Scott," *Playboy*, December, 1980.

236 "He was living . . ." DS interview with Fritz Weaver.

238 ". . . Moby Dick . . ." *Day of the Dolphin* review, *Playboy*, April 1974.

238 "I won't play . . ." GCS quoted by Theodore Mann, *Journeys in the Night: Creating a New American Theatre with Circle in the Square*. New York: Applause Theatre & Cinema Books, 2007, page 251.

238 "If I see one . . ." Ibid.

239 "Nicol Williamson . . ." DS interview with Elizabeth Wilson.

240 "My wife and I . . ." Nicol Williamson quoted by Christopher Sharp, "Nicol Williamson: The Busiest Uncle in Town," *Women's Wear Daily*, June 19, 1973.

240 "One matinee . . ." DS interview with Elizabeth Wilson.

241 "I used to have lunch . . ." Ibid.

241 "He's the most lauded actor . . ." Nicol Williamson quoted by Joyce Haber, "Actors, That Other Imbibing Fraternity," *Los Angeles Times*, Sept. 4, 1973.

241 "How does it feel . . ." Ibid.

242 ". . . simply acts . . ." Martin Gottfried, *Uncle Vanya* review, *Women's Wear Daily*, June 6, 1973.

242 ". . . the charged intensity . . ." T. E. Kalem, "Unrequited Lives," *Time*, June 18, 1973.

242 "Scott radiates . . ." John Simon, *Uncle Vanya* review, *New York*, June 18, 1973.

242 "The turmoil within him . . ." DS interview with David Finkle.

242 "He's lost . . ." GCS quoted by Lewis Funke, *Actors Talk About Theatre: 12 Interviews with Lewis Funke*. Chicago, Westport: The Dramatic Publishing Company, 1977, page 251.

243 "This was the summer . . ." DS interview with Elizabeth Wilson.

243 "For a number of summers . . ." Ibid.

244 "There was a studio . . ." DS interview with Marta Byer-White.

245 "George has to come first . . ." TVD quoted by Judy Klemesrud, "Trish? Mrs. Scott? Both?" *New York Times*, Dec. 31, 1974.

245 ". . . the most middle-of-the-road . . ." TVD quoted in "Couples: Who's Afraid of George C. Scott? Everybody but Trish Van Devere," *People*, Feb. 7, 1977.

246 "George was better casting . . ." DS interview with Bob Balaban.

247 "He made it up . . ." Jess Gregg quoted by John Anthony Gilvey, *Before the Parade Passes By: Gower Champion and the Glorious American Musical*. New York: St. Martin's Press, 2005, page 241.

247 ". . . a dreadful film . . ." GCS interview with Professor Richard Brown, *Reflections on the Silver Screen*, American Movie Classics, 1993, Museum of Broadcast Communications.

15. A TAME *SAVAGE*

249 "Not even when the sun . . ." Aljean Harmetz, "George C. Scott: Controlling the Savage Within," *Cosmopolitan*, April 1975.

250 "Having done that . . ." GCS, "Dialogue on Film: George C. Scott/Trish Van Devere," The American Film Institute, January 1975.

250 "We've hocked the ranch . . ." GCS quoted by John M. McGuire, "George C. Scott Shows the People of Missouri," *People*, Aug. 5, 1974.

250 "They told Henry Ford . . ." Ibid.

251 "It couldn't be too pastoral . . ." TVD quoted by Pierre Cossette, "The Savage Is Loose," *Saturday Evening Post*, December 1974.

252 ". . . overweight . . ." GCS quoted by Aljean Harmetz, "George C. Scott: Controlling the Savage Within," *Cosmopolitan*, April 1975.

252 "I tried to talk him into . . ." DS interview with Clifton James.

253 "Generally . . ." GCS quoted by Jack Richardson, "George C. Scott Among the Hurricanes," *Esquire*, November 1974.

254 "Acting is a very difficult life . . ." GCS quoted by Aljean Harmetz, "Can Scott Sell His Own Movie?" *New York Times*, July 24, 1974.

254 "It was hard . . ." GCS quoted by Jacoba Atlas, "George C. Scott," *Los Angeles Free Press*, Oct. 25, 1974.

255 "When things go wrong here . . ." TVD quoted by Aljean Harmetz, "George C. Scott: Controlling the Savage Within," *Cosmopolitan*, April 1975.

255 "About two in the morning . . ." TVD interview on *The Mike Douglas Show*, Nov. 25, 1974, Paley Center for Media (formerly Museum of Television and Radio).

255 "I think it's a tasteful film . . ." GCS quoted by John M. McGuire, "George C. Scott Shows the People of Missouri," *People*, Aug. 5, 1974.

256 "If I had wanted . . ." GCS quoted by Charles Champlin, "Gen. Scott in War Games," *Los Angeles Times*, Oct. 18, 1974.

257 "One of the members . . ." TVD quoted by Barbara Ettorre, "The Baker's Wife," *Women's Wear Daily*, Sept. 3, 1974.

258 ". . . scared shitless . . ." Peter Marshall and Adrienne Armstrong, *Backstage with the Original Hollywood Square*. Nashville, TN: Rutledge Hill Press, 2002, page 110.

258 "*The Savage* crawls by . . ." Pauline Kael, *Reeling*. New York: Warner Books, 1976, page 509.

258 "Sometimes the worst thing . . ." DS interview with Larry Gelbart.

258 "[N]ow I'm four-walling . . ." GCS quoted by Guy Flatley, "At the Movies: Some of the Things George C. Scott's Been Up To Lately," *New York Times*, Sept. 23, 1977.

259 *"Grand Hotel . . ."* Pauline Kael, *Reeling.* New York: Warner Books, 1976, page 427.

260 ". . . the most dismal . . ." Charles Michener, "Looking Backward," *Newsweek,* Dec. 29, 1975.

260 ". . . dominates the film . . ." *Fear on Trial* review, *Film & Filming,* April 1976.

260 "People assumed . . ." DS interview with Susan L. Schulman.

261 "I thought she was very difficult . . ." DS interview with Judith Barcroft.

261 "Although I've always wanted . . ." GCS quoted by Robert Wahls, "Footlights: In Love with a Play," *New York Sunday News,* March 16, 1975.

262 "This is a very poorly . . ." Clive Barnes, *"All God's Chillun* at Circle in the Square," *New York Times,* March 21, 1975.

262 ". . . a major disaster . . ." John Simon, *All God's Chillun* review, *New York,* April 7, 1975.

262 "Faced with the play's . . ." Walter Kerr, "O'Neill's Uneasy Study in Black and White," *New York Times,* March 30, 1975.

263 "I was roundly criticized . . ." GCS quoted by Michael Reidel, "Great Scott!" *Theatre Week,* Oct. 14–20, 1991.

264 "George wanted Harvey . . ." Chuck Patterson quoted by Marshall Fine, *Harvey Keitel: The Art of Darkness.* New York: Fromm International, 1998, pages 76–77.

264 "That created . . ." Arvin Brown quoted in Ibid., page 77.

264 "Willy doesn't know . . ." GCS interview with Margaret Croyden, "Twenty-five Years at Circle in the Square," *Camera Three,* 1975, Theatre on Film and Television collection, Lincoln Center Library for the Performing Arts.

264 ". . . an embittered, chained . . ." William Glover, *Death of a Salesman* review, Associated Press, July 7, 1975.

264 "When his head is . . ." T. E. Kalem, "A Défi to Fate," *Time,* July 7, 1975.

264 "If there were nothing . . ." Julius Novick, "George C. Scott: His Last Bow?" *Village Voice,* Aug. 25, 1975.

265 "I think it has an enormous effect . . ." Arthur Miller quoted by Christian-Albrecht Gollub in *Conversations with Arthur Miller,* edited by Matthew C. Roudane. Jackson and London: University of Mississippi, 1987, page 276.

265 "I've never forgotten . . ." DS interview with Bob Balaban.

265 "George wants to do the film . . ." James Farentino quoted by Mary Murphy, *Los Angeles Times,* Nov. 19, 1975.

266 "Last night . . ." TVD, "Fiji and Me (And George C. Makes Three)," *Family Weekly,* July 25, 1976.

267 "George C. is a riot . . ." Ibid.

267 "One of the big . . ." GCS quoted in "Couples: Who's Afraid of George C. Scott? Everybody but Trish Van Devere," *People,* Feb. 7, 1977.

267 "We were making each other . . ." Ibid.

267 "He was a good man . . ." Ibid.

16. PAPA, THE BEAST, AND A SLY FOX

269 "I read everything he wrote . . ." GCS quoted in Paramount press release, Franklin J. Schaffner Collection, Franklin & Marshall College Library, Folder 53/2.

269 "He could say the most . . ." Ibid.

269 "George C. Scott is the Ernest Hemingway . . ." Andrew Sarris, "Has the Hemingway Hero Had It?" *Village Voice*, March 28, 1977.

270 "When I write notes . . ." unpublished manuscript, Franklin J. Schaffner Collection, Franklin & Marshall College Library, Folder 53/2.

271 "By the way . . ." Ibid.

272 "Looking at him . . ." Peter Bart and Peter Gruber, *Shoot Out: Surviving Fame and (Mis)Fortune in Hollywood*. New York: G. P. Putnam's Sons, 2002, page 207.

272 "Producers prevent you . . ." Ibid., page 208.

272 "They want to rehash . . ." GCS quoted by Ray Loynd, "A Lion in the Sea," *Los Angeles Herald-Examiner*, Nov. 30, 1975.

273 "I had the most unpleasant experience . . ." GCS quoted by David Brown, *Let Me Entertain You*. Beverly Hills, California: New Millennium Press, 1990, 2003, page 226.

273 "And as for *Rage* . . ." Ibid., page 227.

273 "Scott got thoroughly . . ." Peter Bart and Peter Gruber, *Shoot Out: Surviving Fame and (Mis)Fortune in Hollywood*. New York: G. P. Putnam's Sons, 2002, page 126.

273 "Scott, far from being . . ." Claire Bloom, *Leaving a Doll's House*. Boston, New York: Little, Brown, and Company, 1996, page 145.

275 "The script was sent to him . . ." DS interview with Sherman Yellen.

275 "My God! I'm too old . . ." TVD quoted by Kay Gardella, *New York Daily News*, Nov. 28, 1976.

275 "Once in a while . . ." GCS quoted by Robert Musel, "Ten Hours in a Boar's Head: George C. Scott's Method for Making the Beast Sympathetic Is All in the Eyes," *TV Guide*, Nov. 27, 1976.

276 "He did break out . . ." DS interview with Del Acevedo.

276 "The only one . . ." DS interview with Sherman Yellen.

276 "It's in the eyes . . ." GCS quoted by Robert Musel, "Ten Hours in a Boar's Head: George C. Scott's Method for Making the Beast Sympathetic Is All in the Eyes," *TV Guide*, Nov. 27, 1976.

277 "My work was . . ." Larry Gelbart, *Laughing Matters: On Writing M*A*S*H,*

Tootsie, Oh, God!, and a Few Other Funny Things. New York: Random House, 1998, page 218.

278 "That was his idea . . ." DS interview with Larry Gelbart.

278 ". . . a man might . . ." Clive Barnes, *Sly Fox* review, *New York Times*, Dec. 15, 1976.

279 "George burned with a short fuse . . ." Christopher Lee, *Lord of Misrule: The Autobiography of Christopher Lee.* London: Orion Books, Ltd., 2004, page 322.

279 "Once we were in a tournament . . ." Jack Lemmon quoted in "Tribute: 1999," *TV Guide*, Jan. 1, 2000.

280 "We were very lucky . . ." GCS quoted by Rick Carroll, "Two Film Stars' Close Call at Sea," *San Francisco Chronicle*, Jan. 18, 1978.

281 "There was only one bad day . . ." DS interview with Larry Gelbart.

281 "Gelbart is such a good writer . . ." GCS quoted by Wayne Warga, "Scott Still Foxing the Establishment," *Los Angeles Times*, June 18, 1978.

282 "That was a very depressing film . . ." GCS quoted by Paul Riordan, "The Films of George C. Scott," Images website, 1997, www.imagesjournal.com/issue04/features/georgecscott2.htm.

282 "It was thrilling working . . ." Paul Schrader quoted by Robert J. Emery, *The Directors: Take Three.* New York: Allworth Press, 2003, page 160.

283 "He's simply amazing . . ." Peter Boyle quoted by Paul Schrader in Robert J. Emery, *The Directors: Take Three.* New York: Allworth Press, 2003, page 161.

283 "It was always a big melodrama . . ." Paul Schrader quoted in ibid.

285 "Scott's powerful performance . . ." David Ansen, "Lower Depths," *Newsweek*, Feb. 19, 1979.

285 "The relationship of Larry Gelbart . . ." DS interview with Joe Logrippo.

286 "Next spring . . ." GCS quoted by Wayne Warga, "Scott Still Foxing the Establishment," *Los Angeles Times*, June 18, 1978.

287 "She produced . . ." DS interview with Joe Logrippo.

288 "I decided not to . . ." GCS quoted in "Scott Rises to the Occasion," *US*, April 1, 1980.

289 "You know when you find . . ." DS interview with Karen Truesdell Riehl.

290 "Those who admired . . ." Charles Champlin, *The Changeling* review, *Los Angeles Times*, March 26, 1980.

290 ". . . elegant and scary . . ." David Denby, *The Changeling* review, New York, April 20, 1980.

17. PATTON MEETS THE GODFATHER

294 "I made a big mistake . . ." John Avildsen quoted by Robert J. Emery in *The Directors: Take Two.* New York: Allworth Press, 2002, page 132.

295 "Well, Marlon . . ." Tom Buckley, "At the Movies," *New York Times*, May 30, 1980.

295 "He had a pressure device . . ." John Avildsen quoted by Robert J. Emery in *The Directors: Take Two*. New York: Allworth Press, 2002, page 134.

296 "I was surprised . . ." Steve Shagan quoted by Tom Buckley, "At the Movies," *New York Times*, May 30, 1980.

296 "I sensed . . ." Ibid.

296 "He goes beyond acting . . ." GCS quoted by Darwin Porter, *Brando Unzipped*. New York: Blood Moon Productions, 2005, page 602.

296 "With Marlon . . ." GCS quoted by quoted by Lawrence Grobel, "Playboy Interview: George C. Scott," *Playboy*, December, 1980.

296 "I'd show up in the morning . . ." John Avildsen quoted by Robert J. Emery, *The Directors: Take Two*. New York: Allworth Press, 2002, page 132.

297 ". . . a terrible piece of shit . . ." Marlon Brando quoted by Lawrence Grobel, *Conversations with Brando*, New York: Hyperion, 1991, page 174.

297 "I think I played . . ." GCS quoted by Darwin Porter, *Brando Unzipped*. New York: Blood Moon Productions, 2005, page 602.

298 ". . . clump of sludge . . ." *The Formula* review, *Variety*, Dec. 2, 1980.

298 ". . . so murkily plotted . . ." *The Formula* review, *Newsweek*, Jan. 19, 1981.

298 "I have immense respect . . ." "George C. Scott Out as Director of Paige Vidpic," *Variety*, June 2, 1980.

299 "The only mystery . . ." Frank Rich, *Hot Seat: Theatre Criticism for the New York Times, 1980–1993*. New York: Random House, 1998, page 35.

299 "They seemed to have invented . . ." Lawrence Eisenberg, "Hollywood Babble-On," *Modern Maturity*, March–April, 2001.

299 "How dare you!" GCS quoted, ibid.

299 "We decided that the company . . ." DS interview with Merle Debuskey.

302 "It was a terrible mistake . . ." TVD quoted by Roderick Mann, "Trish Van Devere Chooses a Different Port in the Storm," *Los Angeles Times*, May 11, 1985.

304 "He knew exactly what he wanted . . ." DS interview with Kate Burton.

304 "I was just this kid . . ." DS interview with Nathan Lane.

304 "Mr. Scott is pickled . . ." Frank Rich, "Stage: Scott in a Noel Coward Play," *New York Times*, July 16, 1982.

304 "It just split my skull . . ." Paul Newman quoted in "Playboy Interview: Paul Newman," *Playboy*, April 1983.

305 "I've been in plays where I've drunk . . ." GCS quoted by Michiko Kakutani, "Is This a Different George C. Scott?" *New York Times*, July 11, 1982.

305 "That's it . . ." DS interview with Nathan Lane.

305 "It's just not the same . . ." DS interview with Dana Ivey.

305 "I was too afraid . . ." DS interview with Nathan Lane.

306 "Eva La Gallienne!" DS interview with Kate Burton.

306 "Every person . . ." DS interview with Nathan Lane.

306 "I'd never before . . ." DS interview with Dana Ivey.

307 "I was feeling poor . . ." DS interview with Karen Truesdell Riehl.

307 "He told me he was . . ." Ibid.

307 "He was getting very tired and very angry . . ." Ibid.

308 "They were not . . ." DS interview with David Epstein.

309 "If nothing else . . ." John J. O'Connor, "TV: Quest in the Orient with George C. Scott," *New York Times*, Oct. 18, 1983.

309 "Your Oscar is waiting . . ." Mason Wiley and Damien Bona, *Inside Oscar: The Unofficial History of the Academy Awards*. New York: Ballantine Books, 1986, 1987, page 623.

18. "ALL I GET IS JUNK"

311 "All I get is junk . . ." GCS quoted by Stephen Farber, "Scott Puts On His Patton Stars Again," *New York Times*, Aug. 13, 1986.

311 "My impression . . ." DS interview with David Epstein.

312 ". . . a big man . . ." Drew Barrymore, with Todd Gold, *Little Girl Lost*. New York: Pocket Books, 1990, page 73.

312 "It was never . . ." Ibid.

313 ". . . one of those half-assed . . ." GCS quoted by Paul Riordan, "The Films of George C. Scott," Images website, 1997, www.imagesjournal.com/issue04/features/georgecscott2.htm.

313 "I admire him from a distance . . ." Frank Finlay quoted by Joan Barthel, "George C. Scott Sweet and Happy? Bah, Humbug!" *TV Guide*, Dec. 15, 1984.

313 "I think we classically . . ." GCS quoted by Tom Viola, "The New Scrooge: George C. Scott," *Horizon*, December 1984.

314 "Loneliness has exhausted . . ." Ibid.

315 ". . . because I don't have Latin blood," GCS quoted by Jay Sharbutt, "George C. Scott Will Cross WWII Battle Lines Again," *Los Angeles Times*, Nov. 15, 1985.

315 "If you watch him . . ." GCS quoted by Lawrence Eisenberg, "A Psychotic Monster," *TV Guide*, Nov. 23, 1985.

316 "In my experience with George . . ." DS interview with Lee Grant.

316 "He was like a puppy . . ." Ibid.

316 "This is history . . ." John J. O'Connor, "TV Weekend: George C. Scott as Mussolini on NBC," *New York Times*, Nov. 22, 1985.

317 "I couldn't sell the damn thing . . ." GCS quoted by Bill Davidson, "This Time George C. Scott Is Playing Patton *His* Way," *TV Guide*, Sept. 6, 1986.

317 "This is the Patton . . ." GCS quoted by Stu Schreiberg. "He Patented Patton, but Says He's a Pussycat," *USA Weekend*, Sept. 5–7, 1986.

317 "That was a very difficult shoot . . ." DS interview with Eva Marie Saint.

318 "I figured what the hell . . ." GCS quoted by Bill Davidson, "This Time George C. Scott Is Playing Patton *His* Way," *TV Guide*, Sept. 6, 1986.

319 ". . . both gruesome and pointless . . ." "Cheers 'n' Jeers," *TV Guide*, Oct. 25, 1986.

319 "Why hang on . . ." GCS quoted by Stephen Farber, "Scott Puts On His Patton Stars Again," *New York Times*, Aug. 13, 1986.

320 ". . . an intimidating person . . ." DS interview with John Cullum.

322 ". . . fundamentally dull . . ." *Choices* review, *Daily Variety*, Feb. 19, 1986.

322 "Despite some sharp performances . . ." Gail Williams, *Choices* review, *Hollywood Reporter*, Feb. 14, 1986.

323 "We didn't understand . . ." Garth Ancier quoted by Daniel M. Kimmel, *The Fourth Network: How Fox Broke the Rules and Reinvented Television*. Chicago: Ivan R. Dee, 2004, pages 60–61.

324 "It was Johnny Carson's flagship show . . ." DS interview with Carlin Glynn.

325 "[I]t's a little painful . . ." *Mr. President* review, *Variety*, Sept. 29, 1987.

326 "The working situation was positively Byzantine . . ." GCS, "The Casual Assassination of *Mr. President*," *Los Angeles Times*, April 3, 1988.

327 "Either do it . . ." GCS quoted by Michael Reidel, "Great Scott!" *Theatre Week*, Oct. 14–20, 1991.

327 "I don't have Alzheimer's disease . . ." GCS quoted by Army Archerd, "Just for Variety," *Variety*, Jan. 25, 1991.

328 "There's a sweetness . . ." GCS quoted by Michael Reidel, cited above.

328 "I didn't know the play at all . . ." DS interview with Nathan Lane.

329 "Mr. Scott and his fine company . . ." John Beaufort, "*Borrowed Time* Triumphs," *Christian Science Monitor*, Oct. 25, 1991.

330 "I remember . . ." DS interview with Nathan Lane.

330 "There must have been . . ." DS interview with Elizabeth Wilson.

19. "THE MOST MELLOW SON OF A BITCH YOU'VE EVER SEEN"

331 "Mellow? I've always been mellow . . ." GCS quoted by Mervyn Rothstein, "George C. Scott Takes On a Play About Death," *New York Times*, Sept. 5, 1991.

333 "The laughs . . ." William A. Henry III, "The Patient Is Impatient," *Time*, March 1, 1993.

333 "I used to try . . ." Tony Danza quoted in "Insider: Tribute to George C. Scott," *TV Guide*, Nov. 26, 1999.

333 "We met them at Ernie's . . ." DS interview with Dr. Albert Ackerman.

334 "A mutual friend . . ." DS interview with Piper Laurie.

334 "There is little . . ." John J. O'Connor, *Traps* review, *New York Times*, March 29, 1994.

335 "All of a sudden . . ." DS interview with Del Acevedo.

336 "It was pretty grim . . ." Myrna Katz Frommer and Harvey Frommer, *It Happened on Broadway: An Oral History of the Great White Way*. New York: Harcourt, Brace and Company, 1998, page 205.

337 "Scott is old . . ." John Simon, *Inherit the Wind* review, *New York*, April 15, 1996.

337 "Old and slightly . . ." Michael Feingold, "Past and Pleasant," *Village Voice*, April 23, 1996.

337 "There were nights . . ." Myrna Katz Frommer and Harvey Frommer, *It Happened on Broadway: An Oral History of the Great White Way*, New York: Harcourt, Brace and Company, 1998, page 207.

338 "I need a pack of Luckys . . ." "George C. Scott Accused of Sexual Harassment in $3.1 Milllion Lawsuit," Associated Press, May 2, 1996.

338 "Based on . . ." Salvatore Arena and Helen Kennedy, "*Patton* in Sex Suit," *New York Daily News*, May 3, 1996.

338 ". . . in danger . . ." Ibid.

338 "I am saddened . . ." "Scott Is Excused in Sexual Harassment Suit," Associated Press, run in *New York Times*, May 4, 1996.

338 "I am concerned . . ." Salvatore Arena and Helen Kennedy, "*Patton* in Sex Suit," *New York Daily News*, May 3, 1996.

339 "There is a ninety . . ." Mike Pearl, Ward Morehouse III, Cathy Burke, "Scott Scoots as Doctor Says 'Sex Suit May Kill Him,'" *New York Post*, May 4, 1996.

339 ". . . obvious . . ." Ibid.

340 "There was a great deal of concern . . ." DS interview with Victoria Lewis.

341 "George C. Scott, as the ship's captain . . ." Caryn James, "It Just Keeps On Sinking, and Sinking and Sinking," *New York Times*, Nov. 16, 1996.

342 "[H]e had to do a scene . . ." Jack Lemmon quoted in "Tribute: 1999," *TV Guide*, Jan. 1, 2000.

342 "I must say I had a feeling . . ." William Friedkin quoted by Eric Harris and Susan King, "George C. Scott Dies at 71; Refused Oscar for Patton," *Los Angeles Times*, Sept. 24, 1999.

342 "Scott is explosive . . ." Tom Shales, "Showtime's Magnificent *12*; Lemmon and Scott Remake TV History," *Washington Post*, Aug. 17, 1997.

343 "My doctor asked me not to . . ." GCS quoted by Army Archerd, "Just for Variety," *Variety*, Sept. 4, 1997.

343 "Trish had adopted . . ." DS interview with Victoria Lewis.

344 "His financial manager . . ." DS interview with Del Acevedo.

344 "We were kind of like . . ." Piper Laurie quoted by Michael Sragow, "Piper Laurie Remembers the Smoldering Genius of George C. Scott," Salon.com, Sept. 30, 1999.

344 "Now in his later years . . ." Daniel Petrie quoted by Eric Harris and Susan King, "George C. Scott Dies at 71; Refused Oscar for Patton," *Los Angeles Times*, Sept. 24, 1999.

345 "It was quite extraordinary . . ." DS interview with Piper Laurie.

346 "His manager said to me . . ." DS interview with Tony Giordano.

347 "Rupture of an abdominal . . ." "George C. Scott . . . Died from an Aortic Aneurysm," Medicinenet.com, www.medicinenet.com/script/main/art.asp?articlekey=10650.

347 "He could have had it operated on . . ." Jim Mahoney quoted in "Command Performer," *People*, Oct. 11, 1999.

347 "The last of the big . . ." Rex Reed, "On the Town with Rex Reed: The Soft Side of G.C. Scott," *New York Observer*, Oct. 6, 1999.

348 "I saw a look on his face . . ." Stephen Hunter, "Rage-on-Tap Fueled George C. Scott," *Washington Post*, Sept. 25, 1999.

348 "George, I never knew . . ." Robert Simonson, "Lane, Robards, Burton, Mann, Libin Remember George C. Scott at Memorial," Playbill On-Line, Oct. 29, 1999.

348 "He liked to hang out . . ." Ibid.

BIBLIOGRAPHY

BOOKS

Adams, Cindy. *Lee Strasberg: The Imperfect Genius of the Actors Studio*. Garden City, NY: Doubleday & Company, Inc., 1980.

Arden, Eve. *The Three Phases of Eve*. New York: St. Martin's Press, 1985.

Barrymore, Drew. *Little Girl Lost*. With Todd Gold. New York: Pocket Books, 1990.

Bart, Peter and Peter Guber. *Shoot Out: Surviving Fame and (Mis)Fortune in Hollywood*. New York: G. P. Putnam's Sons, 2002.

Baxter, John. *Stanley Kubrick*. New York: Carroll & Graf Publishers, Inc., 1997.

Bloom, Claire. *Leaving a Doll's House*. Boston, New York: Little, Brown, and Company, 1996.

Bogle, Donald. *Prime Time Blues: African Americans on Network Television*. New York: Farrar, Straus, and Giroux, 2001.

Brown, David. *Let Me Entertain You*. Beverly Hills, CA: New Millennium Press, 1990, 2003.

Brown, Peter H. *The Real Oscar: The Story Behind the Academy Awards*. Westport, CT: Arlington House, 1981.

Bryer, Jackson R., and Richard A. Davison, eds. *The Actor's Art: Conversations with Contemporary American Stage Performers*. New Brunswick, NJ, and London: Rutgers University Press, 2001.

Buhle, Paul and Dave Wagner. *Hide in Plain Sight: The Hollywood Blacklistees in Film and Television, 1950–2002*. New York: Palgrave MacMillan, 2005.

Callen, Michael Feeney. *Julie Christie*. New York: St. Martin's Press, 1984.

Carey, Gary. *Marlon Brando: The Only Contender*. New York: St. Martin's Press, 1985.

Casper, Joseph Andrew. *Stanley Donen*. Metuchen, NJ, and London: The Scare-
    crow Press, Inc., 1983.

Clarkson, Wensley. *Tom Cruise Unauthorized*. Norwalk, CT: Hastings House,
    1997.

Considine, Shaun. *Mad as Hell: The Life and Work of Paddy Chayefsky*. New York:
    Random House, 1994.

Crawford, Cheryl. *One Naked Individual: My Fifty Years in the Theatre*. Indianapo-
    lis/New York: The Bobbs-Merrill Company, Inc., 1977.

Curtis, Tony, and Barry Paris. *Tony Curtis: The Autobiography*. New York: Wil-
    liam Morrow and Company, Inc., 1993.

Dern, Bruce. *Things I've Said, but Probably Shouldn't Have*. With Christopher Fryer
    and Robert Crane. Hoboken, NJ: John Wiley and Sons, Inc., 2007.

Dewhurst, Colleen. *Colleen Dewhurst: Her Autobiography*. Written with and com-
    pleted by Tom Viola. New York: A Lisa Drew Book/Scribner, 1997.

Douglas, Kirk. *The Ragman's Son*. New York: Pocket Books, Simon & Schuster,
    1988, 1989.

Douglas, Melyvn, and Tom Arthur. *See You at the Movies: The Autobiography of
    Melvyn Douglas*. Lanham, NY, and London: University Press of America,
    1986.

Dunaway, Faye. *Looking for Gatsby: My Life*. With Betsy Sharkey. New York: Si-
    mon and Schuster, 1995.

Emery, Robert J. *The Directors: Take Two*. New York: Allworth Press, 2002.

___. *The Directors: Take Three*. New York: Allworth Press, 2003.

Epstein, Helen. *Joe Papp: An American Life*. Boston, New York, Toronto, London:
    Little, Brown, and Company, 1994.

Estrada, Erik. *Erik Estrada: My Road from Harlem to Hollywood*. With David Seay.
    New York: William Morrow and Company, Inc., 1997.

Fine, Marshall. *Harvey Keitel: The Art of Darkness*. New York: Fromm Interna-
    tional, 1998.

Fishgall, Gary. *Pieces of Time: The Life of James Stewart*. New York: A Lisa Drew
    Book/Scribner, 1997.

Flamini, Roland. *Ava: A Biography*. New York: Coward, McCann & Geoghegan,
    1983.

Frommer, Myrna Katz, and Harvey Frommer. *It Happened on Broadway: An Oral
    History of the Great White Way*. New York, San Diego, London: Harcourt,
    Brace and Company, 1998.

Funke, Lewis. *Actors Talk About Theatre: 12 Interviews with Lewis Funke*. Chicago,
    Westport: The Dramatic Publishing Company, 1977.

Gardner, Ava. *Ava: My Story*. New York: Bantam Books, 1990.

Gelbart, Larry. *Laughing Matters: On Writing M*A*S*H, Tootsie, Oh, God!, and a
    Few Other Funny Things*. New York: Random House, 1998.

Gilman, Richard. *The Drama Is Coming Now: The Theater Criticism of Richard Gilman, 1961–1991*. New Haven and London: Yale University Press, 2005.

Gilvey, John Anthony. *Before the Parade Passes By: Gower Champion and the Glorious American Musical*. New York: St. Martin's Press, 2005.

Goldman, William. *The Season: A Candid Look at Broadway*. New York: Harcourt, Brace & World, Inc., 1969.

Gore, Chris. *The 50 Greatest Movies Never Made*. New York: St. Martin's Griffin, 1999.

Greenberger, Howard. *The Off-Broadway Experience*. Englewood Cliffs, NJ: Prentice-Hall, Inc., 1971.

Grobel, Lawrence. *The Hustons*. New York: Avon Books, 1989.

Hagman, Larry. *Hello Darlin': Tall (and Absolutely True) Tales about My Life*. With Todd Gold. New York: Simon and Schuster, 2001.

Hallifax, Michael. *Let Me Set the Scene: Twenty Years at the Heart of British Theatre, 1956–1976*. Hanover, NH: Smith and Krause, Inc., 2004.

Harbinson, W. A. *George C. Scott: The Man, the Actor, and the Legend*. New York: Pinnacle Books, 1977.

Harris, Jay S., ed. *TV Guide: The First 25 Years*. New York: Simon and Schuster, 1978.

Hayward, Anthony. *Julie Christie*. London: Robert Hale, 2000.

Herman, Jan. *A Talent for Trouble: The Life of Hollywood's Most Acclaimed Director, William Wyler*. New York: G. P. Putnam's Sons, 1995.

Higham, Charles. *Ava: A Life Story*. New York: Delacorte Press, 1974.

Hirsch, Foster. *Otto Preminger: The Man Who Would Be King*. New York: Alfred A. Knopf, 2007.

Holden, Anthony. *Behind the Oscar: The Secret History of the Academy Awards*. New York: Penguin Books, 1993.

Hughes, David. *The Complete Kubrick*. London: Virgin Publishing, Ltd., 2000, 2001.

Huston, John. *An Open Book*. New York: Alfred A. Knopf, 1980.

Jacobs, George and William Stadiem. *Mr. S: My Life with Frank Sinatra*. New York: HarperCollins, 2003.

Kael, Pauline. *Deeper Into Movies*. Boston: Bantam Books, 1974.

___. *Reeling*. New York: Warner Books, 1976.

___. *When the Lights Go Down*. New York: Holt, Rhinehart and Winston, 1980.

Kelley, Kitty. *His Way: The Unauthorized Biography of Frank Sinatra*. New York: Bantam Books, 1987.

Kimmel, Daniel M. *The Fourth Network: How Fox Broke the Rules and Reinvented Television*. Chicago: Ivan R. Dee, 2004.

Krampner, Jon. *Female Brando: The Legend of Kim Stanley*. New York: Back Stage Books, Watson-Guptill Publications, 2006.

Lee, Christopher. *Lord of Misrule: The Autobiography of Christopher Lee.* London: Orion Books, Ltd., 2004.

Little, Stuart W. *Off-Broadway: The Prophetic Theater.* New York: Dell Publishing, Inc., 1972.

Litwak, Mark. *Reel Power: The Struggle for Influence and Success in the New Hollywood,* New York and Scarborough, Ontario, 1986,

LoBrutto, Vincent. *Stanley Kubrick: A Biography.* New York: Donald I. Fine Books, 1997.

MacLaine, Shirley. *My Lucky Stars: A Hollywood Memoir.* New York: Bantam Books, 1995.

Madsen, Alex. *John Huston: A Biography.* Garden City, NY: Doubleday & Company, Inc., 1978.

Malden, Karl. *When Do I Start? A Memoir.* With Carla Malden. New York: Simon & Schuster, 1997.

Mann, Theodore. *Journeys in the Night: Creating a New American Theatre with Circle in the Square.* New York: Applause Theatre & Cinema Books, 2007.

Manso, Peter. *Brando: The Biography.* New York: Hyperion, 1994.

Marshall, Garry. *Wake Me When It's Funny: How to Break into Show Business and Stay There.* With Lori Marshall. Holbrook, MA: Adams Publishing, 1995.

McCarty, John. *The Complete Films of John Huston.* Secaucus, NJ: Citadel Press, 1987.

Metz, Robert. *CBS: Reflections in a Bloodshot Eye.* Chicago: Playboy Press, 1975.

Minney, R. J. *The Films of Anthony Asquith.* South Brunswick and New York: A. S. Barnes and Company, 1973.

O'Brien, Daniel. *Paul Newman.* London: Faber and Faber, 2004.

O'Neil, Thomas. *The Emmys: The Ultimate, Unofficial Guide to the Battle of TV's Best Shows and Greatest Stars.* 3rd ed. New York: Berkley Publishing Group, 1992, 1998, 2000.

____. *Movie Awards: The Ultimate, Unofficial Guide to the Oscars, Golden Globes, Critics, Guild & Indie Honors.* New York: Berkley Publishing Group, 2001.

Oumano, Elena. *Paul Newman.* New York: St. Martin's Press, 1989.

Peary, Danny, ed. *Close-Ups: Intimate Profiles of Movie Stars by Their Costars, Directors, Screenwriters and Friends.* New York: Workman Publishing, 1978.

Porter, Darwin. *Brando Unzipped.* New York: Blood Moon Productions, 2005.

Probst, Leonard. *Off Camera: Leveling About Themselves.* New York: Stein and Day, 1975.

Quintero, José. *If You Don't Dance, They Beat You.* Boston, Toronto: Little, Brown and Company, 1974.

Reed, Rex. *Conversations in the Raw: Dialogues, Monologues, and Selected Short Subjects.* New York and Cleveland: The World Publishing Company, 1969.

____. *People Are Crazy Here.* New York: Dell Publishing, Inc. 1974.

Rich, Frank. *Hot Seat: Theatre Criticism for the New York Times, 1980–1993*. New York: Random House, 1998.

Riehl, Karen Truesdell. *Love and Madness: My Private Years with George C. Scott*. Alpine, California: Sands Publishing, LLC, 2003.

Robb, David L. *Operation Hollywood: How the Pentagon Shapes and Censors the Movies*. Amherst, NJ: Prometheus Books, 2004.

Rovin, Jeff. *The Great Television Series*. South Brunswick and New York: A. S. Barnes and Company, 1977.

____. *TV Babylon*. Updated Edition. New York: Penguin Books, 1987.

Schumacher, Michael. *Francis Ford Coppola: A Filmmaker's Life*. New York: Crown Publishers, 1999.

Seldes, Marian. *The Bright Lights: A Theatre Life*. Boston: Houghton Mifflin Company, 1978.

Server, Lee. *Ava Gardner: "Love Is Nothing."* New York: St. Martin's Press, 2006.

____. *Robert Mitchum: "Baby, I Don't Care."* New York: St. Martin's Press, 2001.

Shackelford, Laurel, and Bill Weinberg, eds. *Our Appalachia: An Oral History*. New York: Hill and Wang, 1977.

Shipman, David. *The Great Movie Stars 2: The International Years*. Boston: Little, Brown and Company, 1972, 1980, 1989.

____. *Marlon Brando*. London: Sphere Books, Ltd., 1989.

Silver, Alain, and James Ursini. *Whatever Happened to Robert Aldrich? His Life and His Films*. New York: Limelight Editions, 1995.

Silverman, Stephen M. *The Fox That Got Away: The Last Days of the Zanuck Dynasty at Twentieth Century–Fox*. Secaucus, NJ: Lyle Stuart, Inc., 1988.

Simon, Neil. *Rewrites: A Memoir*. New York: Simon and Schuster, 1996.

Spoto, Donald. *Stanley Kramer: Film Maker*. New York: G. P. Putnam's Sons, 1978.

Stapleton, Maureen. *A Hell of a Life: An Autobiography*. With Jane Scovell. New York: Simon & Schuster, 1995.

Starr, Michael Seth. *Art Carney: A Biography*. New York: Fromm International Publishing Company, 1997.

Steinberg, Cobbett. *Reel Facts: The Movie Book of Records*. Updated Edition. New York: Vintage Books, 1982.

Strasberg, John. *Accidentally on Purpose: Reflections on Life, Acting, and the Nine Natural Laws of Creativity*. New York: Applause Books, 1996.

Stricklyn, Ray. *Angels & Demons: One Actor's Hollywood Journey*. Los Angeles: Belle Publishing, 1999.

Suid, Lawrence H. *Guts and Glory: The Making of the American Military Image in Film*. Lexington, KY: The University Press of Kentucky, 2002.

Taraborrelli, J. Randy. *Sinatra: Behind the Legend*. Secaucus, New Jersey: Carol Publishing Group, 1997.

Thomson, David. *The New Biographical Dictionary of Film*. New York: Knopf, 2004.

Tracy, Kathleen. *Diana Rigg: The Biography*. Dallas, Texas: BenBella Books, 2004.

Wapshott, Nicholas. *Peter O'Toole: A Biography*. New York: Beaufort Books, Inc., 1983.

Wayne, Jane Ellen. *Ava's Men: The Private Life of Ava Gardner*. New York: St. Martin's Press, 1990.

Wiley, Mason and Damien Bona. *Inside Oscar: The Unofficial History of the Academy Awards*. New York: Ballantine Books, 1986, 1987.

Yule, Andrew. *Richard Lester and the Beatles: A Complete Biography of the Man Who Directed "A Hard Day's Night" and "Help!"* New York: Donald I. Fine, Inc., 1994, 1995.

PERIODICALS, PUBLICATIONS, ARTICLES

Albarino, Richard. "Exhibs at NATO Session Asked to Ignore Scott Plea for Use of *Savage* Without R Label." *Variety*, Oct. 8, 1974.

Alpert, Don. "Acting Takes Guts—George Scott." *Los Angeles Times*, Feb. 20, 1966.

Amory, Cleveland. "The Loves and Hates of George C. Scott." *Parade*, Oct. 27, 1985.

Arena, Salvatore and Helen Kennedy. "Patton in Sex Suit." *New York Daily News*, May 3, 1996.

Atlas, Jacoba. "George C. Scott." *Los Angeles Free Press*, Oct. 25, 1974.

Backes, Clarus. "And Now, the Award for Best Actor in a Near-Disaster Filmed by Hollywood on Foreign Soil." *Chicago Tribune Magazine*, April 11, 1971.

Balch, Jack. "George C. Scott." *Theatre Arts*, June, 1960.

Barthel, Joan. "At Grips with an Angry Vagabond; George C. Scott Takes Up Directing Movies with a Suitably Titled Film, *Rage*." *Life*, Sept. 22, 1972.

___. "George C. Scott Sweet and Happy? Bah, Humbug!" *TV Guide*, Dec. 15, 1984.

Bennetts, Leslie. "A Calm George C. Scott Stays Busy." *New York Times*, Oct. 31, 1985.

Billington, Michael. "Back to Bogie and the Forties." *Times of London Saturday Review*, Feb. 27, 1971.

Binsacca, Rich. "George C. Scott: Portrait of the Artist as a Young Man." *Columbia Missourian Sunday Magazine*, March 19, 1987.

Blume, Mary. "Only Crap Game in Town." *New York Herald Tribune*, Aug. 6, 1965.

Blumenfeld, Ralph, "The New Leading Man Has 5 Days, Then B'way." *New York Post*, Feb. 25, 1962.

Borsten, Joan. "*Mussolini*: History for TV's Masses." *Los Angeles Times*, March 31, 1985.

Braun, Saul. "Great Scott." *Playboy*, April 1971.

"Bricks Were Stepping Stones to Stardom for George Scott." *New York World-Telegram and Sun*, Sept. 19, 1959.

Carroll, Rick. "Two Film Stars' Close Call at Sea." *San Francisco Chronicle*, Jan. 18, 1978.

Champlin, Charles. "Gen. Scott in War Games." *Los Angeles Times*, Oct. 18, 1974.

___. "George C. Scott's New Direction Is an Old Goal." *Los Angeles Times*, Nov. 11, 1973.

Christon, Lawrence. "Scott and Van Devere Ply Their Trade in *Tricks*." *Los Angeles Times*, Sept. 14, 1980.

Coffin, Howard A. "George C. Scott and His Mysterious Vanishing Act." *Philadelphia Inquirer*, March 3, 1974.

Cossette, Pierre. "The Savage Is Loose." *Saturday Evening Post*, December, 1974.

"Couples: Who's Afraid of George C. Scott? Everybody but Trish Van Devere." *People*, Feb. 7, 1977.

Cronin, Mary. "George C. Scott: Tempering a Terrible Fire." *Time*, March 22, 1971.

Davidson, Bill. "Great Scott." *Saturday Evening Post*, November 16, 1963.

___. "The Last Days of Patton: This Time, George C. Scott Is Playing Patton *His Way*." *TV Guide*, Sept. 6, 1986.

"Dialogue on Film: George C. Scott/Trish Van Devere." The American Film Institute, January 1975.

Efron, Edith. "Who Killed Neil Brock?" *TV Guide*, March 28, 1964.

Eisenberg, Lawrence. "Hollywood Babble-On." *Modern Maturity*, March–April, 2001.

___. "A Psychotic Monster: Mussolini Was the Most Challenging Role George C. Scott Has Ever Played." *TV Guide*, Nov. 23, 1986.

English, Priscilla. "The Submersible Stars of *Day of the Dolphin*." *Los Angeles Times*, June 24, 1973.

Ettorre, Barbara. "The Baker's Wife." *Women's Wear Daily*, Sept. 3, 1974.

Evans, Greg. "It's Curtains as Scott Exit Knocks Sales Out of *Wind*." *Variety*, May 8, 1996.

Farber, Stephen. "Scott Puts on His Patton Stars Again." *New York Times*, Aug. 13, 1986.

"First Nights: Captain Wirz On-Stage." *Newsweek*, Jan. 11, 1960.

Francis, Paul. "On the Grapevine: Hail (and Farewell) to the Chief." *TV Guide*, Jan. 2, 1988.

Gelb, Barbara. "Great Scott!" *New York Times Magazine*, Jan. 23, 1977.

"George C. Scott Is Fined After Row in Ava's Suite." Associated Press, *New York Post*, Jan. 8, 1965.

Grobel, Lawrence. "Playboy Interview: George C. Scott." *Playboy*, December, 1980.

Gross, Ben. "Great Scott!—A Star Who Pulls No Punches." *Sunday New York News*, Sept. 29, 1963.

Gussow, Mel. "*Patton* Campaign: It Took 19 Years." *New York Times*, April 21, 1971.

Haber, Joyce. "Actors, That Other Imbibing Fraternity." *Los Angeles Times*, Sept. 4, 1973.

———. "Happiness Is George C. Scott on the Stage." *Los Angeles Times*, March 3, 1968.

Harmetz, Aljean. "Can Scott Sell His Own Movie?" *New York Times*, July 24, 1974.

———. "George C. Scott: Controlling the Savage Within." *Cosmopolitan*, April 1975.

Harris, Eric, and Susan King. "George C. Scott Dies at 71; Refused Oscar for *Patton*." *Los Angeles Times*, Sept. 24, 1999.

Harrity, Richard. "Make-Believe Murder." *Cosmopolitan*, March, 1960.

Haun, Harry. "A Kinder, Gentler George C." *New York Daily News*, Aug. 26, 1991.

"Heavy Star." *Time*, Feb. 23, 1962.

Herridge, Frances, "Across the Footlights: George C. Scott Reverts to Acting." *New York Post*, June 25, 1962.

"Home Q & A: George C. Scott and Trish Van Devere." *Los Angeles Times*, Nov. 24, 1974.

Hopper, Hedda, "The Actor Who Scorned the Oscar." *Chicago Sunday Tribune Magazine*, Oct. 14, 1962.

"In Memoriam: George C. Scott." *In Theater*, Oct. 11, 1999.

Kakutani, Michiko, "Is This a Different George C. Scott?" *New York Times*, July 11, 1982.

Kass, Carole. *Variety*, March 10, 1971 (article title obscured, *Patton* clipping file, Billy Rose Theatre Collection, Lincoln Center Library for the Performing Arts).

Kaye, Joseph. "George Scott Recalls M.U. Days as the Start of His Acting Career." *Kansas City Star*, Feb. 10, 1963.

Kilday, Gregg. "Guess Who's Coming to a New Film Concept." *Los Angeles Times*, Jan. 7, 1973.

Kirk, Christina. "The Real George C. Scott Stands Up." *Sunday New York News*, March 8, 1970.

Kiss, Margo. "The Year George C. Scott Won Everything . . . But Lost the Woman He Loves." *Modern Screen*, August 1971.

Klemesrud, Judy. "Trish? Mrs. Scott? Both?" *New York Times*, Dec. 31, 1972.

Koven, Stan. "George C. Scott vs. the Oscars." *New York Post*, March 6, 1962.

Jones, James Earl. "A Bombardier's Reflection on *Strangelove*." *Wall Street Journal*, Nov. 16, 2004.

Lewin, David. "The Inside Story of a Take-Over." *Today's Cinema*, March 9, 1971.

Loydn, Ray. "A Lion in the Sea." *Los Angeles Herald-Examiner*, Nov. 30, 1975.

Luft, Herbert C. "World Cinema: George C. Scott." *Canyon Crier*, Nov. 26, 1972.

Mann, Roderick. "Scott Tackles Patton—On His Own Terms This Time." *Los Angeles Times*, July 21, 1985.

___. "Trish, George—Loving Ties That Bind." *Los Angeles Times*, March 11, 1979.

___. "Trish Van Devere Chooses a Different Port in the Storm." *Los Angeles Times*, May 11, 1985.

Manville, W. H. "Mister George C. Scott." *Cosmopolitan*, October 1968.

McGuire, John M. "George C. Scott Shows the People of Missouri." *People*, Aug. 5, 1974.

McManus, Margaret. "Actors Scott and Dewhurst—Steel and Fire." *St. Louis Post-Dispatch*. Jan. 31, 1971.

Morrison, Hobe. "*Sly Fox* Can Net 25G a Week; Due to Recoup 300G in March." *Variety*, Dec. 22, 1976.

Mothner, Ira. "George C. Scott: Don Quixote on Broadway." *Look*, Nov. 6, 1962.

Musel, Robert. "Miss Bronte Would Be Pleased: Her *Jane Eyre* Has Been Re-created in Its Original Surroundings." *TV Guide*, March 20, 1971.

___. "Ten Hours in a Boar's Head: George C. Scott's Method for Making the Beast Sympathetic Is All in the Eyes." *TV Guide*, Nov. 27, 1976.

"No One Really Cares About George C. Scott." *Pageant*, December, 1966.

Novick, Julius. "George C. Scott: His Last Bow?" *Village Voice*, Aug. 25, 1975.

Oppenheimer, Peter J. "The Explosive Mr. Scott." *Family Weekly*, May 15, 1966.

___, "George C. Scott: 'I Hope My Children Never Become Actors.'" *Family Weekly*, Dec. 23, 1973.

Owen, Michael. "I Won't Join the Oscar Meat Parade.' *Evening Standard*, Feb. 9, 1971.

Pearl, Mike, Ward Morehouse III, and Cathy Burke. "Scott Scoots as Doctor Says 'Sex Suit May Kill Him.'" *New York Post*, May 4, 1996.

Peterson, Percy. "The Terrible Tempered George C. Scott." *Motion Picture*, May 1972.

Reed, Rex. "On the Town with Rex Reed: The Soft Side of George C. Scott." *New York Observer*, Oct. 6, 1999.

Reidel, Michael. "Great Scott!" *TheatreWeek*, Oct. 14–20, 1991.

Richardson, Jack. "George C. Scott Among the Hurricanes," *Esquire*, November, 1974.

"A Risk Actor Cuts Loose: Blooming Big Year for George C. Scott." *Life*, March 8, 1968.

Rollin, Betty. "George C. Scott: Nothing Ever Really Helps." *Look*, April 20, 1971.

Rosenfield, Paul. "For Scott—A New Cause Celebre." *Los Angeles Times*, March 9, 1979.

Rothstein, Mervyn. "George C. Scott Takes On a Play about Death." *New York Times*, Sept. 5. 1991.

Schickel, Richard. "I've Been as Obnoxious as Humanly Possible." *TV Guide,* Nov. 30, 1963.

Schreiberg, Stu. "He Patented Patton, but Says He's a Pussycat." *USA Weekend*, Sept. 5–7, 1986.

Scott, George C. "The Casual Assassination of *Mr. President.*" *Los Angeles Times*, April 3, 1988.

____ "Sorry About That." *Esquire*, December 1965.

Seitz, Matt Zoller. "Framed." *New York Press*, Sept. 29–Oct. 5, 1999.

Sharbutt, Jay. "George C. Scott to Cross WWII Battle Lines Again." *Los Angeles Times*, Nov. 15, 1985.

"The Show Is Over, but the Actor Is Still Fuming: George C. Scott Gets Some of His Frustrations Off His Chest." *TV Guide*, July 18, 1964.

Simon, Marion. "The Wild Man of Broadway: Fear of Failure Is What Makes George Run," *National Observer*, May 27, 1968.

Simonson, Robert. "Lane, Robards, Burton, Mann, Libin Remember George C. Scott at Memorial." Playbill Online, Oct. 29, 1999.

Smith, Kyle. "Command Performance." *People*, Oct. 11, 1999.

Smith, Liz. "Oh! . . . Those Movie Meanies." *Cosmopolitan*, September, 1966.

Sragow, Michael. "Piper Laurie Remembers the Smoldering Genius of George C. Scott." Salon.com, Sept. 30, 1999.

Stephens, Shelby. "George C. Scott Talks." *Photo Screen*, May 1971.

Steuer, Joseph. "Scott Departs *Wind* with Aneurysm, Suit." *Hollywood Reporter*, May 6, 1996.

St. Pierre, Brian. "After *The Bible*, a Little *Flim-Flam.*" *New York Times*, Nov. 13, 1966.

Sullivan, Jerry. "He's Come a Long Way from the Old 'Apple Barn.'" *Detroit News Pictorial Magazine*, Feb. 11, 1962.

Sweeney, Louise. "George C. Scott: The Vanishing Ego." *Christian Science Monitor*, Nov. 12, 1980.

Thomas, Bob, "Scott Views Oscars." Associated Press, March 5, 1965.

Tusher, Will. "Scott Revs Up War on Ratings." *Hollywood Reporter*, Oct. 4, 1974.

Van Devere, Trish. "Fiji and Me (And George C. Makes Three)." *Family Weekly*, July 25, 1976.

Viola, Tom. "The New Scrooge: George C. Scott." *Horizon*, December 1984.

Wahls, Robert. "Footlights: In Love with a Play." *New York Sunday News*, March 16, 1975.

Walker, Alexander. "Shagan + Secrets + Brando = *The Formula*." *Los Angeles Times*, April 20, 1980.

Warga, Wayne. "Scott Still Foxing the Establishment." *Los Angeles Times*, June 18, 1978.

Wedman, Les. "*The Changeling*: Film to Haunt Hollywood." *Los Angeles Times*, Feb. 11, 1979.

____. "Genie Awards a Confusing Affair." *Vancouver Free Press*, March 21–27, 1980.

Weisman, John. "Penthouse Interview: George C. Scott." *Penthouse*, May 1973.

Williams, Ashley. "Prodigious Career Nurtured Locally." *Columbia Daily Tribune*, Sept. 23, 1999.

Wilson, John M. "The Script That Just Won't Die." *Los Angeles Times*, Aug. 23, 1981.

Wolf, Jeanne. "Insider: Tribute to George C. Scott." *TV Guide*, Nov. 20, 1999.

Zolotow, Maurice. "Cleopatra in the Park and Home." *New York Times*, June 9, 1963.

DVD, VIDEOS

The Day of the Dolphin, commentary/interviews, DVD. Studio Canal, 2003.

The Formula, commentary/interviews, DVD. Warner Brothers, 2006.

George C. Scott: Power and Glory, videocassette. Twentieth Century Fox Film Corporation, 1998.

Patton, commentary/interviews, DVD. Twentieth Century Fox Home Entertainment, 2006.

"Twenty-Five Years at Circle in the Square," *Camera Three*, 1975, Theatre on Film and Television collection, Lincoln Center Library for the Performing Arts.

INDEX